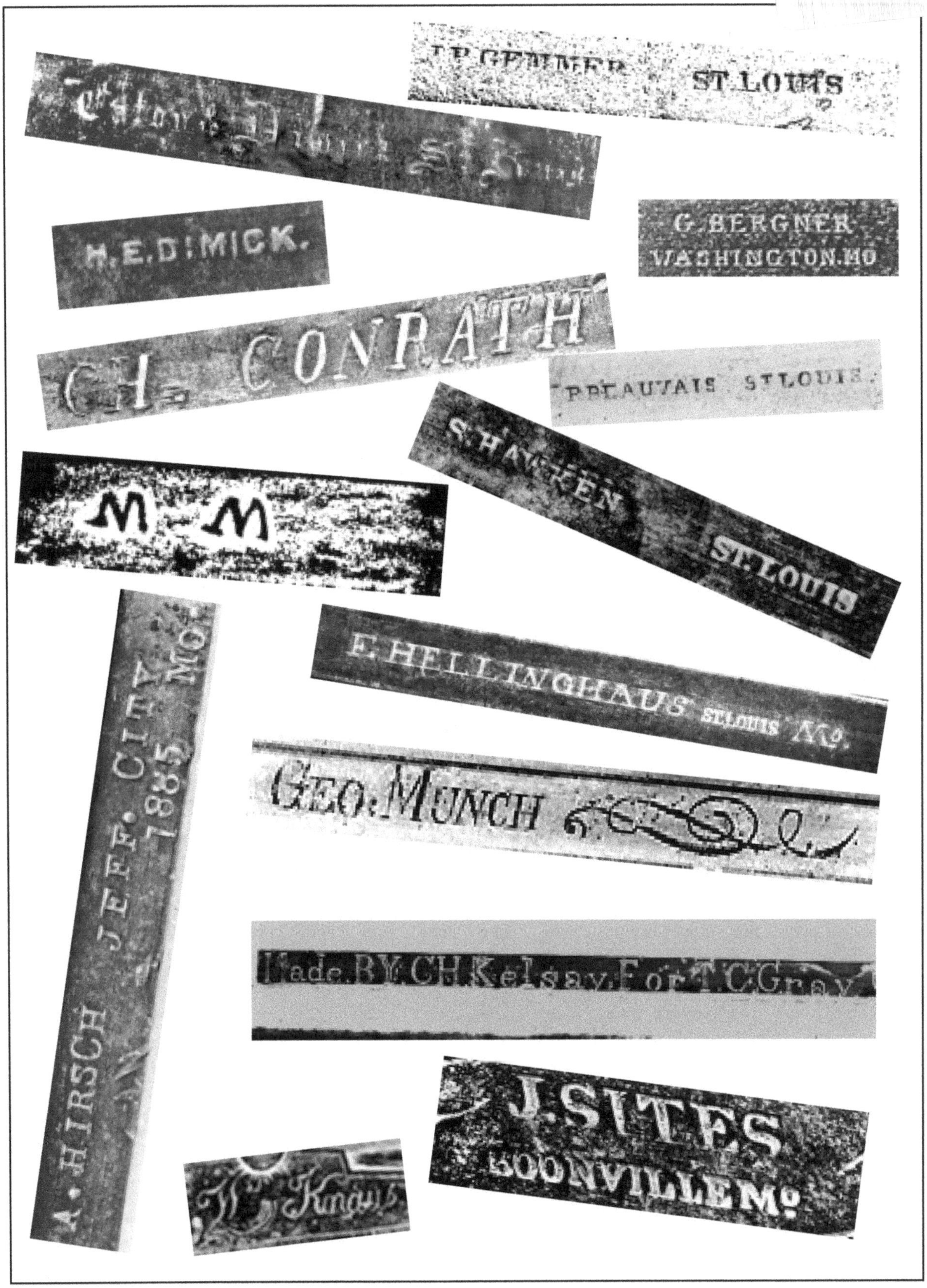
ST. LOUIS
H.E.DIMICK.
G. BERGNER
WASHINGTON.MO
CONRATH
ST. LOUIS
S. HAWKEN
ST. LOUIS
E. HELLINGHAUS ST. LOUIS Mo.
A. HIRSCH JEFF. CITY MO.
1885
GEO. MUNCH
J. SITES
BOONVILLE Mo

MISSOURI GUNSMITHS
to 1900

by Victor A. Paul

Obscure Place Publishing
P. O. Box 3111
Quincy, Illinois 62305-3111

© 1999
by Author
All rights reserved

ISBN 978-0967726038

INTRODUCTION

This book is the culmination of a comprehensive study on gunsmiths and the firearms trade in the State of Missouri.

The over 1100 entries represents the best possible accounting of Missouri gunsmiths and the trade available as of the publication date (1999). It is the finalization of the second of two works previously published by the author.

The first, GATEWAY GUNSMITHS, co-written with DeWitt Pourie, was published in 1990 and dealt only with the City and County of St. Louis. It also concerned itself to a much greater extent with gun dealers than this work.

The second, An Index of Missouri Gunsmiths by Counties of Residence, a pamphlet printing, was a precursor of this publication and is contained here as Appendix III. Neither of the prior works contained the extensive illustrations or the recopying of historical and informative articles as contained herein.

For continuity with these previously published works, some dealers have been listed in this book.

Historically, the first permanent notice of firearms in what is now the State of Missouri comes at Ste. Genevieve where fourteen fusils were present on a 1752 census. The first gunsmith known to have settled in the State was John Baptiste Heverieux. He came from Cahokia in 1764, with the founding of St. Louis. Mentions of gunsmiths other than Heverieux are not found until 1795, a number of French and Spanish blacksmiths have been noted. 1795 marks the first recorded manufacture of firearms in the state by Francois Migneron and Andre Landreville at Manchester, Mo. The earliest known surviving firearms are those attributed to Mosias Maupin of Franklin Co., Mo. and Philip Creamer in nearby Illinois.

Missouri, as a place name, was not commonly used until the creation of Missouri Territory, both French and Spanish authorities calling the area Illinois. European population was small and restricted to narrow strips of land bordering both shores of the Mississippi River. There were essentially five major communities and some smaller satellites in the middle of the wilderness. (See map Appendix I.) Any listing of Missouri gunsmiths is incomplete without the consideration of the gunsmiths who served on the Illinois side of the Mississippi River, as these communities relied on each other for local trade. In Illinois there was Kaskaskia, Fort Chartres and Cahokia. In Missouri, St. Louis, across from Cahokia, and Ste. Genevieve, near Kaskaskia and Fort Chartres.

The following is a partial list of Illinois gunsmiths near the Mississippi river prior to 1810. Further details of their careers are available in Curt Johnson's GUNSMITHS OF ILLINOIS.

Bowerman, Jacob
Creamer, Daniel
Creamer, Philip*
DeMarrais, Joseph
Goings, William, Sr.
Goings, William, Jr.
Heverieux, J. B.*
Judy, Jacob
Moore, George*
Moore, William
Quesnel, Charles
Thorn, Solomon

* later in Missouri

The period of greatest firearm production in St. Louis and Missouri was from the late 1830's to the Civil War with several distinct markets being served. Target shooters, local and transient hunters, military personnel, and western traders all had their particular needs.

As the majority of Missouri gunsmiths were immigrants to the State, this study is a slight departure from previous checklists. An attempt has been made to more fully utilize the data which is present on the 1850 and later censuses.

The material is presented in the following manner: Name, and if known, Year of Birth/Death, Place of Birth, Known Locations prior to Missouri, Missouri Locations, and Known Locations after Missouri.

NAME: As censuses were written longhand and are at times illegible a "?" means just that. Whatever immediately precedes it is open to question and represents a "best guess". A name in parentheses represents a known or possible alternate spelling for the listed name. As gunsmithing was frequently a family business, fathers, sons, and brothers are identified whenever possible. No unnoted assumptions were made. The abbreviations; prob. (probable) and poss. (possible), were used wherever it seemed appropriate. To cite one case, Carter Markham is almost certainly the father of Thomas Markham. As they are separate on the censuses, that assumption was not made. However, since they were in the same county at the same time, "prob." is used to show their probable relationship.

YEAR OF BIRTH-DEATH: Year of birth is generally the least accurate information on the censuses. Several years differences are common on succeeding censuses. Previously published years of birth were used whenever possible. Georgia born Joseph Bivens' age is given as 51 when he appears on the 1850 Tennessee census, on the 1870 Missouri census his age is given as 65. His Tennessee born wife, Rebecca, shows a more normal two year difference in age between the two censuses.

PLACE OF BIRTH: Slightly more reliable is the place of birth. However, once again, it is a guide - not absolute fact. The records on Dan Drew well illustrate this problem. The 1850 Missouri census shows Ireland as his birthplace while the 1870 Illinois census shows Virginia. Other documents related to his death in Illinois, found by Curt Johnson, show Maryland as his birthplace, this last is presumed to be accurate. We may surmise from the two censuses some additional information. Probably born of Irish parents in Maryland, he worked or lived in Virginia at some time in his life. Indeed, his name appears on a September 1813 list of armorers employed at Harpers Ferry. Similarly, Springfield, Missouri's longtime pistolsmith, Jacob Painter's place of birth on the 1850 Mo. census is shown as Illinois, while North Carolina is listed on the 1860 Mo. census. Further information found shows he was born in North Carolina. His father took him to Tennessee when he was two, and again to Illinois about 1826 where he probably served his apprenticeship. In 1831 he once again moved with his father to Greene County, Missouri where he lived many years.

KNOWN LOCATIONS PRIOR TO MISSOURI, MISSOURI LOCATIONS and KNOWN LOCATIONS AFTER MISSOURI:

This information is gleaned from published books, directories, censuses, and unpublished sources.

The birthplace of children is potentially the most reliable information on the censuses. While years of birth are probably slightly more accurate than that of the parents, the birthplace gives us a way of tracking the movements of gunsmiths prior to their arrival in Missouri and often the approximate date of arrival. However, this information may be flawed in several ways. Apprentices may be counted as sons, adoptions may not be noted or it may be simply bad data collected by the census taker and/or misread by the researcher.

Abbreviations used are as follows,
- c. = census.
- dir. = directory.
- ic. = industrial census.
- perc. = percussion
- prob. = probable
- poss. = possible
- unl. = unlocated (from census data)

The states are abbreviated using the standard two letter abbreviations, the foreign countries should be self explanatory. The German State of birth is sometimes given for German born gunsmiths. However, here they are all listed as GER. Austria is abbreviated as AUS, as no Missouri gunsmiths are known to have emigrated from Australia.

SOURCES

This checklist is somewhat larger than other works of it's type as it benefits from previously published works as well as the unpublished research of others.

AMERICAN GUNSMITHS by Frank M. Sellers, The Gun Room Press, 1983, an excellent nationwide list, was used as a baseline to begin this work. An attempt was made to confirm every entry. However, not every source used by Sellers has been found by this writer.

A conscious effort was made to follow the same source notation as Sellers' AMERICAN GUNSMITHS. One exception is (Sellers) always refers to AMERICAN GUNSMITHS, while (Sellers 1) refers to AMERICAN PERCUSSION REVOLVERS.

Charles. E. Hanson, Jr.s' THE HAWKEN RIFLE: ITS PLACE IN HISTORY, The Fur Press, 1979, must be considered required reading by anyone interested in the Missouri gun trade; it is referred to as (Hanson2) Although THE PLAINS RIFLE (Hanson) by the same author contains errors, it has much valid information and is recommended with the proviso that THE HAWKEN RIFLE be read first. An article "Geminien P. Beauvais" by Charles E. Hanson Jr. was not used in AMERICAN GUNSMITHS, and is referred to as (Hanson 3). It is available in THE MOUNTAIN MEN AND THE FUR TRADE OF THE FAR WEST, Arthur H. Clark Company, 1969, Vol. VII., pp. 35-43.

Volume I of Curtis Johnson's GUNSMITHS OF ILLINOIS, (A-K) Shumway, 1997 has been released. Volume II will be released in the future.

(Noble) refers to Volumes I & II of Jerry Noble's NOTES ON SOUTHERN LONG RIFLES.

Magazine sources are cited by an abbreviation of the title followed by month and year of publication.
AR = American Rifleman   GR = Gun Report
MB = Muzzle Blasts

The Federal censuses of 1850, 1860, 1870 and 1880, as well as the industrial censuses for Missouri of 1850, 1860 and 1870 were used in the preparation of this work. Census data from other states, usually furnished by others, was also utilized.

Over 60 directories and gazetteers were used, the majority from St. Louis.

As mentioned, this writer is far from the first to study Missouri gunsmiths and has benefited from the freely shared research of others. As they shared this information with each other, it was not always possible to identify the original source. Research of the late Dr. L. E. Monroe, the late L. G. Osborne, and that of Jim Blackburn (now of Alabama), and Gordon Lewis (unknown current address) have been received second hand. DeWitt Pourie of Missouri, Curt Johnson and Jerry Noble of Illinois, and the late Dan Wallace of Tennessee have also shared unpublished research. Dave Radcliffe of Kirkwood, Mo., the editor of this book and Gateway Gunsmiths, has furnished varous minutia culled from his notes and knowledge of the Civil War in Missouri

ACKNOWLEDGMENTS: INSTITUTIONS

St. Louis, Missouri is a researcher's dream as it is home to three remarkable institutions, sometimes overlapping but always complimentary in research material. The St. Louis Mercantile Library, a private library founded 1846, The Missouri Historical Society founded 1866 and the St. Louis Public Library founded 1865. The staffs at all three bent over backwards to help in every way they could, sometimes answering questions this writer had not the wit to ask. The majority of the research has been performed at these three fine facilities.

Similarly, the staff at the State Historical Society of Missouri, in Columbia, Mo., were happy to help.

The author would be remiss if he did not mention the oldest continuous circulating library in the State of Illinois, The Belleville Public Library, Belleville, IL. A large amount of the preparatory work was performed at this library.

The support of the St. Louis Antique Arms Association Inc. and its individual members is greatly appreciated.

ACKNOWLEDGMENTS: INDIVIDUALS

A number of people have provided information contained in this book. The following have provided a significant amount of help.

It is difficult to assess DeWitt Pourie's most important contribution. He provided suggestions, corrections, names to contact, free access to his own research and reviewed the manuscript more than once. All unacknowledged photos are from his files and this includes his conversion of them to digital form for inclusion in this book. The offer to put his name "on the cover" was made on more than one occasion. Put simply, it would have taken longer to prepare and would have been of much less value without his help.

The late Charles E. Hanson Jr., former Director of the Museum of the Fur Trade, had many suggestions for sources and content. Curt Johnson had numerous suggestions on avoiding problems he had encountered as well as free access to his research materials, including unpublished material principally about, but not restricted to, the state of Iowa. George McCluney provided format detail and many suggestions on the graphics. Jerry Noble provided access to a number of articles as well as considerable information. Bill Quick acted as my first sounding board and his personal suffering avoided much the same for the reader. David V. Radcliffe, perhaps foolishly, volunteered editorial help, a task not to be envied. George Shumway had suggestions and provided the final push which turned a rather innocent interest in gunsmith Philip Creamer into the MONSTER which devours old books but lives on huge quantities of microfilm. The late Dan Wallace provided information on a number of gunsmiths from southern states.

The above named individuals as well as Bob Browner, Jerry Gnemi, Bob McHale, and Kip Rapp of Missouri, Bob Dunbar of Idaho and Gene Rourke of Texas provided the push that finally brought this work to completion.

The author is still actively seeking any information related to Missouri gunsmiths and the Missouri gun trade. All assistance will be acknowledged.

Victor A. Paul
P. O. Box 2026
Washington, MO 63090
December, 1999

" ...As the pronuciation of a name will often admit of various modes of spelling it, the reader is requested not to relinquish his search, should he not find it on the first attempt; but to seek for it under every possible variety the ear may dictate."
The St. Louis Directory and Register, 1821, John A. Paxton

A

ABBOTT, ASA McFARLAND
  (1820-1889) Springfield Armory, Ma. 1839, Richmond, Ky. 1840. St. Louis, Mo. 1841-1843. Oquawka, Henderson Co., Il. 1844-1848. Ustick twp.,Whiteside Co., Il. (Johnson)
ABE, AUGUSTUS
  (1848-1895) ? St. Louis, Mo. 1869, 1871 dir.-1895 dir. 1869 with Louis Waechter.
  1870 Industrial Census
  St. Louis
  Name. Abe, Augustus
  Name of Business,Manufacture or Product.
    Gunsmith
  Cost of Raw Materials. $ 100
  Number of Employees. 1
  Monthly wages   Not Given
  Annual Gross Product. $ 1200
ABILL (ASBILL), ROSS
  (1802-) NC unl. Ky. 1834-1848. Putnam Co., Mo. 1850c.
ADAMS, JOHN
  St. Charles, Mo. ca. 1820/21.

ADAMS, JULIUS
  (-1869) GER Washington, Franklin Co., Mo. Step-son of George Bergner and nephew of Edward Reichard.
ADAMS, ROBERT W.
  (1842-) IL Henry Co., Mo. 1860c. Apprenticed to J. Morgan Hurst.
AHRENS, AUGUST
  Moberly, Randolph Co., Mo. 1876/77 dir.
ALBRIGHT, HENRY T. See p. 2
ALBRIGHT, JOSHUA
  (1814-) NC Otsego, Ray Co., Mo. 1850c.-1855 dir.
ALBRIGHT, THOMAS JOHN See p. 2
ALBRIGHT, WILLIAM A. See p. 2
ALDINGER, A.
  St. Louis, Mo. 1840/41 dir. Probably C. Altinger or other family member.
ALLEN STAMP AND SEAL CO.
  Kansas City, Mo. 1893/94 dir.
ALLEN, EDWARD
  Kansas City, Mo. 1891 dir.-1893 dir.

Letterhead from Missouri Historical Society Files

Top barrel flat stamping

T. J. ALBRIGHT,
NO. 50 FOURTH STREET,

Near the Planter's House,   ST. LOUIS.

GUNS, PISTOLS,
FISHING TACKLE, POCKET CUTLERY, &C.,
HENRY'S REPEATING RIFLES
AND WILMOT GUNS.

Campbell & Richard's 1863 St. Louis Directory

ALBRIGHT, HENRY T.
(1848-) MO St. Louis, Mo., 1850c., 1860c.-1878 dir. Son of T. J. Later directories list him as bookkeeper for various non-firearms related firms. Attended Washington University, St. Louis.

ALBRIGHT, THOMAS JOHN
(1808-1890) OH Stroudsburg, Pa., 1835-1840. St. Louis, Mo. 1844-1877 dir., 1850c., ic., 1860c. Son of Henry Albright and grandson of Andrew Albright, both noted gunmakers.

ALBRIGHT, THOMAS JOHN, JR.
Reported St. Louis, Mo. 1849 dir.-1866 dir. No evidence found of a T. J. Jr. . T.J. was listed at home and at factory.

ALBRIGHT, WILLIAM A.
(1835-) PA St. Louis, Mo. 1850c., 1860c., 1854 dir.-1896 dir. Son of T.J. Salesman for C. J. Chapin Arms Co., 1886 dir.-1887 dir. Salesman for E. C. Meachem Arms Co., 1888 dir.-1895 dir. Kirkwood, St. Louis Co., Mo. 1896, no occupation given. Secretary St. Louis Patent Shell Mfg. Co.

Company names, from directories:
  T. J. Albright 1844-1857
    (1844 from letterhead)
  T. J. Albright and Son 1857-1860
    (T. J. & Wm. A.)
  T. J. Albright 1863, 1864
  T. J. Albright and Son 1865-1872
    (T. J. & Wm. A.)
  Albright and Rudolph 1873
    (Wm. A. and Thomas W. Rudolph)
  T. J. Albright and Sons, 1874-1876
    (T. J., Wm. A. & Henry T.)
  Albright Bros. 1877-78
    (Wm. A. & Henry T.)
  William A. Albright 1879-1885

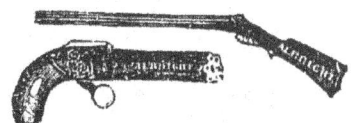

Keemle's 1848 St. Louis Directory

1850 Industrial Census:
St. Louis, Ward 3
Name. T. Albright
Name of Business, Manufacture, or Product.
  Gunsmith
Capital invested in Real and Personal Estate in the Business. $1000
Raw Material used, including Fuel.
Quantities.   Kinds.   Values.
  5000ft.   lumber
  500lb.   iron   } $600
  300lb.   steel
  3000bu.   coal
Average number of hands employed.
  Male. 5
Wages. Average Monthly cost of male labor.
  $200
Annual Product.
Quantities.   Kinds.   Values.
  300   Guns & Pistols $8,000

Known Albright employees:
  Duncan, Wilson, 1850 census
  Bateman, Thomas, 54-57 dir.
  Sieber, Charles R., 73 & 75 dir.
  Sieber, Robert C., 74 (prob. same as abv.)

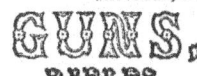

Greene's 1854-55 St. Louis Directory

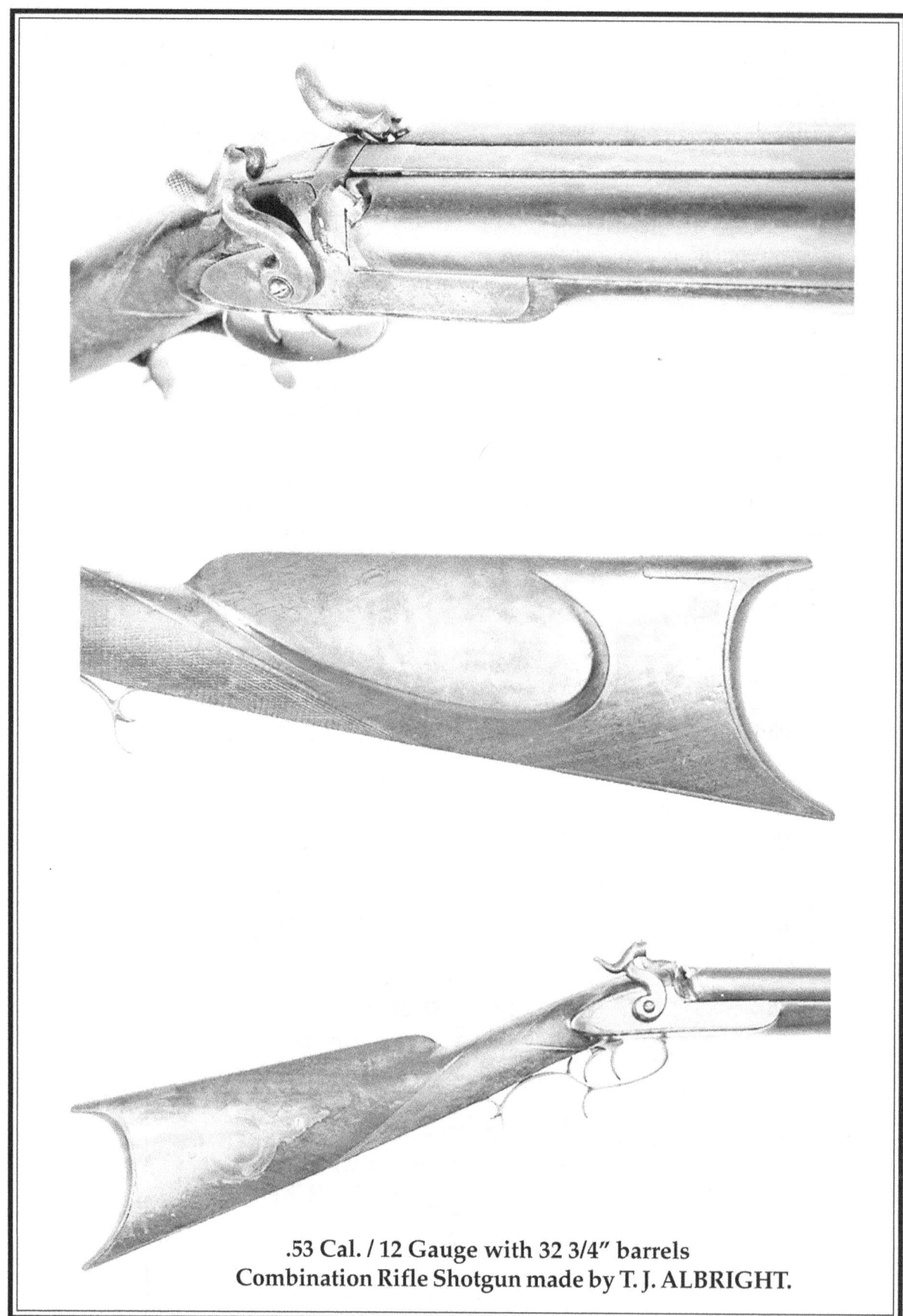

.53 Cal. / 12 Gauge with 32 3/4" barrels
Combination Rifle Shotgun made by T. J. ALBRIGHT.

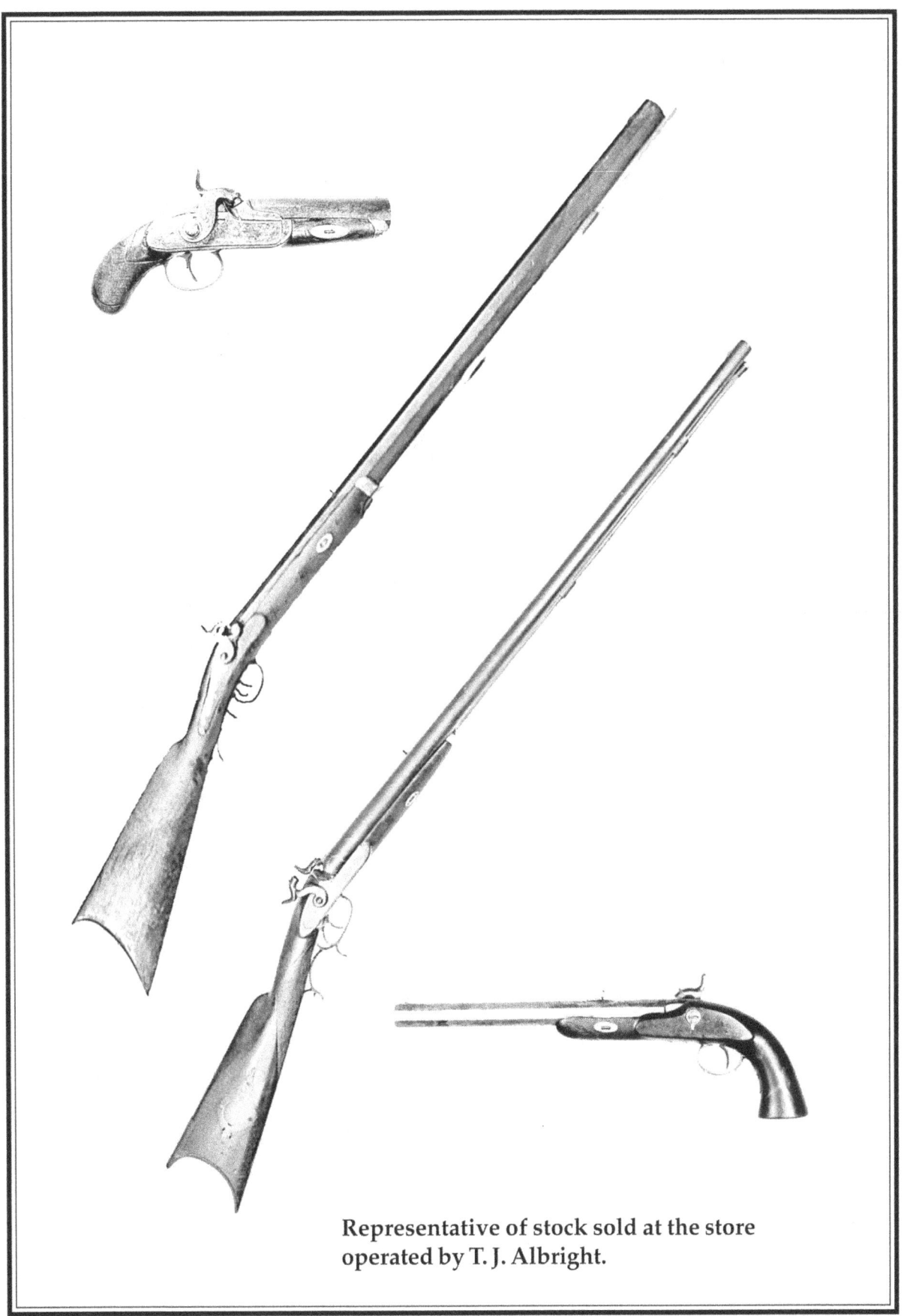

Representative of stock sold at the store operated by T. J. Albright.

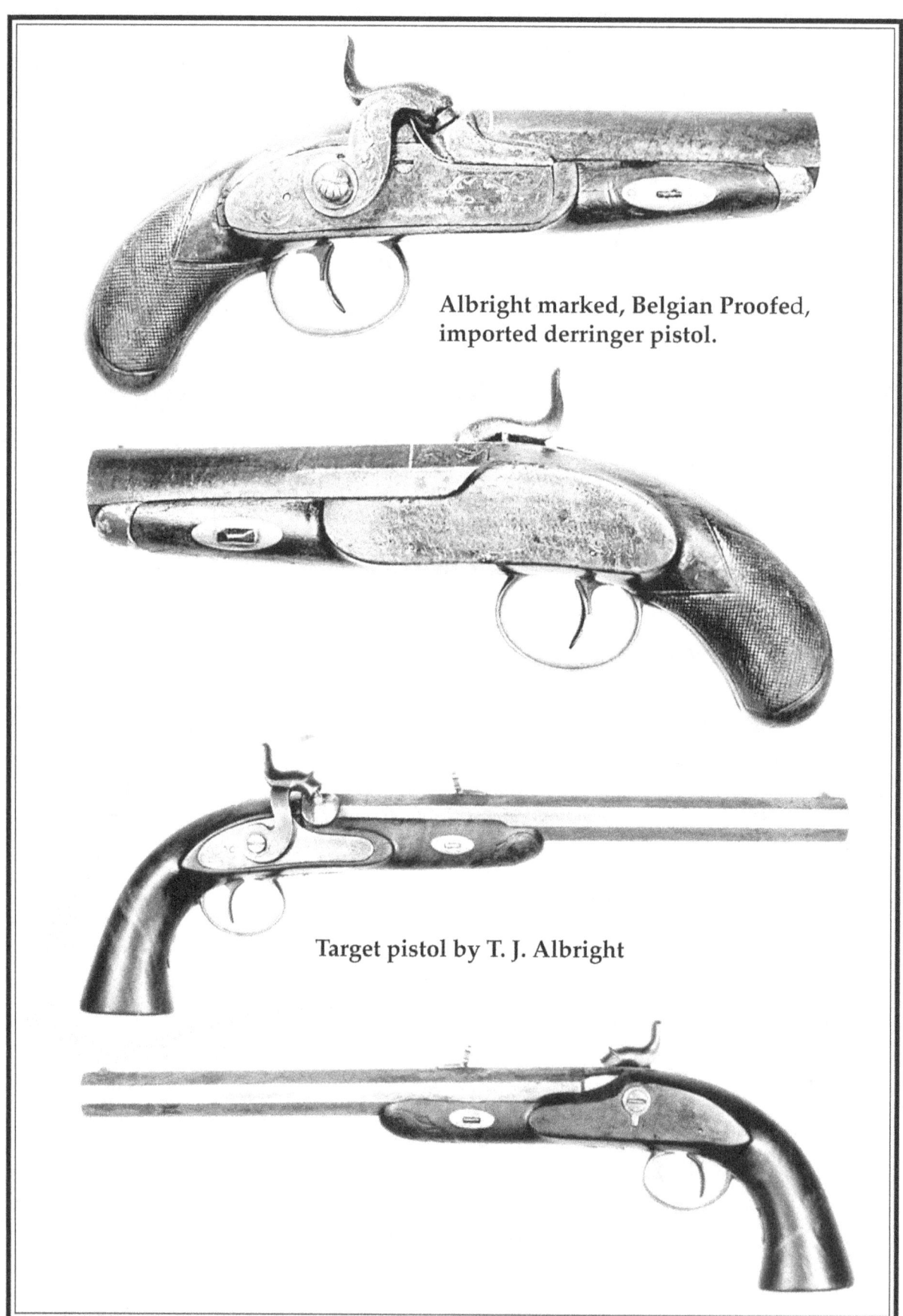

Albright marked, Belgian Proofed, imported derringer pistol.

Target pistol by T. J. Albright

ALTINGER, ADOLPH
MO St. Louis, Mo. 1869 dir.-1870 dir. Son of Charles.

ALTINGER, ALEXANDER
MO St. Louis, Mo. 1869 dir.-1870 dir. Son of Charles.

ALTINGER, CHARLES
(1818-1889) GER St. Louis, Mo. 1842 dir.-1860 dir., Lebanon, Il. 1864 dir. Stockton, Ca. 1867 dir. St. Louis, Mo. 1869 dir.-1870 dir. Springfield, Mo. 1876/77 dir.-1885/86 dir. A. Aldinger, St. Louis 40/41 dir. may be him, 1848 dir. Alkin prob. him. Related to George, Ignatius and Joseph, relationships not yet determined. Brother in-law of George de Hodiamont and worked with him. Perc. dbl. shotgun marked " C. ATTINGER, St. Louis ", probably a mismark by barrel manufacturer. Called his store the New York Gunstore 57-59. Jacob Baumann at same address 1842. Emmanuel Burgan with him 1860. Poss. associated with Jacob Painter after moving to Springfield, Mo.

ALTINGER, GEORGE
GER St. Louis, Mo. 1845 dir.-1847 dir. Sellers reported perc. dbl. shotgun.

ALTINGER, IGNATIUS
GER St. Louis, Mo. 1842 dir.-1851 dir.

ALTINGER, JOSEPH
GER St. Louis, Mo. 1838 dir.-1845 dir.

AMICK, WILLIAM
(1803-) NC Mo. 1837. Howard Co., Mo. 1850c.

AMRITH?, WILLIAM
(1823-) NC Mo. 1838. Johnson Co., Mo. 1860c.

ANDERSON & COYLE
St. Louis, Mo. 1860 dir.-1866 dir. Locksmiths & bellhangers. Listed as gunsmiths in 1864 dir. George Anderson and James C. Coyle.

ANDERSON, GEORGE
St. Louis, Mo. 1859 dir.-1867 dir. Primarily a locksmith.

ANDERSON, R. S.
(1818-) MO Carondolet, St. Louis Co., Mo. 1850c.

ANSCHUTZ, AUGUST
Chillicothe, Livingston Co., Mo. 1879 dir.-1881 dir. New Frankfort, Mo. 1883/84 dir.-1885/86 dir.
1870 Industrial Census
Livingston Co.
Name. Anschutz, August
Name of Business, Manufacture or Product. Gunsmith
Cost of Raw Materials   Not Given
Number of employees Not Given
Monthly Wages   Not Given
Annual Gross Product $600

APPEL, CHARLES
Pa. prior to 1838. Apple Creek, near Appleton, Cape Girardeau Co., Mo. .32 cal. 1/2 stock.

ARN, EDWARD
Marietta, Oh. 1862-1865. Boonville, Cooper Co., Mo. 1870-1889/90 dir.

ARN, F.E.
Boonville, Cooper Co., Mo., 1891 dir.-1898/99 dir. Son of Edward.

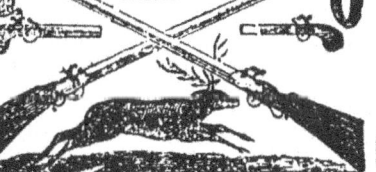

Kennedy's 1857 St. Louis Directory

Arnold-Avis

ARNOLD, THOMAS
(1820-   ) KY unl Ky. prior to 1848. Platte Co., Mo. 1850c. St. Louis, Mo., 1853/54 dir. Mitchelville, Harrison Co., Mo. 1867/68 dir. St. Louis, Mo. 1869 dir.

ARNOLD, WILLIAM
(1841-   ) ENG unl. Ia. 1859? Mo. 1852. Hannibal, Marion Co., Mo. 1860c.

ASBECK, JULIUS
St. Louis, Mo., 1882 dir.-1885/86 dir.

ASBILL, A.
Middle Fabius, Scotland Co., Mo. 1860 dir.

ASH, S.
St. Joseph, Buchanan Co., Mo. Fullstock perc. conversion.

ATCHLEY, T. V.
Oakland, LaClede Co., Mo. 1860 dir.

AUSTERSNELL, LOUIS
(1806-   ) GER Mo. 1848. Hermann, Gasconade Co., Mo. 1854 dir., 1860c. As Austermell, merchant, 1860.

AVIS, S.
VA? Marked some firearms and parts, St. Louis. Is not believed to have worked in Mo., rather had an agent, perhaps Dimick. (Johnson)

NOTES

NOTES

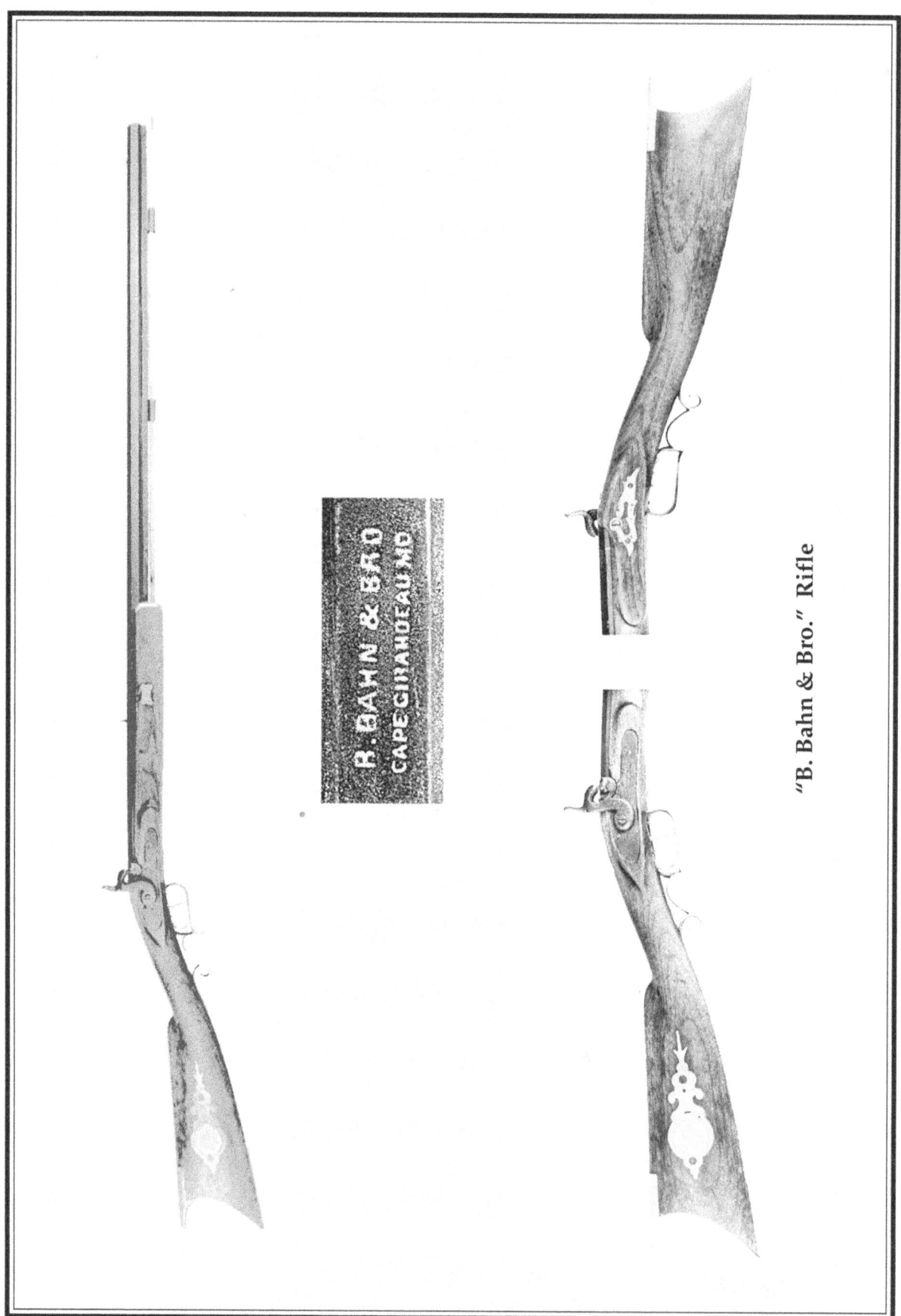

"B. Bahn & Bro." Rifle

B

BACHELOR, JOSIAH see BATCHELLER

BAHN, B. & BRO.
Cape Girardeau, Mo. 1875 dir.-1889/90 dir. Albaugh, in Confederate Arms, cites an " R. BAHN & BRO." and several sources have seen 2 other rifles marked " R. BAHN & BRO. Cape Girardeau, Mo.", in one line. These rifles have the bottom of the "B" missing. One rifle seen could be read "L. BAHN & BRO." , but on closer examination it is a "B", poorly stamped.

BAIRD (BEARD), JAMES
St. Louis, Mo. 1811-12. Large blacksmith shop. Barrel maker? Same as James Baird/Beard who made 1812 trip to Santa Fe and was jailed there by Spanish authorities. See p. 30

BAIRD, JAMES
Auburn, Lincoln Co., Mo. 1860 dir.

BAKER, SOLOMON
(1803-) VA Henry Co., Mo. 1860c.

BAKER, THOMAS H.
(1801-) TN Mo. 1839. Osage Co., Mo. 1860c.

BALDWIN, CHARLES
St. Joseph, Buchanan Co., Mo. 1860 dir. As Baldwin and Bro.

BALTHASAR, FLOERL
Union, Franklin Co., Mo. 1870ic. Ste. Genevieve, Mo. 1879 dir.-1891/92 dir. Primarily a jeweler, occasionally listed as a gunsmith. Balthasar, Balthazar and Balthauer as given name or surname.

**1870 Industrial Census
Franklin Co. (Union)**

Name. Balthaur, Flor.
Name of Business, Manufacture or Product.
    Jewelry
Cost of Raw Materials. $ 200
Number of Employees.   1
Monthly wages $ 800
Annual Gross Product. $ 1300

BALTZOR & ESLINGER
Virgil City, Cedar Co., Mo. 1893/94 dir.

Bamberg-Beall

BAMBERG, JULIUS
  St. Louis, Mo. 1860 dir. as armourer.
BARBER, EPHRAIM
  St. Louis, Mo. 1842 dir. as armourer.
BARGDOLL, JOEL
  (1823-) OH Randolph Co., Mo. 1850c. Chillicothe, Livingston Co., Mo., 1860 dir.-1867/68 dir.
BARGDOLL, LOUIS
  Chillicothe, Livingston Co., Mo. 1885/86 dir.-1898/99 dir.
BARICHTER, ,
  Mo.? Muzzle Blasts 4/64 p. 32 ad for 100 yr. old rifling machine. see Bauerichter
BARKMAN, JOEL CHARLES
  (1819-) GER St. Louis, Mo. 1850c.
BARNES, ERASMUS
  Monticello, Lewis Co., Mo. 1881 dir.-1883/84 dir.
BARNETT, D.
  (1815-) ENG unl. Wi. 1849-1854. unl. Il. 1856. Brunswick, Chariton Co., Mo. 1860c.
BARNETT, P. J.
  Isabella, Ozark Co., Mo. 1883/84 dir.-1885/86 dir.
BARNWELL, R. M.
  Little Prairie, Phelps Co., Mo. 1860 dir.
BARTH, GEORGE F.
  (1816-) GER St. Louis, Mo. 1860c.
BARTHOLOMEW, H. M.
  Richmond, Ray Co., Mo. 1881 dir. as H. H., 1883/84 dir.
BARTON, D. C.
  Rocheport, Boone Co., Mo. 1885/86 dir.
BASLER & DENK
  St. Louis, Mo. 1859 dir. John Basler and Emmanuel Denk, air guns. (Wolff)

BASLER, JOHN
  (1837-) GER N.Y., N.Y. 1855 dir. St. Louis, Mo. 1859 dir., 1860c., dir., as Basler & Denk with Emmanuel Denk. Sacramento, Ca. 1863-1868. Hamilton, Nv. 1871 dir. Ely, Nv. 1872 dir. Ward, Nv. 1878 dir.-1880 dir. (Shelton)
BASTMANN see BATEMAN
BATCHELLER, JOSIAH W., SR.
  (1836-) VA Oregon City, Holt Co., Mo. 1860c. St. Joseph, Buchanan Co., Mo. 1883/84 dir.-1898/99 dir. As Bachelor 60c.
  1870 Industrial Census
  Holt Co.
  Name. Batcheller, Joseph
  Name of Business, Manufacture or Product.
      Gun Shop
  Cost of Raw Materials. $ 60
  Number of Employees.   1
  Monthly wages   Not Given
  Annual Gross Product. $ 500 (repair)
BATCHELLER, JOSIAH, JR.
  MO? St. Joseph, Buchanan Co., Mo. 1898/99 dir.
BATEMAN, THOMAS
  (1821-) ENG St. Louis, Mo. 1850c., 1860c., 1842 dir.-1866 dir. For T. J. Albright 1854-1857. Bastmann in census probably the same man.
BAUERICHTER, FREDERICK (FRITZ)
  (-1881) GER Warren Co., Mo. 1854-1881. Also found spelled Baurichter. see Barichter.
BAUMANNN, JACOB
  St. Louis, Mo. 1842 dir. With Charles and Ignatius Altinger.
BAUMBACH, HENRY EMIL
  St. Louis, Mo. 1879 dir.-1908 dir.
BEALL, HOWARD C.
  St. Louis, Mo. 1899 dir.-1900 dir.

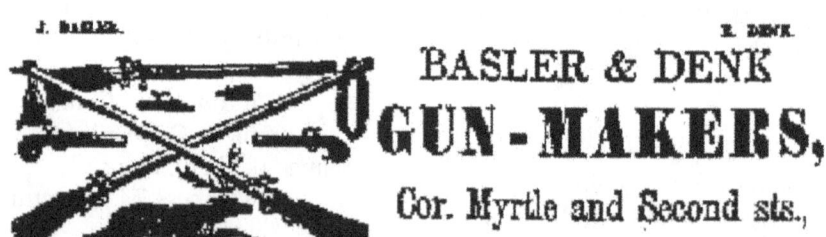

Kennedy's 1859 St. Louis Directory

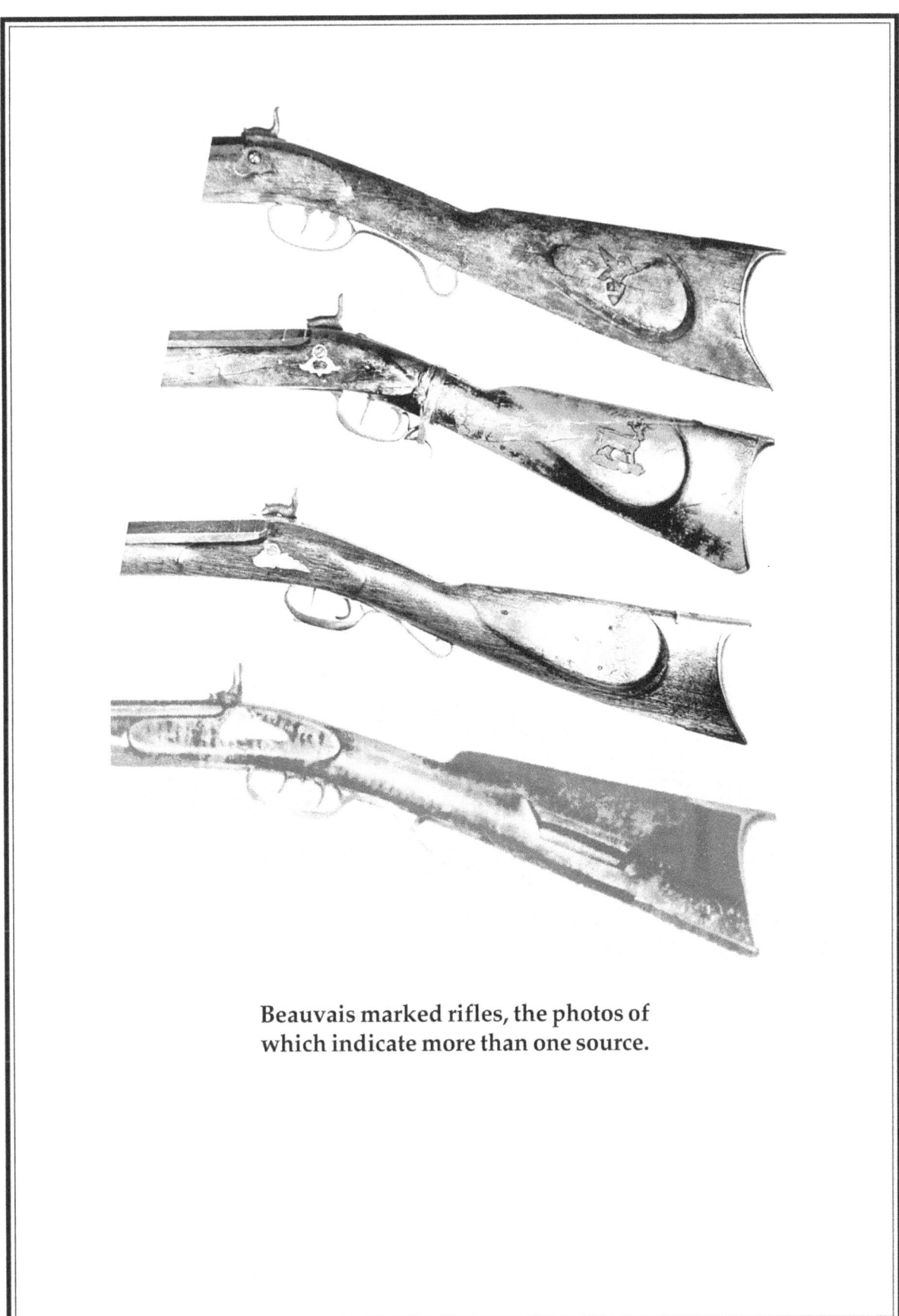

Beauvais marked rifles, the photos of which indicate more than one source.

Beauvais

BEAUVAIS, FRANCIS AUGUST
  MO St. Louis, Mo. 1847 dir., 1851 dir. St. Joseph, Mo. 1855-1864. St. Louis, Mo. 1864 dir.-1869 dir. 47 dir. with brother Renault as R & A Beauvais. 51 dir. as Francis A., a silversmith. St. Joseph store believed to be a branch store of Renault's operation. 1864-1869 with Renault. Not known as a gunsmith. Son of Jemien. (Hanson 3)

BEAUVAIS, JEMIEN (GEMIEN)
  (-1841?) CAN St. Louis, Mo. 1799-1807? Ste. Genevieve, Mo. 1807?-1841. Blacksmith and gunsmith to Indians on Currant River, Mo. 1822. Father of Renault & Francis A. Listed in early records as blacksmith and cabinet maker. See p.142 for map of St. Louis land grant. Another son, Geminien, was a well known mountain man and trader. (Hanson 3)

BEAUVAIS, JULES (JULIAN)
  (1840-) MO St. Louis, Mo. 1850c.-60c.- 1878 dir. Son of Renault. Not known as a gunsmith. Continued in business while Renault's estate was being settled.

BEAUVAIS, RENAULT (RENO, RENAUD)
  (1820-1876) MO St. Louis, Mo. 1840-1874 dir., 1850c., 1860c. (Known by the American community as "Reno" because of the similarity of pronunciation.) Jeweler and silversmith in most dir. Son of Gemien and son in-law of J.B. LeBeau Sr. Listed as gunsmith 1864-68 dir. Uncertain if he was actively a gunsmith but he probably employed some. Also imported guns and marked them with his name. DeWitt Pourie believes the majority of Beauvais marked guns were not made in St. Louis. Easily one of the wealthiest men on this list. Was among the group of St. Louis citizens who met to found the Missouri Historical Society. (Hanson 3)

Names associated with Renault Beauvais:
  John Baptiste LeBeau Sr. is the only one of those listed below who was known as a gunsmith. The others certainly possessed the skills; however, it is uncertain if they used them. There is a perc. pistol marked "J. N. SCOTT", possibly by John Scott below.

  Beauvais, Francis August (brother)
  Beauvais, Jules (Julius) (son)
  LeBeau, John Baptiste Sr. (father in-law)
  LeBeau, John Baptiste Jr. (brother in-law)
  Scott, John

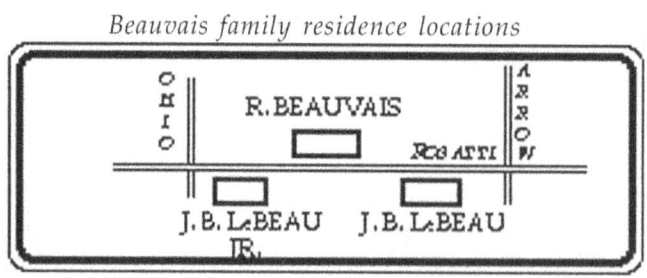

ca. 1870 business card, from Missouri Historical Society files

Beauvais family residence locations

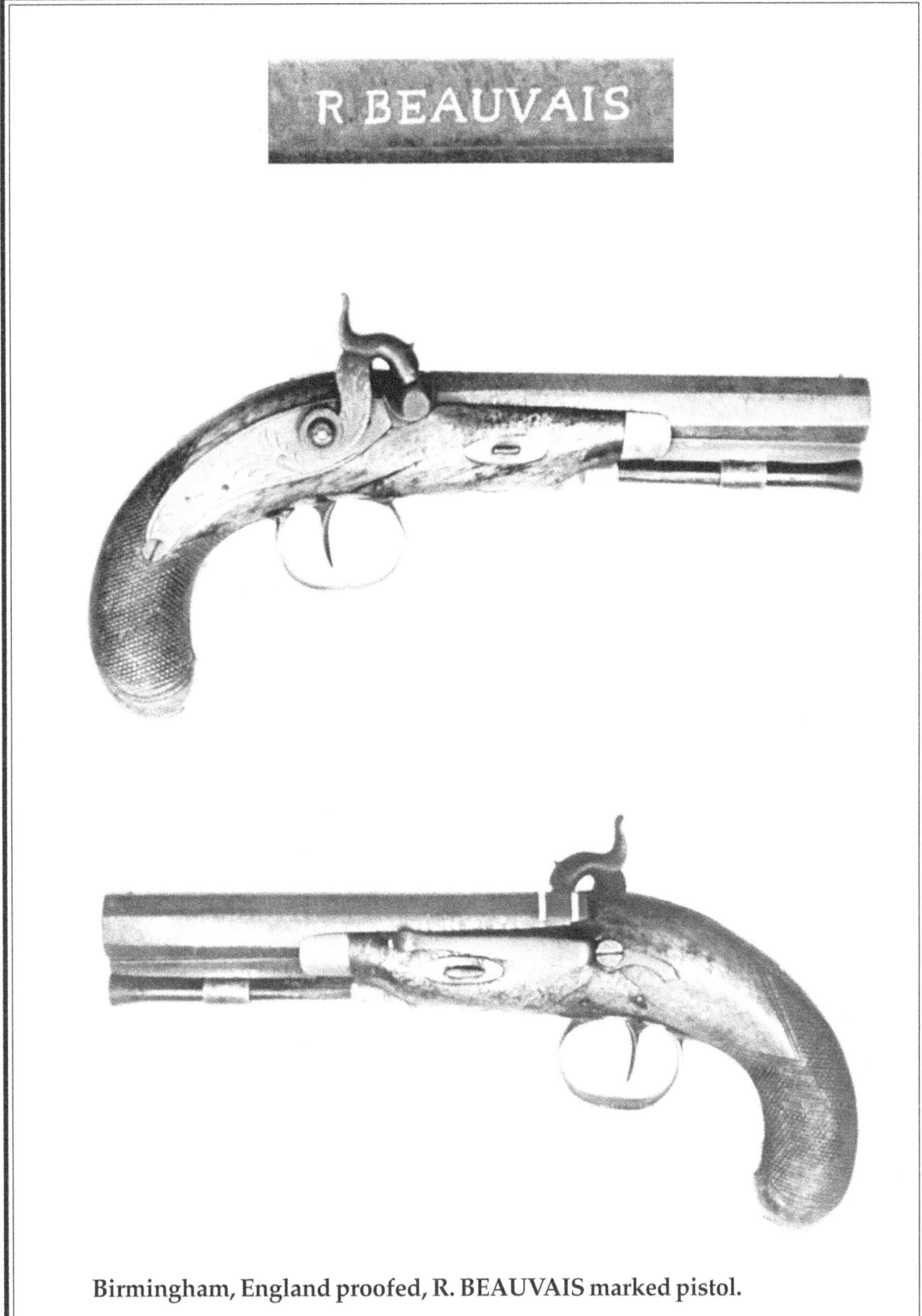

Birmingham, England proofed, R. BEAUVAIS marked pistol.

BEARDEN (BEARDON), ELIAS M.
(1819-) ? Mo. 1842. Greene Co., Mo. 1850c. Son of Pleasant Bearden, gunmaker who operated in S.C., TN. and MS.

BEAN, AHAB
(1778-1857) TN Ste. Genevieve District (Lead Mines), Mo. ca. 1810. Son of William Bean jr. Uncertain if he was a gunsmith. Two rifles marked "A. Bean" are known. Iowa Co., Wi. 1826. (Noble)

BEAN, JOSEPH RUSSEL
(1807?-1868) TN Ste. Genevieve District (Lead Mines), Mo. 1820's. Son of Russel Bean. Uncertain if he made guns while in Mo. Later in Jo Daviess Co., Il. (Johnson)

BEATTY, WILLIAM T.
(1805-) KY Mo. 1839. Calhoun, Henry Co., Mo., 1860c., dir.

BECKETT, WILLIAM
St. Louis, Mo. 1858 dir.-1871 dir.

BEEMAN, O. H.
Kirksville, Adair Co., Mo. 1893 dir.-1898/99 dir.

BEFORD, ARTER
Jefferson City, Cole Co., Mo. Reported by Dean as Beford, by Dillin as Redford. (Sellers)

BEHR, PETER N.
St. Louis, Mo. 1894 dir.-1900 dir.

BEHRLE, JOSEPH
(1804-) GER Mo. 1862. Perry Co., Mo. 1870c.

BENEDICT, ALBERT
(1812-) NY Mo. 1840. Lincoln Co., Mo. 1850c., 1860c.

BENNETT, JOAB W.
(1824-) KY Mo. 1843. Pulaski Co., Mo. 1850c. Lawrence Co., Mo. 1860c. Father Richard (1799-) VA and brother James (1827-) KY are listed in 50 census as blacksmiths. Tennessee style rifle marked "J. W. & T. Bennett"

BENNETT, R.
Mt. Vernon, Lawrence Co., Mo. 1860 dir.

BENNETT, THOMAS
(1826-) KY Pulaski Co., Mo. 1850c. Brother of Joab W. 1850c. See WATT & BENNETT

BENNETT, WILLIAM H.
Lexington, LaFayette Co., Mo. 1876/77 dir.

BERG, CHARLES J.
St. Louis, Mo. 1889 dir.-1898/99 dir. As Bird 1893 directory. Locksmith in most directories.

BERGESOIDES, RUDOLPH
Ste. Genevieve, Mo. 1854 dir. (Sellers)

BERGHOUSEN, CHARLES
Kansas City, Mo. 1891 dir. -1893/94 dir.

BERGNER, GEORGE
(1830-1905) GER Washington, Franklin Co., Mo., 1853, 1860c., 1876/77 dir.-1885/86 dir., Stepfather of Julius Adams and brother in-law of Edward Reichard. Held seven patents not related to firearms. Gunsmith Joseph Etterle(Etterly) boarding with him in 1860 census. See p. 129.

BERGNER, HENRY
Washington, Franklin Co., Mo. 1860 dir.

BERKLY, JOHN R.
Globe, Johnson Co., Mo. 1860 dir.

BETTS, JESSE F.P.
(1833-) KY Mo. 1858. Bowling Green, Pike Co., Mo. 1860c., dir. Louisiana, Pike Co., Mo. 1879 dir. Also reported as Jesse M., gunmaker & jailer.

BILLINGS, F. C.
Kansas City, Mo. 1898/99 dir.

BIRCHER, CASPER
(-1876?) St. Louis, Mo. 1874 dir.-1876 dir. Perc. Schuetzen rifle. Dealer 1876.

BIRCHER, ELIZABETH
St. Louis, Mo. 1877 dir. Casper's widow.

BIRD, CHARLES see BERG

BISCHENS, BENJAMIN
St. Louis, Mo. 1847 dir.

BISHOP, ANDREW J.
(1833-) KY New Market, Platte Co., Mo. 1860c., dir.

BISHOP, ROBERT
(1815-) ENG St. Louis, Mo 1840/41 dir. Petersburg, Il. 1841-1888 dir. (Johnson)

BIVENS, JOSEPH
(1805-) GA Lawrence Co., Tn. 1841-1850c., ic. Woodbury, Webster Co., Mo. 1860 dir. Webster Co., Mo. 1870c. Perc. fullstock.

1870 Industrial Census
Webster Co.
Name. Bivens, Joseph
Name of Business, Manufacture or Product. Gunsmith & Wheelwright
Cost of Raw Materials. $ 100
Number of Employees. 1
Monthly wages Not Given
Annual Gross Product. $ 400 (60 Guns)

BLACK, CENAS
St. Louis, Mo. 1848 dir.

BLACK, HENRY
St. Louis, Mo. 1847 dir.

BLACK, JOHN
(1786-) NC unl. Tn. prior to 1827. unl. Il. 1835. Hickory Co., Mo. 1850c.

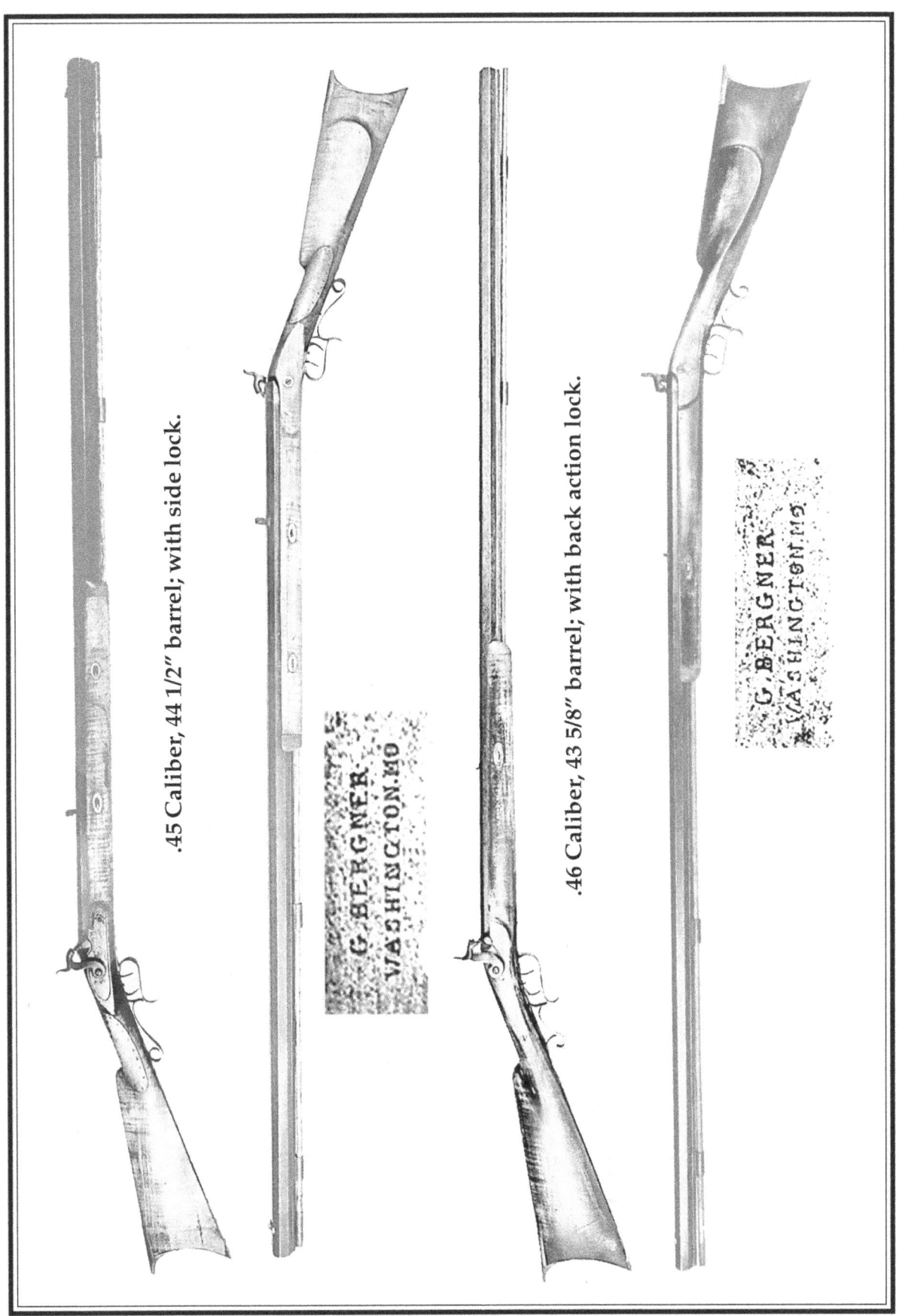

.45 Caliber, 44 1/2" barrel; with side lock.

.46 Caliber, 43 5/8" barrel; with back action lock.

BLACKFISH, PETER
  Quapaw, Newton Co., Mo. 1881 dir.-1883/84 dir.
BLAKEMORE, GEORGE
  (1833-) VA Henry Co., Mo. 1860c.
BLEGARD, ROBERT
  Linden, Atchison Co., Mo. 1898 dir. (Sellers)
BLEHA, WILLIAM V.
  St. Louis, Mo. Patents, #633,949 Sept. 26, 1899, #657,052, Aug. 28, 1900, breechloading firearms.
BLICKENSDOERFER & SCHILLING
  St. Louis, Mo. 1869 dir.-1874 dir. Perc. schuetzen rifles, airguns, shotguns, all well made.
BLICKENDOERFER, A.
  St. Louis, Mo. 1864 dir.
BLICKENSDOERFER, JOHN B.
  (1835?-) GER New Madrid, Mo. 1860c. St. Louis, Mo. 1863 dir.-1874 dir., 1870c. Employed J. P. Schimpf 1866 at 7 S. 3rd. Same address used by Fredk. Schilling in 1865. As Blickensdoerfer & Schilling 1869 dir,-1874 dir. Signed air gun # 125 " J. BLICKENSDOERFER and air gun # 124 "J. BLICKENSDORFER". (stamped) (Pourie)

1870 Industrial Census
St. Louis
Name. [as listed on census]
  "Plickendorf, John"
Name of Business,Manufacture or Product.
  Gunsmith

Cost of Raw Materials.	$ 3000
Number of Employees.	2
Wages	$ 2424
Annual Gross Product.	$ 8000

JOHN BLICKENSDORFER,
Manufacturer of

Guns, Rifles, Pistols & Air Guns,

NO. 7 SOUTH THIRD ST.,

Bet. Market and Walnut,

ST. LOUIS, - - - MO.

Repairing done with neatness and dispatch, and at the shortest notice.

Edward's 1865 St. Louis Directory

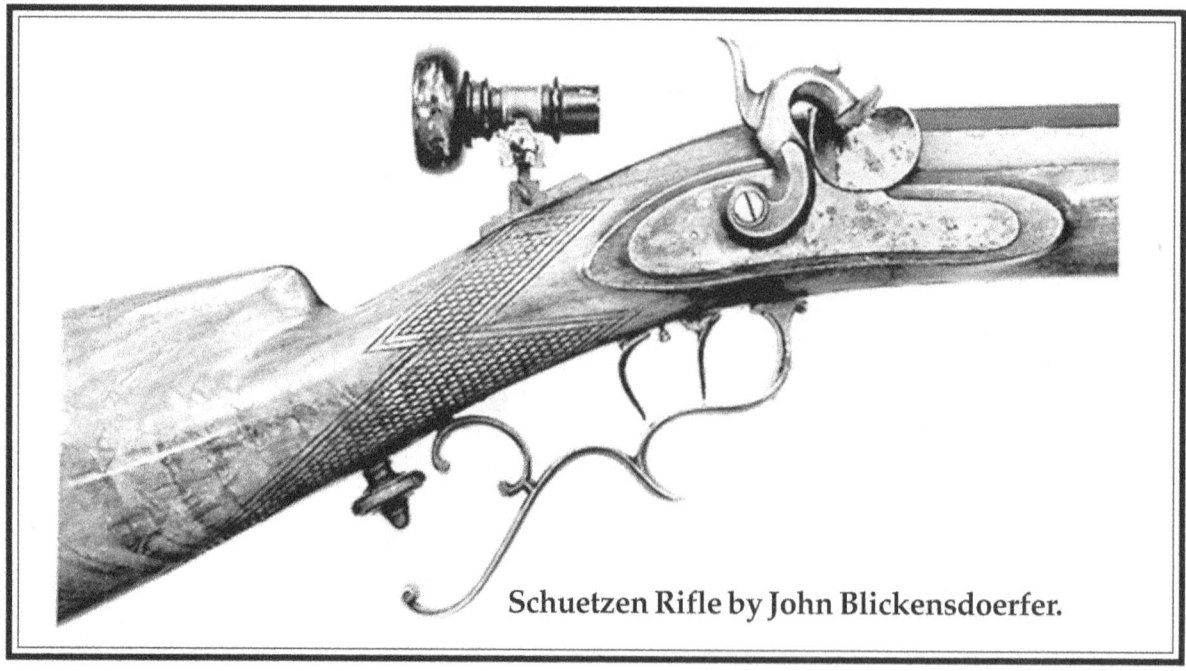

Schuetzen Rifle by John Blickensdoerfer.

BLURTON, JOHN JR.
   Queen City, Schuyler Co., Mo. 1889/90 dir.
BOESCH, JACOB
   (1846-1931) MO? Swiss, Gasconade Co., Mo. 1860c. 2 rifles marked "JACOB BOESCH Swiss, Mo." and dated 1895 have been reported.

BRACKLOW, THEODORE F.
   (1814-) DEN St. Louis, Mo. 1850-1855 dir. Pekin, Il. 1860 dir.-1880 dir. St. Louis, Mo. 1884 dir. Percussion 1/2 stock with St. Louis address. (Johnson)
BRADLEY, AMBROSE
   (1791-) NC unl. SC 1820-1827, unl. Tn. 1829-1839. Mo. 1840. Polk Co., Mo. 1850c., 1860c. As farmer on 1860c.

BOETTCHER, FREDERICK
   (1817-) GER Mo. 1848. Shelbyville, Mo. 1850c., 1867/68 dir. as Bottcher. 1/2 stock, smoothbore. See Butcher, F. T.
BOISAUBIN, VINCENT
   (1831-) WEST INDIES St. Louis, Mo. 1857 dir., 1858, 1860c. No known firearms. However, he entered a rifle by M. Gauchez in the 1858 Agricultural and Mechanical Fair.
BOLIN, WILLIAM G.
   California, Moniteau Co., Mo. 1879 dir.-1891/92 dir.
BONKER, GEORGE
   Sedalia, Pettis Co., Mo. 1898/99 dir.
BOTTS, WILLIAM
   (1809-) KY. unl. Ky. prior to 1844, Mo. 1845. Jackson Co., Mo. 1850c., 1860c.
BOUIS, J. V.
   St. Louis, Mo. prior to 1819. 1819 ad. ending business. No further information found on anyone with those initials. Possibly a typo for either Antoine Vincent Bouis or Andrew Vincent Bouis. See rent receipt p. 143.
BOUTEL, S. M.
   Orleans, Polk Co., Mo. 1860 dir.
BOWEN, J. R.
   Edina, Knox Co., Mo. 1889 dir.-1898/99 dir. As George 1891/92 directory.
BOWLING?, JUSTUS
   (1820-) KY unl. Ky. 1844-1850. Mo. 1852. Nodaway Co., Mo. 1860c.
BRACE, DELOS R.
   Hannibal, Marion Co., Mo. Patent # 426, 916 April 29, 1890, Auto gun (self cocking double barrel) with R. W. Cash.

BRADSHAW, BURTON
   Hermitage, Hickory Co., Mo. 1879 dir. (Sellers)
BRAKE, WILLIAM
   (1808-) GER St. Louis, Mo. 1850c.
BRAMLEY, E.D.
   Logans Creek, Reynolds Co., Mo. 1860 dir.
BRANHAM, JOHN
   (1819-) KY unl. Ky. prior to 1849. Monroe Co., Mo. 1850c.
BRANTLINGER, D. F.
   (1825-) OH Pittsfield, Pike Co., Il. 1850c.-1856 . Mo. 1857. Louisiana, Pike Co., Mo. 1860c. Census definately reads Brantington, data very closely matches that of D. F. Brantlinger, prob. same. (Johnson)
BRANTINGTON, D. F. see BRANTLINGER
BRAWLEY BROTHERS
   Ellington, Mo. ca. Civil War.
BRAWLEY, ELIJAH
   Reynolds Co., Mo., 1870ic.
   1870 Industrial Census Reynolds Co.
   Name. Brawley, Elijah
   Name of Business, Manufacture or Product.
           Gunsmith (Part Time)
   Cost of Raw Materials. $ 575
   Number of Employees.   1
   Monthly wages   Not Given
   Annual Gross Product. $ 700
BRAWLEY, JOHN
   (1790-) NC unl. Tn. 1824-1830. Mo. 1840. Reynolds Co., Mo. 1850c.
BRAWNER, GEORGE
   (1805-) KY unl. Ky. prior to 1834. Mo. 1836. Chariton Co., Mo. 1850c.

BRECHT, GUSTAV V.
(1825-) GER St. Louis, Mo. 1850c.-1854 dir. 1864 dir., 1867 dir. As mechanic on census. As mechanic and mfr. of butchers equipment 1864. As mechanic 1867. Signed later butcher knives "Brecht & Co."

BRECHT, GUSTAVUS V.
(1821-) GER St. Charles, Mo. 1850c., 1854 dir., 1875 dir. As Von Brecht, August 1854 dir., not certain if this same man as above or if there were two gunsmiths with very similar names, one operating in St. Charles, one in St. Louis.

BRECHT, WILLIAM
St. Louis, Mo. 1848 dir.-1851 dir.

BRECK, WILLIAM
(1800-) St. Louis, Mo. 1845 dir.-1850 Santa Barbara, Ca., 1850-1870. (Shelton)

BREITENBAUGH, MARTIN
Harpers Ferry armorer 1813 as Britenbaugh? St. Louis, Mo. 1842 dir.

BREITENSTEIN, JACOB
(1841-) MO Farmington, Ia. 1865 dir. Warsaw, Il. 1866-1870, 1869a., 1870c. St. Louis, Mo. 1871 dir.-1873 dir. Warsaw, Il. 1874-1903. Born in St. Louis. (Johnson)

BREMERMAN, RASCHOE & CO.
St. Louis, Mo. 1854 dir.-1860 dir., dealers.

BRENNAN, HUGH
St. Louis, Mo. 1857 dir.-1859 dir. Marked rifle not his own manufacture.

BRENTZEL, WILLIAM
Bloomfield, Stoddard Co., Mo. 1898/99 dir.

BRICKSEY, WILLIAM
Waldo, Webster Co., Mo. 1854 dir. (Sellers)

BRIDGER, JAMES
(1804?-1881) VA Madison & St. Clair cos., Il. 1817-1822. Apprentice to Philip Creamer. Best evidence indicates he never worked as a smith in Mo. Unknown if he sold firearms at his Westport, Mo. store. Not known to have been active as a gunsmith after he left Creamer. Famous mountain man, trader, scout and guide.

BRISCOE, JOHN
(1824-) VA Brunswick, Chariton Co., Mo. 1850c.

BRISON, BENJAMIN
(-1859) Harpers Ferry, Va. 1830, 1835. St. Louis, Mo. 1842 dir.-1859 dir., 1842-1848 at St. Louis Arsenal. 1859 dir. as Webb, Brison & Co.

BRITTON, J.
(1836-) NY Warrensburg, Johnson Co., Mo. 1860c.

BROOKE, EDWARD
St. Louis, Mo. 1868 dir.-1870 dir. Son of John B. Brooke.

BROOKE, JOHN B.
St. Louis, Mo. 1845 dir.-1870 dir. Lock & gunsmith. Locksmith and bellhanger in most directories. Father of Edward.

BROOKS, JOSEPH
Harpers Ferry, Va., 1821, 1830, 1835, St. Louis, Mo. 1848 dir., at St. Louis Arsenal.

BROWN, EVAN B.
(1810-) KY unl. Ky. prior to 1842. Mo. 1844. Savannah, Andrew Co., Mo. 1850c., ic.

1850 Industrial Census:
Andrew Co.
Name. E. B. Brown
Name of Business, Manufacture, or Product.
  Gunsmithing
Capital invested in the Business. $ 1245
Raw Material used, including Fuel.
Quantities. Kinds. Values.
(not given) Iron & other articles $ 900
Average number of hands employed. Male. 4
Wages. $ 100
Annual Product.
Quantities. Kinds. Values.
(not given) Guns & other articles $ 2,500

BROWN, GEORGE
(1798-) TN Utica, Livingston Co., Mo. 1860c.

BROWN, HENRY M.
(1814-) NY St. Louis, Mo. 1838/39 dir.-1850c.

Keemle's 1840-41 St. Louis Directory

BROWN, JOHN
(1814-) KY Mo. 1844. Boone Co., Mo. 1860c.

BROWN, L. J.
(1806-) KY Lawrence Co., Mo. 1860c.

BRUCE, W.
Louisiana, Pike Co., Mo. 1867/68 dir.

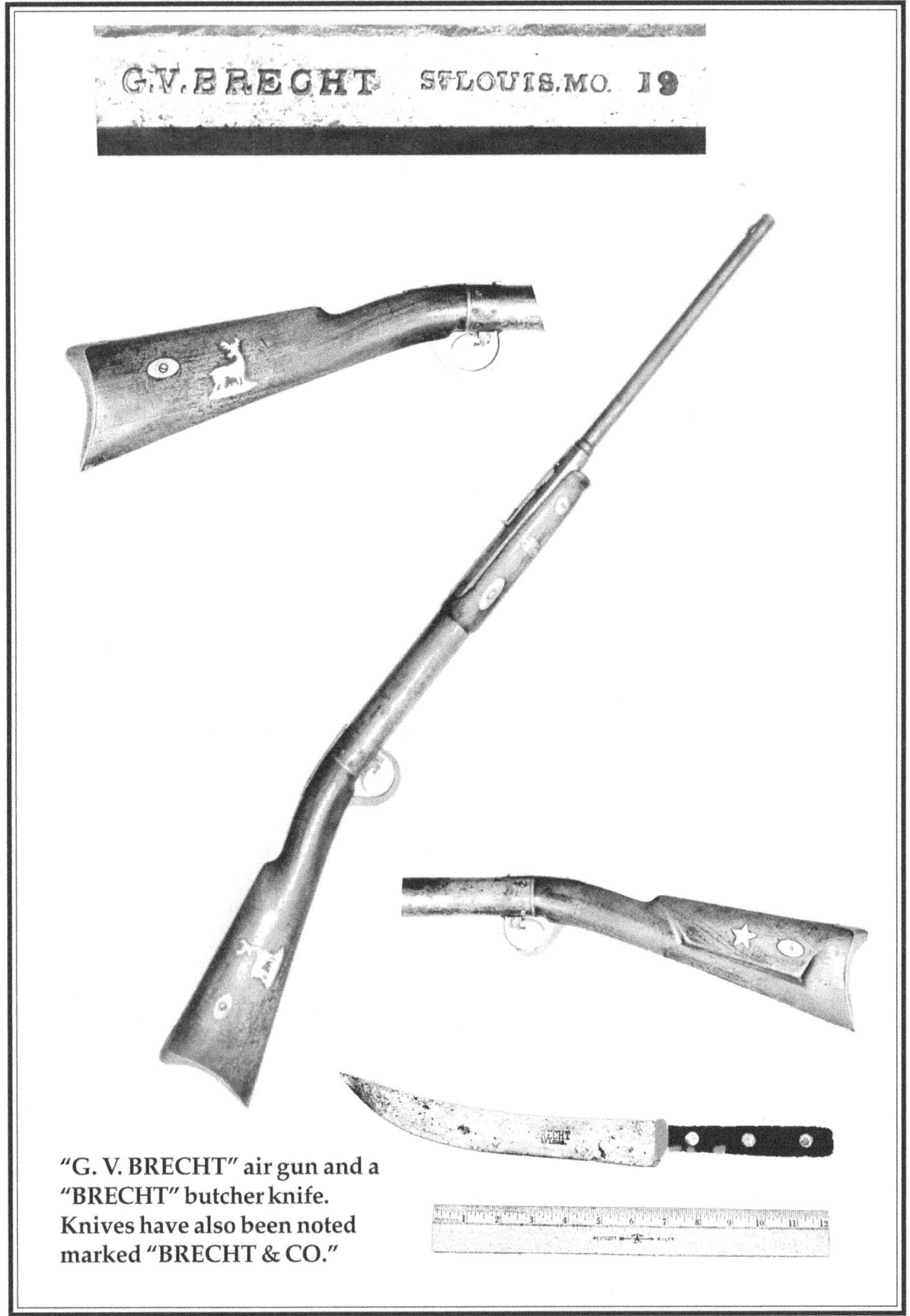

"G. V. BRECHT" air gun and a "BRECHT" butcher knife. Knives have also been noted marked "BRECHT & CO."

BRUNDAGE, HENRY
    Atcheson Co., Mo., 1870 ic.
1870 Industrial Census
Franklin Co.   (Union)
Name. Brundage, Henry
Name of Business, Manufacture or Product.
        Gun Smith
Cost of Raw Materials. $ 180
Number of Employees.   1
Monthly wages $ 200
Annual Gross Product. $ 600

BRUNER, J.
    Woodville, Macon Co., Mo. 1860 dir.

BRUNN, J. G.
    Kansas City, Mo. 1885/86 dir.

BRUNNER, JOSEPH
    (1800-1869) GER New York, New York 1834-1838. St. Louis, Mo. 1840/41 dir.- 1869 dir., 1850c., ic. Gunsmith & trussmaker. 1860 last gunsmith entry found.
1850 Industrial Census
St. Louis, Ward 2
Name. Joseph Brunner
Name of Business, Manufacture, or Product.
        Gunsmith & Trussmaker
Capital invested in the Business. $ 800
Raw Material used, including Fuel.
Quantities.   Kinds.   Values.
(not given) Iron & other materials $ 200
Employees. Male. 2
Wages. $ 40 (20 crossed out)
Annual Product.

Quantities.	Kinds.	Values.
2 doz.	Rifles	$ 480
(not given)	Trusses	$ 800
(Total)		$ 1,280

BRUNNER, JOSEPH JR.
    (1834-1906) NY 1850c.-1900 dir.+. Only gunsmith listing found was on census. Many dir. listings, usually as machinist.

BRUNTY, JESSE
    (1831-) MO Carrol Co., Mo. 1850c. Son of William.

BRUNTY, WILLIAM
    (1801-) KY Mo. 1831. Carroll Co., Mo. 1850c.

BRUTON, JACKSON W.
    Guthrie, Callaway Co., Mo. Patent # 440, 538 Nov. 11, 1890, target (rubber band) gun.

BUCHANAN, JAMES
    Malden, Dunklin Co., Mo. 1879 dir. (Sellers)

BUCHANAN, JOHN
    Pochahantas, Cape Girardeau Co., Mo. 1860 dir.

BUCKMINSTER, L. W.
    Craig, Holt Co., Mo. 1881 dir.-1885/86 dir.

BUCHEIT, JOE
    Appleton, Cape Girardeau Co., Mo., ca. 1860, identified by Bob Favier

BUECHEL, F. W.
    Kirkwood, St. Louis Co., Mo. 1881 dir.-1883/84 dir. Kansas City, Mo.1885/86 dir.

BUFFINGTON, A. R., Lt. U.S.A.
    (1838-1922) VA St. Louis, Mo. Asst. to Callender at Arsenal, 1861. West Point Class of May 1861. Arsenal duties 61-66 (poss. not all in St. Louis). Later Commanding Officer of Springfield Armory 1881-92. Developed Buffington wind gauge sight for Model 1884 US trapdoor rifle, first U.S. military sight adjustable for windage. Thought to be responsible for 1884 US 45/70 rod bayonet rifle development.

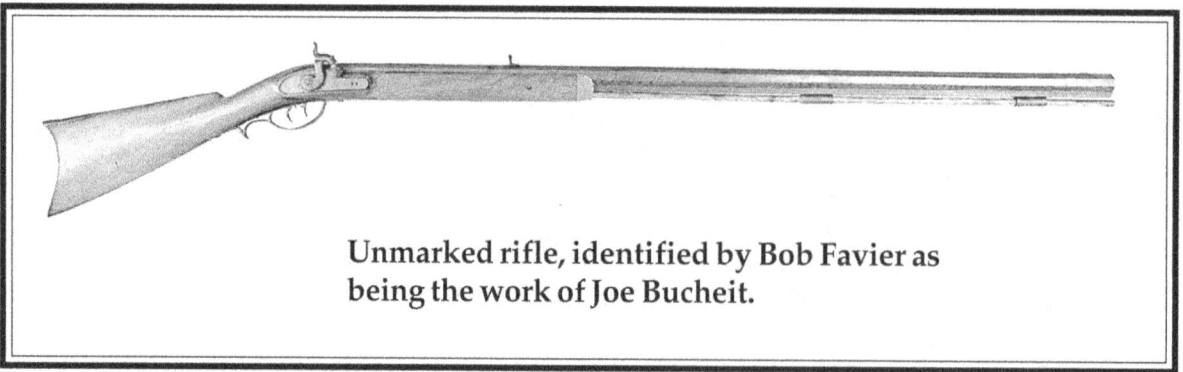

Unmarked rifle, identified by Bob Favier as being the work of Joe Bucheit.

BURGAN, EMMANUEL
   St. Louis, Mo. 1860 dir. With Charles Altinger.
BURGESS, L.
   (1832-) MO St. Louis, Mo. 1870c.
BURKE, WILLIAM
   Harpers Ferry, Va., 1830. St. Louis, Mo. 1848 dir., at St. Louis Arsenal.
BURKHARD?, MEYER?
   Canton, Lewis Co., Mo., 1870ic.
   1870 Industrial Census
   Lewis Co. (Canton)
   Name. Burkhard?, Meyer?
   Name of Business, Manufacture or Product.
         Gunsmith
   Cost of Raw Materials. $ 200
   Number of Employees.   1
   Monthly wages   Not Given
   Annual Gross Product. $ 550
BURN, J.
   Eustace, Mo. Derringer. Unable to locate Missouri town with that name. (Sellers)
BURNS, WILLIAM
   St. Louis, Mo. 1859 dir.-1867 dir. 1859, 1860 as shotmaker. 1864-66 at same address used by Thomas Corbett in 63. With Walter Corbett 66-67.

BURCHET, THEODORIC
   (1803-) VA Polk Co., Ia. 1850c.-1855. Harrison Co., Mo. 1860c.
BURNS, JOSEPH S.
   (1803-) GA unl. Tn. 1845. Webster Co., Mo. 1860c.
BUSCH, OSCAR
   Union, Franklin Co., Mo. 1869dir.-1898dir. Fine percussion target rifle.
BUSCH, ROBERT
   (1795-) VA unl. Ar. 1843-1850. Ozark Co., Mo. 1860c.
BUTCHER, F. T.
   Shelbyville, Shelby Co., Mo. 1860 dir. Kansas City, Mo. 1891/92 dir.
   See Boettcher.
   1870 Industrial Census
   Shelby Co.
   Name. Butcher, Fred.
   Name of Business, Manufacture or Product.
         Gunsmith
   Cost of Raw Materials. $ 200
   Number of Employees.   1
   Monthly wages   Not Given
   Annual Gross Product. $ 700

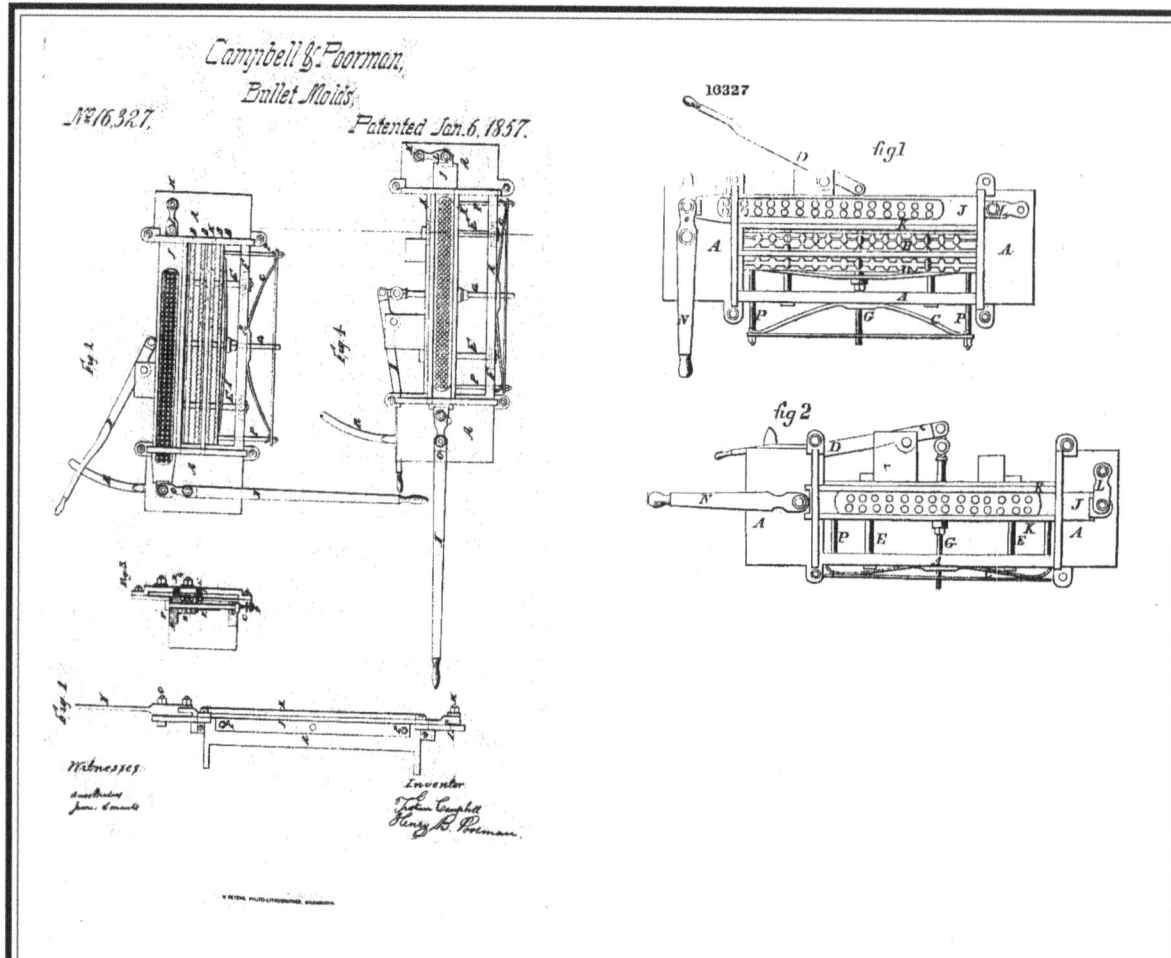

Two views of the Campbell-Poorman bullet casting machine. The patent did not claim the uses of a sprue-cutter or the mold block arrangement. Claimed as patentable were the arrangement of lever D, drawbar G and spring C. The left drawing accompanied the patent application.

Tristam or Tristram? One of the places one would expect to find the prefered spelling of a man's name is in his signature. The above is an enlargement of the signature on the patent drawing above left.

C

CALKINS, ELI
Hermitage, Hickory Co., Mo. 1876/77 dir.

CALLENDER, F. D., Capt. U.S.A. (1861)
(1816-1882) NY West Point Class of July, 1839. St. Louis, Mo. 1861-1870. In charge of St. Louis Arsenal workshop 1861. Commanding Officer of the Arsenal 1862-1870. Breveted BG April, 1865.

CAMERON, E. P.
Albany, Gentry Co., Mo. 1889/90 dir.

CAMPBELL, ROBERT
(1805-1879) IRE St. Louis, Mo., 1835-1879. Long career in St. Louis after returning from the mountains. One of wealthiest men in city. Dry goods and Indian goods merchant and land investor. Purchased Hawken Shop real estate from Sam Hawken in 1853. His sale of property not yet located. House, purchased in 1854, and lived in for the remainder of his life, has been turned into a museum. Located at 1508 Locust st., St. Louis, Mo., it contains original furniture and other items from his life.

CAMPBELL, TRISTRAM
(1813-) PA? St. Louis, Mo. 1842 dir.-1860 dir. Denver, Co. 1860c. Patent #16,327 Jan. 6, 1857 with Henry B. Poorman, bullet mould. With J&S Hawken 1842, Hoffman & Campbell 1845 dir.-1848 dir., Hawken & Campbell 1854 dir. (Hanson 2)

CARDIFF?, DENNIS
(1827-) MO Montgomery Co., Mo. 1860c.

CARLISLE, A. A., MRS
. Columbia, Boone Co., Mo. 1891/92 dir.-1893/94 dir.

CARLISLE, JOHN W.
Columbia, Boone Co., Mo. 1876/77 dir.-1898/99 dir.

CARMAN, D.
Quapaw, Newton Co., Mo. 1879 dir. (Sellers) see Cornman.

CARNS, A.
Ayersville, Putnam Co., Mo. 1860 dir.

CARSON, JOSEPH
(1801-) KY unl. Ky. prior to 1854. Clay Co., Mo. 1860c.

CARTER, HENRY
(1803-) VA unl. Ky. 1830. Mo. 1835. Benton Co., Mo. 1850c.

CARTER, JAMES F.
(1830-) KY Benton Co., Mo. 1850c. Son of Henry.

CASH, ROBERT W.
Hannibal, Marion Co., Mo. 1879 dir.-1893/94 dir. Patent # 426,916 April 29, 1890, with D. R. Brace, self cocking double barrel.

CASPARI, CHARLES
(1846-) GER St. Louis, Mo. 1860c.- 1866 dir. Son of Frederick.

CASPARI, FREDERICK
(1804-) GER St. Louis, Mo. 1850c., 1860c., 1851 dir.-1866 dir. 1854 dir. as Caspan.

CASPARI, WILLIAM
(1842-) GER St. Louis, Mo. 1860c., 1866 dir.-1909 dir. Son of Frederick.

CASTNER, GEORGE
St. Charles, Mo. 1812.

CHADWICK & CRIGLER
Monroe City, Mo. 1889/90 dir.

CHAMBERLIN, HOWARD
(1808-) MA unl. Ma. prior to 1846. St. Louis, Mo. 1860c.

CHAPIN, C. J., ARMS CO.
St. Louis, Mo., 1882 dir.-1891 dir. Retail only? Employed Wm. A. Albright 1886 & 1887.

CHAPIN, CHARLES J.
St. Louis, Mo., 1880 dir.-1891 dir. Rep. for Oriental Powder Co.

CHAPMAN, W. S.
Brookfield, Linn Co., Mo. 1867/68 dir. Brownsville, Saline Co., Mo. 1876/77 dir.

CHEDESTER, JOSEPH
New Madrid, Mo. 1879 dir.-1881 dir.

CHEEVER & BURGHARD CUTLERY CO.
St. Louis, Mo. Single barrel shotgun and suicide special by T. J. Ryan. (Sellers)

CHERLIN, CHRIST
Dardenne (now St. Peters), St. Charles Co., Mo. 1867/68 dir. See Scherlin.

CHESTER, M.
(1809-) IL Jefferson City, Cole Co., Mo. 1860c.

CHIDESTER, MARTIN
New Madrid, Mo. 1883/84 dir.

CHILD, ALONZO
St. Louis, Mo. 1838-1861. A. Child & Co., 1838-1846. Child, Farr & Co., 1847-51. Child, Pratt & Co. 1852-1860. Child, Pratt & Fox, 1861. All as Hardware Merchants.

CHILDERS, M.
Alexandria, Clark Co., Mo. 1867/68 dir.

CHISMAN, JOHN
(1810-) NY Jefferson City, Cole Co., Mo. 1860c.

CHISMORE, H.
Rockford, Il. 18??. Jefferson City, Cole Co., Mo. 1860? Linn Creek, Camden Co., Mo. 1860-1873. Target rifle dated Nov. 8, 1860 and marked " H. CHISMORE LINN CREEK, MO." At least 3 other similar known, one marked " ROCKFORD, IL." no date. (Johnson)

CLABROUGH, JOHN P.
St. Louis, Mo. 1860 dir. San Francisco, Ca. 1863-1896. (Shelton)

CLARK, A. B.
Whiterock Prairie, McDonald Co., Mo. 1860 dir.

CLARK, BARNES
(1812-1892) Clarksdale, Mo. 1836-1882. Perc. 1/2 stock, perc. dbl. rifle/shotgun. (MB 10-62)

CLARK, M. O.
St. Louis, Mo. Perc. pistol.

CLARK, MATHIAS B.
St. Louis, Mo. 1842 dir. As journeyman locksmith at same address as Samuel Shawk. Prob. same as above.

CLARKE, A. P.
Louisiana, Pike Co., Mo. 1867/68 dir.

CLARY, A.
Dimple, Jasper Co., Mo. 1898/99 dir.

CLAWSON, GEORGE
(1843-) IN Trenton Grundy Co., Mo. 1860c. As apprentice to father James.

CLAWSON, JAMES
(1810-) VA unl. In. 1843-1851. Trenton, Grundy Co., Mo. 1860c. Prob. brother of John Clawson (Johnson) and Robert Clawson, Johnson Co., Tn. 1850c. (Noble)

CLEFF, HENRY R.
(1813-) GER Lexington, Lafayette Co., Mo. 1850c.

CLEVER, P. J.
Brunswick, Chariton Co., Mo. 1876/77 dir.-1898/99 dir.

CLIFTON, WILLIAM
Barry Co., Mo. 1850c.

CLINES, JOHN
St. Louis, Mo. 1860 dir.

COCHRAN, FREDERICK G.
St. Louis, Mo. Patent #116,559 revolver.

COGSHALL, CALEB
Little Black, Ripley Co., Mo. 1879 dir.

COHEN, JOHN
(1834-) PA St. Louis, Mo. 1860c.

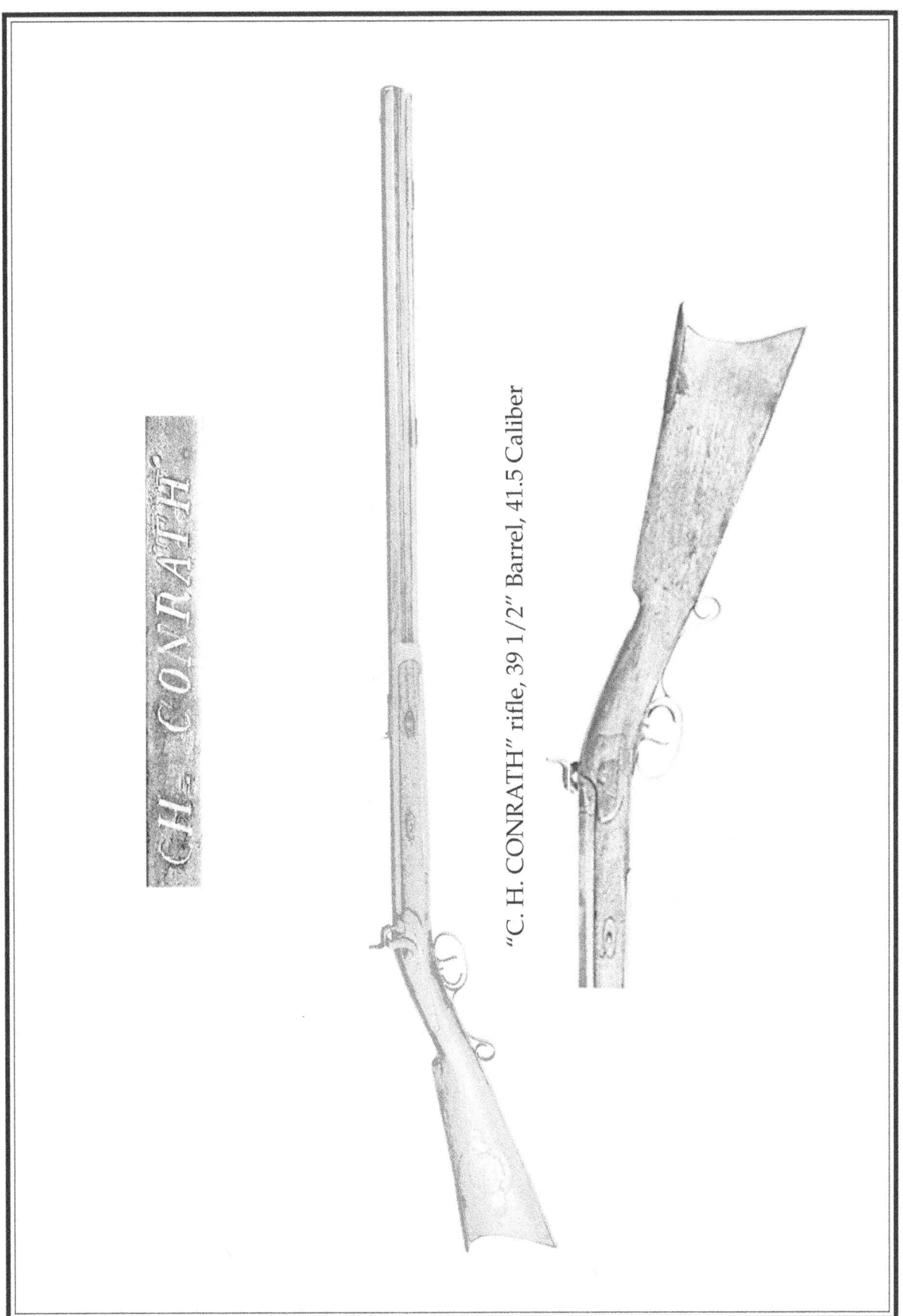

"C. H. CONRATH" rifle, 39 1/2" Barrel, 41.5 Caliber

COLE, WILLIAM
(1787-1868) VA Salem, Va. until ca. 1819. Mo., 1819? Caledonia, Washington Co., Mo. 1854 dir.-1860c., dir.

COLONEY, MYRON
(1832-) OH St. Louis, Mo. 1865 dir.-1877 dir. A "newspaperman", 1865 listed as commercial editor "St. Louis Evening News". 1875 Com'l editor, "Democrat" and sec. and treas. St. Louis Cotton Exchange. 1877 reporter for "Republican". Assigned to James H. McLean 7/8 of all rights, title and interest in and to certain improvements in "Time Shells" and "breechloading cannons". Filed for record in U. S. Patent Office, Nov. 19, 1880, Liber C 26, page 27 of transfer of patents. Coloney agreed on April 15, 1878, to work for McLean " towards the perfecting and bringing into practical operation said inventions and each of them". He granted McLean full agency to sign his name. It appears that Coloney was the inventor and developer of shells, cannons and machine guns, and McLean was the financier and licensee of them. McLean agreed to pay an allowance of $75.00 per month, payable weekly, to Coloney along with exceptional monies as required. Coloney had moved to New Haven, Ct. by time patents were granted. See McLean, p. 80, p. 176 and p. 212.

COLTRIN, WILLIAM H.
Neosho, Newton Co., Mo. 1889/90 dir.

COMPTON, W. J.?
(1817-) SC unl. Tn. prior to 1856. Greene Co., Mo. 1860c.

CONDOR, ADDISON
(1817-) KY Philadelphia, Marion Co., Mo. 1860c., dir. As gunsmith dir., shoemaker in census.

CONNER, ARMSTRONG
(1800-) SC Mo. 1829. Jackson Co., Mo. 1850c.

CONRATH, C. H.
Hannibal, Marion Co., Mo. 1854 dir. Halfstock percussion rifle.

CONWAY, JOSEPH
(1806-) KY Mo. 1831. Hannibal, Marion Co., Mo. 1850c., 1860c.

COOK, JOHN W.
Quitman, Nodaway Co., Mo. 1898/99 dir.

COOPER, J.
South West City, McDonald Co., Mo. 1881 dir.-1885/86 dir.

COPE, JAMES
West Plains, Howell Co., Mo. 1898/99 dir.

CORBETT, THOMAS
(-1863) ? St. Louis, Mo. 1860 dir.-1863 dir. Succeeded by Wm. Burns.

THOMAS CORBETT,
GUN & LOCKSMITH,
DEALER IN
HARDWARE AND BELL HANGINGS.
N. B.—All kinds of New and Second Hand Tools, bought, sold and exchanged.
Repairing Done on Short Notice.

Campbell & Richard's 1863 St. Louis directory

CORBETT, WALTER
St. Louis, Mo. 1866 dir.-1867 dir. Same address as Wm. Burns. Son of Thomas.

CORBIN, H.
Ozark, Christian Co., Mo. 1860 dir.

COREY, CHESTER
(1814-) NY Mo. 1847. Reynolds Co., Mo. 1850c.

CORNMAN, DAVID
Quapaw, Newton Co., Mo. 1881 dir.-1883/84 dir. See Carman.

CORY, RANDOLPH
Union City, In. 1881. Patent # 245,792 Aug. 1881, revolver. St. Louis, Mo. 1890-1907, Patents for choke attachments # 555,432 Feb. 28, 1896, #633,428 Sept.19, 1899 and #847,911 Mar.19, 1907. Made cartridge shotguns.

COTTEM, PAUL
St. Louis, Mo. 1888 dir.

COTTET, EUGENE
Nevada, Vernon Co., Mo. 1898/99 dir.

COTTON, WM.
Oregon, Holt Co., Mo. 1867/68 dir. Same as Wm. Cotten, Topeka, Ks. 1888 dir.-1894 dir. (Sellers)

COUCH, TETYRE
(1839-) NH Marshfield, Webster Co., Mo. 1870c. With John Zink?

COUNT (COURT?), LAWRENCE H.
(1809-) IRE St. Louis, Mo. 1850c. Armorer at St. Louis Arsenal. Possibly McCourt.

COURTNEY, R. H.
Memphis, Scotland Co., Mo. 1860 dir. Canton, Lewis Co., Mo. 1867/68 as R. H. Coutney.

COX, JESSE R.
(1812-) IL unl. Tn. 1834-1838. Mo. 1840. Knox Co., Mo. 1850c.

COYLE, JAMES C. (1824-) IRE St. Louis, Mo., 1850c.-1851 dir.-1869 dir., locksmith & bell-hanger, Anderson & Coyle 1860 dir.-1866 dir.

CRABEN, WILLIAM
(1832-) GER Warren Co., Mo. 1850c., with William Harrison.

CRAIG, JOHN W.
(1834-) OH Randolph Co., Mo. 1860c. Knoxville, Il. 1867 dir., Kirkwood, Il. 1870-1910. Perc. 1/2 stock.

CREAMER, JOSEPH N.
(1810-1856) IL St. Louis, Mo. 1827-1835, St. Clair Co., Il. 1840c.-1850c. St. Louis Co., Mo. 1854-55? Son of Philip. Listed as farmer on 1850c. Perc. pistol signed "J. N. CREAMER". Also several rifles recently reported, "J" or "J. N. CREAMER "(Johnson) See p. 133.

CREAMER, PHILIP
(1775-1845) MD Taneytown, Md. 1799-1805. St. Clair Co., Il. 1805-1816, and 1818-1825. Madison Co., Il. 1816-1821. Harpers Ferry, Va. 1825-1826. (for Indian Dept. in Madison Co. and "civilian" shop in St. Clair Co. during over-lap period) St. Louis, Mo. 1826-1835, two shops again as in Il. Civilian shop at 4th. & Olive 1827-1835. 1826-1833 worked for Indian Dept. as gunsmith. Indian shop just south of Pine on Front. St. Clair Co., Il. 1836- . "P. CREAMER" stamped or signed on barrel and on some locks. Known western guns are stamped. Noted for the high quality of his locks (flint). " He's as sure as a Creamer lock". [John Reynolds] (Johnson) See pp. 133-140

CREAMER, WILLIAM
(1790-) PA unl. Oh. 1824-1838. Mo. 1840. Morgan Co., Mo. 1850c.

CREASEY, MASON
Mexico, Audrain Co., Mo. 1893/94 dir.

CREASON, NICK B.
(1811-) MO Sullivan Co., Mo.1850c.-1860c., dir. As Niles B. on 60c., V. B. Creson 60 dir. Prob. all same man.

CREISSEN, EDWARD
St. Louis, Mo. 1879 dir.-1883 dir.

CRITQUELHOEF?, WILLIAM
St. Louis, Mo. 1850 ic. Surname ending could also be hoff, hass or haff.

**1850 Industrial Census:
St. Louis, Ward 3**

Name. William Critquelhoef ?
Name of Business, Manufacture, or Product.
            Gunsmith
Capital invested in the Business. $ 400
Raw Material used, including Fuel.
    Quantities.   Kinds.   Values.
    1 ton   iron
                   wood, brass } $ 200
                   steel & silver
Average hands employed.   Male. 2
Wages. $ 60
Annual Product.
    Quantities.   Kinds.   Values.
    (not given)   Guns, Rifles & Pistols $ 1,800

CROCKER, JOHN
Cameron, Clinton Co., Mo. 1883/84 dir.-1885/86 dir.

CROSIER, JESSE L.
(1838-) IL Texas Co., Mo. 1860c.

CURTAIN, JOSEPH
St. Louis, Mo. 1842 dir.-1848 dir. at St. Louis Arsenal, 1848 as Kirton.

Left and right views of the oldest known St. Louis rifle, that is to say a rifle of a generic type manufactured in and about St. Louis for use in the West. It was probably made in Illinois ca. 1820 or earlier. The crude "snake" sideplate may mean this rifle was intended for the Indian trade.

The barrel, stamped on the top flat "P. CREAMER", on the underside is crudely stamped "J.A.B. ..ker" (maker?). This may indicate that Jim Bridger, the famed mountain man and known Creamer employee, made the barrel.

Less romantic, though tending to date the rifle earlier, is that the "J.A.B." stands for James Baird who in 1811 opened a blacksmithing shop in what was then the largest building in St. Louis. Baird's business closed in 1812, Baird going to Santa Fe where he was jailed by Spanish authorities. The building soon became "The Theater" in St. Louis.

The pictured rifle has, of course, been converted from flintlock to percussion

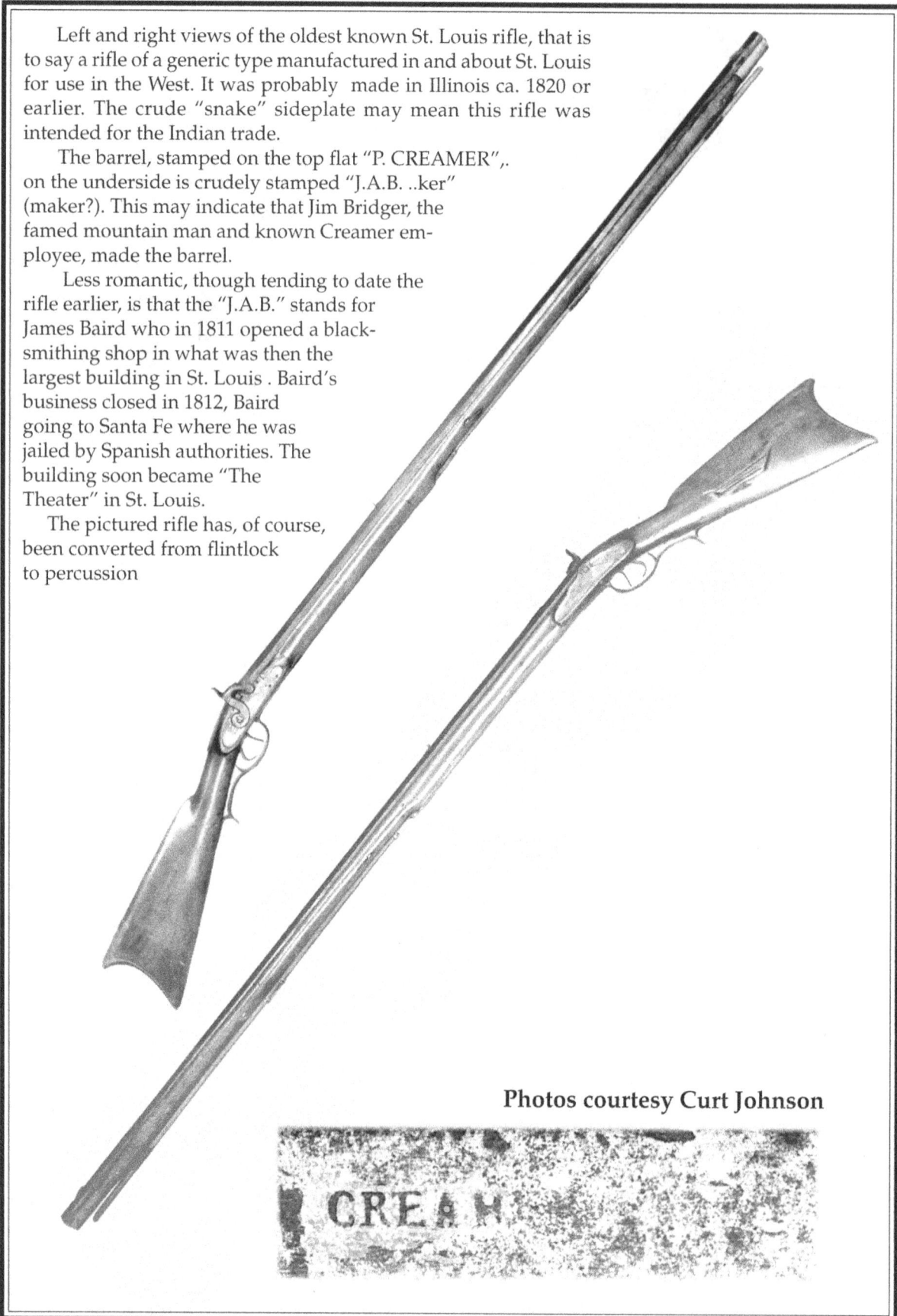

Photos courtesy Curt Johnson

D

DAFT & HAGUE
   St. Louis, Mo. 1851 dir.-1852 dir. Alexander Daft and James Hague.
DAFT, ALEXANDER
   (1826-) ENG St. Louis, Mo. 1850c.-1852 dir. Brother of Robert. See abv.
DAFT, ROBERT
   (1824-) ENG St. Louis, Mo. 1850c.-1851 dir.
DAHN, A.
   Dittmer's Store, Jefferson Co., Mo. 1883/84 dir. See Dohn.
DANNE, JOHN F.
   (1795-) GER Ray Co., Mo. 1850c.
DAVE (DAVEY) (SLAVE OF JOHN SMITH T.)
   Ste. Genevieve district, Mo. (lead mines) ca. 1808. John Smith T. reportedly set Dave up in a shop where five men were kept busy repairing guns. Another source says 2 slaves. Pistols used in the Crittenden-Fenwick duel belonged to Smith T., See Smith , A.

DAVENPORT, JAMES
   (1814-) KY unl Ky. prior to 1840. Mo. 1842. Jackson Co., Mo. 1860c.
DAVIDSON, ALFRED
   (1814-) KY Mo. 1841. Montgomery Co., Mo. 1850c.
DAVIS, G. W.
   Unionville, Putnam Co., Mo. 1898/99 dir.
DAVIS, HARMAN
   NC Mo. before 1830. 1830 at Indian Agency for the Delawares.
DAVIS, JAMES
   St. Louis, Mo. 1847 dir.
DAVIS, W. P. & SON
   Kansas City, Mo. 1878 dir. (Sellers)
DAWSON, J. G.
   Lecoma, Dent Co., Mo. 1898/99 dir.
DAWSON. W. H.
   Paris, Monroe Co., Mo. 1867/68 dir.
DAY, DANIEL & Co.
   Malta Bend, Saline Co., Mo. 1883/84 dir.-1885/86 dir.

DAY, JAMES
(1812-   ) VA Mo. 1837. St. Francois Co., Mo. 1850c.

DAY, THOMAS
St. Louis, Mo. 1848 dir.-1860 dir. as Shapleigh, Day & Co. N.Y., N.Y. 1867 dir.-1880 dir. as Day & Halsey. (Sellers)

De FORD, ISAAC
Forest City, Holt Co., Mo. 1898/99 dir.

de HODIAMONT, GEORGE see HODMOND

DEITERICH, LOUIS see DIETRICH

DEMPSEY, A. B.
Sedalia, Pettis Co., Mo. 1876/77 dir.-1898/99 dir. Sedalia Gun and Machine Co. 1898/99 dir.

DENK, EMMANUEL
St. Louis, Mo. 1859 dir. As Basler & Denk.

DENNIS, ISAAC
(1797-   ) KY unl. Ky. prior to 1828. Mo. 1830. Marion Co., Mo. 1850c.

DENNIS, WILLIAM
(1826-   ) KY LaGrange, Marion Co., Mo. 1860c., dir., son of Isaac.

DENNISON, JAMES
(1815-   ) VA unl. Ky. prior to 1839. His family moved there before 1823. Mo. 1840. St. Francois Co., Mo. 1850c.

DETCHENENG?, LAWRENCE
(1809-   ) MO unl. Wi. 1842-1850. Mo. 1852. Ste. Genevieve, Mo. 1860c.

DICKENSON, JOHN C.
(1835-   ) MO Arrow Rock, Saline Co., Mo. 1850c. With John P. Sites Jr., his uncle.

DICKSON, MOSES
(1825-   ) KY Louisville, Ky. 1848-1860 dir., as Dickson & Gilmore. Liberty, Clay Co., Mo., 1860c., dir.-1867/68 dir. (Sellers)

DIETRICH, LOUIS
(1818-   ) GER Mo. 1858. Wittenburg, Perry Co., Mo. 1870c.-1883/84 dir. 1879 as Deiterich, 1883/84 as Deietrich.

DIETTRICH, JOHN F. see DITTRICH

DIMICK H. E. & CO. see p. 34.

DIMICK, EDWARD E. see p. 34.

DIMICK, HORACE E. see p. 34.

DIMICK, R. E. & CO.
St. Louis, Mo., 1888 dir., listed as gun dealer, Richard E., son of Horace. Not known as gunsmith.

DIMITT, FRANK
Rocheport, Boone Co., Mo. Patent # 306,593, Oct. 14, 1884, shotgun.

DIMMRICK, H. C.
(1821?-   ) ENG St. Louis, Mo. 1850c.

DINKLE, CHRIS
(1820-   ) GER Mo. 1843. Howard Co., Mo. 1850c.

DITTRICH, JOHN F.
(1827-1875) GER St Louis, Mo. 1850c.-1859 dir. Resided with Martin Flesch. Mobile, Al. 1860c. 1861 dir.-1868 dir. New Orleans, La. 1868-1875 dir. Made and imported percussion guns. (Sellers)

DOBY, ALSEY
Sarvis Point, Webster Co., Mo. 1885/86 dir.

DODSWORTH, ROBERT
(1823-   ) ENG St. Louis, Mo. 1857 dir.-1879 dir. Listed as engineer 1860c. Listed as locksmith, bellhanger and gunsmith in various directories.

DOELL, GOTTFRIED
(1830-   ) GER Mo. 1860. St. Louis, Mo. 1870c.-1874 dir.

DOHN, N. A.
Ditmer's Store, Jefferson Co., Mo. 1893/94 dir. See Dahn.

DOHRMANN, FREDERICK
St. Louis, Mo. 1840-1842 dir. Lock and gunsmith.

DOLL, J. A.
(1820-   ) GER Neosho, Newton Co., Mo. 1860c.

DOUGLAS, ,
St. Louis Co., Mo. 1816.

DOUGLAS, DANIEL
Clarksville, Pike Co., Mo. 1879 dir. Perc. full stock.

DOUGLASS, ASA B.
(1804-   ) TN Beech, Dunklin Co., Mo. 1860c., dir. Farmer on census.

DOWLING, JESSE
(1781-   ) MI Mo. 1821. Jefferson Co., Mo. 1850c.

DOWLING, NAPOLEAN
(1821-   ) MO Jefferson Co., Mo. 1850c. Listed as blacksmith with father Jesse.

DRESSER, SAMUEL R.
(1835-1915) ? Mt. Pleasant, Miller Co., Mo. 1866-1868, also at Eldon and Bagnell, Mo. Small rifle with 25 inlays made 1894 signed " S. DRESSER ".

DREW, ANDREW
(-   ) ? Caledonia, Washington Co., Mo. Rifle dated Feb. 1898 (Monroe)

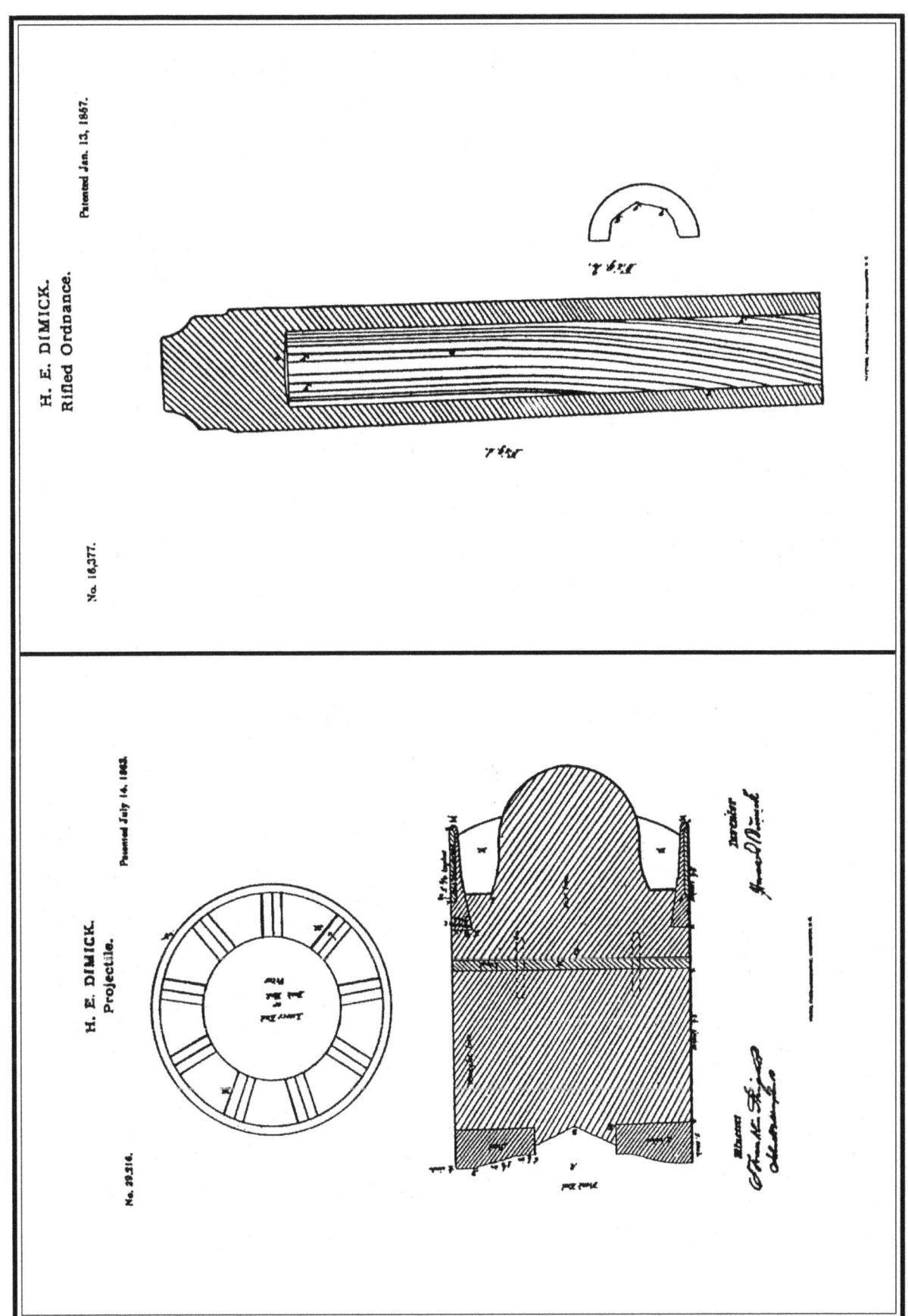

DIMICK, EDWARD E.
St. Louis, Mo. 1852 dir. As H. E. Dimick & Co. Not known as a gunsmith.

DIMICK, HORACE E.
(1809-1873) VT Lexington, Ky. 1838 dir. St. Louis, Mo. 1849-1873. Patents, # 16,377, Jan. 13, 1857, rifling cannon and # 39,216, July 14, 1863, cannon projectile. Well made rifles and pistols of various types. Sold guns made elsewhere marked with his name. Is believed to have acted as agent for other area gunsmiths. Sold gunsmithing supplies. He employed the most skilled gunsmiths available. Firearms of all types stamped " H. E. DIMICK & CO. " and "H. E. DIMICK ". (AR 4-58) See ad p. 171.

    Directory listings for firm:
    H. E. Dimick & Co. 1851-1859
        (Horace and Edward Dimick 52)
        (Horace and H. Folsom 54-59)
    Horace E. Dimick 1860
    Horace E. Dimick & Co. 1863, 1864
        (Horace & Daniel Eaton)
        (EATON & DIMICK see Daniel Eaton)
    Horace E. Dimick 1865-1873
    Rudolph & Co. 1874-1875
        (Thomas W. Rudolph & ——)

Dimick Partners:
    Dimick, Edward E. 1852
    Eaton, Daniel 1864
        (in dir. only 64)
    Folsom, George 1852
    Folsom, Henry 1854-59

Known Dimick employees:
    Kersey, Levi Charles 1869-70
    Knoder, T.
    Linzel, August Edward 1857*
    Palmer, Henry C. 1868*
    Schanz, Henry 1868
    Schilling, Frederick 1868
    Seibert, C. (poss. Charles R. Sieber)
    Shamich, ,
    Talman (Tolman), James
        (bookeeper)
    Wirsing, Christian A.

* job work for Dimick after leaving him.

The drawing previous page top is that of Dimick's cannon patent. It was "free bored, gain twist". Dimick claimed neither of these as his innovation.

    "I claim-
    A system of straight grooves extending from the base of the bore to about the position of the trunnions, and twisting from thence to the muzzle, in combination with a freed bore, substantially as described, as an improved mode of applying the rifle principle to ordnance.
    In testimony whereof I have hereunto signed my name before two subscribing witnesses."
HORACE E. DIMICK
    Witnesses:
        Geo. Patten,
        John S. Hollingshead.

Letters of Patent No. 16,377, Jan. 13, 1857

The drawing previous page bottom is a shell Dimick designed for use against armor. It was a composite of cast steel, wrought iron, cast iron, lead, and babbitt, the babbitt acting as bearing surface for the rifling.

    "I do not claim a concave front; neither do I claim the spaces in the rear for inviting the explosive force of the charge; but
    What I claim as my invention , and desire to secure by Letter Patent is-
    The construction and shape of the steel and wrought-iron front, in combination with the lead and cast-iron portion, as arranged with the bands N and P, for the purpose of giving the projectile perfect rotation and making it more certain in its action, as herein described."
HORACE E. DIMICK
Witnesses:
        J. Franklin Reigart,
        John S. Hollingshead.

Letters of Patent No. 39,216, July 14, 1863

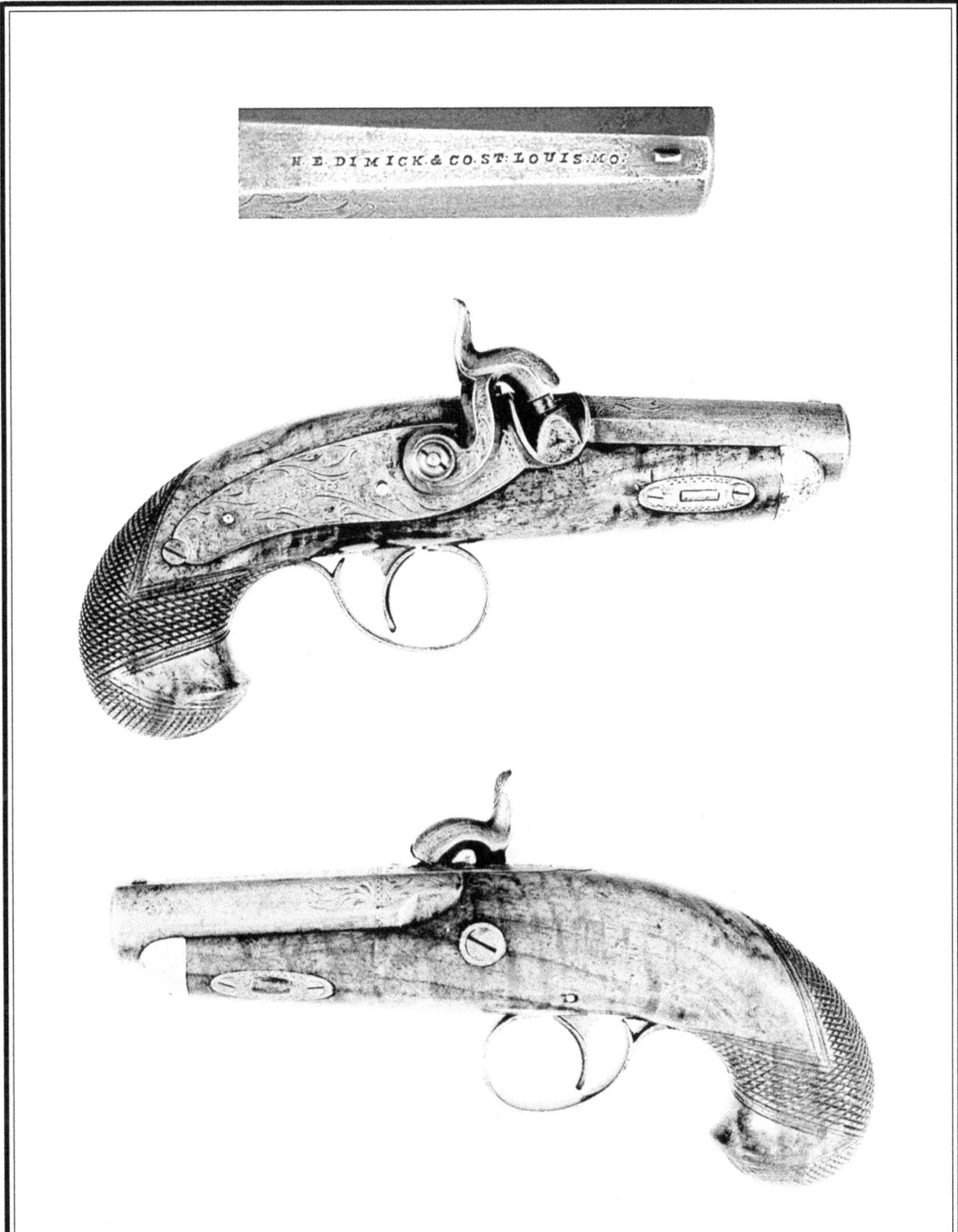

A Dimick/Wirsing derringer. The "WIRSING" mark is visible when the hammer is pulled back, unfortunately not readable in the photo.

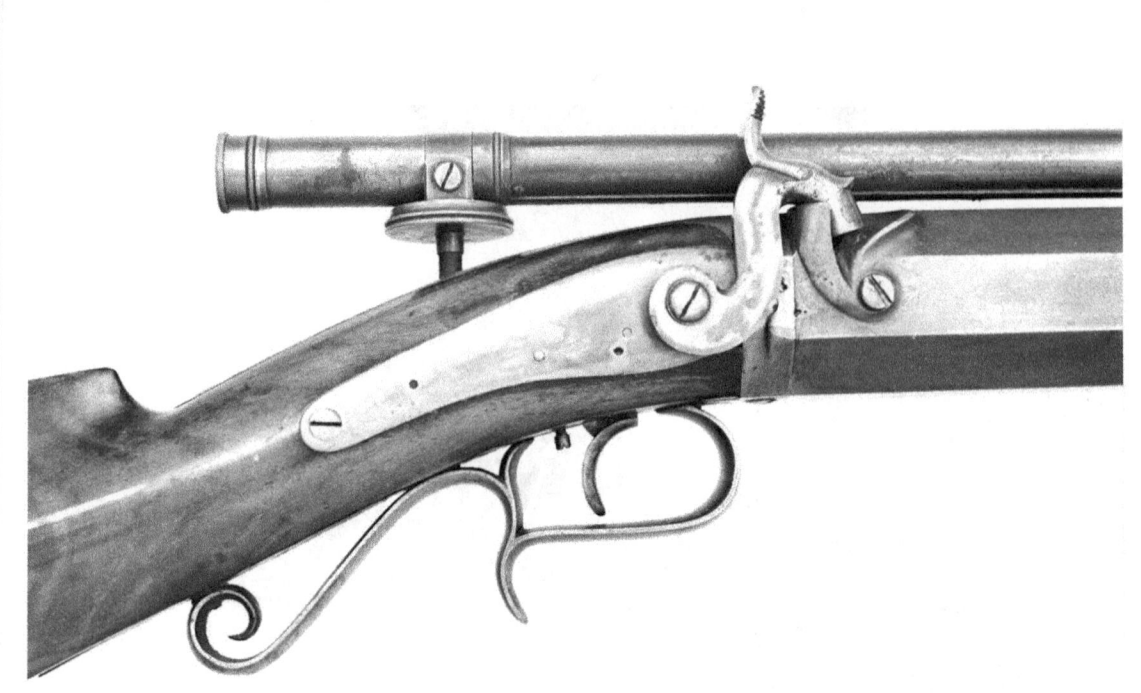

Close-up of breech area of a "H. E. DIMICK" bench rest rifle

Medallion on a "H. E. DIMICK" schuetzen rifle, shooting match prize

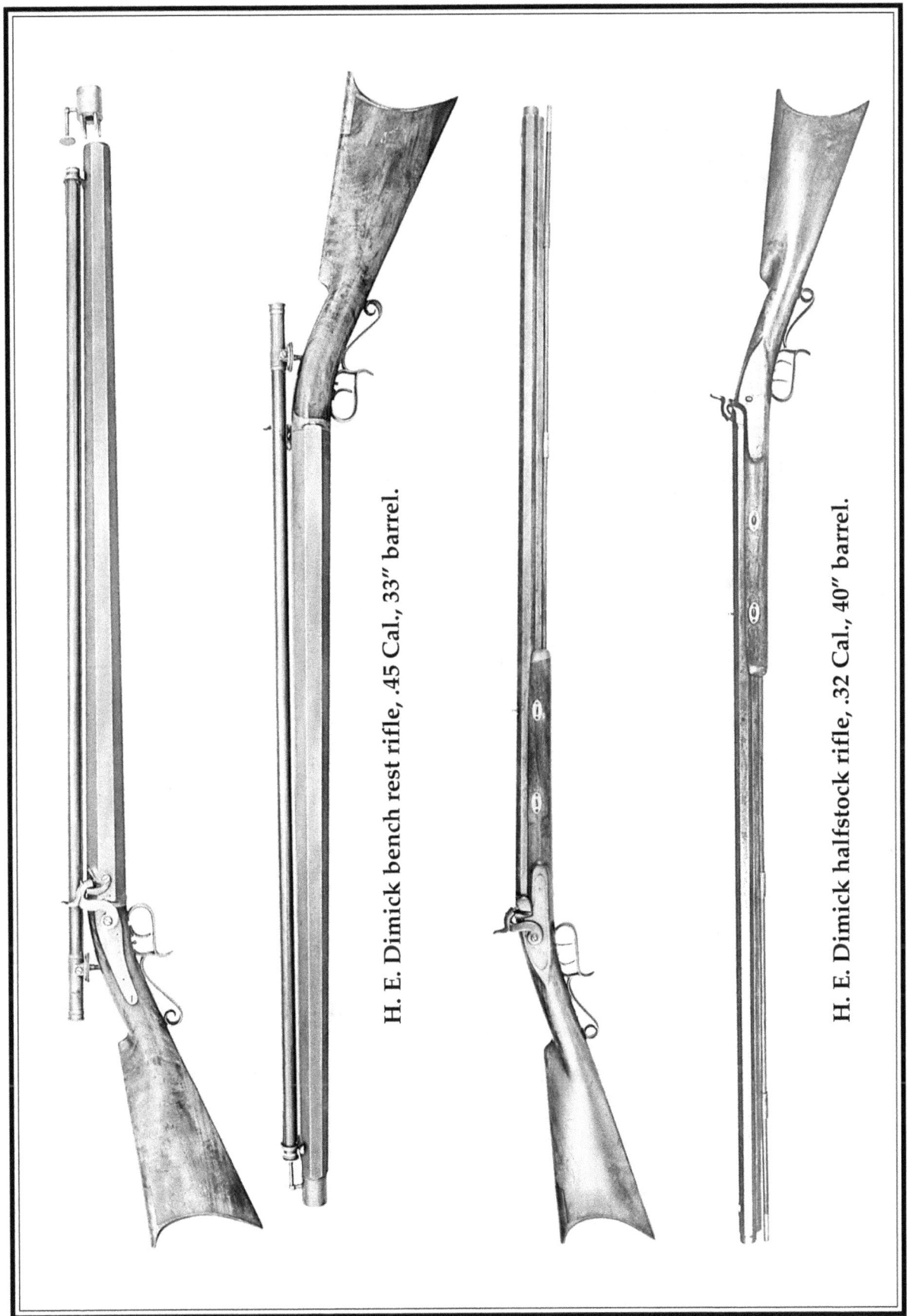

H. E. Dimick bench rest rifle, .45 Cal., 33" barrel.

H. E. Dimick halfstock rifle, .32 Cal., 40" barrel.

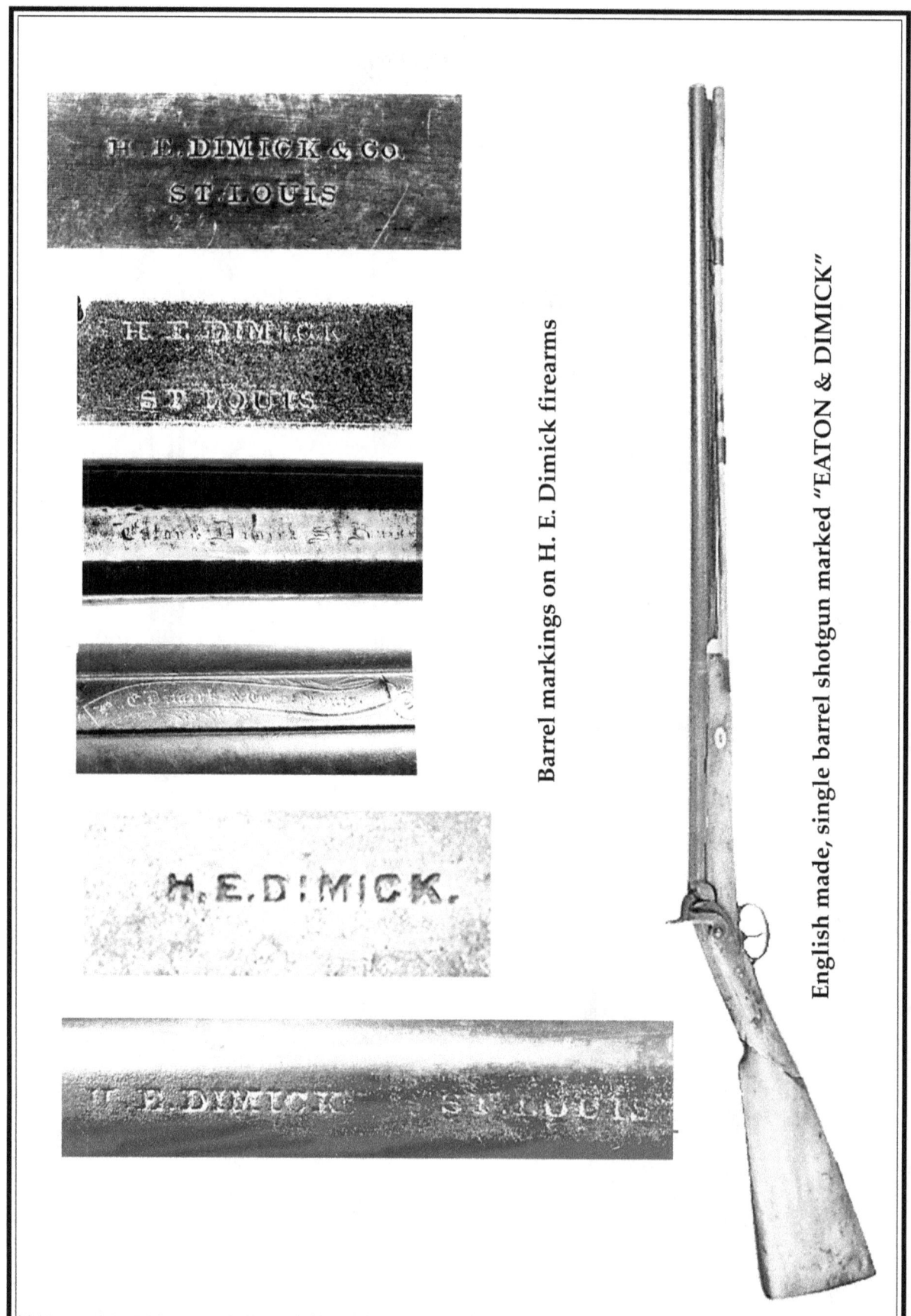

Barrel markings on H. E. Dimick firearms

English made, single barrel shotgun marked "EATON & DIMICK"

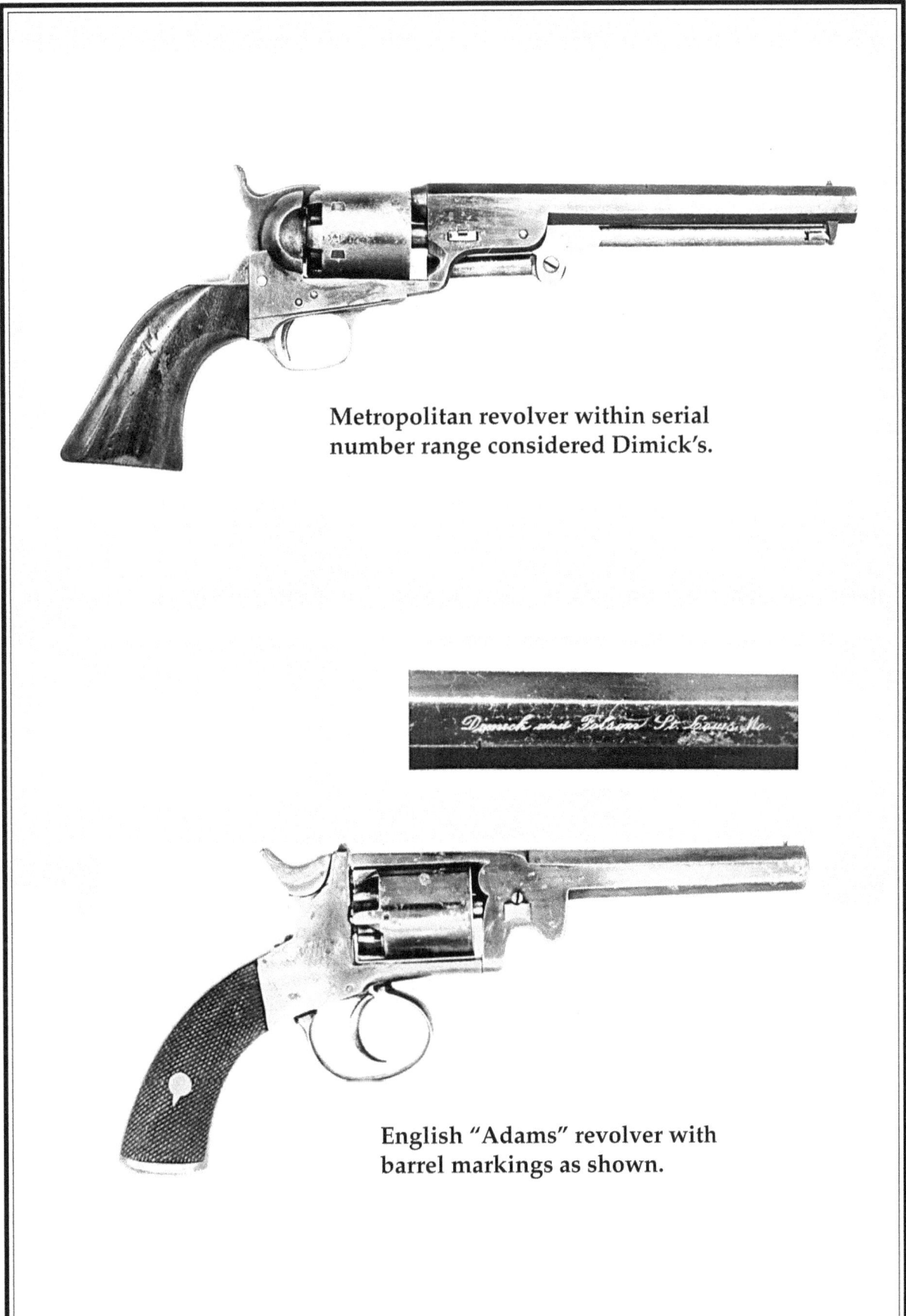

Metropolitan revolver within serial number range considered Dimick's.

English "Adams" revolver with barrel markings as shown.

DREW, DAN
(1794-1870) MD Harpers Ferry, Va. 1813 at Arsenal. Mo. 1832. St. Louis, Mo., 1848 dir.-1850c. Sagetown (now Gladstone), Henderson Co., Il. 1870c. 1848 at St. Louis Arsenal. 50c. shows Ireland as birthplace, 70 shows Va. Maryland is believed to be correct. (Johnson)

DRUMMOND, N. SIEGELE
Butler, Bates Co., Mo. 1879 dir.-1883 dir.

DRUMMOND, F. J.
Bates Co., Mo., 1870ic.

1870 Industrial Census
Butler Co.

Name.	Drummond, F. J.
Name of Business, Manufacture or Product.	Gunsmith
Cost of Raw Materials.	$ 200
Number of Employees.	1
Wages	Not Given
Annual Gross Product.	$ 500

DUCHENE, JOHN
St. Louis, Mo., 1883/84 dir.

DUENCKEL, GEORGE F. S.
St. Louis, Mo., 1864 dir.-1888 dir. Perc. dbl. shotgun. As Duenckels in 75 dir.

1870 Industrial Census
St. Louis

Name.	Duenckel G.
Name of Business, Manufacture or Product.	Gunsmith
Cost of Raw Materials.	$ 55?
Number of Employees.	1
Wages	$ 500
Annual Gross Product.	$ 8000

DUENCKLE, AUGUSTUS
(1814-) GER unl. Ar. 1841. Mo. 1844. Boonville, Cooper, Co., Mo. 1860c., dir. Heavy St. Louis rifle, signed " A. DUENKELE ". (Blackburn)

DUFFY, BARTHOLOMEW
(1820-) IRE unl. N.Y. 1842-1845. Mo. 1847. St. Louis, Mo. 1850c.-1851 dir. As locksmith 1851.

DUFFY, JOHN
(1826-) IRE St. Louis, Mo. 1850c. at St. Louis Arsenal.

DUMAS, JOHN S.
(1800-) VA Mo. 1841. Clark Co., Mo. 1860c.

DUNCAN,   ,
Jenkins Ridge, St. Clair Co., Mo. 1860 dir.

DUNCAN, WILSON
(1833-1913) NY St. Louis, Mo. 1850c. with T. J. Albright. St. Joseph, Buchanan Co., Mo. 1852-1854 with Carlos Gove. Quincy, Il. 1854 dir.-1857. Osceola, St. Clair Co., Mo. 1860c., dir. Council Bluffs, Ia. 1854, 1857-1913. Worked for Carlos Gove in St. Joseph and Council Bluffs, staying in Council Bluffs when Gove left for Denver in 1862. (see Sellers 3 and see Johnson)

DUNN, JOHN H.
(1842-) VA Callaway Co., Mo. 1860c. As apprentice to his father William.

DUNN, WILLIAM
(1814-) VA unl. Va. prior to 1848. Callaway Co., Mo. 1860c.-1870ic.

1870 Industrial Census
Callaway Co.

Name.	Dunn, William
Name of Business, Manufacture or Product.	Gunsmith (part time)
Cost of Raw Materials.	$ 50
Number of Employees.	1
Wages	Not Given
Annual Gross Product.	$ 800

DUNSETH, A
St. Louis, Mo. Flint period? A rifle is on display in the state capitol which belonged to the first governor of Missouri. Converted to percussion by Hawken Shop. Reputed to have been the most accurate rifle in the state.

DURJK, JOHN
(-) ? St. Louis, Mo. 1872 dir.

DUTY, HIRAM
(1802-) NC unl. Tn. 1834. unl. Mo. 1841-1845. unl. Ky. 1846-1848. Lafayette Co., Mo. 1850c.

E

EARL, WILL
(1821-) MD unl. Va. 1847. St. Louis, Mo. 1850c.

EARLY, JACOB H.
(1816-1886) TN Washington Co., Tn. Bent's Fort, Co. 1839. Kane twp., Jackson Co., Mo., 1848-1850c. Ft. St. Vrain, Co. 1855. Marias des Cygnes, Ks. 1860. Westport, Jackson Co., Mo., 1860c. Atchison, Ks. 1864-1886 dir. (Sellers 3)

EASTER, ALLEN
(1817-) KY unl. Ky. prior to 1845. Pettis Co., Mo. 1850c.

EATON, DANIEL E.
Cincinnati, Oh. 1849 dir.-1853 dir. with Kittredge as partner. Chicago, Il. 1853-1855 as D. Eaton & Co. St. Louis, Mo. 1862?-1867 dir. 1864 dir. Shown as partner, H. E. Dimick & Co. No occ. listed 1865 dir. Clerk for G. S. Saxton 1866 dir. Salesman same 1867 dir. Further dir. listing indicate he left gun business. Logan credits him with rifles. Some question if he was a gunsmith. His forte' was as merchant. Import single barrel perc. shotgun marked "EATON & DIMICK". Theory is he ordered them marked this way by manufacturer, without permission of Dimick. This in turn may have led to his short stay with Dimick & Co. (Johnson, AR 4-58)

EBERLY, J. E.
Platte City, Mo. 1881 dir.

ECKHARDT, HENRY
(1833-1909) St. Joseph, Buchanan Co., Mo. 1860 dir.-1869 dir. Sacramento, Ca. 1870-1896. Perc. & breechloading shotguns. (Shelton)

ECKHARDT, WILLIAM
St. Joseph, Buchanan Co., Mo. 1860 dir.-1879 dir.
Eckhardt Bros. 1860-1866 (Henry & William)
Eckhardt & Rein 1866-1867/8 dir.(William &, , Rein)
Eckhardt & Hopkins 1869 dir. (Henry & Frank Hopkins)

EDWIN, WILLIAM J.
Chillicothe, Livingston Co., Mo. 1876/77 dir.

EGGELSTON, C. J.
St. Joseph, Buchanan Co., Mo. 1885/86 dir.

EISPRICH, CHARLES
(1836-) NH unl. Oh. 1849. St. Louis, Mo. 1860c.

ELDRIDGE, WILLIAM W.
Bowling Green, Pike Co., Mo. 1876/77 dir. As photographer & gunsmith.

ELK, J. F.
Warrensburg, Johnson Co., Mo. 1885/86 dir.-1898 dir. Kunkle & Elk?

ELLINGER, HENRY
St. Joseph, Buchanan Co., Mo. 1883/84 dir. St. Louis, Mo. 1894 dir.-1907 dir.

ELLIS, WILLIAM
(1784-) NC unl. Tn. 1825. Scott Co., Mo. 1850c. Flintlock fowlers.

ELVINS, RALPH
Farmington, St. Francois Co., Mo. 1893 dir.-1898/99 dir.

ELY, LEWIS A.
(1819-1911) OH? Chesterville, Oh. 1847-1856. St. Joseph, Buchanan Co., Mo. 1856-1870. Leadville, Co. 1870 dir.-1872 dir. Cardington, Oh. 1896 dir. Made guns only in Oh. & Mo. (Hutslar)

ELY, LYMAN H.
Nevada, Vernon Co., Mo. 1876/77 dir.-1885/86 dir. As L.M. on 1879 dir.

ENGELS, NATHANIEL
(1812-) GER Mo. 1852. St. Louis, Mo. 1860c. Listed as Master Armorer at Arsenal.

ENGLE, E. W.
(1832-) VA Jefferson Co., Mo. 1860c.

ENGLES, DAN?
(1814-) GER St. Louis, Mo. 1850c. See Ingles.

ENGLISH, WILLY
(1846-) TX St. Louis, Mo. 1870c.

ENHOLM, J. H.
St. Louis, Mo. Patent # 28,977 July 3, 1860, alarm gun.

ENKE, E.
Norma, Webster Co., Mo. 1879 dir.

ETTERLE (ETTERLY, ETERLE), JOSEPH
(1804-1881) GER Washington, Franklin Co., Mo. 1860c. St. Louis, Mo. 1867, 1869-1870 dir. As "Etterly" on 60 census, with Geo. Bergner. As "Eterle" with Gemmer 1870. See p. 129.

EUREKA GUN WORKS
Kahoka, Clark Co., Mo. 1885/86 dir. John F. and Horace C. Longanaecker.

EUSTACE, THOMAS F.
St. Louis, Mo. Patent #488,627, Dec. 27, 1892., cartridge.

EVERHART, P.
Breckenridge, Caldwell Co., Mo. 1881 dir.

EVERTZ, FREDERICK
St. Louis, Mo. 1880 dir.-1912 dir.

F

FALKENRATH, RUDOLPH
   St. Louis, Mo. 1887 dir.- 1913 dir. 1887 dir. as finisher. Gunsmith or locksmith in other directories.
FANN. J. W.
   Independence, Jackson Co., Mo. 1883/84 dir.-1898/99 dir.
FARMER, EDWIN
   Greenville, Oh. 1875 dir., Carthage, Jasper Co., Mo. 1881 dir.-1898/99 dir. (Sellers)
FAXON (FAXTON), A. M.
   (1810-) NY Mo. 1846. Clark Co., Mo. 1850c. St. Francis, Mo. 1854 dir. Athens, Clark Co., Mo. 1881 dir.-1883/84 dir. Census as Faxton.
FEA & HAMILTON
   St. Louis, Mo. 1854 dir. Thomas Fea & John Hamilton.
FEA, THOMAS
   (1815-) SCOT St. Louis, Mo. 1854- 1859 dir. Washington Co., Mo. 1860c.
FEEL, JAMES E.
   Havana, Gentry Co., Mo. 1876/77 dir.-1881 dir. Fell 1881 dir., Peel 76/77 dir.
FELTON, S.
   Meramec Iron Works, Phelps Co., Mo. 1860 dir.
FISHER, LAWRENCE
   (1832-) GER Warren Co., Mo. 1850c. With William Harrison.
FLESCH (FLESH), MARTIN
   (1829-) GER St. Louis, Mo. 1850c., 1870c. John F. Dittrich with him 1850c.
   1870 Industrial Census
   St. Louis
   Name. Flesh, Martin
   Name of Business, Manufacture or Product.
         Gunsmith
   Cost of Raw Materials. $ 3000
   Number of Employees.   4
   Wages $ 4000
   Annual Gross Product. $ 8500
FLETCHALL, P.
   Hopkins, Nodaway Co., Mo. 1876/77 dir.
FLOERL, BALTHAZAR see BALTHASAR
FLOHR, ANDREW
   (1824-1896) Mo. 1850. Sacramento, Ca. 1851-1893. Flohr &Wendell 1858-1860. Perc. and breechloading rifles and shotguns. (Shelton)

Flood-Furlong

FLOOD, JOHN
Montgomery City, Mo. 1867/68 dir.

FLUHMANN, GOTTLIEB H.
St. Louis, Mo. prior to 1861. Died in Colorado (Noble)

FOGGERSON, LLOYD?
(1823-   ) GER Mo. 1855. St. Francois Co., Mo. 1860c.

FOLSOM, H. & CO.
St. Louis, Mo. 1860 dir.-1881 dir. Listed as gunsmiths 1866 dir. James H. McCulloch managing partner 1869-1881.

FOLSOM, DAVID
St. Louis, Mo. 1865-1868 dir. Son of Henry.

FOLSOM, HENRY
(-1887) St. Louis, Mo. 1854-1865 dir. With Dimick in H.E. Dimick & Co. 1854-1859. H. Folsom & Co. 1860 (with Grant Burrows). Kept St. Louis Store until at least 1881. Memphis, Tn. 1862-1866. New Orleans, La. 1864-1887. See p 39 & p. 186. (Sellers)

FOPAY, FREDERICK
St. Louis, Mo. 1860 dir.

FOSLER, E.
Rinkelville, Mo. (inside corporate limits City of St. Louis) 1881 dir.-1885/86 dir.

FREDERICKS, FREDERICK
(-1887) ? Kansas City, Mo. 1869 dir.-1885/86 dir. As T. in 76/77 dir.

   1870 Industrial Census
   Jackson Co.   (Kansas City)
Name. Fredericks, Frederick.
Name of Business, Manufacture or Product.
   Gunsmith (repair)

Cost of Raw Materials.	$ 700
Number of Employees.	1
Wages	Not Given
Annual Gross Product.	$ 2000

FREEMAN. J.
Coulter's Store, Macon Co., Mo. 1860 dir.

FRICKE, HENRY (HEINRICH)
(-1890) GER? St. Louis, Mo. 1873 dir.-1889 dir.

FRICKE, HENRY
St. Louis, Mo. 1900 dir.-1904 dir. Son of Henry.

FRICKE, MINNA
St. Louis, Mo. 1890 dir.-1891 dir. Widow of Henry.

FRIEDE, MEYER
(1821-   ) GER St. Louis, Mo. 1848 dir.-1860c., ic., dir. Jewelry and rifle manufacturer.

FRIEDE, M. & CO.
St. Louis, Mo. 1860ic., dir. Meyer Friede and Leopold Schoen.

   1860 Industrial census:
   St. Louis, Ward 8
   Name. M. Friede & Co.
Name of Business, Manufacture, or Product.
   "Jewellry & Rifle Manufacury"
Capital invested in the Business.
   $ 500 ($ 1000 crossed out. Figures separated for jewelry and rifle manf.)
Raw Material used, including Fuel.

Quantities.	Kinds.	Values.
40 oz.	Gold	$ 720
10 lb.	Silver	$ 150
500 "	Steel & Iron	$ 125

Average number of hands employed.
   Male. 4 (Jewelry)
          2 (Rifle)
Wages. Average Monthly cost of male labor.
   $ 150 (Jewelry)
   $ 75 (Rifles)
Annual Product.

Quantities.	Kinds.	Values.
175	Rifles	$ 1,750
400	G. Rings	$ 400
	"Miscell."	$ 3,160

FROELICH, LOUIS
St. Louis, Mo., 1898/99 dir.

FUNK, FOLDEN
(1830-   ) GER Mo. 1855. St. Louis Co., Meramec twp., Mo. 1860c.

FUNKE, CHARLES
Union, Franklin Co., Mo. 1876/77 dir.-1885/86 dir. As tinner & gunsmith 1876/77 dir.

FURLONG, HENRY
(1819?-   ) LA St. Louis, Mo. 1850c. Poss. 1829 as year of birth.

FURLONG, MARTIN
Carthage, Jasper Co., Mo. 1876/77 dir.-1879 dir.

G

GANDERS, LOUIS
  Brookfield, Linn Co., Mo., 1870ic.
  1870 Industrial Census
  Linn Co. (Brookfield)
  Name. Ganders, Louis
  Name of Business, Manufacture or Product.
    Gunsmith (part time)
  Cost of Raw Materials. $ 50
  Number of Employees.   1
  Wages   Not Given
  Annual Gross Product. $ 250

GARRETT, ROBERT A.
  (1822-) KY unl. Ky. prior to 1848. Adair Co., Mo. 1850c., 1860c.

GAUCHEZ, M.
  Rifle entered by Boisaubin in 1858 Ag. & Mech. Fair. See p. 19

GAYLOR, CALVIN
  (-1866) TN unl. Mo. 1840-1844. unl. Ar. 1847. unl. Mo. 1850. Taney Co., Mo. 1860c.

GEESEY, J. N.
  Plattsburgh, Clinton Co., Mo. 1883/84 dir.

GEMMER, JOHN PHILIP see following pages and p. 129.

GEMMER, JULIUS P. H. see following page and p.129.

GEORGE, J. H.
  St. Louis, Mo. 1884 dir.

GERMAN, HENRY
  Hermann, Gasconade Co., Mo. 1891/92 dir.

GERNGROSS, STEPHEN
  St. Louis, Mo. Patent #110,353, Dec. 10, 1870, breechloading firearm. (bolt)

GERO?, JACOB
  (1812-) FR Mo. 1846. Clay Co., Mo. 1860c.

GERTNER, XAVIER
  St. Louis, Mo. 1893 dir.-1898/99 dir.

GIBBONS, THOMAS
  (1827-) ENG unl. Pa. 1841-1844? Covington, Ky. 1850c. St. Louis, Mo. 1859 dir. -1879 dir., 1885/86 dir., 1860c. Perc. 1/2 stock & locks Ky. & Mo.

J. P. GEMMER,
WHOLESALE AND RETAIL DEALER IN
Guns, Pistols
AMMUNITION and SPORTING GOODS.

700 North Third St., - **ST. LOUIS, MO.**

Polk's 1893-94 State Directory

GEMMER, JOHN PHILIP
(1838-1919) GER Boonville, Cooper Co., Mo. 1855-1859. St. Louis, Mo. 1859-1915. Apprenticed at Booneville? 1860 with Kleinhenn. 1860c. listed as gunmaker. Took Hawken shop over from Watt about 1865 and operated it until 1915. Skilled and innovative. Four Rimfire breechloading St. Louis Rifles known, marked patent applied for. No evidence found that he was granted a patent.
See P. 58 for "Spencer-Hawken" conversion.

1870 Industrial Census
St. Louis
Name. Gemmer, J. P.
Name of Business, Manufacture or Product.
    Gunsmith
Cost of Raw Materials. $ 1315
Number of Employees.   3
Wages $ 2080
Annual Gross Product. $ 9250

Known Employees:
    William L. Watt 1865-1870
    Joseph Etterle 1867-1870

GEMMER, JULIUS P. H.
(1873-1956) MO St. Louis, Mo. son of John P. listed as gunsmith 1890's dir.'s. Winchester representative for many years. Cartridge dbl. shotgun marked " JULIUS P. GEMMER ".

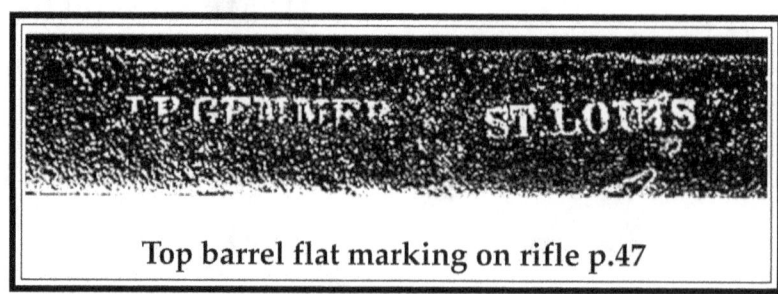

Top barrel flat marking on rifle p.47

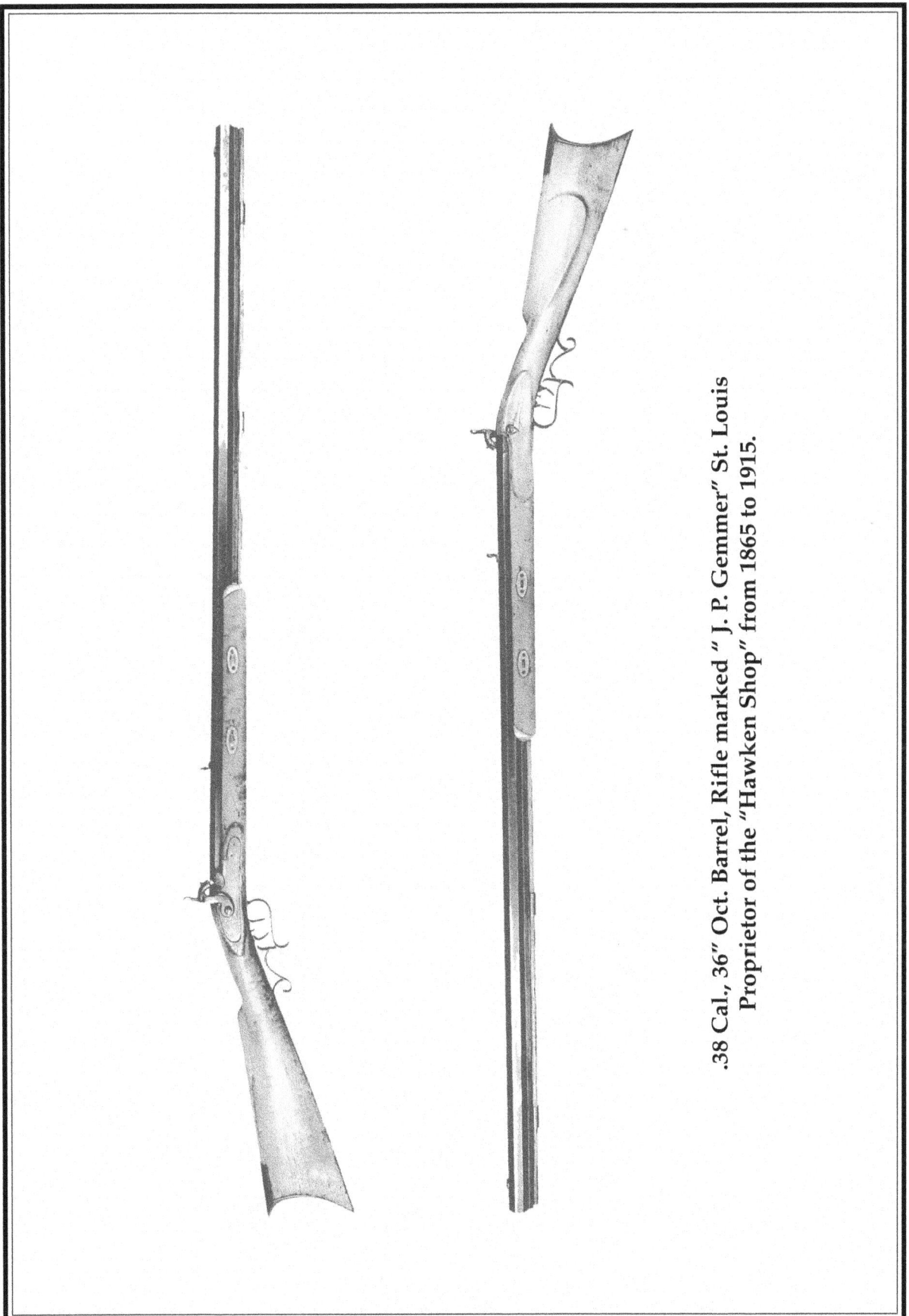

.38 Cal., 36" Oct. Barrel, Rifle marked "J. P. Gemmer" St. Louis Proprietor of the "Hawken Shop" from 1865 to 1915.

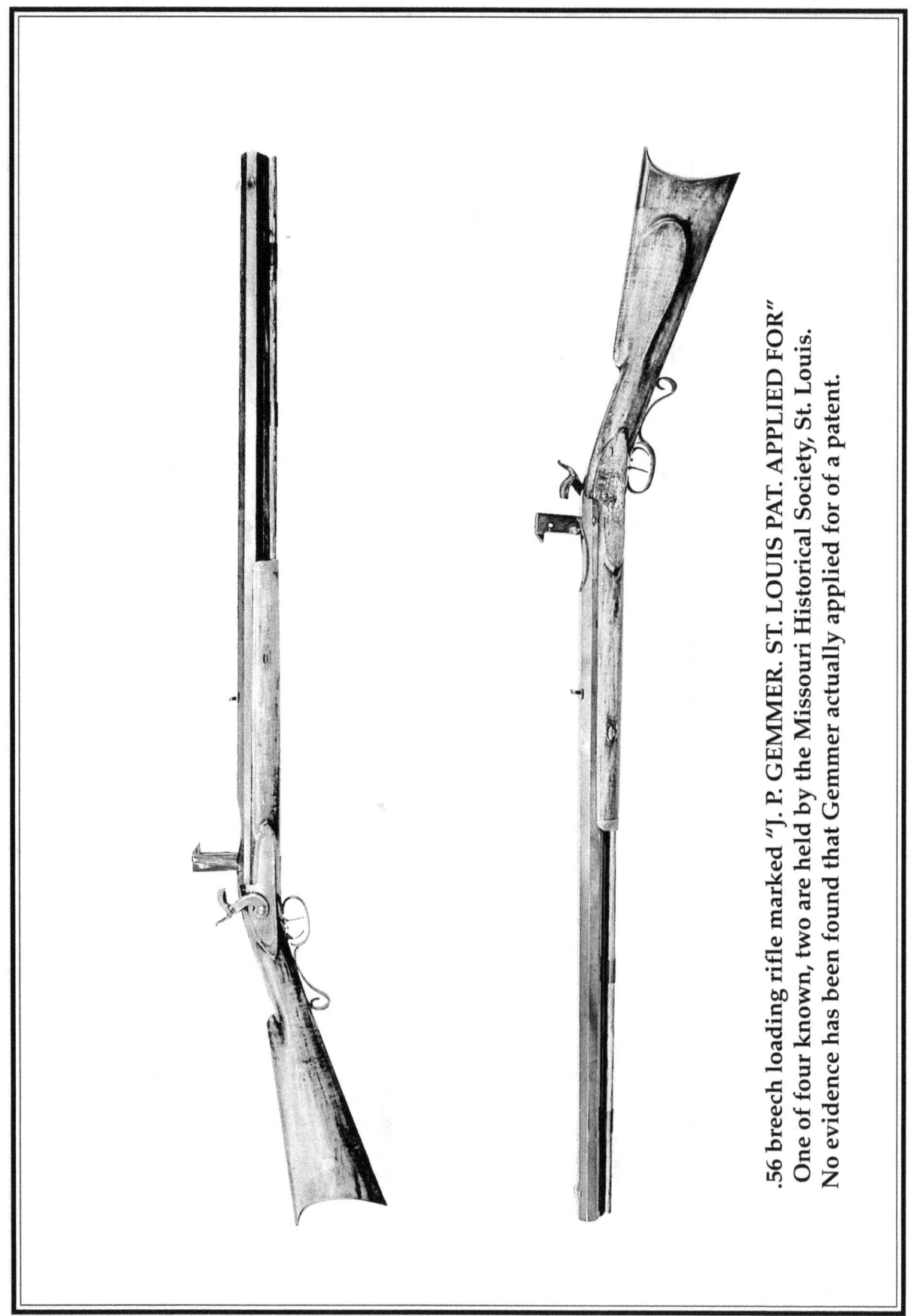

.56 breech loading rifle marked "J. P. GEMMER. ST. LOUIS PAT. APPLIED FOR" One of four known, two are held by the Missouri Historical Society, St. Louis. No evidence has been found that Gemmer actually applied for of a patent.

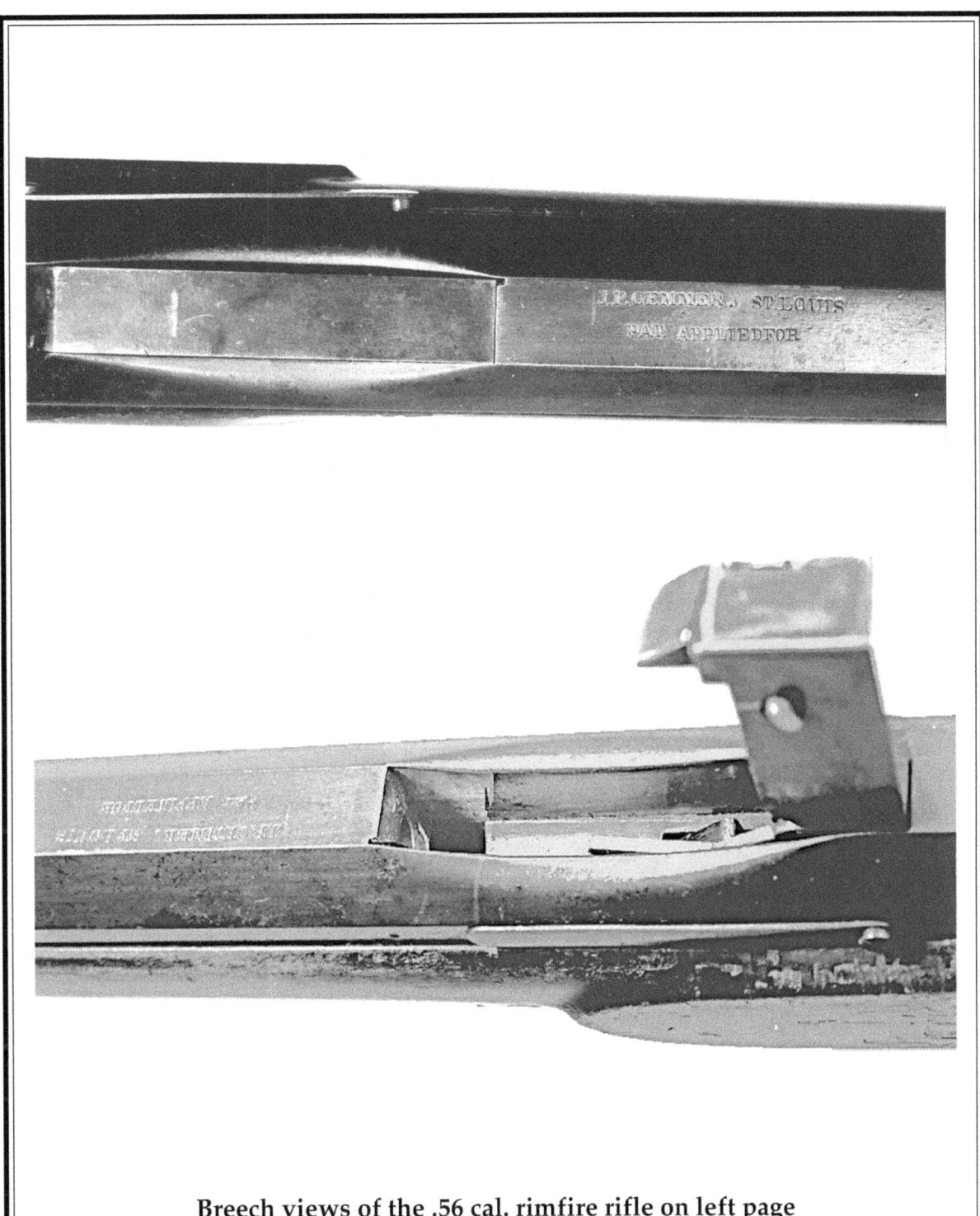

Breech views of the .56 cal. rimfire rifle on left page

GIBBS, EDWIN
  Macon City, Mo. 1860 dir.
GIBSON, L. L.
  (Rock Prairie, Dade Co., Mo. 1879 dir.-1881 dir. Everton, Dade Co., Mo. 1883/84 dir. French Village, St. Francois Co., Mo. 1885/86 dir.-1889/90 dir.
GILL, PRISLEY (PRESLEY)
  (1805-) VA Portland, Callaway Co., Mo. 1835- 1850c., ic., 1854 dir. As Gill & Blackburn 1854 dir. Lincoln Co., Mo. 1860c., ic.

  1850 Industrial Census:
  Callaway Co.
  Name. P. Gill
  Name of Business, Manufacture, or Product.
      Gunsmith & Blacksmith
  Capital invested in Real and Personal Estate in the Business. $ 300
  Raw Material used, including Fuel.
      Quantities.   Kinds.   Values.
      25   Gun Barrels
              Stocks & C. $ 100
      5 ton   Iron $ 500
  Number of hands employed. Male.   2
  Average Monthly cost of male labor. $ 60
  Annual Product.
      Quantities.   Kinds.   Values.
      25   Guns $ 450
              Sundry Work $ 1,000

  1860 Industrial Census:
  Bedford Township, Lincoln Co.
  Name. Presley Gill
  Name of Business, Manufacture, or Product.
      Gunsmith
  Capital invested in Real and Personal Estate in the Business. $ 800
  Raw Material used, including Fuel.
      Quantities.   Kinds.   Values.
      20   Gun Barrels $ 60
      500 lbs. Iron, steel $ 30
      100 bu.   Coal $ 80
  Average number of hands employed. Male. 1
  Average Monthly cost of male labor. $ 30
  Annual Product.
      Quantities.   Kinds.   Values.
      20   Rifles $ 320
              Other Work $ 200

GILLIS, GEORGE
  Osceola, St. Clair Co., Mo. ca. 1860. Knife and gunmaker.
GINGER, GEORGE W.
  (1837?-) ? Boonville, Cooper Co., Mo. 1879 dir.-1885/86 dir.

GIVENS, THOS.
  Butler Co., Mo. 1870ic.

  1870 Industrial Census
  Butler Co.
  Name. Givens, Thos.
  Name of Business, Manufacture or Product.
      Pistols & Guns
  Cost of Raw Materials. $ 600
  Number of Employees.   2
  Wages   Not Given
  Annual Gross Product. $ 1000

GLANZ, JOHN
  (1835-) GER unl. In. 1861-1863. Mo. 1867. St. Louis, Mo. 1870c.
GLIDEWELL, WILLIAM J.
  (1832-) TN unl. Tn. until 1859. Cape Girardeau Co., Mo. 1860c.
GLORE, JAMES R.
  (1828-) KY Mo. 1848, Troy, Lincoln Co., Mo. 1860c., dir. Gunsmith and jailer.
GOBBELS, MATHIAS
  St. Louis, Mo. 1848 dir.-1859 dir. As Gobbes 1848 dir. Goebels 1859 dir.
GODSPEED, THOMAS see GOODSPEED
GOEKEN, EWALDUS
  St. Louis, Mo. 1848 dir.-1878 dir. Given name also listed as Ewald and Edward. Surname also listed as Gocken.
GOOD, J. J.
  Warrensburg, Johnson Co., Mo. 1860 dir. Cythiana, Ky. 1879 dir.-1896 dir.
GOOD, HENRY M.
  (1825-) KY Stoddard Co., Mo. 1860c.
GOODLINE, J.
  St. Joseph, Buchanan Co., Mo. 1869 dir.-1873 dir.
GOODMAN, HENRY
  St. Louis, Mo. 1877 dir.-1905 dir. Patents # 185,912, Jan. 2,1877, # 212,459, Feb. 18, 1879, # 267,876, Nov. 21, 1882, breechloading firearms, # 274,093, Mar. 13, 1883, # 288,939, Nov. 9, 1883, # 352,185, Nov. 9, 1886 revolvers. Descendants closed gunstore in early 1980's. In its heyday the gunstore was a major safari supplier, popular with Hollywood stars. The walls were adorned with signed photographs of celebrities taken when they shopped at the store.
GOODRICH, ASAPH
  (1810-) MO Lincoln Co., Mo. 1850c.
GOODSPEED, THOMAS
  Isadora, Worth Co., Mo. 1889 dir.-1898/99 dir. As Godspeed 89 dir.

GOVE, CARLOS
(1817-1900) NH Council Bluffs, Ia. 1840-1852? St. Joseph, Buchanan Co., Mo. 1850 ic., 1852-1854. Council Bluffs, Ia. 1854-1862. Denver, Co. 1862-84. For a time worked for Indian Dept. in Iowa and had his own shop in Mo. Perc. and cartridge guns. Perc. double rifle marked " C. GOVE " prob. Ia. or Mo. mfg. Wilson Duncan with him part of the time in St. Joseph and Council Bluffs. (Sellers 3, Johnson)

1850 Industrial Census:
Buchanan Co. (St. Joseph)

Name. C. Gove
Name of Business, Manufacture, or Product.
                    Gunsmith
Capital invested in Real and Personal Estate in the Business. $ 1,000
Raw Material used, including Fuel.
    Quantities.   Kinds.   Values.
    2500 lbs.   Iron Steel & c. $ 300
                    Gun stocks $ 300
Average number of hands employed. Male. 2
Average Monthly cost of male labor. $ 50
Annual Product.
    Quantities.   Kinds.   Values.
    (not given)   Guns, Pistols & c. $ 3,500

GRATIOT MFG. CO.
St. Louis, Mo. 1860, perc. revolvers of doubtful authenticity. (Sellers 1)

GREEN. ARTHUR
(1821-) ENG unl. Me. 1858-1863. Mo. 1867. St. Louis, Mo. 1870c.

GREEN, ALFRED
Wayne Co., Mo. ca. Civil War?

GREENAN, BARNEY
(1838-) IRE St. Louis, Mo. 1860c.

GREENSTRED, Z.
Humbolt, Pulaski co, Mo. 1860 dir.

GREENUP. F. M.
Mexico, Audrain Co., Mo. 1893/94 dir.

GRIDNER, CHARLES
St. Louis, Mo. 1860 dir.

GRIEFELT, STEPHEN
(1848-) GER Mo. 1863. St. Louis, Mo. 1870c.

GRISEMAUER, C.
St. Charles, Mo. 1860 dir.

GROSS, A. P. M.
Sedalia, Pettis Co., Mo. 1898/99 dir.

GROSS, FREDERICK
(1832-) GER Warren Co., Mo. 1850c. With George Munch.

GROTJAN, J. A.
Moberly, Randolph Co., Mo. 1898/99 dir.

GRUENINGER?, J.
(1819-) GER Mo. 1848. Westport, Jackson Co., Mo. 1860c.

GULLY, JOHN J.
(1833-) TN Bollinger Co., Mo. 1860c.

GUNTEMAN, JOSEPH
(1821-) GER St. Louis, Mo. 1850c.

GUNTEMAN, WILLIAM
(1823-) GER St. Louis, Mo. 1850c.

GUSCOYLE, TAYLOR
(-) GER Warren Co., Mo. 1860c.

H

HAAS, C.
Holden, Johnson Co., Mo. 1879/80 dir.-1881 dir. As Hast 81.

HAGUE, JAMES
(1823-) ENG St. Louis, Mo. 1850c.-1852 dir. As Daft & Hague 1852.

HAMILTON, JOHN
(1836-) KY Platte Co., Mo. 1860c. St. Joseph, Buchanan Co., Mo. 1860 dir.

HAMILTON, JOHN M.
St. Louis, Mo. 1850c.-1869 dir., 1854 as Fea & Hamilton. As gunsmith only on 1859 dir. Locksmith on others.

HAMLIN, J.
Knob Lick, St. Francois Co., Mo. 1889/90 dir.

HAMS, JOHN
St. Louis, Mo., 1870ic.
 1870 Industrial Census
 St. Louis
 Name.   Hams, John
 Name of Business,Manufacture or Product.
  Gunsmith (repair)
 Cost of Raw Materials. $ 300
 Number of Employees.   1
 Wages   Not Given
 Annual Gross Product. $ 1000

HARDING, B.
(1845-) VA St. Louis, Mo. 1870c.

HARDSHELL, CHARLES
Dry Creek, Crawford Co., Mo. 1885/86 dir.-1889/90 dir.

HARMON, DAVID
DeKalb, Jackson Co., Mo. 1891 dir.-1898/99 dir.

HARMON, GEORGE
(1820-) TN Mo. 1842. Atchison Co., Mo. 1850c.

HARMON, JOHN L.
(1815-) KY unl. Ky. 1844-1849. DeKalb, Jackson Co., Mo. 1860c.

HARRINGTON, J. C.
Frumet, Jefferson Co., Mo. 1893/94 dir. Herrington?

HARRIS, JOHN
(1821-) ENG N.Y., N.Y. 1848-1852. Mo. 1856. St. Louis, Mo. 1870c. (Sellers)

HARRIS, ROBERT, H.
(1831-) DEL Kirksville, Adair Co., Mo. 1860c., dir.-1898/99 dir. John C. Short as his apprentice 1860.

HARRISON, MARSHAL
(1805-) NC Linn Co., Mo. 1860c.

1847 St. Louis Directory

HAWKEN, CHRISTOPHER MILLER
(1825-1905) MO St. Louis, Mo. Son of Jacob. 1860c. listed as farmer.

HAWKEN, JACOB
(1786-1849) MD Harpers Ferry, Va. 1808-1818. St. Louis, Mo. 1818-1849. (Hanson 2)

HAWKEN, JAMES M.
(1836-) MO St. Louis, Mo. 1865 dir. as Hawkins. Son of Samuel.

HAWKEN RIFLE FACTORY see GEMMER

HAWKEN, SAMUEL T.
(1793-1884) MD Hagerstown, Md. 1815-1816. Xenia, Oh. 1816-1822. St. Louis, Mo. 1822-1859. Denver, Co. 1859-1862. St. Louis, Mo. 1863 to death, not active in firearms trade. Birth from family bible. (Hanson 2, Hartzler)

HAWKEN, WILLIAM STEWART
(1825-1900) MO St. Louis, Mo. 1850c.-1860c., 1859 dir. Denver, Co. 1860-1864. 1893 dir. Sutter, St. Louis Co., Mo., 1897 dir. Hillside, St. Louis Co., Mo. Son of Samuel T. (Hanson 2)

Various names of shop and proprietors:
    Lakenan & Hawken 1818-1825
        (James Lakenan and Jacob)
    J & S Hawken 1825-1849
        (Jacob & Samuel)
    S Hawken 1849-1853
    Hawken & Campbell 1854-1856
        (Wm. S. & Tristram Campbell)
    Wm. S. Hawken 1857-1859
    Watt & Bennett
        (ca. 1860, not found in directory, from extant business cards)
    Wm. L. Watt 1860-1864
    J. P. Gemmer 1864-1915

    Hawken Rifle Factory (date unknown, from a photo, p.42, *The Plains Rifle*)

1850 industrial census:
St. Louis, Ward 4
Name. Sam'l. Hawken
Name of Business, Manufacture, or Product. Gunsmith
Capital invested in Real and Personal Estate in the Business. $1,000
Raw Material used, including Fuel.
Quantities. Kinds. Values.
  2000ft.   lumber
  1 ton   iron
  500lb.   steel   } $500
  2200lb. charcoal
  50lb.   brass

Average number of hands employed. Male. 4
Average Monthly cost of male labor. $120
Annual Product.
Quantities. Kinds. Values.
  100   Rifles   } $2,700
  20   Shot Guns

Employees from directories:

Campbell, Tristram 1842
    partner of Wm. S. 1854-56
Hoffman, Christian 1842
Lenghorner (Lenzhaner?), Frederick 1857
    (31 Washington)
Nutz, L. N. 1857
    (21 Washington)
Schwarz, Frederick 1857
    (31 Washington)
Sieber, Robert (Charles R.?) 1857
    (31 Washington)
Tegethoff, William 1857
    (31 Washington)

S. Hawken-pre 1826

Hawken-Spencer

S. Hawken-1849/1853 and later

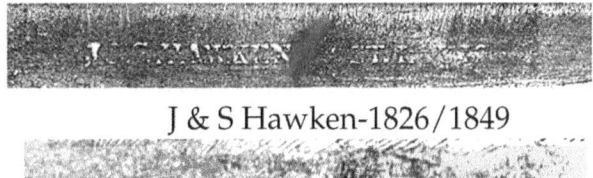
J & S Hawken-1826/1849

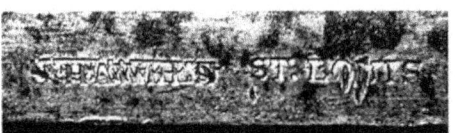
S. Hawken-Overstamped

* Hawken-Colorado?

Jacob and Samuel Hawken, two of the best known makers of plains rifles, began their careers apprenticed to their father, Christian Hawken, in Hagerstown, Maryland. Jacob continued his education, working at the Harpers Ferry Arsenal, where the well known U. S. Model 1803 Rifle was manufactured and this background is reflected in the large bore, hard hitting rifles coveted by men whose lives depended upon them. Samuel enlisted in the Army during the War of 1812 and was discharged in 1815 after which he married and opened a gunshop in Xenia, Ohio. After his wife's death in about 1821, he returned with his three daughters to Hagerstown and in 1822 came to St. Louis.

Jacob arrived in St. Louis in 1818 and set up shop with James Lakenan, doing general gunsmithing, making guns and doing repair work for the Indian Department. This partnership lasted until Lakenan's death in 1825 when, upon Lakenan's death, Jacob and Samuel in 1826 formed a partnership which lasted until Jacob's death from Cholera in 1849. Samuel continued operating the shop until 1853, when he sold the shop to his son William and the property on which it was built to Robert Campbell. See pp. 141-144 for details of the purchase and sale of the property as well as William S. Hawken's bankruptcy in 1857.

Other than the fact that Jacob was survived by his wife, Catherine, and three of his four children, little is known of his personal life. Samuel, on the other hand, took an active part in the organizing and operation of Union Fire Company No. 2 and was the subject of an editorial in the Missouri Republican newspaper, promoting him as a candidate for Mayor.

At the age of 67 in 1859, Sam, according to his own words, walked to Denver where he and son William opened a gun shop. Sam returned to St. Louis after the death of his wife in 1861.

Sam died in 1884, at the age of 92 (From the family bible, Sam was born in 1792) and was buried in Bellefontaine Cemetary, St. Louis.

Jacob and Samuel lived and worked during the colorful years of the 19th Century which included the development of the Santa Fe Trail, the Fur Trade era, the opening of the Oregon Trail, the War with Mexico and the acquisition of Texas and, of course, the discovery of Gold in California. Certainly the most important period of western expansion and a period where the Hawken Rifle played its part.

---

* It was reported that the "Hawken Colorado ?" rifle was brought to Missouri by a man returning from Colorado during th 19th century. The rifle has all the characteristics of the S.Hawken rifle of the 1850's except for the unique barrel marking, of which only two have been reported. The trigger assembly is marked J.P. Lower (Colorado) and knowing that Sam and son William had set up shop in Colorado led to the surmise that the rifle had originated there. Hence the question mark. (D. Pourie)

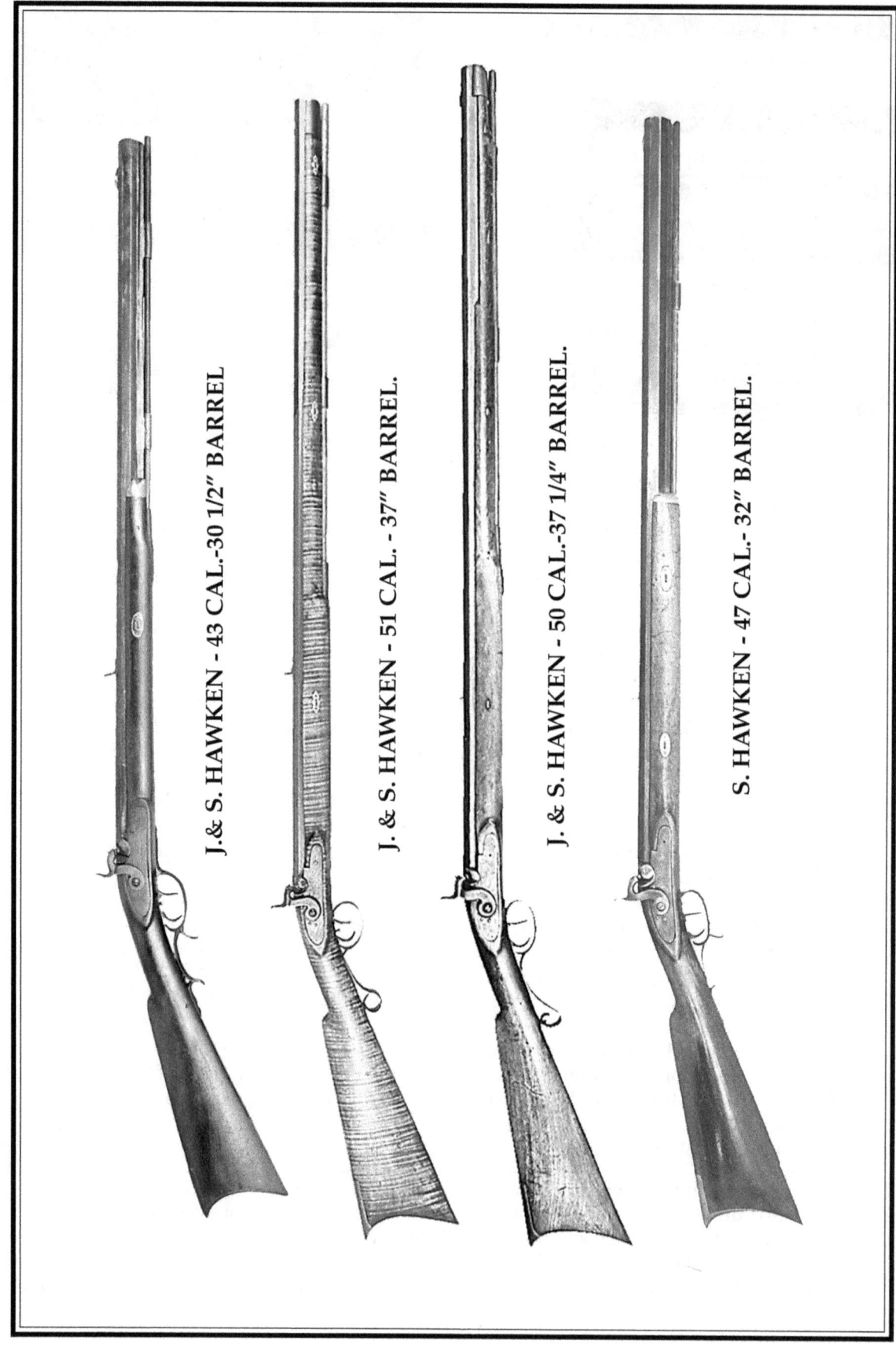

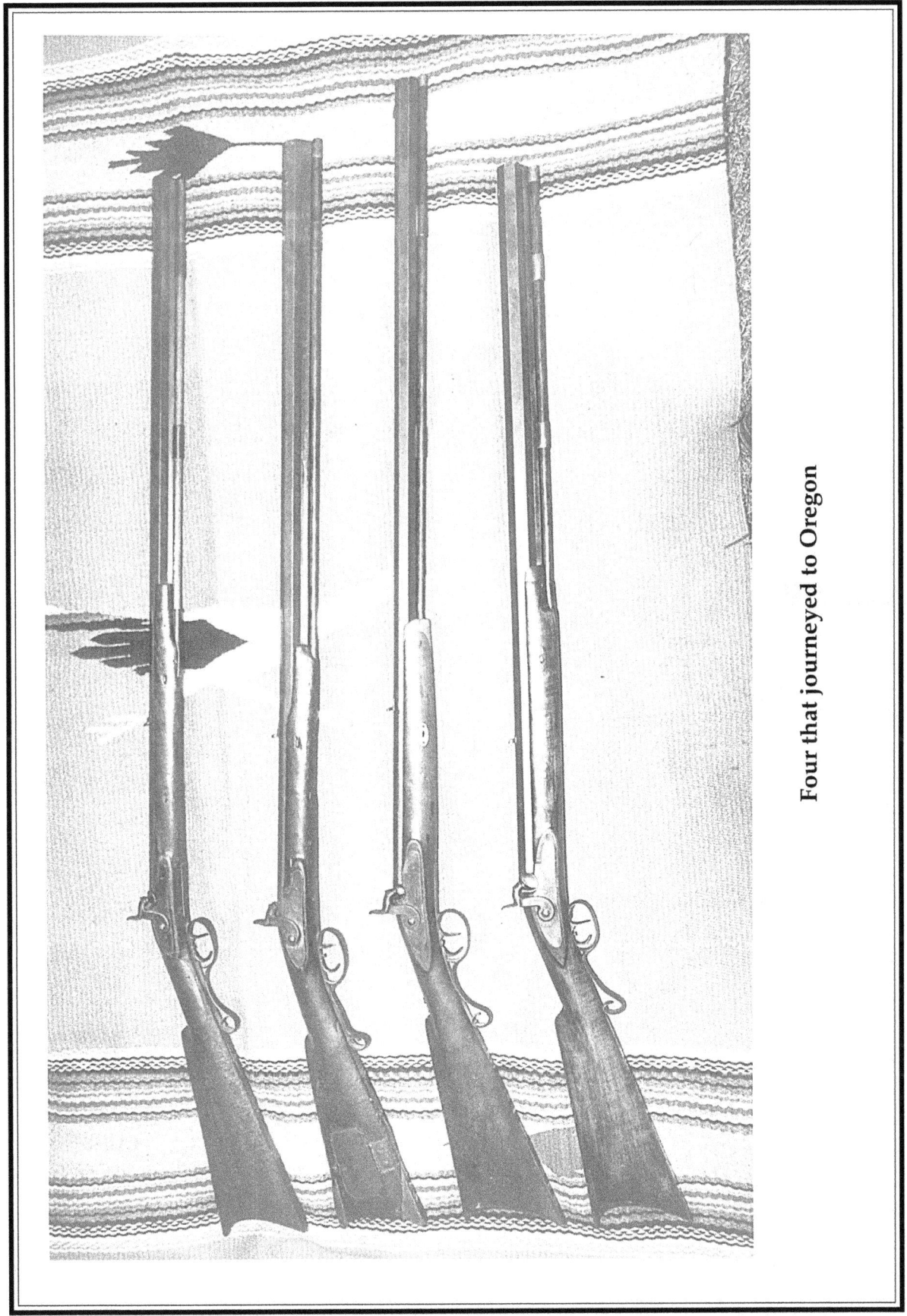
Four that journeyed to Oregon

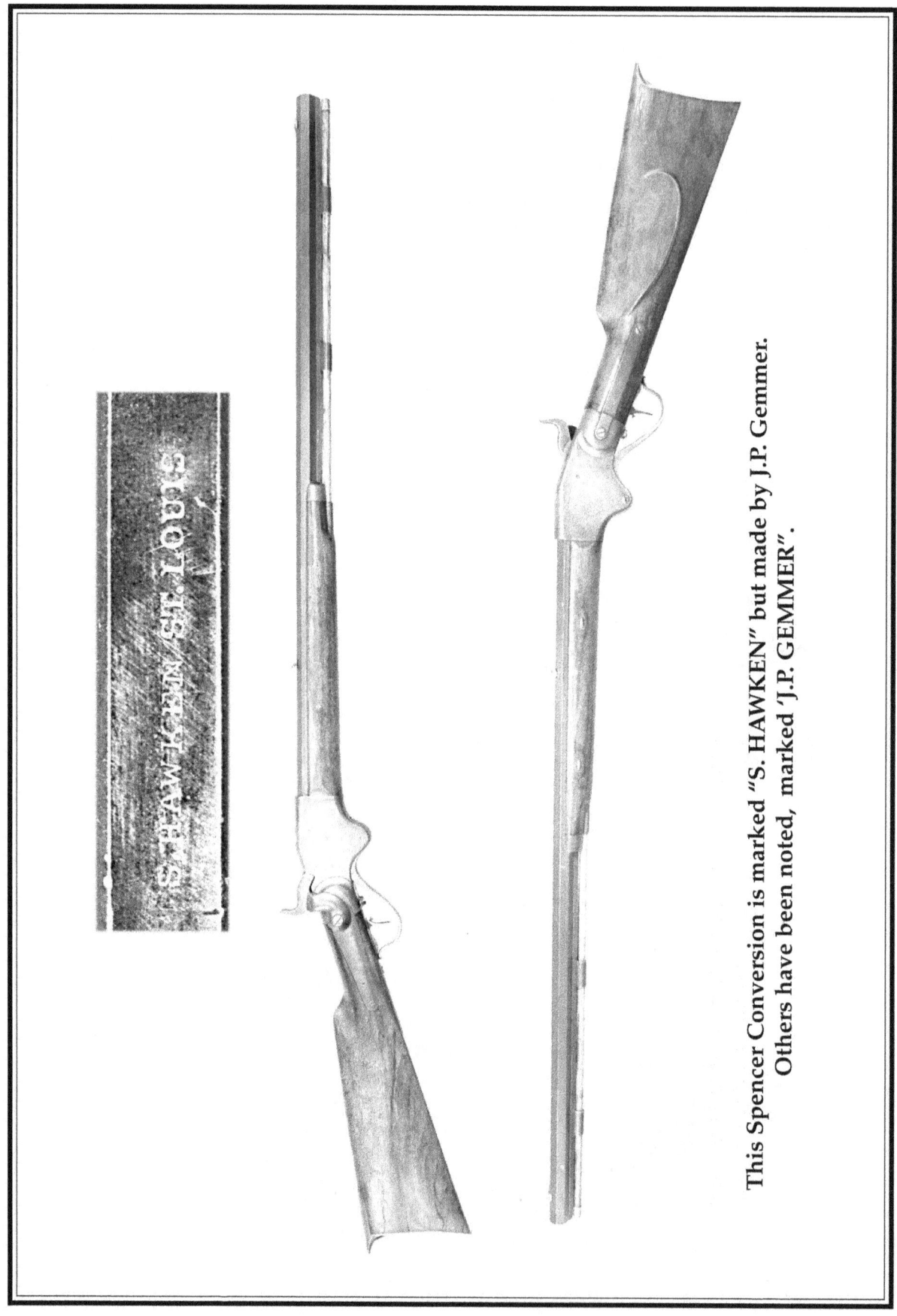

This Spencer Conversion is marked "S. HAWKEN" but made by J.P. Gemmer. Others have been noted, marked "J.P. GEMMER".

HARRISON, WILLIAM
(1812-) OH Warren Co. Mo. 1850c. Gunsmiths Lawrence Fisher and William Craben have same address.

HARRISON, WILLIAM
(1822-) NC Linneus, Linn Co., Mo. 1850c., 1860c., dir.

HARSTROTTER, JNO.
St. Louis, Mo., 1870ic. Same as Herkstroeter?

1870 Industrial Census
St. Louis
Name. Harstrotter, Jno.
Name of Business, Manufacture or Product.
    Gun & Locksmith
Cost of Raw Materials. $ 250
Number of Employees.   1
Wages   Not Given
Annual Gross Product. $ 1500

HARTKOFF, DANIEL
New London, Ralls Co., Mo. 1867/68 dir. Fredericktown, Madison Co., Mo. 1885/86 dir.

HARTUNG, GOTTFRIED
Cape Girardeau, Mo. 1889 dir.-1898/99 dir.

HARVEY, J. M.
Mound City, Holt Co., Mo. 1889/90 dir.

HASENJAGER, FREDERICK
Holstein, Warren Co., Mo. 1879 dir.-1898/99 dir.

1870 Industrial Census
Warren Co.
Name. Hasenjager, (first name not given)
Name of Business, Manufacture or Product.
    Gunsmith
Cost of Raw Materials. $ 200
Number of Employees.   1
Wages   Not Given
Annual Gross Product. $ 1000

HAST, C. see HAAS

HASTINGS, GARDNER P.
(-) ? Springfield, Greene Co., Mo. Patent # 576, 964, Feb. 9, 1897, magazine gun.

HATFIELD, R .P.
(1819-) KY Mo. 1846. Horse Creek, Barton Co. 1860c., dir. As blacksmith in census.

HAUPTMAN, JOSEPH (SR)
(1813-) GER St. Louis, Mo. 1860c., dir.-1867 dir. Listed as Hoffman in census and 1864 dir.

HAUPTMAN, JOSEPH JR.
(1838-) GER St. Louis, Mo. 1860c.-1866 dir. With father in census.

HAWKEN see previous pages and pp. 141-144.

HAWKINS, WILLIAM
(1817-) KY Callaway Co., Mo. 1823. Bloomfield, Callaway Co., Mo. 1850c.

HAWKSLEY, WILLIAM
(1832-) ENG St. Louis, Mo. 1859 dir.-1860c., dir.

HAYES, WILLIAM
(1813-) OH unl. Mo. 1840? unl. Oh. 1845-1849. Warsaw, Benton Co., Mo. 1850c., 1860c., ic., dir., 1883/84 dir.-1893/94 dir. see Samuel Hays

1860 industrial census:
Warsaw City, Benton Co.
Name. William Hayes
Name of Business, Manufacture, or Product.
    Gun Manufacturer
Capital invested in Real and Personal Estate in the Business. $ 600
Raw Material used, including Fuel.
    Quantities.   Kinds.   Values.
    3 doz.   Gun Barrels $ 100
    3 doz.   Locks $ 36
    3 doz.   Mountings $ 9
Average number of hands employed. Male. 1
Average Monthly cost of male labor. $ 40
Annual Product.
    Quantities.   Kinds.   Values.
    3 doz.   Guns $ 648

HAYS, CHARLES
(1818-) IL Mo. 1848. Callaway Co., Mo. 1850c.

HAYS, SAMUEL
(Benton Co., Mo., 1870ic., son of William?

1870 Industrial Census
Benton Co.
Name. Hays, Samuel
Name of Business, Manufacture or Product.
    Gunsmith (part time)
Cost of Raw Materials. $ 100
Number of Employees.   1
Wages   Not Given
Annual Gross Product. $ 450

HAZLEWOOD, H. B.
(1829-) ENG unl. Oh. 1863-1865. Mo. 1867. St. Louis, Mo. 1870c.

HEAD, L. D.
(1819-) KY Marion Co., Il. 1850c. Louisville, Lincoln Co., Mo. 1860 dir. (see Johnson)

HEBB, E. T.
St. Louis, Mo. Perc. fullstock.

HEBERER, ANTON
St. Louis, Mo. 1897 dir.-1899 dir.+

HEBERLEIN, A.
St. Louis, Mo. ca. 1870. St. Louis style air guns marked " R. SIEBER and A. HEBERLEIN " and "A. HEBERLEIN ". See p. 130.

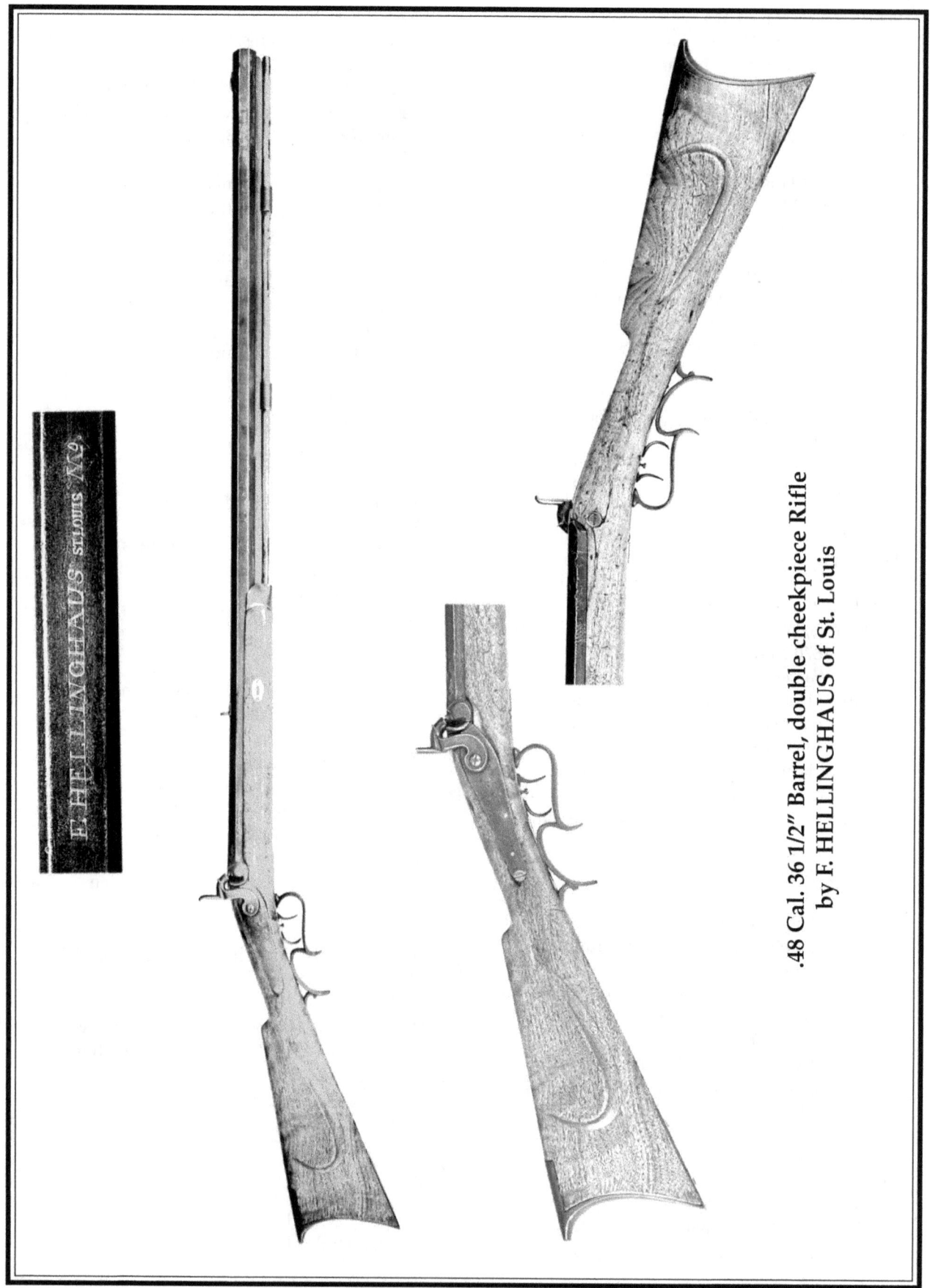

.48 Cal. 36 1/2" Barrel, double cheekpiece Rifle by F. HELLINGHAUS of St. Louis

HEDRICH, C.
   Hermann, Gasconade Co., Mo. 1881 dir.
HEEHNART see KEENHART
HEEMAN, FRED
   (1840-   ) GER St. Louis, Mo. 1860c.
HEIAD, DAN
   (1815-   ) IN unl. In 1853. Lincoln Co., Mo. 1860c.
HEISEL, JAMES L.
   (1819-   ) FR Cole Co., Mo. 1850c.
HEISS, PHILIP
   St. Louis, Mo. 1845 dir.
HELLER, RUDOLPH
   Palmyra, Marion Co., Mo. 1867/68 dir.
HELLINGHAUS, FREDERICK
   (1811-   ) AUS Baltimore, Md., 1832-1835. St. Louis, Mo. 1840/41 dir.-1847 dir. Sacramento, Ca. 1851 dir. San Francisco, Ca. 1856-1857. With John Pearson in Md. With Henry Morgan in St. Louis. Dalles City, Wasco Co., Or. 1860c. (Shelton)
Jerry Gnemi turned up this interesting piece on Hellinghaus, attributed to the June, 20, 1844 issue of The Pittsburgh [Pa.} Morning Chronicle

MORE SHOOTING IN ST. LOUIS

   The Missouri Republican of the 10th. inst. says: "About noon yesterday, a young man, named James Howard, residing on Oak street near Third, threw some water from a window, which fell on the person of a gun smith, named F. Hellinghaus, who resided in the adjoining building. The latter immediately entered the dwelling in which Howard was - met him on the stairs, and, after a few words of altercation with him, shot him in the head. The ball broke the skull, and inflicted a wound which his physicians believe will prove fatal. Hellinghaus was taken into custody, and committed to await an examination today.
   The wounded man says that the wetting of Hellinghaus' person was an accident, and that he was not aware of the fact until accosted in an angry manner by him on the stair landing. On perceiving Hellinghaus draw a pistol, Howard struck him, and the former instantly fired. The wounded is a native of New Hampshire - his antagonist is a German.

HEMMES, STEPHEN
   (1804-   ) GER St. Charles, Mo. 1854 dir.-1860c., dir.-1867/68 dir. 1860 dir. as Hamas, 1867/68 as Hammes.
HENDERSON, BUGGY
   Kaiser, Mo. Perc. rifles.
HENKEL, WILLIAM
   St. Louis, Mo. 1878 dir.-1890 dir. As Kenkel 1878.
HENSLAG, HERMAN
   (1802-   ) St. Louis, Mo. 1850c. (Lewis)
HEPPERT, HENRY
   Hannibal, Marion Co., Mo. 1885/86 dir.-1889/90 dir.
HERKSTROETER & STAHLBERG
   St. Louis, Mo. 1870 dir.-1871 dir. Frederick Herkstroeter and William Stahlberg.
HERKSTROETER, FREDERICK
   St. Louis, Mo. 1860 dir., 1865 dir.- 1874 dir. See above. Same as Harstrotter?
HERMAN, JOHN
   St. Louis, Mo. 1895-1905. Tip-up rifles & pistols. One dated 1905, (pictured GR 4-72)
HERRINGTON, JOHN C.
   (1819-   ) MO Jefferson Co., Mo. 1860c.
HERRINGTON, WILLIAM
   (1788-   ) KY Mo. 1830. Jefferson Co., Mo. 1850c.-1860c.
HESTON, T. J.
   St. Mary's, Ste. Genevieve Co., Mo. Very heavy fullstock.
HETCHALL, P.
   Grant City, Worth Co., Mo. 1883/84 dir.
HEVERIEUX, JOHN BAPTISTE
   (-1775) CAN? Cahokia, Il. prior to 1764? St. Louis, Mo. 1764-1775, sources differ. Either a member of the founding party of St. Louis or a very early immigrant from the Il. side of river. Called royal armorer in one source, gunsmith in others. See MALTA BEND GUNSMITH'S CACHE.
HILLSTEAD, F. W. see MILSTEAD
HINGLE, JOHN
   St. Louis, Mo. 1840/41 dir.
HINTSCHE, WILLIAM
   Kansas City, Mo. 1888 dir.-1898/99 dir.
HIRSCH, ADAM
   Jefferson City, Cole Co., Mo. 1869-1885/86 dir. Perc. 1/2 stock dated Sept. 1869.
HITTON, E. J.
   (1817-   ) VA unl. Ia. 1840-1843. unl. Oh. 1845. Mo. 1847. Pike Co., Mo. 1850c.
HOBLIT, LYMAN
   Sheldon, Vernon Co., Mo. 1889/90 dir.

HOCKENSMITH, K. D.
(1811-) KY Mo. 1836. Independence, Jackson Co., Mo. 1850c., ic., 1860c.
1850 industrial census:
Jackson Co.,
Name. K. D. Hockensmith
Name of Business, Manufacture, or Product.
Gunsmith
Capital invested in Real and Personal Estate in the Business. $ 175
Raw Material used, including Fuel.

Quantities.	Kinds.	Values.
24	Gun Stocks	$ 9
12	" Bls.	$ 48

Average number of hands employed. Male. 1
Average Monthly cost of male labor. $ 50
Annual Product.

Quantities.	Kinds.	Values.
6	Guns	$ 120
	Miscellan.	$ 500

HOCKENSMITH, WILLIAM
(1798-) KY Mo. 1839. Ray Co., Mo. 1850c. Bro. of K. D. ?

HOCKENSMITH, WILLIAM C.
(1836-) MO Independence, Jackson Co., Mo. 1850c. Crab Orchard, Mo. 1876/77 dir., 1883/84 dir. Son of K. D.

HOCKENSMITH, WILLIAM W.
Lawson, Ray Co., Mo. 1898/99 dir.

HODGE, G. W.
Clarence, Shelby Co., Mo.,1883/84 dir.-1889/90 dir.

HODMOND, GEORGE (deHodiamont, George)
(-1866) ? St. Louis, Mo. 1857 dir. E. St. Louis, Il. 1866. Son of Baron Emmanuel de Hodiamont. Listed in dir. as Hodmond. Worked with and was a brother-in-law of Charles Altinger.

HOFFMAN & CAMPBELL
St. Louis, Mo. 1845 dir-1848 dir. Christian Hoffman and Tristram Campbell, plains rifles. [St. Louis rifles] (Hanson 2)

HOFFMAN, CHRISTIAN
Philadelphia, Pa. 1824 dir.-1833 dir. St. Louis, Mo. 1836 dir.-1860 dir. As Huber & Hoffman 1836/37 dir. With Hawken 1842. As Hoffman & Campbell 1845 dir.-1848 dir. 1857-1860 occupation listed as slater, with John Austwick in 1857. He is mentioned as one of the major creditors in Wm. S. Hawken bankruptcy. See p. 144.

HOFFMAN, JOSEPH see HAUPTMAN

HOFFMAN, JOSEPH JR. see HAUPTMAN

HOFFSTETHER, F.
(1825-) GER St. Louis, Mo. 1850c.

HOGAN, JOSEPH
St. Louis, Mo. 1868 dir. As Shone & Hogan.

HOLBERT, JOSHUA
(1804-) SC Mo. 1839. Crawford Co., Mo. 1860c.

HOLMES, SAMUEL C.
(1833-) IN unl. In. prior to 1858. Saline Co., Mo. 1860c.

HOLMES, SILVESTER
(1808-) NY Mo. 1840. Monroe Co., Mo. 1850c.

HOMA, CONRAD
(1840-) GER Mo. 1867. St. Louis, Mo. 1870c., ic.
1870 Industrial Census
St. Louis
Name. Homa, Conrad
Name of Business,Manufacture or Product.
Gunsmith

Cost of Raw Materials.	$ 3000
Number of Employees.	2
Wages	$ 2424
Annual Gross Product.	$ 7800

HONEY, JOHN W.
Herculaneum, Jefferson Co., Mo. Patent, not numbered, Feb. 10, 1825, shot table.

HOOK, ELIJAH
(1810-) VA Boonville, Cooper Co., Mo. 1849, 1850c. Florence, Morgan Co., Mo. 1860c., dir.-1889 dir.

HOPKINS, DAVID
(1821-) VA Eagle, Harrison Co., Mo. 1860 dir., c.? As farmer on census.

HOPKINS, FRANK G.
St. Joseph, Buchanan Co., Mo. 1869 dir.-1879 dir. As Eckhardt & Hopkins 1869-1870.

HOPPENAU, HENRY
Kansas City, Mo. 1873-1878 dir. Patent # 136,998, Mar. 18,1873. Paola, Ks. 1884 dir. (Sellers)

HOPPER, R.
Caverna, McDonald Co., Mo. 1898/99 dir.

HOUDLETTE, FREDERICK M.
St. Louis, Mo. 1899 dir.

HOWARD, DEGRATTA?
(1835-) KY Mo. 1847. Charleston, Mississippi Co., Mo. 1860c., dir.

HOWARD, JAMES
(1825-) KY New Madrid, Mo. 1850c. With H. L. Walker.

HOWARD, LAWSON H.
(1829?-) IN? Louisiana, Pike Co., Mo. 1850c., 1860c.,1876/77 dir.-1889 dir.

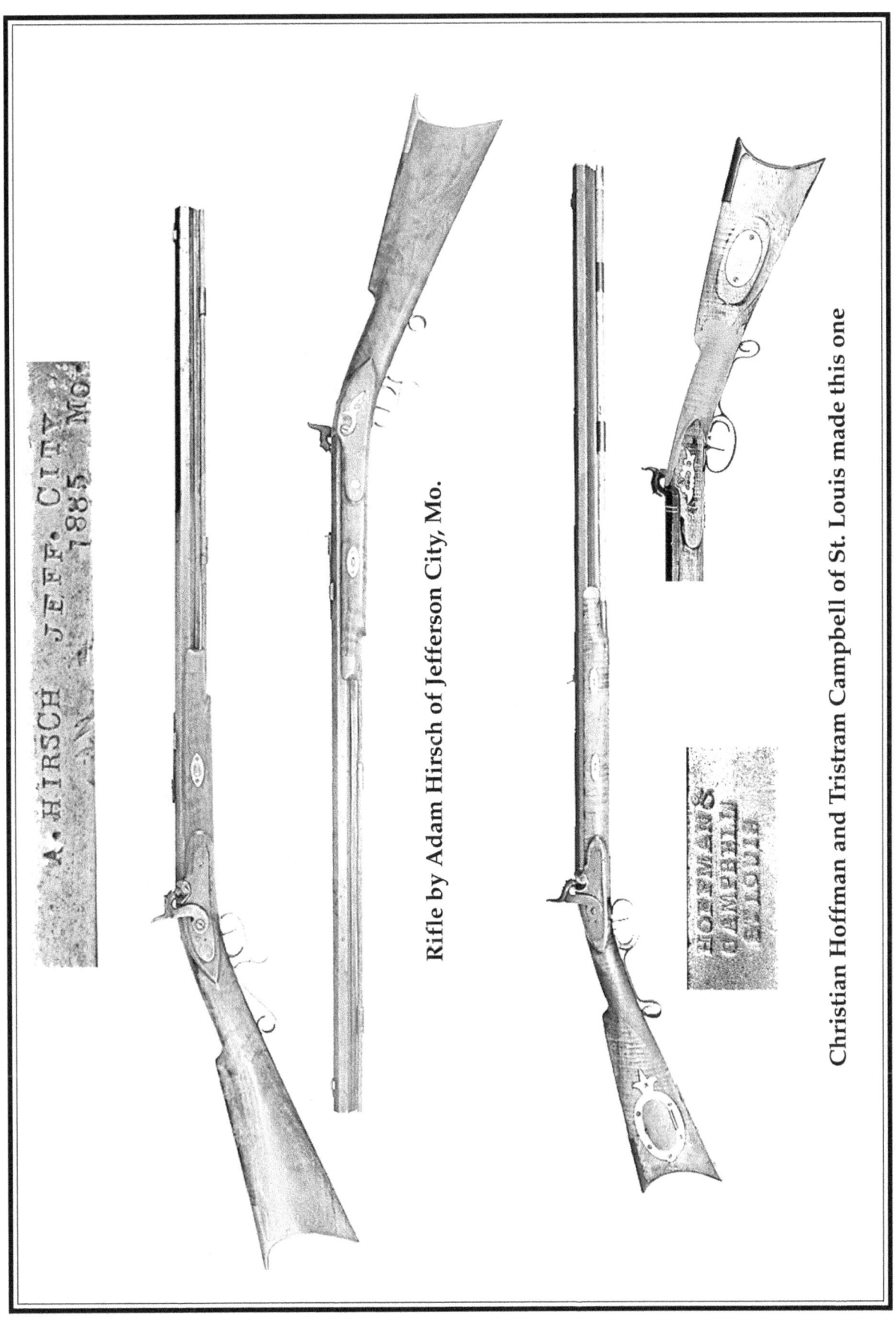

Rifle by Adam Hirsch of Jefferson City, Mo.

Christian Hoffman and Tristram Campbell of St. Louis made this one

HOWE, OLIVER R.
(1821-   ) NY Mo. 1849. Cooper Co., Mo. 1850c. Amazonia, Andrew Co., Mo. 1860c., dir. Amazonia, Mo. 1891/92 dir.

HOWELL, JOHN
(1825-   ) KY Parkville, Platte Co., Mo. 1850c., 1860 dir.

HOWELL, WILLIAM B.
(1819-   ) VA Parkville, Platte Co., Mo. 1850c. Albany, Gentry Co., Mo. 1867/68 dir. Brother of John.

HOWLETT, ROBERT W.
(1826-   ) ENG unl. Il. 1850-1859. Hannibal, Marion Co., Mo. 1859-1860c., dir. Barry, Il. 1864 dir.-1880 dir. (Johnson)

HUBER & HOFFMAN
St. Louis, Mo. 1836/37 dir. J. Huber & Christian Hoffman.

HUBER, FELIX
DeSoto, Jefferson Co., Mo. 1876/77 dir. St. Louis, Mo. 1878 dir.-1885/86 dir.

HUBER, J.
St. Louis, Mo. 1836/37 dir.-1838/39 dir. As Huber & Hoffman 1836/37 dir.

HUEBLER, REINHART
Chamois, Osage Co., Mo. 1885/86 dir.

HUGGINS, CALVERT
(1838-   ) MO Liberty, Clay Co., Mo. 1860c. With Moses Dickson.

HUNT, JOHN
(1818-   ) OH Mo. 1842. Gentryville, Gentry Co., Mo. 1850c.

HUNTER, WILLIAM
Nevada, Vernon Co., Mo.1891/92 dir.

HUNTINGTON, CHATTON Z.?
(1827-   ) IL unl. Il. 1855. Mo. 1858. Wayne Co., Mo. 1860c.

HURST, J. MORGAN
(1830-   ) OH Vigo Co., In. 1850c., with Henry Fairbanks. Paris, Il. 1851-1882., Rich Hill, Bates Co., Mo. 1883/84 dir.-1898/99 dir. (see Johnson for details of Il. career)

HUSKY, D. F.
California, Moniteau Co., Mo. 1879 dir.-1893/94 dir. 1883/84 dir. as Huskoi.

HUSLAGE, HERMAN G.
(1799-   ) GER St. Louis, Mo. 1838 dir.-1859 dir. Carondolet, Mo. (s. St. Louis) 1860c., dir. Name spelled differently in almost every directory. 1854 dir. listing as Huslage & Herman is certainly an error.

HUSS, JOHN ADAM
(1830-   ) GER St. Louis, Mo. 1859 dir.-1860c., dir. As Adam Locksmith 1859 dir. and John A. 1860 dir. John, engineer, on c.

HUTTON, JAMES
Beemont, Franklin Co., Mo. 1879 dir.

HUXOL, SIMON
Hermann, Gasconade Co., Mo. 1898/99 dir.

I

IDDINGS, ISAAC A.
(1813-1868) NC Guilford Co., NC to 1835, Fulton Co., In. 1836-1843, Holt Co., Mo. 1844-1868. Listed as a Wagonmaker and gunsmith. Not believed to have been a gunmaker. Also a Judge in Mo. (Ray Iddings)

INGALLS, ALBERT P.
(1841-) PA Shelbyville, Il. 1870c. Portland, Me. 1880-1889. Stewardson, Shelby Co., Il. 1890. St. Louis, Mo. 1898 dir.-1900 dir.+ (Johnson)

INGLES, DAVID
St. Louis, Mo. 1848 dir. See Engles.

IRELAND, J. F.
St. Joseph, Buchanan Co., Mo. 1859 dir.-1860 dir.

ITH, RUDOLPH (RANDOLPH)
(1825-) SWITZ Fulton, Callaway Co., Mo. 1860c., dir.-1889 dir. Perc. 1/2 stock.

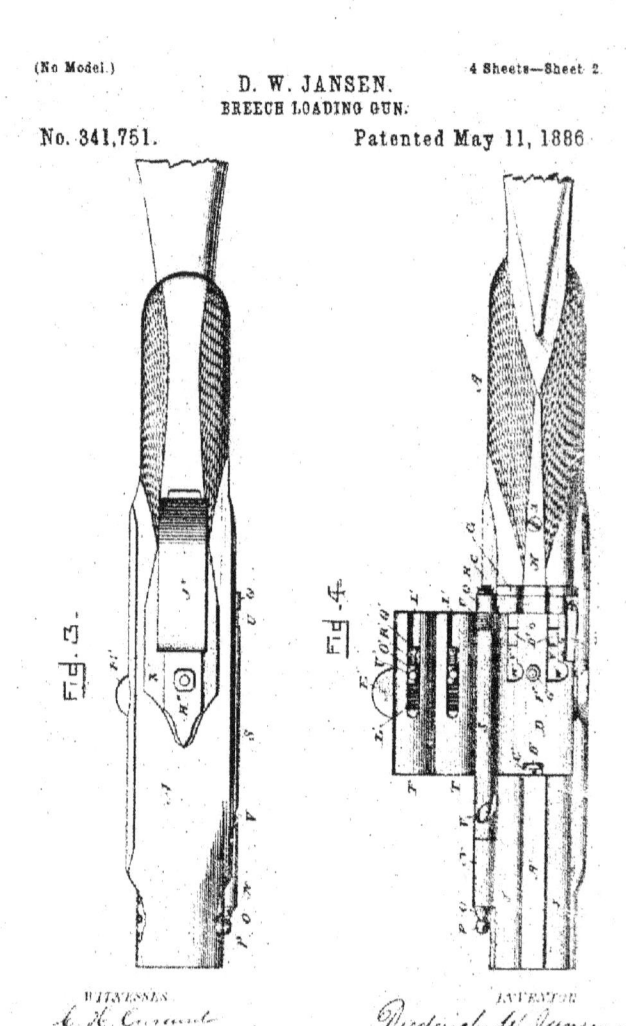

D. W. JANSEN,
G·U·N·S·M·I·T·H
And Patent Model Maker.
217 Main Street,
JOPLIN.   -   -   MISSOURI.

Polk's 1893-94 State directory

J

JACKSON, E. T.
(1805-   ) MA Bangor, Me. 1834 , St. Louis, Mo. 1838/39 dir. New Orleans, La. 1842 dir. Limestone Co., Tx. 1850c. Thomas Jackson, who advertised as a dealer, St. Louis, Mo. 1838-1840 prob. same. (Hanson 2)

JACKSON, GEORGE R.
(1839-   ) PA Jerseyville, Il. 1859-1860, Lithchfield, Il. 1861-1862, Co. H, 97th. Illinois, 1862-1865, Jerseyville, IL. 1865-1866, Charleston, Il. 1866-1867, Clinton, Henry Co., Mo. 1876, 1876/77 dir.-1893/94 dir. Chillicothe, Livingston Co., Mo. 1898/99 dir.

JACKSON, JOHN J.
(1809-   ) VA unl. Il. 1844-1859. Clarksville, Pike Co., Mo. 1860c.

JACOBY, FRED
O'Fallon, St. Charles Co., Mo. 1889/90 dir.

JAMES, H.
Scopus, Bollinger Co., Mo. 1898/99 dir.

JAMES, H. A.
Sedalia, Pettis Co., Mo. 1889 dir.-1898/99 dir. As White & James 1889 dir.

JAMISON, ALLEN
Gower, Clinton Co., Mo.1898/99 dir.

JANSEN, DIEDERICH W.
Joplin, Jasper Co., Mo. 1872 dir.-1899 dir. Patent # 341,751, May 11, 1886, breechloading firearm. Listed as locksmith in some directories. As Johnson 1883/84 dir. See p. 66.

JETT, STEPHEN C.
(1819-   ) KY 1842 dir.-1860c. Watchmaker & jeweler. As S. C. & J. S. Jett on 1857 dir. Retail guns, not known as gunsmith. Sold gunsmithing supplies. 1848 dir. listed as Jelt. With Edw. Mead & Co. 1842.

JICHA, FRANK
St. Mary's, Ste. Genevieve Co., Mo. 1879 dir.-1883/84 dir.

JOHNS, HENRY see SCHANTZ

JOHNSON, A. & CO.
St. Louis, Mo. perc. pistol. Prob. E. A. & Co. (GR 6-64)

JOHNSON, C.
   Kansas City, Mo. 1898/99 dir.
JOHNSON, JAMES Y.
   (1827-) MO Louisiana, Pike Co., Mo. 1850c.
JOHNSON, GUNDER
   Cape Girardeau, Mo. 1848 dir. St. Paul, Mn. 1856-1878 dir. (Sellers)
JOHNSTON, COLUMBUS (JOHNSON)
   Clarksville, Pike Co., Mo. 1861-1879 dir. Patent # 32,067, 4/16/61, shot pouch, Patent # 68,512, 9/3/67, *Charger for Shot Pouches*.
JOKERST, EMIL
   MO? Minnith, Ste. Genevieve Co., Mo.

JOLLY, WILLIAM
   (1800-) KY Family moved to Saline twp., Cooper Co., Mo. 1812. 1850c. Also a wheelwright, cooper, miller, distiller, doctor, farmer, and preacher.
JONES, HENRY H.
   (1792-) NC unl. In. 1819? Mo. 1828., Jefferson Co., Mo. 1850c.
JONES, JESSE
   (1819-) IN Mo. 1840. Jefferson Co., Mo. 1850c. Son of Henry H. ?
JUGHARDT, CHARLES
   St. Louis, Mo. 1859 dir.-1860 dir. Fostoria, Oh. 1859-1869. 1860 dir. as Tughardt. (Sellers)
JUNKER, EDWARD
   St. Louis, Mo. 1885 dir.-1898/99 dir.

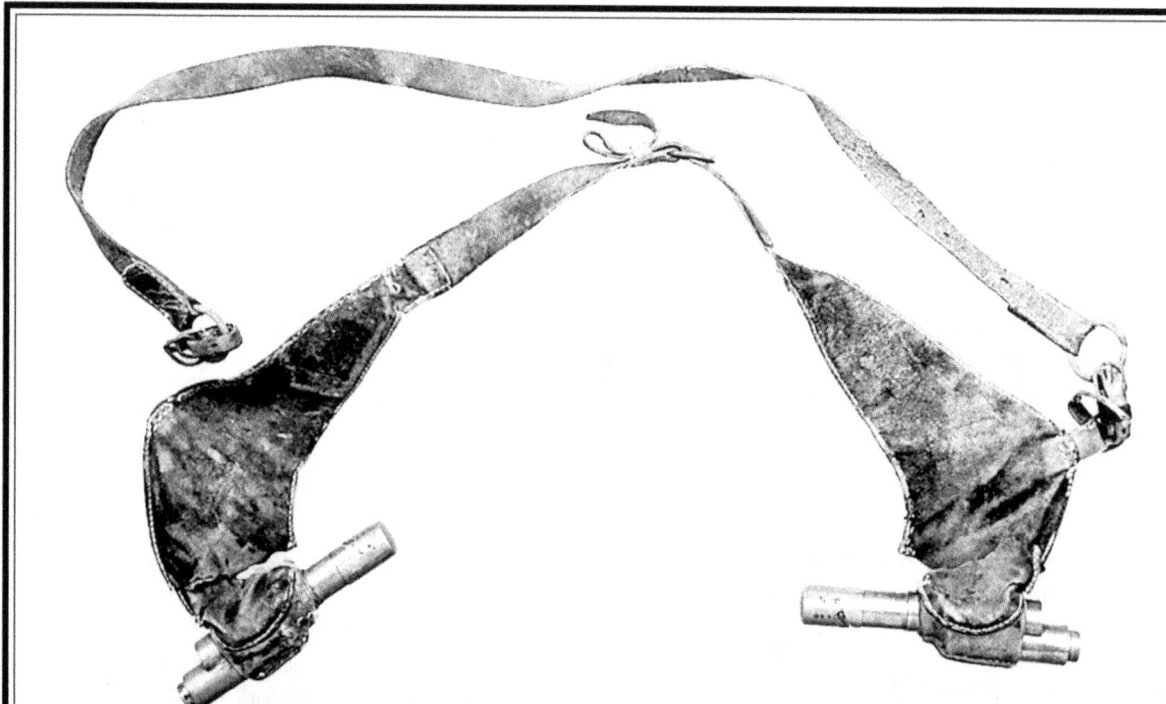

   An original set of Columbus Johnson patented shot measures, with pouches. The Patent application is as follows:
   68,512.-Columbus Johnson, Clarksville, Mo.-Charger for Shot Pouches.- September 3, 1867.-
   By forcing down the plunger the communication with the pouch is closed, and the charge is allowed to pass to the tube, which conducts it to the gun. The piston head is adjustable to vary the capacity of the charge chamber.

Claim,- First, the combination of the inner and outer tubes A and B, having
       side ports and discharge tubes I, when all are arranged together substantially as and for the purpose described.
Second, the adjustable plunger or piston head N to the inner tube A, substantially as described for the purpose specified.

K

KABLER, JOHN G.
(1797-) GER Mo. 1846. Perry Co., Mo. 1850c. Curt Johnson has seen a 24 lb. "chunk gun".

KACER, MARTIN V.
St. Louis, Mo. Patents # 273,288, Mar. 6, 1883, breechloading firearm (four- barrel shotgun rifle) and # 282,328, July 31, 1883, magazine gun. Both with William Kriz.

KAISER, ,
Bear Creek, Cedar Co., Mo. rifle signed "....KAISER ". (Blackburn)

KALBITZ, JUSTICE
GER Jefferson Co., Mo. 1850c. Brother of Robert.

KALBITZ, ROBERT
(1829-) GER Jefferson Co., Mo. 1850c. unl. Il. 1855. St. Louis, Mo. 1857 dir.-1878 dir. Listed as laborer on 1850c. Also a musician, 1879 dir. lists him as leader of the Empire String Band.

KALER, JOHN
(1788-) PA unl. Va. 1809-1845. Mo. 1849. Schuyler Co., Mo. 1860c.

KANSTEINER, WILLIAM
(1827-) ? Hannibal, Marion Co., Mo. 1847-1890. (Sellers)

KARNS, H.
Lancaster, Schuyler Co., Mo. 1867/68 dir.

KARNS, LEWIS
Pekin, Il. 1860 dir. Carthage, Jasper Co., Mo. ca. 1880. (Johnson)

KARTHAGO, STEPHEN
Kansas City, Mo. 1898/99 dir. As Western Bicycle Works, advertised gunsmithing.

KASEL, G.
Washington, Franklin Co., Mo. 1898/99 dir.

KEATING, E. C.
Sedalia, Pettis Co., Mo. 1885/86 dir.

KEEHNART, CHARLES
(1812-) GER St. Louis, Mo. 1850c. Poss. Heehnart.

KEENEY, J. T.
Belton, Cass Co., Mo. 1891 dir.-1898/99 dir.

KEISSIG & SCHMIDT
Kansas City, Mo. 1868 dir. (Sellers)

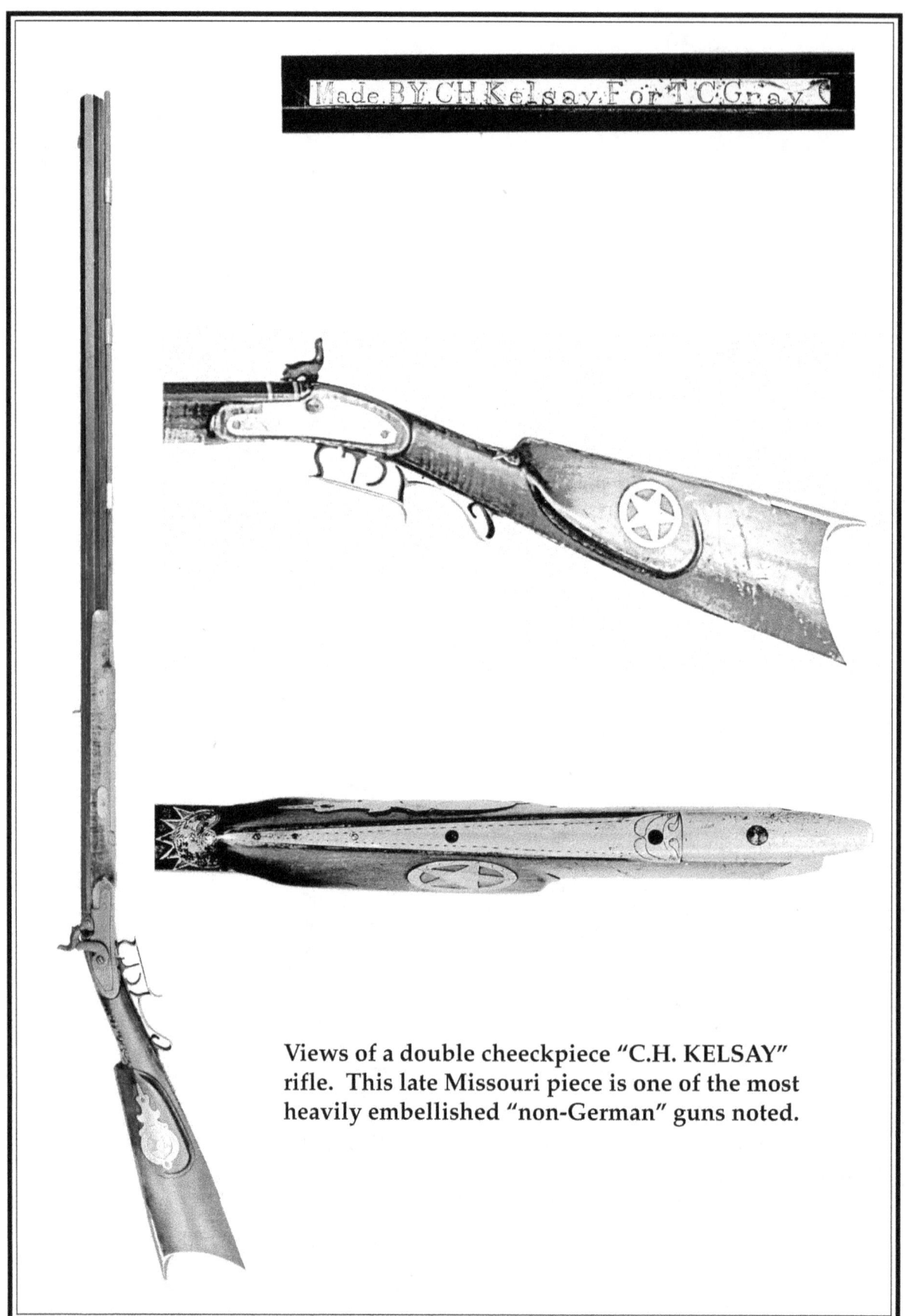

Views of a double cheeckpiece "C.H. KELSAY" rifle. This late Missouri piece is one of the most heavily embellished "non-German" guns noted.

KELLER, JAMES M.
(1809-) KY unl. Ky. 1839. Mo. 1841.
Liberty, Clay Co., Mo. 1850c., ic. Missouri City,
Clay Co., Mo. 1860c.
1850 Industrial Census:
Clay Co.
Name.   James M. Keller
Name of Business, Manufacture, or Product.
           Gun Maker
Capital invested in Real and Personal Estate in
the Business. $ 840
Raw Material used, including Fuel.
    Quantities.   Kinds.   Values.
    (not given) Iron, Steel, Brass $ 800
Average number of hands employed. Male. 2
Wages. Average Monthly cost of male labor.
    $ 15 (prob. should be $ 30)
Annual Product.
    Quantities. Kinds.   Values.
    (not given) Guns $ 1,000

KELSAY, C. H. ("KILL")
(1822-1882) ? Lathrop, Clinton Co., Mo. 1881 dir.
Holt, Clay Co., Mo. Perc. 1/2 stock. (MB 9-63)

KELSEY, JOHN
(1819-1899) KY Ray Co., Mo. 1840-1873. Kelseyville,
Ca. 1873-1899. Perc. & breechloading rifles. (Shelton)
1850 Industrial Census:
Ray Co.
Name.   John Kelsey
Name of Business, Manufacture, or Product.
           Gunsmith
Capital invested in Real and Personal Estate in
the Business. $ 250
Raw Material used, including Fuel.
    Quantities.   Kinds.   Values.
    200 lb.   Iron $ 150
Average number of hands employed. Male. 2
Average Monthly cost of male labor. $ 50
Annual Product.
    Quantities.   Kinds.   Values.
    50   Guns & C. $ 750

KELSEY, NATHANIEL
(1825-) KY Ray Co., Mo. 1850c., 1860c.
Kelseyville, Ca. 1867-1873 . (Shelton)

KELSEY, WILLIAM
(1792-) TN Pioneer, Oh. 1850c.? Ray Co.,
Mo. 1860c. Huntington Oh. 1868 dir.?
Kelseyville, Ca. 1867-1879. (Shelton)

KEMP, A. (ALEXANDER?)
(1820-) PA St. Joseph, Buchanan Co., Mo. 1850ic.,
1860c. Helena, Mt. 1871 dir. As gentleman on
census.
1850 Industrial Census:
Buchanan Co.
Name. A. Kemp
Name of Business, Manufacture, or Product.
           Gunsmith
Capital invested in Real and Personal Estate in
the Business. $ 1,000
Raw Material used, including Fuel.
    Quantities.   Kinds.   Values.
    50   Gun Bbls $ 150
    100   " Stocks $ 30
Average number of hands employed. Male. 2
Average Monthly cost of male labor. $ 60
Annual Product.
    Quantities.   Kinds.   Values.
    80   Guns $ 400
                  Misc. $ 1,500

KENNEDY, THOMAS I. (J.)
(1801-) TN unl. Tn. 1828-1839. Mo. 1841. Newton
Co., Mo. 1850c.

KERKROESER, F. & CO.
reported, not verified, 1848 St. Louis, Mo.,
barrels.

KENDRICK, WILLIAM
(1796-) SC unl. Ky. 1826-1838. Neosho, New-
ton Co., Mo. 1850c., ic., 1860c., dir. As black &
gunsmith on 1850ic. Gunsmith William H.
Turner with him on 1850 census.
1850 Industrial Census:
Newton Co.
Name. William Kendrick
Name of Business, Manufacture, or Product.
           "B & Gun Smith"
Capital invested in Real and Personal Estate in
the Business. $ 250
Raw Material used, including Fuel.
    Quantities.   Kinds.   Values.
    3200 lb.   Iron & Steel $ 250
    400 bu.   Coal $ 50
Average number of hands employed. Male. 4
Wages. Average Monthly cost of male labor.
    $ 40 ($ 10 crossed out)
Annual Product.
    Quantities.   Kinds.   Values.
    (not given) Wagons, Ploughs, } $ 500
                 Hoes & job work

KERSEY, LEVI CHARLES
(1827-) Rochester, N.Y. 1855-1857. Elmira, N.Y. 1859. St. Louis, Mo. 1869-1870 dir. San Francisco, Ca. 1874-1877. Red Bluff, Ca. 1877-1885. With Dimick 1869. Dimick rifle with "KERSEY" on underside of barrel. (Pourie) Perc. guns, primarily multi-barrel. (Shelton, Eich)

KERSTEINS, HENRY
(1816-) GER St. Louis, Mo. 1850c.-1854 dir.

KESSLER, JOHN
Weston, Platte Co., Mo. 1848-1858. (Sellers)

KESTER, JOHN
(1825-) OH Weston, Platte Co., Mo. 1860c., dir.-1879 dir. Note similiarity to abv. name

KILE, JOHN
(1816-) KY unl. Tn. 1837-1845. Monroe Co. Tn. 1850c. unl. Ar. 1852. Mo. 1854. Greene Co., Mo. 1860c. (Wallace)

KILEY, F. J.
Huntsville, Randolph Co., Mo. 1860 dir.

KIMBALL, R. A.
New Madrid, Mo. 1898/99 dir.

KINCHLER (KINCHLOW), EZEKIAL
(1793-) KY unl. Ky. prior to 1829. St. Francois Co., Mo. 1850c., 1860c. 1860c. as Kinchlow.

KINZY, CHRISTIAN
Higginsville, LaFayette Co., Mo. 1885/86 dir.-1889/90 dir.

KIRLIN, THOMAS
(1805-) MD Mo. 1832. St. Louis, Mo. 1850c.

KIRTON, JOSEPH
St. Louis, Mo. 1848 dir. See Curtain.

KISH, MICHAEL
(1785-) GER Atchison Co., Mo. 1850c. Linden, Atchison Co., Mo. 1860 dir. As blacksmith 1850 c.

KITTREDGE, CHARLES
(St. Louis, Mo. 1859- 1860 dir., 1867 dir. -1868 dir. Agent for Tranter revolver. As gunsmith 1867 & 1868 directories.

KLEINHENN, EMANUEL
(1806-) GER Mo. 1836. Boonville, Mo. prior to St. Louis? St. Louis, Mo. 1845 dir.-1860c., dir. E. St. Louis, Il. 1874 dir.-1884 dir. (Johnson)

KLINE, P.
St. Louis, Mo. Perc. 1/2 stock. (Noble)

KLINGLESMITH, JOHN F.
St. Louis, Mo. Patent #398,265, Feb. 19, 1889, spring gun. (toy gun)

KLOCKER, JOHN
St. Louis, Mo. 1860 dir.-1867 dir. With Franz Lunsmann 1864 & 1867. Dyersville, Ia. Fine perc. Schuetzens. (Johnson)

KNAUS, J. H.
Franklin, Howard Co., Mo. 1867/68 dir.-1879 dir.

KNAUS, WILLIAM
(1823-) MO Otterville, Cooper Co., Mo. 1844-1850c.-1860c.-1889/90 dir.

1870 Industrial Census
Cooper Co.

Name.	Knaus, William
Name of Business, Manufacture or Product.	Blacksmith
Cost of Raw Materials.	$ 1150
Number of Employees.	3
Wages	$ 800
Annual Gross Product.	$ 2800

KNEUBUEHLER, JULIUS
Hermann, Gasconade Co., Mo. 1885/86 dir.

KNIDLER?, JULICO?
(1825-) GER St. Louis, Mo. 1860c.

KNODER, T.
St. Louis, Mo. machinist for Dimick. (AR 4-58)

KNOTZEL, ANTON
(1815-) SWITZ St. Louis, Mo. 1854 dir.-1860c., dir. Jerseyville, Il. 1880 dir.-1888 dir. Name spelled Knotzel, Anton; Knetcel, Anton; Knetzel, Antoine and Knetzel, Anthony in 4 different sources (Johnson)

KOEPPENS, ERNST
St. Louis, Mo. 1870 dir.-1872 dir., 1894 dir.-1901 dir. As Ernst H. C. 1894-1901.

KOHNE, CHARLES
(1829-) GER Platte City, Mo. 1860c.

KRAG, GUSTUS
(1839-) GER Henry Co., Mo. 1860c.

KRATTLI (KRATTLE), JOHN
(1830-) SWITZ unl. N. J. 1855. Hermann, Gasconade Co., Mo. 1860c., dir.

KRIZ, WILLIAM J.
St. Louis, Mo. Patents with Martin Kacer.

KUMM, LOUIS
Sedalia, Pettis Co., Mo. 1881 dir.

KUNKLE & ELK
Warrensburgh, Johnson Co., Mo. 1893/94 dir.-1898 dir. J. H. Kunkle and J. F. Elk

KUNKLE, J. H.
Warrensburgh, Johnson Co., Mo. 1889 dir.-1898/99 dir.

KUNKLE, MATHIAS
(1850-) MO St. Louis, Mo. 1870c.

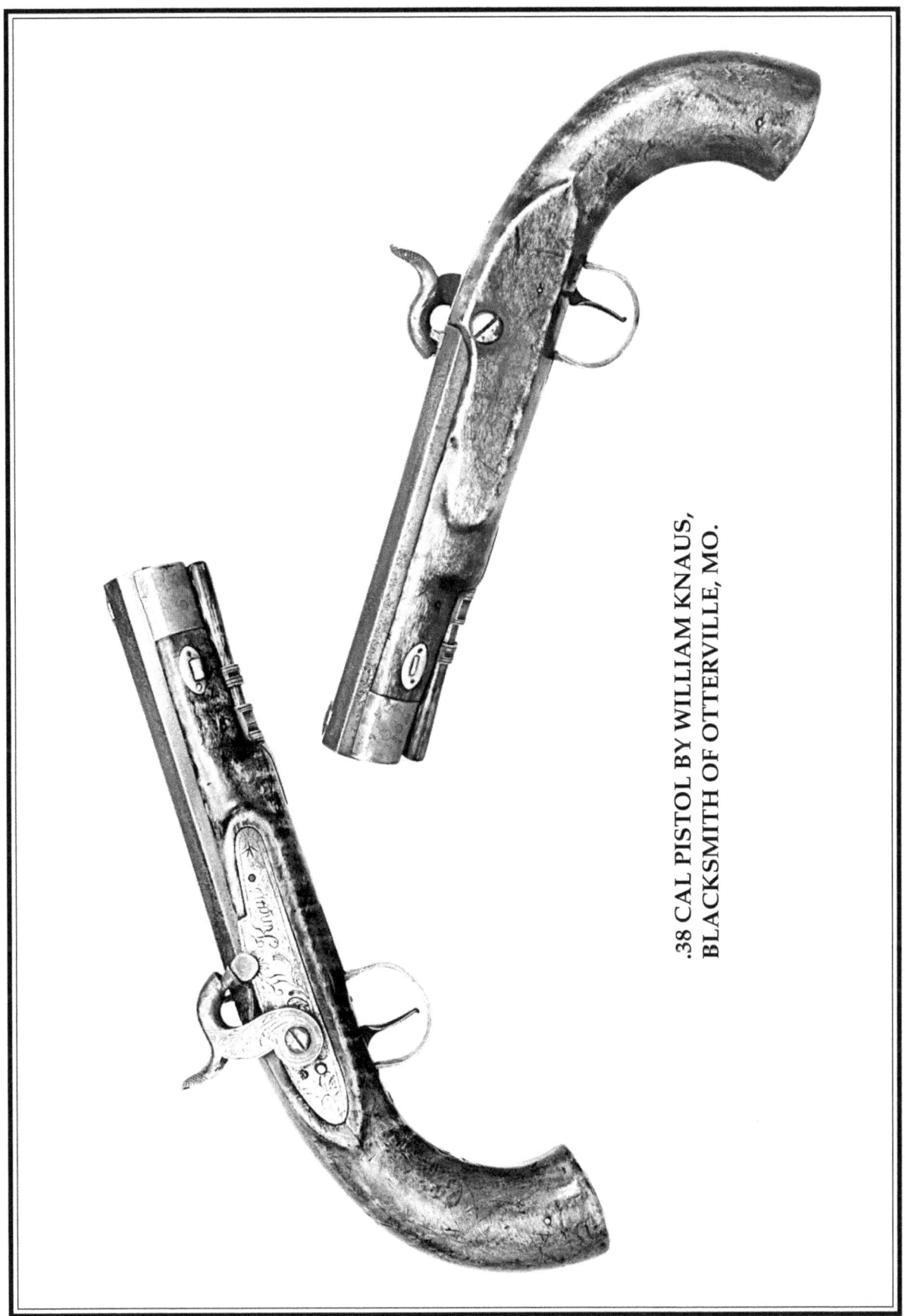

.38 CAL PISTOL BY WILLIAM KNAUS, BLACKSMITH OF OTTERVILLE, MO.

NOTES

L

LAFFERTY, SMITH
(1824-) OH Belleville, Oh. 1850c.-1853 dir. Bethany, Harrison Co., Mo. 1860c., dir. Winterset, Ia. 1882 dir.-1892 dir. (Sellers)

LAGRAIN, WILLIAM
South Fork, Howell Co., Mo. 1883/84 dir.-1891/92 dir. As Lagain 1885/86 and 1891/92.

LAIRD, D. C. (DAVID C.)
Freeport, Stephenson Co., Il. 1867-1868 dir. Montgomery City, Mo. 1891 dir.-1893/94 dir. (Johnson)

LAIRD, WILLIAM
Montgomery City, Mo. 1889/90 dir.

LAKENAN, JAMES
(-1825) VA? Richmond, Va. 1802-1818. St. Louis, Mo. 1818-1825. As Lakenan & Hawken. See p. 142. (Hanson 2)

LAMB, JOAB
(1810-) NC Mo. 1832. Butler Co., Mo. 1850c. Clinton Co. Mo. 1860c. As blacksmith in 1860 census.

LaMOTT, JOHN
(1828-) FR Cole Co., Mo. 1850c. In state pen for grand larceny, went in 1849.

LANDREVILLE, ANDRE
(-1834) ? Manchester, St. Louis Co., Mo. 1795. St. Louis, Mo. 1797- 1834. As partner of Francois Migneron 1795. Primarily a merchant. Name previously reported as Lauderville. Also noted Landville, Landerville and L'Andreville. Step-father of J. B. LeBeau Sr.

LANGE, WILLIAM
(1832-) GER Warren Co., Mo. 1850c. With George Munch.

LANGEN, THOMAS
St. Louis, Mo. 1848 dir. At Arsenal.

LAPTHORNE, S. J.
St. Joseph, Buchanan Co., Mo.1898/99 dir. Proprietor of the St. Joseph Gun and Bicycle Factory.

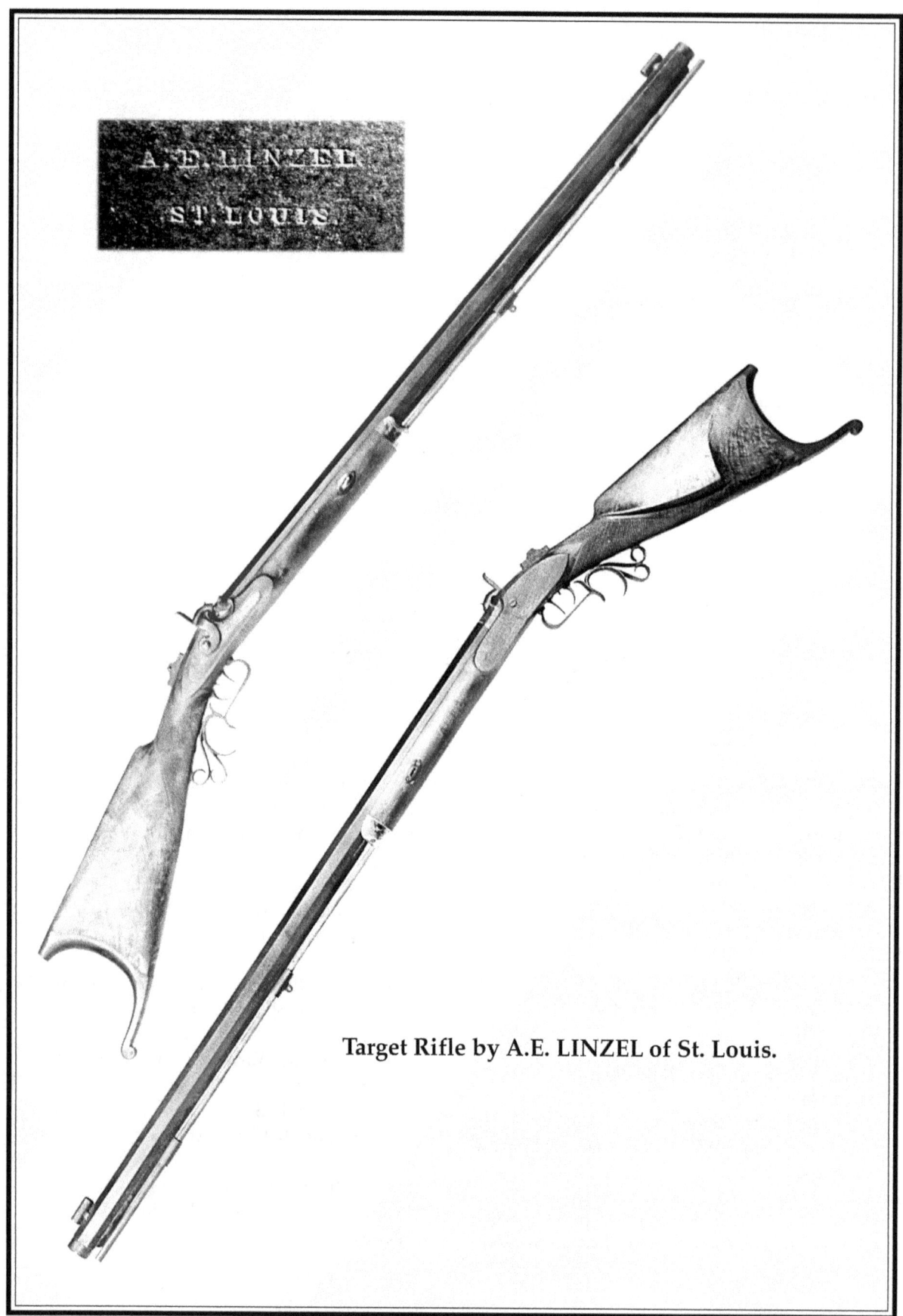

Target Rifle by A.E. LINZEL of St. Louis.

LARD, ALLEN E.
St. Joseph, Buchanan Co., Mo. Patents # 630,061, Aug. 1, 1899, # 636,050, Oct. 31, 1899, # 668,526, Feb.19, 1901, # 674,508, May 21, 1901 and # 747,191, Dec. 15, 1903. All for single triggers. (for dbl. guns)

LASH, JOHN
(1823-) OH Ohio until 1856. Dallas Co., Mo. 1860c. Poss. same as John H. Lash, Marysville, Oh. 1854-1859 dir. Son of J. B. Lash. (Hutslar) Age on census indicates he may be father of John H. and son of John B. Also prob. same as John Lash, Ft. Scott, Ks. 1866 dir.-1876 dir., Girard, Ks. 1884 dir.-1888 dir. (Sellers)

LAUDERVILLE see LANDREVILLE

LAUGHLIN, G. O.
Missouri City, Clay Co., Mo. 1860 dir.

LeBEAU, JOHN BAPTISTE
Three men bore this name in St. Louis, Mo.

LeBEAU, JOHN BAPTISTE (ELDER)
(-1815?) ? St. Louis, Mo. 1799-1802, -1815? Master blacksmith. Father of John Baptiste LeBeau Sr.

LeBEAU, JOHN BAPTISTE SR.
(1803-1872) MO St. Louis, Mo. 1823a., 1827 one week at Indian Affairs St. Louis gunsmith shop. Rock Island, Il. 1828 for Indian Dept. Jo Daviess Co., (Rock Island) Il. 1830c. St. Louis, Mo. 1835a-1850c.-1860c.-1870 dir. 1850c. listed as mechanic, all other listings as gunsmith. May be overlaps between him and his son. Referred to as Sr. late 60's and in obit. Step-son of Andre Landreville. Father in-law of Reno Beauvais. Majority of career in Mo. Son Alexander (1834-) shows Il. as birthplace on 1860c. (Mo. on 1850c.) Name also found spelled LaBeau.

LeBEAU, JOHN BAPTISTE JR.
St. Louis, Mo. 1848 dir.-1864 dir. 1848 dir. as jeweler. 1851 dir. as silversmith with Francis A. Beauvais. 1854 dir. independant silversmith. 1857 dir. as jeweler (at Migneron's former address) 1859-1860 dir. bookkeeper for Reno Beauvais. Referred to as Jr. in most dir. Not known as a gunsmith.

LeCONTE
St. Louis, Mo. 1804. Gunsmith for the Indians. An alias in the French manner. Probably a member of the Herbert/Hebert family. (Hanson)

LEEMAN, JULIUS
St. Louis, Mo. Patent # 295,564, Mar. 25, 1884, magazine gun.

LEHZAHNEN, FRITZ
(1838-) GER St. Louis, Mo. at Arsenal, 1860c. Poss. Lenzahner.

LEICH, GEORGE J. H.
St. Louis, Mo. 1876 dir.-1900 dir.

LENZHANER & OTTO
St. Louis, Mo. 1864 dir. Frederick Lenzhaner and A. G. Otto.

LENZHANER, FREDERICK
(1838?-) GER? St. Louis, Mo. 1857 dir.-1866 dir. As Lenzhaner & Otto 1864 dir.

LESCHER, G.
South West City, McDonald Co., Mo. 1881 dir.

LETTEY, WILLIAM
(1836-) PA California, Moniteau Co., Mo. 1860c. Prob. associated with J. W. Palmer.

LEVISY, SIMPSON
(1826-) OH unl. Oh. 1852-1854. Mo. 1856. Nodaway Co., Mo. 1860c.

LEWIS & SWAN
St. Louis, Mo. 1867 dir.

LEWIS,
St. Joseph, Mo.? Rifle with fancy eagle patchbox, 1837 under barrel. (Blackburn)

LEWIS, CHARLES L.
(1800-) MA unl. Va. 1848-1851. unl. Oh. 1854. Mo. 1858. Concord, Callaway Co., Mo. 1860c., dir.

LEWIS, IRA
(1793-) SC unl. Tn. 1832-1834., Mississippi Co., Mo. 1850c.

LEWIS, J. B.
Lone Dell, Franklin Co., Mo. 1891 dir.-1893/94 dir.

LEWIS, PETER
(1814-) KY Lawrence Co., Mo. 1850c.

LINBERG, CHARLES J
St. Louis, Mo. Patent #109,914, Dec. 6,1870, revolver. With Wm. J. Philips.

LINDSAY, E. H.
Lathrop, Clinton Co., Mo. 1885/86 dir.

LINDSAY, EDWARD
(1832-) GER unl. Pa. 1855. Mo. 1857. St. Louis, Mo. 1860c.

LINZEL, AUGUSTUS EDWARD
(1831-1904) GER St. Louis, Mo. 1857 dir.-1869 dir. With Dimick 1857, did job work for him after opening own shop. Little Rock, Ar. 1869-1904. Perc. pistols, rifles, perc. Schuetzens and airguns. One of finest gunsmiths ever in Mo. (Elias, Wolff)

LIVINGSTON, T. E.
West Plains, Howell Co., Mo. 1883/84 dir.-1898/99 dir.

LOCKWEILER, F. A.
Kansas City, Mo. 1885/86 dir.

LOGAN, ALEXANDER
(1826-) MO Warren Co. Mo. 1850c.

LOHR, BENJAMIN
Morrison, Gasconade Co., Mo. 1876/77 dir.

LONDON, BYRON
Butler, Bates Co., Mo. 1889 dir.-1891/92 dir.

LONG, ROBERT
(1827-) GER Kansas City, Mo. 1859 dir., 1860c., dir.-1870 dir.

LONGANECKER, HORACE C.
Kahoka, Clark Co., Mo. 1883/84 dir.-1891/92 dir. Proprieter Eureka Gun Works 1885/86 dir.

LONGANECKER, JOHN F.
Kahoka, Clark Co., Mo. 1881 dir.-1898/99 dir. Superintendent for above 1885/86 dir.

LORENZ, FRED
(1836-) GER unl. In. 1856-1861. Mo. 1866. St. Louis, Mo. 1870c.

LOVE, LYCIAN B.
(1829-) KY Middletown, Montgomery Co., Mo. 1854 dir.-1860c.

LOWERY, M. T.
New Point, Holt Co., Mo. 1879 dir.-1885/86 dir.

LOWRY, THOMAS
Lancaster, Schuyler Co., Mo. 1860 dir.

LUNSMANN, FRANZ (FRANCIS)
(1820-) GER St. Louis, Mo. 1847, 1850c., ic., 1860c., 1865-1872 dir. Henry Morrow at same address 1850c. Employed J. Klocker, 1864 & 67.
   1850 Industrial Census:
   St. Louis, Ward 2
Name. Franz Lunsman
Name of Business, Manufacture, or Product.
   Gunsmith
Capital invested in Real and Personal Estate in the Business. $ 500
Raw Material used, including Fuel.
   Quantities.   Kinds.   Values.
   100   gun barrels ⎫
   100   locks   ⎬ $ 400
                      ⎭

Average number of hands employed. Male. 1
Average Monthly cost of male labor. $ 36
Annual Product.
   Quantities.   Kinds.   Values.
   150   Rifles & ⎫ $ 1,500
         Pistols ⎭

LUTES, WILLIAM
(1787-) NC Bullitt Co., Ky. 1825. unl. In. 1830. Mercer Co., Mo. 1850c. (MB11-66)

LUTZ, D.
St. Louis, Mo. Perc. 1/2 stock, air gun. Poss. only barrel maker. (Pourie)

LYNCH, WILLIAM
(1819-) TN Mo. 1843. Cape Girardeau, Mo.

LYON, JOHN
(1816-) IRE St. Louis, Mo., 1850c. At Arsenal.

M

McALISTER, ALBERT
  Marshall, Saline Co., Mo. 1876/77 dir.
McBLAIR, W.
  St. Louis, Mo. 1880 dir. As W. McBlair & Co.
McCALLUM, DAVID
  (1779-) VA unl. Ky. 1829-1840. Mo. 1844. Linn Co., Mo. 1850c.
McCANN (McCANE), GEORGE A.
  (1826-) KY unl. Ky. prior to 1858. Howard Co., Mo. 1860c.
McCANN, J. E.
  Neosho, Newton Co., Mo. 1876/77 dir.-1883/84 dir.
McCARD see McCORD
McCAUGHIE, THOMAS
  (-1859) ? St. Louis, Mo. 1857 dir.-1859 dir.
McCLANE (McCLURE), ANDREW
  (1804-) KY Mo. 1841. Meramec twp., St. Louis Co., Mo. 1850c. Pacific, Franklin Co., Mo. 1860c., dir.

McCORD, DORASTUS
  (1797-) PA St. Louis, Mo. 1850c.
McCOURT, LAWRENCE see COURT
McCOY, JOHN
  Chillicothe, Ohio prior to Mo. Independence, Jackson Co., Mo. 1842 dir.-1854 dir. As McCoys & Lee 1842. (Sellers)
McCOY, WILLIAM
  Chillicothe, Ohio prior to Mo. Independence, Jackson Co., Mo. 1842 dir.-1854 dir. As McCoys & Lee 1842. (Sellers)
McCULLOCH, JAMES, H.
  St. Louis, Mo. 1869 dir.-1881 dir. With H. Folsom & Co. Managing partner of St. Louis store.
McDONALD, D. W.
  Allenton, St. Louis Co., Mo. 1898/99 dir.
McFALL, JAMES
  (1833-) NY unl. N. Y. prior to 1865. Mo. 1866. St. Louis, Mo. 1870c., dir.
McFARLAND, GEORGE W.
  (1808-) NC Mo. 1834. Austin, Cass Co., Mo. 1850c.

McFARLAND, R.
(1831-) MO Chamois, Osage Co., Mo. 1860c., dir.

McINNES, JAMES
St. Louis, Mo. 1859 dir. Same address as Charles Webb.

McKAIN, SAMUEL see below

McKEAN, S. L.
Mexico, Audrain Co., Mo. 1870ic.? 1879 dir.- 1889/90 dir.

1870 Industrial Census
Audrain Co.
Name. McKain, Samuel
Name of Business, Manufacture or Product.
    Gun Smith
Cost of Raw Materials. $ 200
Number of Employees.   1
Wages   Not Given
Annual Gross Product. $ 1000

McKINNEY, JOHN R.
(1806-) TN unl. Me. 1838? unl. Ky. 1833. unl. Al. 1848. Medoc, Jasper Co., Mo. 1860c., dir.

McLANAHAN, J. K.
St. Louis, Mo. 1858-61 as Shawk & McLanahan.

McLANE, ANDREW see **McCLANE**

McLAREN, WILLIAMS & CO.
St. Louis, Mo. 1870 dir. Shotgun lockplate.

McLEAN, DR. JAMES HENRY
(1829-) SCOT St. Louis, Mo. 1859 dir.-1898 dir. Occupation listings vary, physician, physician & druggist, mfr. patent medicine, wholesale drugs and medicines, soap mfr. Not certain what input he had in the design of the following. Patents, # 282, 548, breechloading gun (cannon) and # 282,549, machine gun, both with Myron Coloney. # 282,550 cartridge. #'s 282, 551 & 282,553, machine guns. # 282,552 & # 282,554 magazine guns. All Aug. 7, 1883. # 290,905 Dec. 25, 1883, breechloading firearm. See Coloney, p. 26, p. 176 and p. 212.

McMANNAMA, J. B.
Norma, Webster Co., Mo. 1881 dir.

McMILLAN, EDWARD
(1800-) VA Mo. 1843. Bem, Gasconade Co., Mo. 1860c., dir. As blacksmith on c.

McMILLIAN, E.
Canaan, Gasconade Co., Mo. 1881 dir.-1883/84 dir.

McMILLIAN, W. R.
Salem, Dent Co., Mo. 1893/94 dir.-1898/99 dir.

McMULLEN, THOMAS S.
(1823-) KY Farmington, St. Francois Co., Mo. 1838-1848. Mariposa Co., Ca. 1852c. Farmington, Mo. 1857-1860c., dir. (Shelton)

McPARTLAND, P.
(1831-) IRE St. Louis, Mo. 1860c. At Arsenal.

MACHTER, JOHN see **WACHTER**

MAGNIEN, GEORGE
(-) ? Springfield, Greene Co., Mo. 1898/99 dir.

MALKIN?, PETER
(1828-) IN Chariton Co., Mo. 1850c.

MALTA BEND GUNSMITH'S CACHE
Near Malta Bend, Saline Co., Mo., discovered in 1933, the remains of what was probably a gunsmith's wood chest, containing a large number of locks, some other gun parts and 16 gunsmiths tools. Buried about 1,000 yards from a Little Osage village which was occupied roughly 1725-1775. No documentation exists to connect him with the village but note the "convenient" death of Jean Baptiste Heverieux at St. Louis in 1775. If not Heverieux, some unknown gunsmith, probably Indian or French, cached these parts and tools for later retrieval and never picked them up. These artifacts represent the earliest evidence thus far discovered of a "full service" gunsmith in Missouri. (Hamilton)

MANNON, R. W. (A. W.)
Esper, Putnam Co., Mo. 1893 dir.-1893/94 dir.

MAPLES?, WILLIAM
(1785-) NC Mo. 1849. Morgan Co., Mo. 1860c.

MARCUM see **MARKHAM**

MARKHAM, CARTER
(1777-) VA unl. Tn. 1825-1836. McDonald Co., Mo. 1850c., ic. As Marcum on ic.

1850 Industrial Census:
McDonald Co.
Name. Carter, Marcum
Name of Business, Manufacture, or Product.
    Gunsmith
Capital invested in Real and Personal Estate in the Business. $ 100
Raw Material used, including Fuel.
    Quantities.   Kinds.   Values.
    1000   Iron $ 70
Average number of hands employed. Male. 2
Average Monthly cost of male labor. $ 40
Annual Product.
    Quantities.   Kinds.   Values.
    100   Rifle Guns $ 1,000

MARKHAM, THOMAS
(1808-) VA McDonald Co., Mo. 1850c., ic. Loomisville, McDonald Co., Mo. 1860c., dir. 1850 census as Markum. 1850 ic. as Markham. 1860c., dir. as Marcum. Prob. son of Carter, separate on census & industrial census.
1850 Industrial Census:
McDonald Co.
Name. T. Markham
Name of Business, Manufacture, or Product.
   Gunsmith
Capital invested in Real and Personal Estate in the Business. $ 250
Raw Material used, including Fuel.
   Quantities.   Kinds.   Values.
     1800   Iron $ 146
Average number of hands employed.
   Male. 1 (written heavily over 2)
Average Monthly cost of male labor. $ 20
Annual Product.
   Quantities.   Kinds.   Values.
     80   Guns $ 1,200

MARKWITH, JAMES H.
Lamar, Barton Co., Mo. 1889/90 dir.-1898/99 dir. As Markwick, James on 1889/90.

MARSHOF, JOHN G.
(1835-) IN Bates Co., Mo. 1850c. With father Abraham (1810-) OH, blacksmith.

MARTIN, JOHN J.
(1808-) VA unl. Il. 1834. unl. Ia. 1836-1838. Mo. 1844. Clark Co., Mo. 1850c.

MARTCINAF?, JULIUS
(1833-) GER St. Louis, Mo. 1860c. As gun maker.

MASON, F. M.
Holden, Johnson Co., Mo. 1883/84 dir. Springfield, Greene Co., Mo. 1889/90 dir.

MASUCH, EDWARD
(1823-) SWITZ Kansas City, Mo. 1859/60 dir., 1860c.-1871 dir.

MATHEWS, JAMES
(1804-) TN unl. Tn. 1828-1830. Johnson Co., Mo. 1850c.

MATHEWS, LEMUEL C.
(1828-) TN Johnson Co., Mo. 1850c. Son of James.

MATHEWS, WILLIAM
Sedalia, Pettis Co., Mo. 1876/77 dir.-1893/94 dir.

MATHIS, W.
Mirible, Caldwell Co., Mo. 1860 dir.

MATTHEWS, J. A.
St. Louis, Mo. Patent # 29,437, July 31, 1860, turret gun.

MAUPIN FAMILY
More research needed. Early percussion rifles have been reported, marked "M M", and attributed to Mosias Maupin. Other rifles reported seem to date in the mid-1840's. Brothers John, Amos, William and Daniel are reported as gunsmiths. To add to the confusion the name William was common among the Maupins, at least two and possibly four may have been gunsmiths. A number of other members of the family seem to have operated as blacksmiths and wagonmakers. At this writing it is not known who made the "M M" rifles. It seems possible that several brothers may have produced them using "M M" as a trade name as the Mosias' rifles carried a good reputation. As with others in this book, farming seems to have been their primary summer occupation., gunsmithing was "winter work".(MB 3-71)

Enhanced view of an early 1960's rubbing made at Union, Mo. and provided by Gene Rourke, now of Texas

MAUPIN, AMOS
Franklin Co., Mo. 1816-1820. Son of Mosias. (MB 3-71)

MAUPIN, DANIEL
(1804-1880) KY Infant when family moved to Mo. Son of Mosias. Built house which still stands on original land claim. Most probable maker of "M M" perc. rifles attributed to Mosias.

MAUPIN, JOHN
(-1813) KY? Franklin Co., Mo. 1804-1813. Son of Mosias. (MB 3-71)

MAUPIN, JAMES J.
(1842-) MO Franklin Co., Mo., Son of Daniel, found listed as a blacksmith and reported as a gunsmith.

MAUPIN, MOSIAS
(1758-1816) VA Greenbrier Co., Va. (W, Va.) 1786-1788. Madison Co., Ky. 1800. St. Louis, Mo. ca. 1804. Franklin Co., Mo. 1806-1816. Reported to have been a sometime hunting partner of Daniel Boone. (MB 3-71)

MAUPIN, W. A.
Louisiana, Pike Co., Mo. 1893/94 dir.

MAUPIN, WILLIAM
(-1880) ?? Franklin Co., Mo. 1820 - . Son of Mosias. Reported as riflemaker. (MB 3-71)

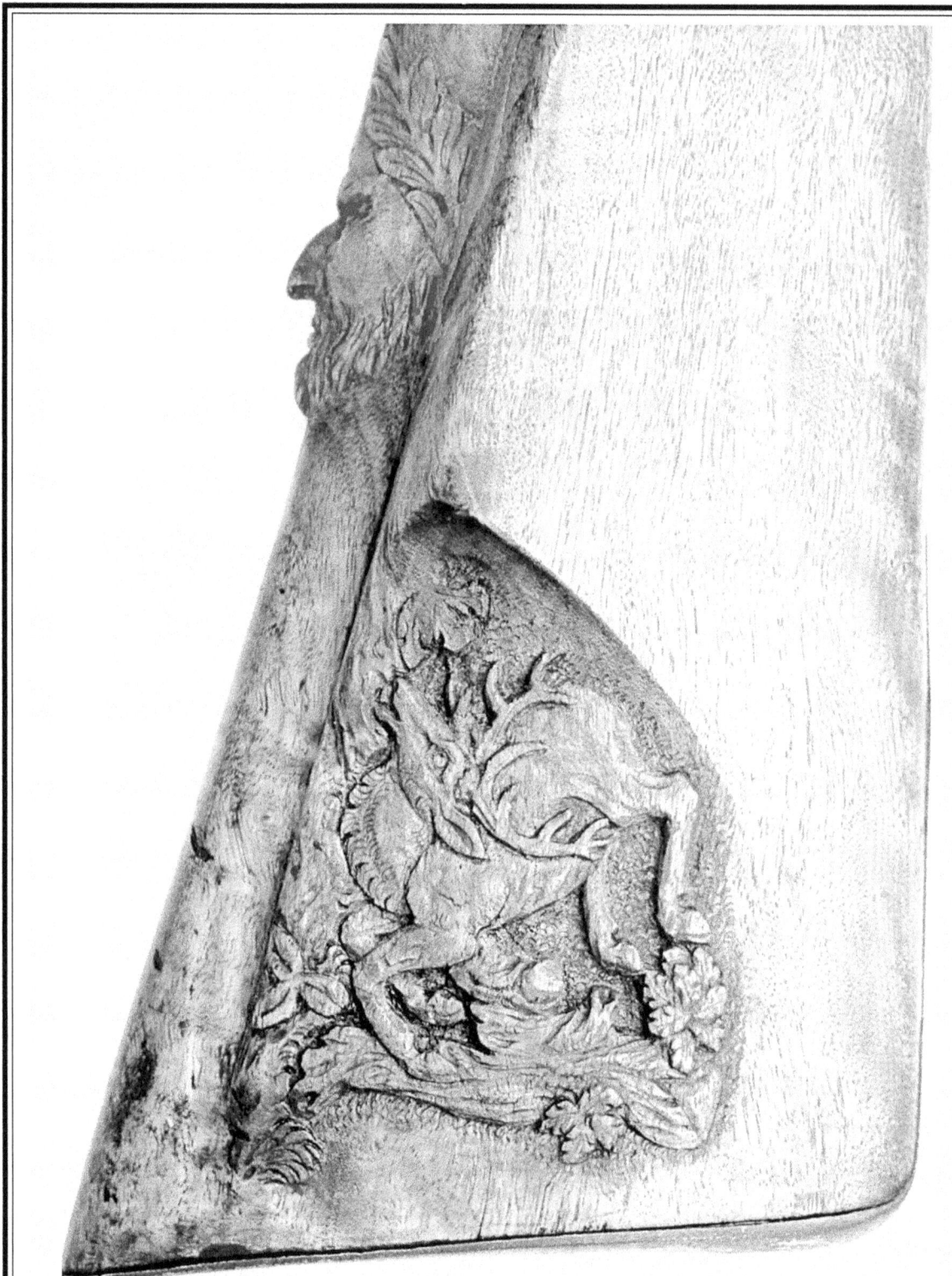

Shotgun stock from the Adolphus Meier Emporium made for Dr. Edward Rose of St. Louis in 1852.

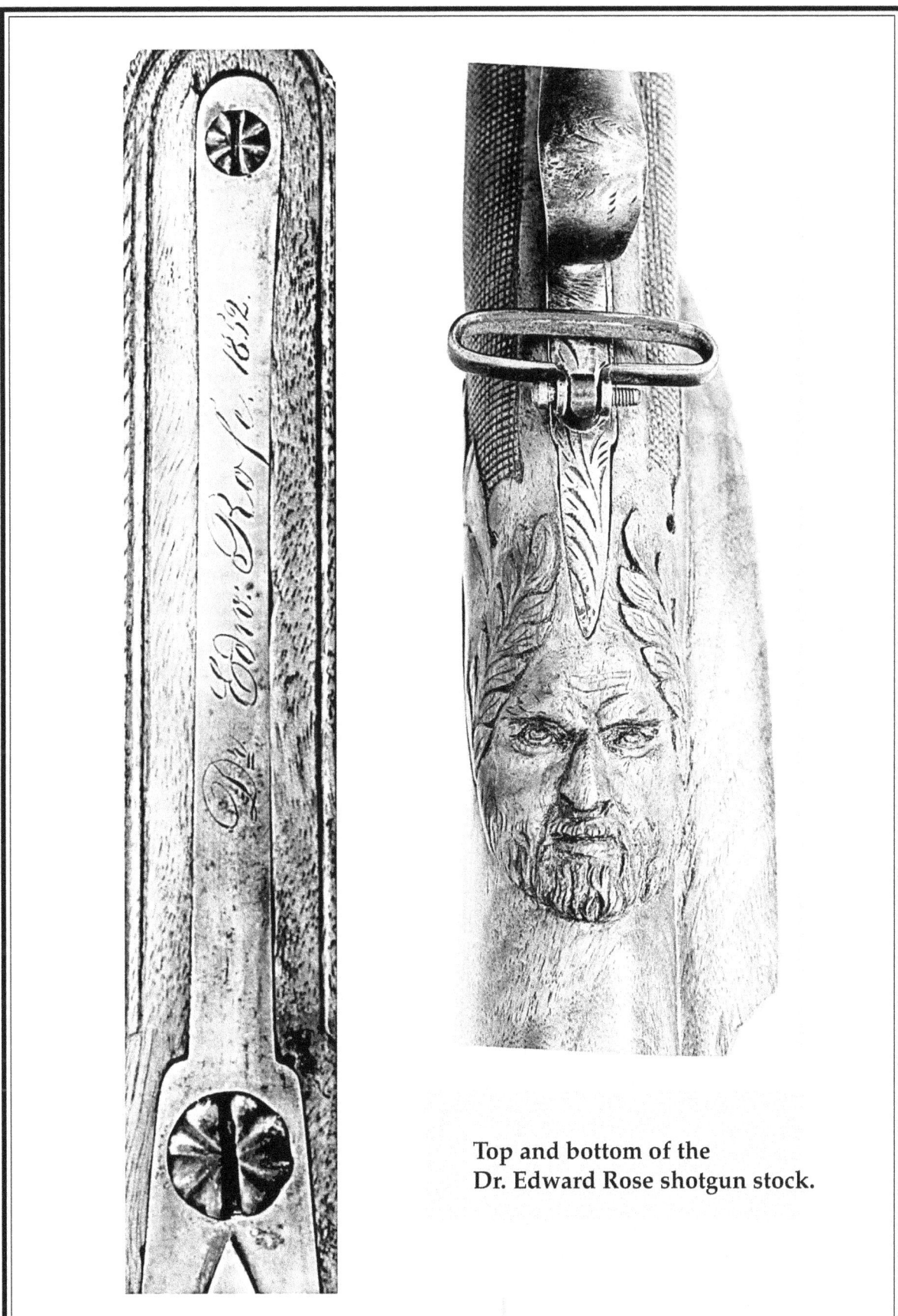

Top and bottom of the Dr. Edward Rose shotgun stock.

MAURER (MOWRER), BERTRAND
  (1824-) GER Ste. Genevieve, Mo. 1854 dir.-1860c. As Mowrer 1860.

MAYO & DURMIAL
  Huntsville, Randolph Co., Mo. 1867/68 dir.

MEACHEM, E. C. & CO.
  St. Louis, Mo. 1878 dir.-1885 dir..

MEACHEM, E. C., ARMS CO.
  St. Louis, Mo. Breechloading double shotgun made by N. R. Davis & Co. Retail only? Employed Wm. A. Albright 1888-1895 as salesman.

MEACHEM, EDWARD C.
  St. Louis, Mo., 1878 dir.-1900 dir.

MEAD & ADRIANCE
  St. Louis, Mo. 1835 dir.-1840 dir. Agent for Allen underhammer.

MEAD, EDWARD
  (1810-1884?) NY Ithaca, NY, 1831-32, St. Louis, Mo. 1835 dir.-1864 dir., as Mead & Adriance 1835-1840 dir. As Edward Mead & Co. 1842 on. Employed Stephen C. Jett 1842. Employed gunsmiths and had a shooting range on third floor of his building 1851. See pp. 149-170.

MEISLANG, JOSEPH see MIESLANG

MELVIN, WILLIAM T.
  Kirksville, Adair Co., Mo. 1876/77 dir. Vinton, Ia. 1880 dir.-1884 dir. Plattsmouth, Ne. 1886 dir. (Sellers)

MENGES, E. E. & CO
  Kansas City, Mo.1883/84 dir.-1889 dir. Listed as gunsmith 1883/84 dir. Dealer only?

MERRICK, JOHN
  St. Louis, Mo. 1870 dir. Retail only?

METROPOLITAN REPAIR CO.
  Springfield, Greene Co., Mo. 1898/99 dir. J. Aug. Rainey and Charles E. Thompson.

MEUR, ADAM
  St. Louis, Mo. 1872 dir. Mueller?

MEYER, JULIUS W.
  St. Louis, Mo. 1864 dir.-1870 dir. Dealer.

MIESLANG, JOSEPH
  (1821-) GER St. Louis, Mo. 1866 dir.-1870c. With Duenkel 1868. Dbl. shotgun. As Meislang in 1866 dir. Signed guns "MIESLANG".

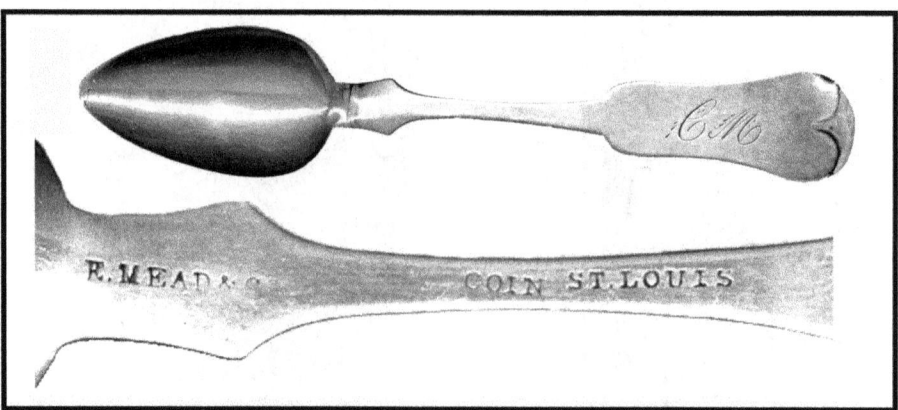

A teaspoon by E. Mead & Co.

MEIER, ADOLPHUS & CO.
  St. Louis, Mo. 1838 dir.-1869 dir. Primarily a hardware dealer, one of largest in St. Louis. May have manufactured as well as marked others guns as theirs. Sold gunsmith supplies. 1859 dir. listed Adolphus Meier, John C. Rust [his brother in-law] and Theodore G. Meier [his son] as partners. Numerous styles of long guns seen with Meier locks including one reported flintlock..

MEIER, ADOLPHUS
  (1813-1888) GER St. Louis, Mo., 1835- . Was merchant, not gunsmith. May have employed some gunsmiths. President of St. Louis Cotton Co. which shipped cotton to Germany in exchange for hardware. 1854 listed as Consul of Hanover.

MIGNERON, FRANCOIS
  Manchester, St. Louis Co., Mo. 1795 with Andre Landreville. Father of L. S. Migneron (Sr.).

MIGNERON, LOUIS SOLOMON (SR?)
  (-1841?) St. Louis, Mo. 1819a.-1821 dir.-1823-1836. Son of Francois.

MIGNERON, LOUIS S. (JR.)
  (1793-) CAN Manchester, St. Louis Co., Mo. 1860c., dir. Son of Louis. S. S. on dir.

MILBURN, NATHAN
  St. Louis, Mo. Patent # 57,751, Sept. 4, 1866, revolving cannon.

MILLER, CHARLES O.
Hannibal, Marion Co., Mo. 1860 dir., 1876/77 dir. Perc. 1/2 stock.
1870 Industrial Census
Marion Co. (Hannibal)
Name. Miller, C. O.
Name of Business,Manufacture or Product.
Gunsmith
Cost of Raw Materials.	$ 400
Number of Employees.	1
Wages	Not Given
Annual Gross Product.	$ 300-400

MILLER, CHARLES
Kansas City, Mo. 1867 dir.-1871 dir.
1870 Industrial Census
Jackson Co. (Kansas City)
Name. Miller, Charles & Co.
Name of Business,Manufacture or Product.
Gunsmith
Cost of Raw Materials.	$ 100
Number of Employees.	2
Wages	Not Given
Annual Gross Product.	$ 1000

MILLER, CHARLES
St. Louis, Mo. 1869 dir.
MILLER, DAVID
(1800-   ) KY Mo. 1830. Pulaski Co., Mo. 1850c.
MILLER, G. C. & CO.
K.C., Mo. 1876 dir.-1898/99 dir. Successors to Charles Miller.
MILLER, JOSEPH
(1814-   ) GER Hermann, Gasconade Co., Mo. 1850c. See Mueller.
MILLER, NICHOLAS
(1817-   ) PA unl. Pa. prior to 1854. Jefferson Co., Mo. 1860c.
MILLER, NOAH
(1804-   ) TN unl. Tn. 1834. Mo. 1853. Bates Co., Mo. 1860c.
MILLIKEN, H. C.
St. Louis, Mo. Maker of underhammer guns. (Logan)
MILLS (WILLS), GEORGE H.
(1818-   ) TN Cole Co., Mo. 1850c. In state pen for larceny, went in 1848.
MILLSTEAD (MILSTED), ALEXANDER I. (J?)
(1837-   ) NY Palmyra, Marion Co., Mo. 1850c., 1860c. Macon City, Mo. 1867/68 dir.-1879 dir. 1860 as a confectioner. Son of Inmet. As Milsted at Macon City.
MILLSTEAD, FREDERICK W.
(1832-   ) ENG Palmyra, Marion Co., Mo. 1850c.-1860c., dir. Son of Inmet. 1854 dir., Milstead & Son. 1860 dir. as Hillstead.
MILLSTEAD (MILSTED), INMET (INMENT)
(1805-   ) ENG unl. N.Y. 1833. Rochester, N. Y. 1838 dir.-1841 dir. (Eich) Palmyra, Marion Co., Mo. 1850c.-1854 dir. As Milstead & Son 1854. Reported as J. Milstead.

MISEL, GEORGE A.
(1813-   ) GER Cole Co., Mo. 1850c.
MISNER, BENJAMIN
(1815-   ) PA Linn Co., Ia. 1850c.-1855. Mo. 1857. Cedar Co., Mo. 1860c.
MITCHELL, D. D.
St. Louis, Mo. 1859 dir.-1860 dir.
MITCHELL, GEORGE
Marshall, Saline Co., Mo. 1879 dir.-1881 dir.
MIX, HARRISON & CO.
Cooper's Hill, Osage Co., Mo. 1879/80 dir. Typo. for Nix, Harrison & Co.
MONTGOMERY, WILLIAM
(1795-   ) KY unl. Ky. 1826-1829. Carroll Co., Mo. 1850c.
MOORE, D. A.
Newton, Putnam Co., Mo. 1860 dir.
MOORE, GEORGE
NC Madison Co., Il. 1809-1836.Independence, Jackson Co., Mo. 1837.(Johnson)
MORGAN, HENRY
(1822-   ) ENG St. Louis, Mo. 1842 dir.-1854 dir. With Frederick Hellinghaus 1842-1844. Perc. 1/2 stock. Mt. Sterling, Il. 1858-1870 (Johnson)
MORLOCH, JACOB
GER Pittsburgh, Pa. Hermann, Gasconade Co., Mo. Pre-civil war.
MORRIS, SMITH & BROTHERS
Eldon and Pleasant Mt., Miller Co., Mo. ca. 1880's.
MORROW, HENRY
(1826-   ) IRE St. Louis, Mo. 1850c. With Franz Lunsman.
MORTON, JOHN
St. Louis, Mo. 1864 dir.-1869 dir. Perc. 1/2 stock.
MOSCH, HERMAN
St. Louis, Mo. 1868 dir.-1875 dir.
MOSER, HENRY
Windsor, Henry Co., Mo. 1885/86 dir.
MOSS, JAMES
Nevada, Vernon Co., Mo. 1860 dir.
MUELLER, ADAM
St. Charles, Mo. 1876/7 dir. 1883/84 dir.-1893/94 dir. As carriage maker 1876/77 dir.
MUELLER, FREDERICK
Boonville, Cooper Co., Mo. 1869/70 dir.
MUELLER (MULLER, MILLER), GEORGE F.
(1812-   ) FR St. Louis, Mo. 1860 dir.-1870c.-1879 dir. Perc. locks. 3 diff. dir. spellings, addresses indicate same man.
MUENCH, GEORGE see MUNCH

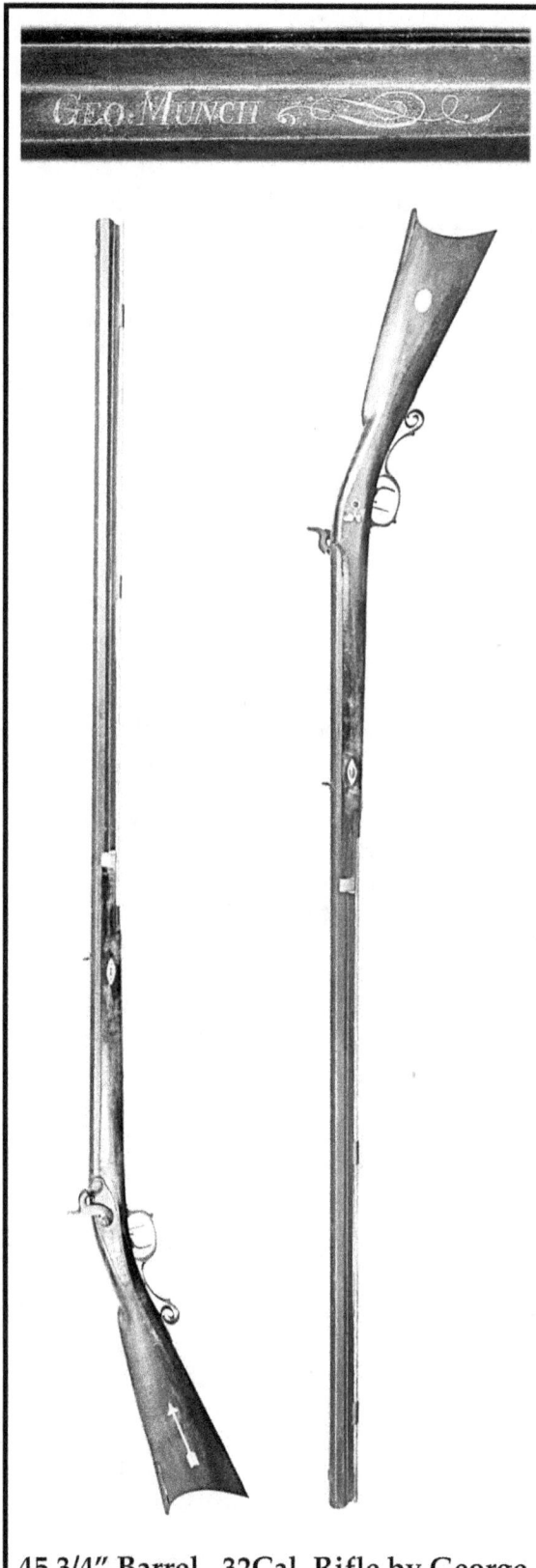

45 3/4" Barrel, .32Cal. Rifle by George Munch, Warren Co., Mo.

MULLER (MUELLER), JOSEPH
(1813-) GER Mo. 1846, Hermann, Gasconade Co., Mo. 1860c., ic., 1870 ic.
1860 Industrial Census:
Gasconade Co. (Hermann)
Name. Joseph Muller
Name of Business, Manufacture, or Product.
          Gunsmith
Capital invested in Real and Personal Estate in the Business. $ 300
Raw Material used, including Fuel.
    Quantities.   Kinds.   Values.
    24   Rifle barrels } $ 150
          Steel, Iron, Fuel
Average number of hands employed. Male. 1
Average Monthly cost of male labor. $ 35
Annual Product.
    Quantities.   Kinds.   Values.
    24   Rifles $ 432
        Other work $ 450

1870 Industrial Census
Gasconade Co. (Hermann)
Name. Muller, Joseph
Name of Business, Manufacture or Product.
          Gunsmith
Cost of Raw Materials. $ 120
Number of Employees.   1
Wages   Not Given
Annual Gross Product. $ 400/350

MULLER, MARCUS
(1825-) FR St. Louis, Mo. 1860c. At Arsenal.

MUNCH, GEORGE
(1801-1879) GER Mo. 1838. Warren Co., Mo. 1850c. St. Charles Co., Mo. 1860c. Gunsmiths Frederick Gross and William Lange living with him on 50 census. Perc. 1/2 stock.

MURPHY, J. G.
St. Clair, Franklin Co., Mo. 1860 dir.

MUSSER, JOSEPH
(1793-) PA Quincy, Adams Co., Il 1835-1860. Died at La Grange, Mo., date unknown. Uncertain if active as gunsmith in Mo. (Johnson)

MYER, F. (P.)
(1832-) GER St. Louis, Mo. 1850c.

N

NATHAN, JOSEPH
(1820-   ) GER St. Louis, Mo. 1850c.

NEAL, ALEXANDER
(1815-   ) TN unl. Mo. 1835-37. unl. Ar. 1839. unl. Mo. 1842. Marion co,, Or. 1845-1850c.

NEFF, JOHN
St. Louis, Mo. 1859 dir. & 1860 dir. As Schillinger & Neff.

NEILSEN, PETER
Kansas City, Jackson Co., Mo., 1870ic.
1870 Industrial Census
Jackson Co. (Kansas City)
Name.   Neilsen, Peter
Name of Business,Manufacture or Product.
         Gunsmith (repair and manufacture)
Cost of Raw Materials. $ 100
Number of Employees.   1
Wages $ 600
Annual Gross Product. $ 1500

NELSON & YOUNQUIST
Kansas City, Jackson Co., Mo., 1870ic., same as P. W. Nelson below?
1870 Industrial Census
Jackson Co. (Kansas City)
Name. Nelson & Youngquist
Name of Business,Manufacture or Product.
         Gunsmith
Cost of Raw Materials. $ 800
Number of Employees.   2
Wage $ 1200
Annual Gross Product. $ 4000

NELSON, P. W.
Kansas City, Mo. 1871 dir. (Sellers)

NETSER, FRANK
(1832-   ) AUS St. Louis, Mo. 1859-1860c., dir. As Nelzer in directory.

NEMOECK?, FRANK
(1847-   ) GER St. Louis, Mo. 1860c. As apprentice gun maker, no affiliation shown.

NEW YORK GUNSTORE
St. Louis, Mo. 1857 dir.-1859 dir. Name Charles Altinger used for his store.

NEWBERRY, WILLIAM
(1814-) OH Mo. 1837. Clarksville, Pike Co., Mo. 1850c.-1860c., dir. 1850 as wagonmaker.

NEWCOMER, MARTIN
(1800-) VA unl. Oh. 1840. Mo. 1852. Piketon, Stoddard Co., Mo.1860c., dir. As blacksmith on census.

NIES, LOUIS
(1825-) GER Buchanan Co., Mo. 1850c.

NIMECK, P. J.
Tipton, Moniteau Co., Mo. 1860 dir.

NIX, HARRISON & CO.
Cooper's Hill, Osage Co., Mo. 1879 dir.-1881 dir. See next.

NIX, THOMAS H.
(1824-) MO Osage Co., Mo. 1860c. Chamois, Osage Co., Mo. 1870. 1879 dir.-1881 dir., as Nix, Haarison & Co.

NORDHEIM, GEORGE ANDREW
(1818-1894) GER Mo. 1849. St. Louis, Mo. 1850c.-1853/54 dir. Burlington, Ia. 1856 dir. Yreka, Ca. 1862-1893. Perc. 1/2 stock prob. Iowa rifle. H. Waechter living same address 1850 census. (Shelton, Johnson)

NOTESTINE, G. W
Kirksville, Adair Co., Mo. 1893/94 dir.

NOWLIN, ABRAM CEPHUS
(1825-1913) Cocke Co., Ky. 1846-1861. Hickory Co., Mo. 1865-1913. (MB 1-49)

NOWLIN, TOM
(1879-1949) MO Fredonia, Benton Co., Mo. 1889-1930. Son of Abram. (MB 1-49)

NULL, THOMAS
(1824-) IRE St. Louis, Mo. 1860c.

NUTZ, L. N.
St. Louis, Mo. 1848dir.-1864dir. 1857 address 21 Washington, as maker of philosophical and mathematical instruments. 2 rifles known, med. cal. perc. 1/2 stock.

O

OATIS, N.
Little Osage, Vernon Co., Mo. 1860 dir.

OBERLE, ,
Weldon Springs, St. Charles Co., Mo. Lock marked "...... OBERLE WELDON SPRINGS , MO." (Blackburn)

OLDHAM, CHARLES
(1838-) TN Howard Co., Mo. 1850c. with father Gabriel. Helena, Mt. 1880 dir.-1898 dir. (Sellers)

OLDHAM, GABRIEL H.
(1816-) TN unl. Tn. prior to 1838. Mo. 1842. Howard Co., Mo. 1850c., ic. Helena, Mt. 1880 dir.-1886 dir . (Sellers)

1850 Industrial Census:
Howard Co.
Name. Gabriel H. Oldham
Name of Business, Manufacture, or Product.
 Gunsmith
Capital invested in Real and Personal Estate in the Business. $ 175
Raw Material used, including Fuel.

Quantities.	Kinds.	Values.
2 doz.	Gun Barrels	
" "	" Lock	$ 208
"	Sheet Brass	

Average number of hands employed. Male. 1
Average Monthly cost of male labor. $ 20
Annual Product.

Quantities.	Kinds.	Values.
24	Rifles	$ 600

OPPELT, A. E. (E.H.?)
St Louis Co., Mo. St. Louis Rifle.

ORREL, JOHN
Jackson, Cape Girardeau Co., Mo. 1880's. Poss. black. Flint rifle signed " JOHN ORREL MAKER, Jackson, Mo." (Blackburn)

OSTERMAN, CHARLES
Kansas City, Mo. 1891/92 dir.

OTTO, AUGUSTUS G.
(1820-) GER unl. Pa. 1838-1840. St. Louis, Mo. 1859 dir.-1864 dir. As locksmith 1860c. Lenzhaner & Otto 1864 dir.

OVERTON, EDWARD
St. Louis, Mo. 1859 dir.

OVREY, JOHN
St. Louis, Mo. 1838 dir. As blacksmith.

OWSLEY, ROBERT
Newark, Knox Co., Mo. 1867/68 dir., 1870ic.

1870 Industrial Census
Knox Co.
Name. Ousley, Robert
Name of Business,Manufacture or Product.
 Gunsmith

Cost of Raw Materials.	$ 800
Number of Employees.	1
Wages	$ 500
Annual Gross Product.	$ 1500

OYLER, COOK
Louisiana, Pike Co., Mo. 1876/77 dir.-1881 dir.

NOTES

P

PAINTER, ELISHA
(1836-) MO Springfield, Greene Co., Mo. 1850c. With father, Jacob. Marionville, Lawrence Co., Mo. 1885/86 dir.-1891/92 dir.

PAINTER, FAELDEN
(1848-) MO Springfield, Greene Co., Mo. 1880c., dir. With father, Jacob.

PAINTER, JACOB
(1810-1896) NC Montgomery Co., Il. 1826-1831. unl. Tn. between Il. and Mo. to 1833? Springfield, Greene Co., Mo. ca. 1831-1889 dir., 1850c., ic., 1860c. Pistolsmith. Possibly associated with Charles Altinger after Altinger moved to Springfield. 1850ic. has only woman (unnamed), thus far found, working for wages in Mo. gun trade.

1850 Industrial Census:
Greene Co.
Name. Jacob Painter
Name of Business, Manufacture, or Product.
        Gunsmith
Capital invested in Real and Personal Estate in the Business. $ 1,000
Raw Material used, including Fuel.
    Quantities.   Kinds.   Values.
    2000 lb.   Iron $ 100
    240 lb.   "Gun Bbls"$ 100
Average number of hands employed.
    Male. 2   Female. 1
Wages.
Average Monthly cost of male labor. $ 50
Average Monthly cost of female labor. $ 5
Annual Product.
    Quantities.   Kinds.   Values.
    300   Pistols $ 1,200
    12   Rifle Guns $ 144
        Job Work $ 250

PAINTER, JOHN
(1841-1919) MO Springfield, Greene Co., Mo. 1850c., 1860c., 1880c. Listed as gunsmith on 1860c. with father, Jacob. As musician on 80c.

PAINTER, JAMES W. see PALMER

PALMER, A. M.
Salisbury, Chariton Co., Mo. 1898/99 dir.

PALMER, E. B.
Stewartville, DeKalb Co., Mo. 1860 dir.

PALMER, HENRY C.
Chicago, Il. 1854 dir. St. Louis, Mo. 1860 dir.-1868 dir. Derringers for Dimick and self. (Johnson, AR 4-58)

PALMER, JAMES W.
(1821-) NC Lafayette Co., Mo. 1850c., ic. Columbia, Boone Co., Mo. 1854 dir. California, Moniteau Co., Mo. 1860c., dir.

1850 Industrial Census:
Lafayette Co.
Name. Jas. W. Palmer
Name of Business, Manufacture, or Product.
        Gunsmith
Capital invested in Real and Personal Estate in the Business. $ 250
Raw Material used, including Fuel.
    Quantities.   Kinds.   Values.
    3 doz.   Gun barrels $ 130
    12 "   Files $ 50
    8 "   Locks $ 100
Average number of hands employed. Male. 4
Average Monthly cost of male labor. $ 60
Annual Product.
    Quantities.   Kinds.   Values.
    (not given) Variety Work $ 2,000

PARKER, A.
Kahoka, Clark Co., Mo. Morgan rifle marked "recut by A. Parker". (Monroe)

PARRE, J. C.
Lamar, Barton Co., Mo. 1860 dir.

PARSCHALL, J. T.
(-) IA Lathrop, Clinton Co., Mo. 1883/84 dir.

PATRICK, J. M.
(1837-) OH Albany, Gentry Co., Mo. 1860c., dir. As clerk on census.

PATTERSON, H. C.
Higginsville, LaFayette Co., Mo. 1881 dir.
Marshall, Saline Co., Mo. 1891 dir.-1898/99 dir.

PATTERSON, JOHN A.
Lindley, Grundy Co., Mo. 1879 dir.-1885/86 dir.
Fairfield, Wayne Co., Il. 1865-1876. (Johnson)

PATTERSON, JOHN
(1832-) VA Grundy Co., Mo. 1860c.

PEABODY, LOREN
(1832-) Georgetown, Oh. 1850c. DeKalb, Buchanan Co., Mo. 1860 dir. Perc. 1/2 stock. (Hutslar)

PEAKE, DANIEL
Madisonville, Ralls Co., Mo. 1854 dir.

PEARSON, JOHN
Baltimore, Md. 1830-1835 dir. Ft. Smith, Ar. 1845-1870. Made first revolvers for Colt and his own perc. guns. Reported St. Louis 1840-45 (Sutherland, Elias)

PEASE, J. S. & CO.
St. Louis, Mo. 1831-1847 dir. Sold gunsmith supplies. Locks marked. Unknown if they employed gunsmiths.

PEEL, JAMES see FEEL

PEERS,
St. Charles, Mo. ca. 1819.

PELTON, THEODORE G.
unl. Mo. 1850's. Jersey Landing, Il. 1860 dir. Clinton, Ia. after. (Johnson)

PENN, GABRIEL
(1773-) VA unl. Va. prior to 1817. Monroe Co., Mo. 1850c.

PENN, SAMUEL
(1803-) VA Monroe Co., Mo. 1850c. Son of Gabriel.

PETERS, JOHN W.
(1804-) GER St. Louis, Mo. 1850c. At Arsenal.

PETTERS, JOHN
(1812-) GER St. Louis, Mo. 1860c. At Arsenal. Poss. same as above.

PHILLIPS, JOHN G.
(1789-) VA Mo. 1829. Boone Co., Mo. 1850c., ic. Small caliber perc. 1/2 stock. Schofield, Wi. 1865. (Sellers)

1850 Industrial Census:
Boone Co.
Name. John G. Phillips
Name of Business, Manufacture, or Product. Gunsmith
Capital invested in Real and Personal Estate in the Business. $ 125
Raw Material used, including Fuel.

Quantities.	Kinds.	Values.
100	Gun Bar.	$ 400
200 bu.	Coal	$ 40

Average number of hands employed. Male. 2
Wages. Average Monthly cost of male labor.
$ 50 ($ 25 crossed out)
Annual Product.

Quantities.	Kinds.	Values.
(not given)	Rifles	$ 2,000
	other Articles	$ 1,000

PHILLIPS, PRESTON
(1829-) MO Boone Co., Mo. 1850c. Son of John G.

PHILLIPS, WILLIAM J.
St. Louis, Mo. Patent # 109,914, Dec. 6, 1870, revolver, with Charles J. Linberg. (Winant)

PIPER, S. P.
Holden, Johnson Co., Mo. 1898/99 dir.

PIPES (PIPER?), JOHN
(1830-) PA Maryville, Nodaway Co., Mo. 1860c. Central City, Ia. 1865 dir.

PIPINO, G. H.
Hannibal, Marion Co., Mo. 1885/86 dir.

PLICKENDORF, JOHN see BLICKENSDORFER

POEPPLEMEYER, WILLIAM
Cedar Fork, Franklin Co., Mo. 1889 dir.-1893/94 dir.

POHL, ALOIS
St. Louis, Mo., 1870ic.

1870 Industrial Census
St. Louis
Name. Pohl, Alois
Name of Business, Manufacture or Product. Lock & Gunsmith

Cost of Raw Materials.	$ 400
Number of Employees.	1
Wages	$ 750
Annual Gross Product.	$ 2400

POLLARD, PHILLIP
    Macon, Mo. 1889/90dir.-1898/99 dir.
POOL, JAMES
    VA Mo. prior to 1830. 1830 at White River Indian Agency.
POORMAN, HENRY B.
    St. Louis, Mo. 1850c.-1857, 1860dir., patent # 16,327, bullet mold with Tristram Campbell. 1860 dir. box manufacturer. See p.24.
PORTER, ALEXANDER A.
    (1802? -) SC? Dunksburg, Pettis Co., Mo. 1860 dir. Johnson Co., Mo. 1864.
POSEGATE, ISAAC F.
    (1802-) VA unl. In. 1835-1838. Weston, Platte Co., Mo. 1850c. St. Joseph, Buchanan Co., Mo. 1860 dir.-1867/68 dir. 1867/68 dir. as I. F. Posegate & Co.
POSEGATE, WILLIAM J.
    St. Joseph, Buchanan Co., Mo. 1869 dir.-1876 dir. Maryville, Nodaway Co., Mo. 1889/90 dir. Prob. son of Isaac.
POTTORF, GEORGE
    (1821-) PA unl. Il. 1848-1852. Vernon Co., Mo. 1860c.

POWELL, C. S.
    Macon, Mo. 1898/99 dir.
POWELL, PETER & CO.
    St. Louis, Mo. 1836-1850dir. Importers of locks and hardware.
POWELL, R. J.
    Palmyra, Marion Co., Mo. 1881 dir.
PRATT & SIMS
    Princeton, Mercer Co. Mo. 1860 dir.
PRIOR, GEORGE W.
    Boeger's Store, Osage Co., Mo. Patent # 264,899, Sept. 26, 1882, sight.
PRISS (PRISSO?), BENJAMIN
    (1815-) VA unl. Va. 1832-1839. Mo. 1843. St. Louis, Mo. 1850c.
PRITCHARD, J. M.
    St. Louis, Mo. 1861. Government rifle contractor.
PROVOST, PETER
    St. Louis, Mo. 1848 dir. As armorer.
PYEATT, JAMES P.
    Jefferson City, Cole Co., Mo. 1876/77 dir.

Q

QUIGLEY, E. F.
    Unionville, Putnam Co., Mo. 1885/86 dir.-1889/90 dir.

QUINEY, FRANK
    St. Louis, Mo. 1848 dir. As armorer.

NOTES

R

RAABE, JULIUS A.
  St. Louis, Mo. 1891 dir.-1900 dir.
RAGG, H.
  Coellda, Camden Co., Mo. 1898/99 dir.
RAINEY, J. AUG.
  Springfield, Greene Co., Mo. 1898/99 dir. As Metropolitan Repair Co., with Charles E. Thompson.
RATRAUFF, H G.
  Warrensburg, Johnson Co., Mo. Perc. 1/2 stock. (Sellers)
READ, O. H. P.
  (1812-) TN Mo. 1838. Taney Co., Mo. 1850c.
REAUBERT, JAMES
  Eldon, Miller Co., Mo. 1883/84 dir.-1885/86 dir.
REBER, H.
  St. Louis, Mo. 1881 dir.
REDFERN, B.
  Lock on R. Beauvais rifle (Pourie)
REDFORD, ARTER
  Jefferson City, Cole Co., Mo., Flint fullstock, reported as Redford by Dillin, Beford by Dean. (Sellers)
REDWINE, JOHN F.
  Lynville, Morgan Co., Il. Utica, Livingston Co., Mo. 1876/77 dir.-1885/86 dir. Chillicothe, Livingston Co., Mo. 1885/86 dir.-1893/94 dir., 1898/99 dir.
REDWINE, WILLIAM J.
  Chillicothe, Livingston Co., Mo. 1881 dir.-1883/84 dir.
REED, ISAAC
  (1811-) PA unl. In. 1844-1853. Mo. 1858. Cravensville, Daviess Co., Mo. 1860c., dir. Farmer on census.
REICHARD, EDWARD
  (1802-1882) GER Washington, Franklin Co., Mo. 1850c., 1860 dir.-1882. Also a watchmaker, silversmith and jeweler.
REICHLING, FRANK
  (1821-) ? Mo. 1848. El Dorado Co., Ca. 1852c. (Shelton)
REINE, JOSEPH
  Marshall, Saline Co., Mo. 1893/94 dir.
REINEKE, FREDERICK
  St. Louis, Mo. 1847 dir.
REINHART, J. W.
  VA Lexington, LaFayette Co., Mo. 1860c. 1889/90 dir. as Rinehart.
RENICK, A. & G.
  Independence, Jackson Co., Mo. 1843-1861. Perc. 1/2 stock.

RENICK, ABRAM
(1814-) KY Independence, Jackson Co., Mo. 1843-1861, 1850ic. Moved to a farm near Independence ca. 1861 and continued in business until at least 1881. See previous page.

1850 Industrial Census:
Jackson Co.
Name.   Abram Renick
Name of Business, Manufacture, or Product.
            Gunsmith
Capital invested in Real and Personal Estate in the Business. $ 200
Raw Material used, including Fuel.

Quantities.	Kinds.	Values.
24	Stocks	$ 12
24	Barrels	$ 75
24	Locks	$ 30
	Hardware	$ 25

Average number of hands employed. Male. 2
Average Monthly cost of male labor. $ 60
Annual Product.

Quantities.	Kinds.	Values.
40	Guns	$ 500
	Other Work	$ 400

RENICK, GEORGE
(1816-1880) KY Independence, Jackson Co., Mo. 1843-1861. Bro. of Abram. See previous.

REST, FREEMAN
Dixon, Pulaski Co., Mo. 1876/77 dir.

RHYNE, ISAAC
Schall's, Perry Co., Mo. 1893/94 dir.

RICH, A. B.
Siloam Springs, Howell Co., Mo. 1885/86 dir.

RICHARD, AUGUST
Washington, Franklin Co., Mo. 1860 dir.

RICHARDSON, E. G.
(1813-) KY Mo. 1845. Memphis, Scotland Co., Mo. 1854 dir.-1860c. As clerk on c.

RICHARDSON, WILLIAM
(1789-) MD St. Louis, Mo. 1860c.

RICHART, EDWIN
(1833-) GER St. Louis, Mo. 1850c.

RICHNER, FREDERICK
(1810-) SWE Mo. 1836. Cape Girardeau, Mo. 1850c.

RICKMERS, A. F.
Cape Girardeau, Mo. 1850-1860 dir. Kansas City, Mo. 1888 dir.-1898/99 dir.

RICKMERS, EDWARD H.
New Melle, St. Charles Co., Mo. 1879 dir.-1898/99 dir.

RIDGEWAY, ZACK
(1807-) VA Mo. 1829. Callaway Co., Mo. 1850c.

RIDGWAY, H. C.
Trenton, Grundy Co., Mo. 1879 dir. (Sellers)

RIGDON, CHARLES H.
(1822-) OH St. Louis, Mo. 1848-1859, 1850c. As scale maker in St. Louis. Made revolvers for the Confederacy in the South during Civil War.

RIGGIN, JOHN
St. Louis, Mo. 1835 (Sellers)

RIGGINS, A. J.
Cassville, Barry Co., Mo. 1860 dir.

RIGGINS, G. W.
Albany, Gentry Co., Mo. 1885/86 dir.

RILEY, FIELDING J.
(1829-) MO Randolph Co., Mo. 1850c., Macon, Mo. 1889/90 dir.-1891/92 dir. Brother of John F.

RILEY, JOHN F.
(1815-) LA Randolph Co., Mo. 1850c., ic.

1850 Industrial Census:
Randolph Co.
Name.   J. Riley
Name of Business, Manufacture, or Product.
            Gunsmith
Capital invested in Real and Personal Estate in the Business. $ 200
Raw Material used, including Fuel.

Quantities.	Kinds.	Values.
(not given)	Sundries	$ 200

Average number of hands employed. Male. 2
Average Monthly cost of male labor. $ 25
Annual Product.

Quantities.	Kinds.	Values.
(not given)	Sundries	$ 1,000

RINEHART, J. W. see REINHART

RINEHART, JESSIE
(1808-) VA unl. Il. 1833-1835. Mo. 1839. Bates Co., Mo. 1850c.

RINGE, FREDERICK
(1815-) GER St. Charles, Mo. 1860c., dir.-1879 dir. Harrisonville, Cass Co., Mo. 1883/84 dir. as Fritz. Norborne, Carroll Co., Mo. 1885/86 dir.

RINGE, HENRY
(1860-) MO St. Charles, Mo. 1883/84 dir.-1898/99 dir. Son of Frederick.

RINGE, LOUIS
(1836-) GER St. Charles, Mo. 1860c., 1867/68 dir.-1893 dir. Son of Frederick.

ROBERTSON, C. P.
Windsor, Henry Co., Mo. 1883/84 dir.

ROBINSON, E. A.
Schell City, Vernon Co., Mo. 1893/94 dir.-1898/99 dir. As Robison 1893/94 dir.

ROBINSON, JOHN
St. Louis, Mo. 1845 dir. Perc. shotgun.

ROEBER, HENRY
St. Louis, Mo. 1880 dir.-1890 dir.

ROESEN W. & J.
Jefferson City, Cole Co. 1881 dir. See below.

ROESEN, JOHN
(1828-   ) GER Mo. 1857. Jefferson City, Cole Co., Mo. 1860c., dir.-1881 dir. Brother of William.

ROESEN, WILLIAM
(1825-   ) GER Jefferson City, Cole Co., Mo. 1860c., 1879 dir.-1891/92 dir.

ROGERS, GEORGE W.
Competetion, LaClede Co., Mo. 1879 dir.

ROLL, FRANCIS X.
(1822-   ) FR Mo. 1853, Liberty, Clay Co., Mo. 1860c.-1865 (Hobbies 6-31) 1870ic. 1893 dir.-1898/99 dir.

1870 Industrial Census
Clay Co. (Liberty)
Name. Roll, Francis X.
Name of Business, Manufacture or Product.
    Lockmaker
Cost of Raw Materials. $ 200
Number of Employees.   1
Wages   Not Given
Annual Gross Product. $ 1800

ROLSTON, JAMES
Kansas City, Mo. 1889/90 dir.

ROMETSH,   ,
Brookfield, Linn Co., Mo. 1883/84 dir. As Tanner & Rometsh.

ROPER, JOHN
(1808-   ) GER St. Louis, Mo. 1836-1850ic.-1860c., dir.-1870c. Listed as retired gunsmith on 1870c.

1850 Industrial Census:
St. Louis, Ward 2
Name. John Roper
Name of Business, Manufacture, or Product.
    Gunsmith
Capital invested in Real and Personal Estate in the Business. $ 300
Raw Material used, including Fuel
    Quantities.   Kinds.   Values.
    25?   Barrels & locks $ 150
Average number of hands employed. Male. 1
Average Monthly cost of male labor. $ 20
Annual Product.
    Quantities.   Kinds.   Values.
    25   guns & rifles $ 550

ROSON, JOHN see ROESEN

ROSTOCK, F. S. jr.
Oregon, Holt Co., Mo. 1889/90 dir.

ROUND, GEORGE
(1811-   ) ENG St. Louis, Mo. 1850c.-1854 dir.

ROUND, JOHN
(1816-   ) St. Louis, Mo. 1850c.-1851 dir.

RUBCORE, FRED
Bilmore, St. Charles Co., Mo. 1891 dir.

RUDOLPH & CO.
St. Louis, Mo. 1874 dir.-1875 dir. Successors to H. E. Dimick. Thomas W. Rudolph and ——. (directory lists no name, simply ——).

RUDOLPH, J. E.
Roscoe, St. Clair Co., Mo. 1893/94 dir.

RUDOLPH, JUSTUS
GER Hermann, Gasconade Co., Mo. ca. 1839.

RUDOLPH, THOMAS W.
St. Louis, Mo. 1865 dir.-1877 dir. 1865, clk., 1866-1870 salesman and 1871 bkpr. for H. Folsom & Co. 1873 Albright & Rudolph. 1874-1875 Rudolph & Co. 1877 McGinnes & Rudolph.

RUDOLPH, VICTOR
(1825-   ) SWITZ St. Joseph, Buchanan Co., Mo. 1860c., 1867 dir.-1874 dir., 1876/7 dir., 1879 dir.-1893/94 dir. Not part of Rudolph & Co., St. Louis. Surname only on census.

1870 Industrial Census
Buchanan Co. (St. Joseph)
Name. Rudolph, Victor
Name of Business, Manufacture or Product.
    Gun Shop (repairs)
Cost of Raw Materials.   300
Number of Employees.   1
Wages   600
Annual Gross Product.   1000

RUGGLES, JAMES
(1822-   ) NY Adair Co., Mo. 1859-1860c.

RUHBOTTOM, EZEKIAL
(1770-1857) NC Greenville, Wayne Co., Mo. 1807-1857. Also a minister, J. P., judge, and surveyor.

RUSS, M. B.
Kansas City, Mo. 1898/99 dir.

RYAN, Patrick
Pierce City, Lawrence Co., Mo. 1898/99 dir. As P. Ryan & Co with wife.

NOTES

S

ST. JOSEPH GUN AND BICYCLE FACTORY
St. Joseph, Buchanan Co., Mo. 1898/99 dir. S. J. Lapthorne, proprietor.

ST. LOUIS ARMS & TOOL CO.
St. Louis, Mo. Name used by Frank Spaedy and Wm. Roessler. 1905-1911. Single shot rifles.

ST. LOUIS ARSENAL
St. Louis, Mo., 1826-1877. Ordnance and repair. Had ability to manfufacture small arms. Rifled guns early Civil War.

ST. LOUIS PATENT SHELL MFG. CO.
St. Louis, Mo. President: Col. Charles L. Hunt. Vice-President: N. S. Chouteau. Sec.: W. A. Albright. Treas.: Theodore Hunt.

ST. LOUIS SUPERINTENDENCY FOR INDIAN AFFAIRS
St. Louis, Mo., 1826-1833. Had a gunsmith shop as well as blacksmith shop to serve visiting Indians. At times also had shops at its various agencies in Missouri, as well as other states.

SACKWITZ, LOUIS
St. Louis, Mo. 1896 dir.

SAMUELS, J. H.
Hannibal, Marion Co., Mo. 1889/90 dir.

SANDERS, LEWIS
Bedford, Livingston Co., Mo. 1860 dir.

SAXTON, GEORGE S.
St. Louis, Mo., 1864 dir.-1869 dir. 1864 dir.-1867 dir. as G. S. Saxton. 1868 dir.-1869 dir. as McLaren, Saxton & Williams. Employed Daniel Eaton 1866 dir.-1867 dir., retail only.

SCAGGS, HENRY
(1801-   ) KY unl. Ky. 1836-37. Mo. 1840. Reynolds Co. Mo. 1860c.

SCEIN, FREDERICK see SWAN

SCHACH, FRANK
Sedalia, Pettis Co., Mo. 1898/99 dir.

SCHADE, JOHN
(1822-1868) St. Louis, Mo., 1850c. Sacramento, Ca. 1851-1868. (Shelton)

SCHAEFER, ANTON
Moberly, Randolph Co., Mo. 1879 dir.-1883/84 dir.

SCHAEFER, P.
Kansas City, Mo. 1869 dir. (Sellers)

SCHAERFF, CHRISTIAN
(1818-) GER St. Louis, Mo., 1850c., ic., 1854 dir.-1865 dir. 1850 ic. 1854 dir. as Schaerff Bros. with brother John. Brothers Wendell & Charles listed as lithographers at same address. Tavern owner 1860 dir. As Sherff on c. As machinist 1865.

1850 industrial census:
St. Louis, Ward 3
Name. C. & J. Schaerff
Name of Business, Manufacture, or Product.
   Gunsmith
Capital invested in Real and Personal Estate in the Business. $ 800
Raw Material used, including Fuel.
   Quantities.   Kinds.   Values.
   1000lbs.   iron and brass, } $ 600
            silver & steel
Average number of hands employed. Male. 3
Wages. Monthly cost of male labor. $ 90
Annual Product.
   Quantities.   Kinds.   Values.
   (not given)   Guns, Rifles } $ 2,600
                & Pistols

SCHAERFF, CHRISTOPHER
(1820-) GER St. Louis, Mo., 1850c. Poss. 2nd. entry for same man as abv. Here living singly, abv. with brothers.

SCHAERFF, JOHN
(1820-) GER St. Louis, Mo., 1850c., ic.-1854 dir. Brother of Christian. As blacksmith on 1850c.

SCHAFER, J. R.
St. Louis, Mo., 1866 dir. Same address as Louis Waechter.

SCHAFERMEYER, JOSEPH B.
St. Louis, Mo. 1896 dir.

SCHAFFER, J. C.
Fruitland, Cape Girardeau Co., Mo. 1893/94 dir.

SCHAMMEL, JOHN
(1812-) GER Palmyra, Marion Co., Mo. 1850c.-1860 dir. Blumfield, Mi., 1863 dir. (Sellers)

SCHAND, FREDERICK & MOLTY
St. Louis, Mo., 1867 dir. Frederick, Molty and another brother Henry. Poss. Schantz.

SCHANN, CHRISTIAN
(1818-) ?? St. Louis, Mo., 1857 dir.1870c., ic., As Schum 1857 dir. and Scham on 1870 census.

1870 Industrial Census
St. Louis
Name. Schann, Christian
Name of Business, Manufacture or Product.
   Gunsmith
Cost of Raw Materials. $ 2000
Number of Employees.   2
Wages $ 2300
Annual Gross Product. $ 6000

SCHANTZ, HENRY
St. Louis, Mo., 1857 dir.-1869 dir. With Dimick 1868.

SCHERLIN, CHRISTIAN
St. Peters, St. Charles Co., Mo. 1875 dir.

SCHERTZER, JULES T.
St. Louis, Mo., 1886 dir.-1887 dir.

SCHILLING, CHARLES F.
(1849-) MO St. Louis, Mo. 1850c. 1875 dir.-1879 dir. Shotguns and air guns. St. Paul, Mn. 1879-1886 dir. Son of Frederick. "C. F. SCHILLING" (Sellers)

SCHILLING, DANIEL
Gayoso, Pemiscot Co., Mo. 1860 dir.-1885/86 dir.

SCHILLING, FREDERICK
(1811-) GER Mo. 1849. St. Charles, Mo. 1850c. St. Louis, Mo., 1860 dir. as blacksmith. Same address as J. P. Schimpf 1865. With Dimick 1868 dir. As Blickensdoerfer & Schilling 1869 dir.-1874 dir. A Frederick Schilling, gunsmith, lived at Blickenderfers Tavern, Lancaster, Pa. 1857. (Pourie)

1870 Industrial Census
St. Louis
Name. Schilling, Fred
Name of Business, Manufacture or Product.
   Gunsmith
Cost of Raw Materials. $ 3000
Number of Employees.   2
Wages $ 2300
Annual Gross Product. $ 8000

SCHILLINGER & NEFF
St. Louis, Mo., 1859 dir. & 1860 dir.

SCHILLINGER, CHARLES
St. Louis, Mo., 1859 dir. & 1860 dir.+. As Schillinger & Neff 1859 dir. & 1860 dir. 1864 dir. as musician.

SCHIMPF, JOHN PETER
(1845-) GER St. Louis, Mo., 1865 dir-1870c., 1881 dir.-1895 dir. At same address as Frederick Schilling 1865. With John Blickensdoerfer 1866 at same address he shared with Schilling in 65.

SCHMIDT, EARNEST
Clinton Co., Mo., 1870ic.

**1870 Industrial Census
Clinton Co.**

Name. Schmidt, Earnest
Name of Business, Manufacture or Product.
    Gunsmith
Cost of Raw Materials.	$ 150
Number of Employees.	1
Wages	Not Given
Annual Gross Product.	$ 700

SCHMIDT, JOHN
Augusta, St. Charles Co., Mo. 1860 dir.

SCHMIDT, WILLIAM
Jefferson City, Cole Co., Mo. 1860 dir., 1898/99 dir.

SCHNEGELSCHEIPEN, J.W.
Warrensburgh, Johnson Co., Mo. 1883/84 dir.-1893/94 dir. As J. H. 1883/84.

SCHOEN, LEOPOLD
St. Louis Mo. 1860 dir.-1872 dir. With M. Friede & Co. 1860. Retail guns and gunsmiths supplies. Not known as gunsmith.

SCHOFIELD, GEORGE L
Lexington, LaFayette Co., Mo. 1876/77 dir.-1883/84 dir.

SCHROEDER, CHARLES F.
St. Louis, Mo., 1889 dir.

SCHUBERT, MARTIN
(1819-) GER Mo. 1857. St. Louis, Mo., 1870c.

SCHULTZ, R. A.
Kansas City, Mo. 1884 dir. (Sellers)

SCHUM, ,
Wellsville, Montgomery Co., Mo. 1867/68 dir.

SCHUMATE, KEMPER
Shelbina, Shelby Co., Mo. 1885/86 dir.-1898/99 dir. As Shumate on some dir.

SCHWANDER, EMIL
(1840-) GER St. Louis, Mo. 1854, 1860c.

SCHWARTZ, FREDERICK F.
(1825-) GER St. Louis, Mo., 1854 dir., 1860c., 1880 dir.-1899 dir.? Very common name in St. Louis. Possibly 3 different men operated as gunsmiths over the years. Frederick F. on c., Frederick W. 1899 dir. At 31 Washington 1857.

SCHWERTFEGER, C.
Palmyra, Marion Co., Mo. 1876/77 dir.

SCOTT, WILLIAM M.
Leadville, Jasper Co., Mo. 1860 dir.

SCOTT, JOHN
St. Louis, Mo., 1845-1848 dir. as silversmith. 1884 mgr. of sporting gds. for Simmons Hardware, prob. same man, neither listed as gunsmith. With R. Beauvais 1848.

SCOTT'S, J. N.
St. Louis, Mo., Simmons Hardware Trade Name on import dbl. cart. & perc. shotguns.

SEAGROVE, JOHN
Neosho, Newton Co., Mo. 1898/99 dir.

SEAR?, ZACHARIAH
(1812-) KY Mo. 1832 ? Knox Co. Mo. 1850c.

SEARCY, BARTLETT
(1805-) KY Knox Co., Mo. 1850c.-1860c.

SECONGOST, J. M.
Boonville, Cooper Co., Mo. 1885/86 dir.-1889/90 dir.

SECOR, OLIVER P.
(1817-) NY unl. N.Y. 1836-1842. unl. Pa. 1846-1849. Weston, Platte Co., Mo. 1850c. Peoria, Il. 1856 dir. Chicago, Il. 1863-1867 dir. Peoria, Il. 1868 dir. Chicago, Il. 1876-1880. Finely made rifles and shotguns. (Johnson)

SEDALIA GUN AND MACHINE CO.
Sedalia, Pettis Co., Mo. 1898/99 dir. A. B. Dempsey mgr.

SEELE, HENRY
Rolla, Phelps Co., Mo. 1879 dir.-1883/84 dir.

SEIBERT, C.
St. Louis, Mo. machinist for Dimick. (AR 4-58)

SEIDNER, PHILLIP
Gasconade Co., Mo. pre-Civil War, inlaid .38 cal. 1/2 stock. (Blackburn)

SEIFERTH, FREDERICK E.
St. Louis, Mo., 1865 dir.-1890 dir. 1865 as gunsmith and air gun spring maker. Name spelled various ways, the one used occurs most frequently.

SEIFERTH, T. EDWARD
1859 dir.-1864 dir. 1859, engineer, 1860, Edward, gunmaker and air gun spring maker, 1863, tool maker.

SEILER, CHARLES
Springfield, Greene Co., Mo. 1898/99 dir.

SHADWICK, CHARLES
Hannibal, Marion Co., Mo. 1881 dir.

SHAEFER, AUGUST
Moberly, Randolph Co., Mo. 1885/86 dir.

SHAFF see SCHAERFF

SHAMICH,
St. Louis, Mo., 1850's? Made rifle barrels for Dimick. (AR 5-58)

SHAPLEIGH HARDWARE
1843-1900+ Rogers & Shapleigh 1843 Shapleigh, Day & Co. 1848-1860, A. F. Shapleigh & Co. 1863-1900+. Major importer and wholesaler.

SHARPE, DANIEL
(1815-) NY St. Louis, Mo., 1860c. Listed as a gun & pistol repairer.

SHAVIERE, ISAAC R.
(1801-) FR St. Louis, Mo., 1868 dir.-1880 dir., 1870c. Sometimes listed as Sheviere or Shavier and once as Juvier.

SHAW, JAMES
St. Louis, Mo., 1853 dir. & 1854 dir. 1853 as gunsmith, 1854 as locksmith.

SHAW, ROBERT
(1829-) MA Mo. 1861. St. Louis, Mo., 1870c.

SHAW, SAMUEL B.
St. Louis, Mo., 1864 dir. Listed under firearms, retail only?

SHAWK & McLANAHAN
St. Louis, Mo., 1858 dir.-1861. Abel Shawk and J. K. McLanahan, perc. revolvers.

SHAWK, ABEL
St. Louis, Mo. Shawk & McClanahan 1858-1861. Brought first steam fire engine to St. Louis from Cincinnati, Sam Hawken was Captain of the Union Fire Co. No. 2, which received it.

SHAWK, SAMUEL
St. Louis, Mo. 1836/37 dir.-1842 dir. As locksmith. Mathias B. Clark at same address 1842. Crude St. Louis rifle, brass trigger guard very similar to that used by Hawkens. Marked "S. SHAWK"

SHAROZ?, HENRY
St. Louis, Mo., 1870ic., same as Schantz?

1870 Industrial Census
St. Louis
Name. Sharoz?, Henry
Name of Business, Manufacture or Product.
    Gun & Locksmith
Cost of Raw Materials. $ 275
Number of Employees.   1
Wages $ 800
Annual Gross Product. $ 2200

SHEETS, DANIEL
(1811-) OH Union, Oh. -184?. Clarksville, Pike Co., Mo. 1848?-1850c. Went to Ca., leaving family in care of Benjamin F. Woodward. Suisun, Ca. 1860-1875. (Hutslar, Shelton)

SHEETS, JOHN
Gallatin, Daviess Co., Mo. 1867/68 dir. Pilot Grove, Cooper Co., Mo. 1881 dir.-1883/84 dir. J.P. Sheety 1881, J. P. Sheetz 1883/84.

SHEETZ, HENRY
(1795-) VA Mo. 1839. Lexington, LaFayette Co., Mo. 1850c. Gallatin, Daviess Co., Mo. 1860 dir. As Sheets on dir.

SHILLINGER & MEFF
Typo for Schillinger & Neff, 1859 dir.

SHONE & HOGAN
St. Louis, Mo. 1868 dir. Geo. Shone & Joseph M. Hogan.

SHONE, GEORGE
St. Louis, Mo., 1868 dir. As Shone & Hogan with Joseph M. Hogan

SHORT, JAMES C.
Pleasant Hill, Cass Co., Mo. 1870 dir.,ic.-1876/77 dir.

1870 Industrial Census
Cass Co. (Pleasant Hill)
Name.   Short, James C.
Name of Business, Manufacture or Product.
    Gunsmith
Cost of Raw Materials. $ 40
Number of Employees.   1
Wages $ 80
Annual Gross Product. $ 2500

SHORT, JOHN C.
(1841-) MO Kirksville, Adair Co., Mo. 1860c. As apprentice to Robt. H. Harris.

SHULER, V.
Chillicothe, Livingston Co., Mo. 1860 dir.

SHUMATE, KEMPER see SCHUMATE

SIEBEN, GUSTAV
Kansas City, Mo. 1881 dir.-1883/84 dir. As Gustav Sieben & Son.

SIEBER & HEBERLEIN
St. Louis, Mo. ca. 1870. Air rifle marked "R. SIEBER & A. HEBERLEIN ".

SIEBER, CARL R. See below

SIEBER, CHARLES R. (BISMARK)
(1826-1911) GER St. Louis, Mo., arrived St. Louis ca. 1856. 1857 dir. 1867 dir.-1906 dir. Worked for Hawken 1857-1860? Albright & Rudolph 1873, Albright & Sons 1875. Prob. same as Robert C. Listed as Carl R. in some dir. No known guns marked Charles R. or C. R. Sieber. Nicknamed "Bismark" due to strong resemblence to German Chancellor. See p. 178.

SIEBER, EDWARD ROBERT
(1828-) GER St. Louis, Mo., 1857 dir.?-1879 dir.?, Poss. brother of Charles, Nashville, Tn. ordnance inspector for Union, made some guns while there. Jacksonville, Morgan Co., Il. 1865-1906. Listed in *Gateway Gunsmiths* as with Albright & Sons, in error. Signed known guns "E. R. SIEBER". See p. 178. (Johnson)

SIEBER, ROBERT
St. Louis, Mo., 1857 dir.-1886 dir., duplicate listings for Charles R.? See p. 178.

SIEBER, ROBERT C.
St. Louis, Mo. 1874 dir., 1875 dir. & 1879 dir. As gunmaker for Albright & Sons 1874. See p. 178.

SIEGMUND, LOUIS
St. Louis, Mo., 1864 dir.-1887 dir. Foreman at Armory 1864. Gunsmith at Armory 1870. As gunsmith most others.

SIMMONS HARDWARE
St. Louis, Mo. 1875-1900+, wholesale.

SITES, ANDREW J.
(1828-) VA Mo. 1846. Jackson Co., Mo. 1850c. Not son of John.

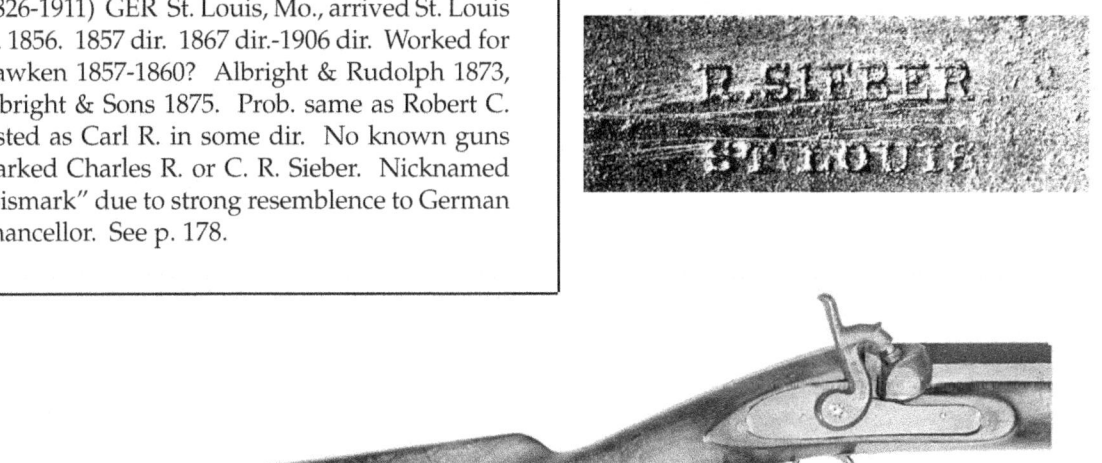

R. Sieber Target Rifle

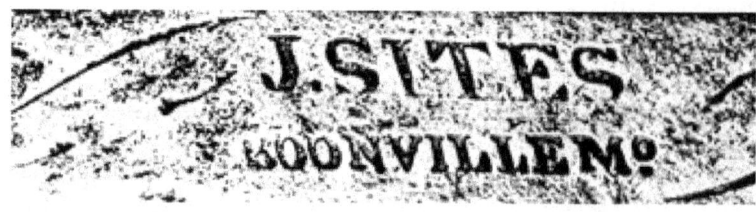

The above are markings on a half-round half-octagon barrel that was found with no stock. It presents a slight problem in that it is atypical of Missouri marked barrels of its time period, no later than 1853, length 30" including breech, .46 cal., .90' at muzzle, .985' at breech. The first thought was that it was from an English made rifle marked by John Sites Sr. The reversed "J L" stamp appeared to be similar to the mark used by James Leigh, a 'setter-up' for the East India Company. DeWitt Pourie was kind enough to share the answer he received from a letter of enquiry he sent to David F. Harding, of London, author of *Smallarms of the East India Company*, Vol. I and II. He consulted with DeWitt Bailey, author of *English Gunmakers*, and they feel that both the breech snail and the size and crudeness of the reversed "J. L." appeared to be more typical of Belgian work, of that time.

D. F. Harding to D. R. Pourie, June 2, 1997

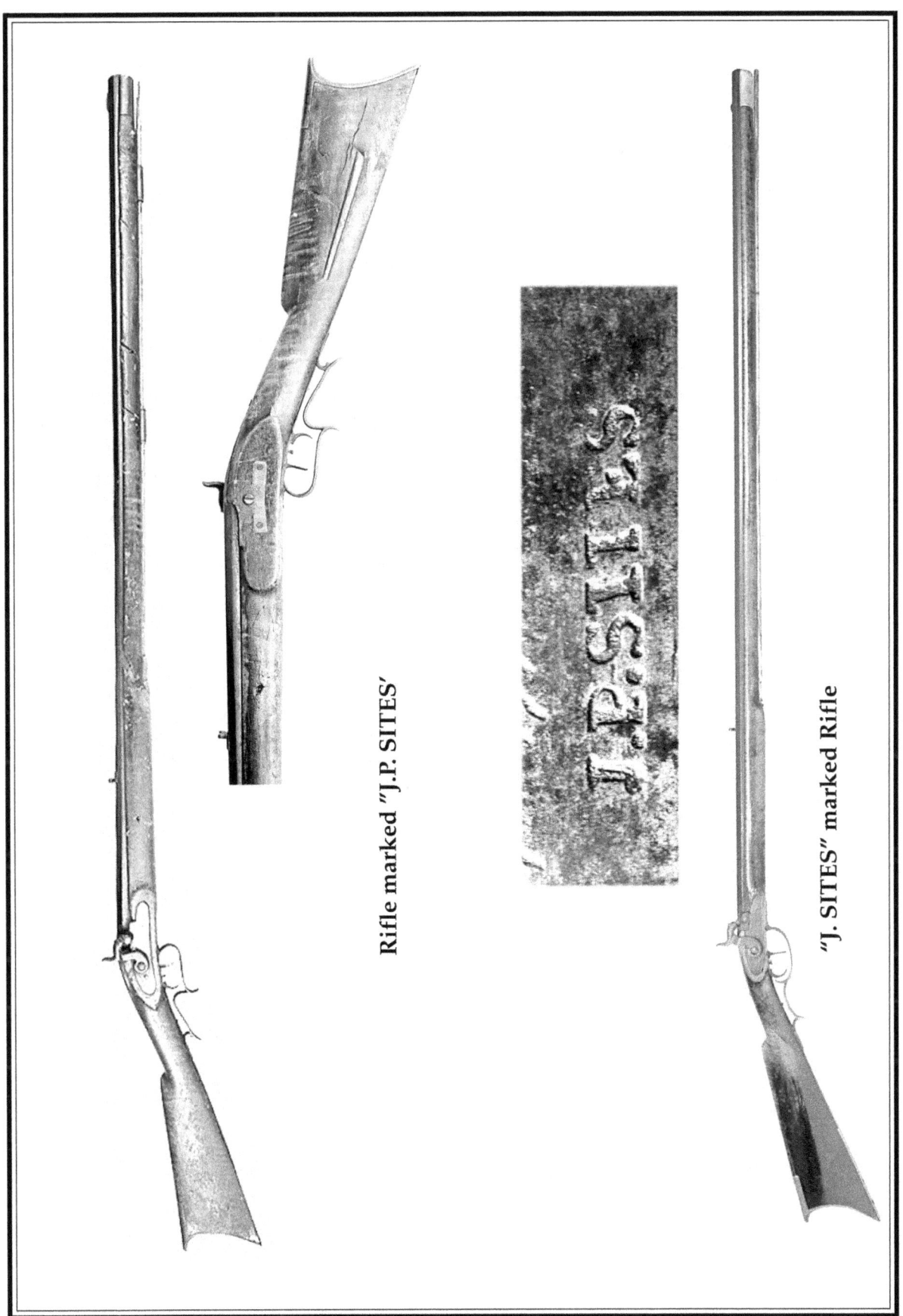

Rifle marked "J.P. SITES"

"J. SITES" marked Rifle

SITES, CHESTER P.
(1834-1899) MO Boonville, Cooper Co., Mo. 1850c. Osceola, St. Clair Co., Mo. Otterville, Cooper Co., Mo. Son of John P. See pp. 179-185.

SITES, JOHN P.
(1784-1853) VA Fincastle, Va. 1804-1833 Marion, Cole Co., Mo. 1834. Boonville, Cooper Co., Mo. 1835-1853. Flint & perc. Kentuckies.

   1850 Industrial Census:
     Cooper Co., City of Boonville

Name. J. P. Sites
Name of Business, Manufacture, or Product.
        Gunsmith
Capital invested in Real and Personal Estate in the Business. $ 300
Raw Material used, including Fuel.
   Quantities.   Kinds.   Values.
   (not given)   Iron & Steel $ 250
Average number of hands employed. Male. 2
Average Monthly cost of male labor. $ 50
Annual Product.
   Quantities.   Kinds.   Values.
   (not given)   Guns Rifles & c. $ 800
See pp. 179-185.

SITES, JOHN P. JR.
(1821-1904) VA Boonville, Cooper Co., Mo. 1835-1841. Clifton, Cooper Co., Mo. 1841-1844. Arrow Rock, Saline Co., Mo. 1844-1900. Nephew, John C. Dickenson living with him on 1850 census. His gunshop at Arrow Rock, Mo. has been restored. See pp. 179-185.

SKAGGS, J. M.
Plattin, Jefferson Co., Mo. 1885/86 dir.

SMITH, A.
ca. 1840 Gasconade Co., Mo. Slave, later freed. Made rifles between Washington and Hermann. (Blackburn)

SMITH, BENJAMIN
(1819-) PA unl. Pa. 1842. Utica, Livingston Co., Mo. 1860c.

SMITH, FRANK M.
Atchison, Ks. 1880 dir. Independence, Jackson Co., Mo. 1898/99 dir. (Sellers)

SMITH, JAMES M.
(1815-) KY unl. Ky. 1842. Mo.1848. Daviess Co. Mo. 1850c.

SMITH, NATHAN
(1818-) ENG St. Louis, Mo. At Arsenal 1850c.

SMITH, ROBERT
(1793-) VA unl. Ky. 1828. Mo. 1833. Monroe Co., Mo. 1850c.

SMITH, WILEY B.
(1807-) TN Mo. 1837, Ray Co., Mo. 1850c.

SMITH T., JOHN
(-1836) VA Ste. Genevieve District (lead mines) Mo. 1805-1836. One of the more notorious characters ever in Missouri. Reportedly fought numerous duels. 3 are recorded, at least 3 others are legend only. Kept slaves who were trained gunsmiths. See DAVE.

SMITHERS, S. A.
Hannibal, Marion Co., Mo. 1885/86 dir.

SNELL, JOSEPH
(1824-) KY Monroe Co., Mo. 1850c.

SNELL, ROBERT M.
(1793-) VA Mo. 1832. La Plata, Macon Co., Mo.1860c., dir. Son Hugh M. (1832-) Mo. Listed as Master blacksmith on census.

SNELLINGS
Bear Creek, Cedar Co., Mo. Perc. rifle. (Noble)

SONCHIN, SONNENSCHEIN, SONNSCHEIN, SONNSHIN, SUNSHER, SUNSHIN, SUNSHNER
On 1860c. Westport, Mo., 4 males living in adjacent houses, 2 in each house. Listed on census as Sonnshin. It is apparent the 3 elder were brothers. In 1863 two moved to St. Louis, Mo., and used the name spelled Sonnenschein while the two who stayed in Westport styled themselves Sonnschein. The other spellings are some of the alternate spellings noted. Ca. 1894 the family changed the preferred spelling to Sunshine, though the shop continued to be listed as Sonnenschein. (D. Sunshine)

SONNENSCHEIN, CHARLES
(1812-1892) GER unl. La. 1846? Westport, Mo. 1860c. St. Louis, Mo., 1870c. 1860c. as physician, gunsmith 1870c. Brother of Henry & William. Worked with Henry.

SONNENSCHEIN, HENRY
(1820-1891) GER unl. Tx. 1846, Westport, Mo. 1860c. St. Louis, Mo., 1870c., 1863 dir.-1897 dir. Brother of Charles & William. Gunsmith Edward Valrat (Vollrath, Ernest) living with him 1870 census.

   1870 Industrial Census
   St. Louis

Name. Sunshin, Henry
Name of Business, Manufacture or Product.
        Gunsmith

Cost of Raw Materials.	$ 100
Number of Employees.	1
Wages	Not Given
Annual Gross Product.	$ 800

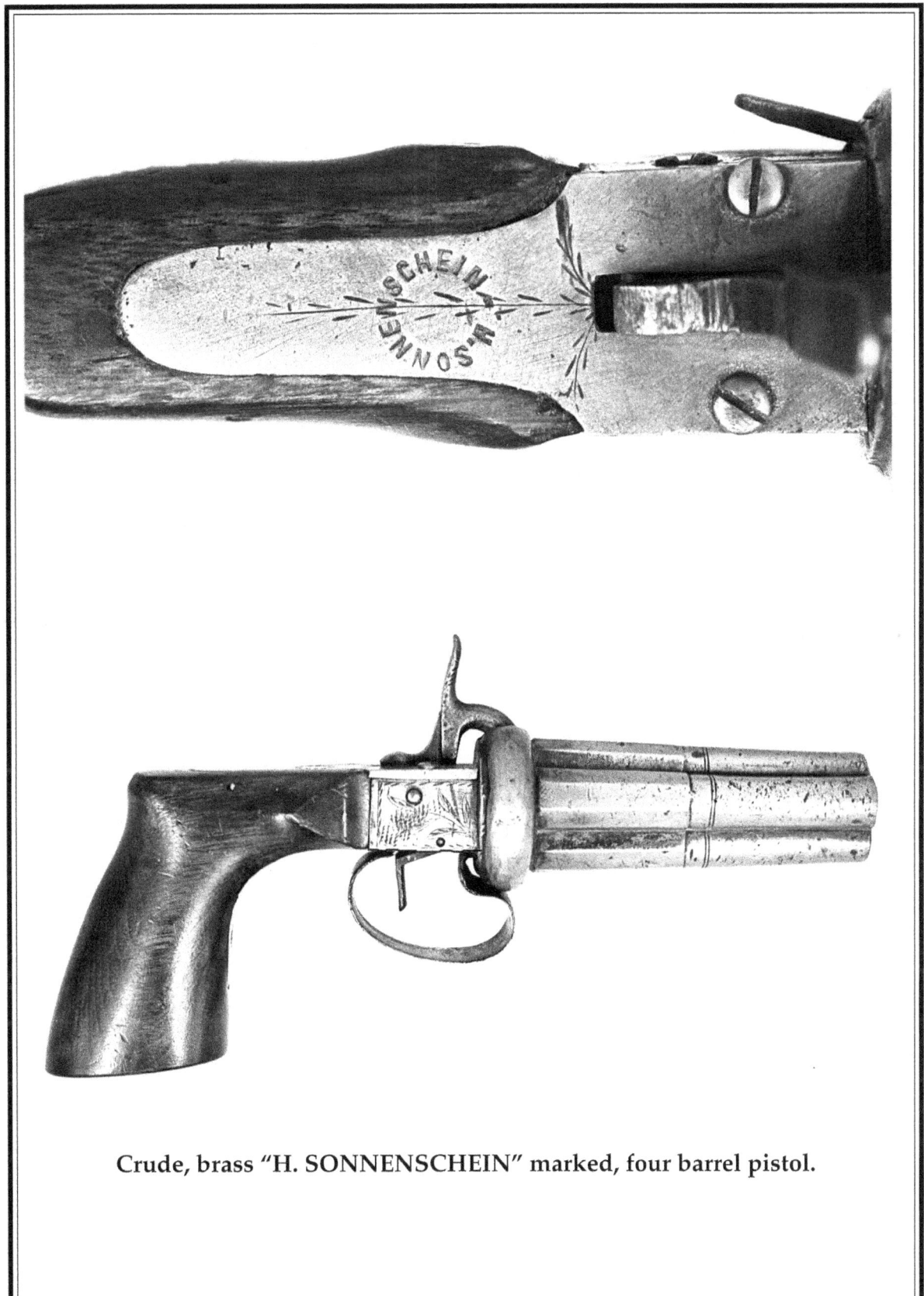

Crude, brass "H. SONNENSCHEIN" marked, four barrel pistol.

SONNENSCHEIN, HENRY (shop name)
Following Henry's death in 1891 the shop was taken over by his son in-law, Ernst Vollrath who operated it until his death in 1928. The shop was listed in dir. under Henry's name for the entire period.

SONNENSCHEIN, LOUIS
Listed as gunsmith in Gateway Gunsmiths in error. Henry's daughter Louise was found listed as a gunsmith once, family sources state this is in error.

SONNSCHEIN, HERMAN
(1846-) LA Westport, Mo. 1860c. Kansas City, Mo. 1876/77 dir.-1898/99 dir. Son of William.

SONNSCHEIN, WILLIAM
(1810-) GER unl. La. 1846. Westport, Mo. 1860c.-1876/77.

SOUDERS, NATHAN
Oak Hill, Crawford Co., Mo. 1883/84 dir.-1889/90 dir.

SOUTHARD, A. M.
Savannah, Andrew Co., Mo. 1867/68 dir. Marshaltown, Ia. 1882 dir.

SPAEDY, FRANK J.
St. Louis, Mo. 1894 dir.-1912 dir. Target rifles and pistols. Noted marksman.

SPECK, JOAB
St. Louis, Mo., 1870 dir.

SPRANGLE, ,
Trenton, Grundy Co., Mo.1867/68 dir.

SPRINKLE, GEORGE
(1820-) VA Cole Co., Mo. 1850c. In state pen., went in 1848.

SPROULLE, R. H.
(1817-) VA Mo. 1842, St. Clair Co., Mo. 1850c.

SREFEE, BOSEMORE
unl. Mo. 1860's. Gilroy, Ca. 1867-1879. (Shelton)

STACY, M. H.
Trace Creek, Madison Co., Mo. 1889/90 dir.

STAHLBERG, WILLIAM
St. Louis, Mo., 1868 dir.-1871 dir. As Herkstroeter & Stahlberg 1870 & 1871.

STAIR, W. H.
Verona, Lawrence Co., Mo. 1883/84 dir.-1885/86 dir.

STANLEY, C. W.
Springfield, Greene Co., Mo. 1898/99 dir.

STAPH, G(odaleper?)
(1790-) GER St. Louis, Mo., 1850c.

STAPHS?, GEORGE E.
(1826-) VA unl. Va. 1853. unl. Il. 1855. Mo. 1857. Morgan Co., Mo. 1860c.

STARDTLEP, AUGUST
(1828-) GER St. Louis, Mo., 1850c.

STARKEY, C. O.
E. Bon Terre, St. Francois Co., Mo. 1893/94 dir.

STAUF, CONRAD
St. Louis, Mo. Patent #34,017, Dec. 24, 1861, portable cannon, with C. J. Steinbach.

STEDMAN, THOMAS
Harpers Ferry, Va., 1821, 1822, 1830, 1835. St, Louis, Mo. 1848 dir., as armorer.

STEIN, FREDERICK see SWAN

STEINBACH, CRISTIAN JOSEF
St. Louis, Mo. see Stauf abv.

STEMPLE, LAWRENCE
Carrollton, Carroll Co., Mo. 1883/84 dir.-1898/99 dir. Son of Louis.

STEMPLE, LOUIS
Carrollton, Carroll Co., Mo. 1866-1881 dir.

STILES, JOHN(ATHAN?) A.
(1829-) ? Savannah, Andrew Co., Mo. 1850c. Birth state unreadable on census.

STIPES, EZEKIAL H.
(1824-) VA Brunswick, Chariton Co., Mo. 1850c. Saline Co., Mo. 1860c.

STOCK, THEODORE
(1831-) GER Mo. 1851, St. Louis,Mo., 1857 dir.-1860c., dir. Kansas City, Mo. 1887 dir.-1898 dir. with G. C. Miller and Co.

STONE, THOMAS
(1796-) ENG LaFayette Co., Mo., 1850c., ic. 1860c.
1850 Industrial Census:
Lafayette Co.
Name. Thos. Stone
Name of Business, Manufacture, or Product.
   Gunsmith
Capital invested in Real and Personal Estate in the Business. $1,000
Raw Material used, including Fuel.
Quantities.	Kinds.	Values.
30	Gun Locks	$75
30	"Setts" Mounting	$25
12 doz.	Files	$50
50 Bush.	Coal	$15

Average number of hands employed. Male. 1
Wages. Average Monthly cost of male labor.
 (not given, prob. worked solo)
Annual Product.
Quantities.	Kinds.	Values.
(not given)	Manufacture and Repair Guns	$800

STRAHORN, J. K.
(1825-) TN unl. Tn. 1847. Mo. 1849. Hopewell, Mississippi Co., Mo. 1860c., dir. As farmer on census.

STRECKER, ANTON
(1838-) GER Mo. 1864. St. Louis, Mo., 1870c.
1870 Industrial Census
St. Louis
Name. Strecks, Anton
Name of Business, Manufacture or Product.
   Gunsmith
Cost of Raw Materials.	$2000
Number of Employees.	3
Wages	$2700
Annual Gross Product.	$6000

STREET, JOHN M.
(1797-) KY unl. Ky. prior to 1833. Mo. 1842. Weston, Platte Co., Mo. 1850c. Son John F. (1831-) KY listed as blacksmith on census.

SUNEMALL, FRANK
(1820-) GER Mo. 1852. St. Louis, Mo., 1870c.

SWAN ?, FREDERICK
(1821-) GER St. Louis, Mo., 1850c. Poss. Stein or Scein.

T

TAL, J. E.
  Gentry Co., Mo., 1870ic.
  1870 Industrial Census
  Gentry Co.
  Name. Tal, J. E.
  Name of Business,Manufacture or Product.
            Gunsmith
  Cost of Raw Materials. $ 125
  Number of Employees.   1
  Wages   Not Given
  Annual Gross Product. $ 600

TALMAN (TOLMAN), JAMES
  (1828-) MA St. Louis, Mo., 1860c. Census lists him as gunsmith. On census with Dimick. Other sources state he was bookkeeper for Dimick. (AR 4-58)

TANNER & ROMETSH (ROMTREH)
  Brookfield, Linn Co., Mo. 1883/84 dir. August Tanner & ? Rometsh.

TANNER, AUGUST
  St. Catherine, Linn Co., Mo. 1876/77 dir.-1881 dir. Brookfield, Linn Co., Mo. 1883/84 dir.-1898/99 dir.

TANNER, WILLIAM
  (1800-) VA unl. Ar. 1847. Nodaway Co., Mo. 1860c.

TATE, JOHN
  (1828-) KY Adair Co., Mo. 1850c. With Robt. A. Garrett.

TAYLOR, WILLIAM
  Bem, Gasconade Co., Mo. 1860 dir.

TEGETHOFF, WILLIAM
  St. Louis, Mo., 1857 dir. at 31 Washington. Name appears on a Shawk & McLanahan revolver. (1858-1861).

TEWKSBURY, JOSIAH
  Webb City, Jasper Co., Mo. 1898/99 dir.

TEXAN, A. M.
  St. Francisville, Clark Co., Mo. 1860 dir.

THANI, SEBASTIAN
  Woollam, Gasconade Co., Mo. 1883/84 dir.

THEIDE, FRED
  Centralia, Il. 1864 dir.-65. Brunswick, Chariton Co., Mo. 1867/68 dir. (Johnson)

THOMAS, J. E.
   Richmond, Ray Co., Mo. 1885/86 dir.

THOMPSON, CHARLES E.
   Springfield, Greene Co., Mo. 1898/99 dir. With J. Aug. Rainey.

THOMPSON, CHARLES I.
   (1858-) Havana, Il. 1880 dir. Mason City, Il., 1880c.-1881 dir. Macon City, Mo. 1883/84 dir. Peoria, Il. 1893. Perc. 1/2 stock. (Johnson)

THOMPSON, F.
   St. Louis, Mo., 1840/41 dir. As lock & gunsmith.

THORMANN, JOHANN
   St. Louis, Mo., 1868 dir.

THORWALD, AUGUST
   (1820-) GER St. Louis, Mo., 1854 dir.-1860c., 1865 dir.,

THURSTIN & JACOBY
   O'Fallon, St. Charles Co., Mo. 1883/84 dir.

THURSTIN, A.
   Foley, Lincoln Co., Mo. 1891/92 dir.-1893/94 dir.

TILFORD, SAMUEL K.
   (1782-) VA unl. Tn. 1827-1835. Lincoln Co., Mo. 1850c.

TIRY, WILLIAM E.
   Beaufort, Franklin Co., Mo. 1860 dir.

TODD, J. T.
   Neosho, Newton Co., Mo. 1898/99 dir.

TOMPKINS, W.
   Hunnewell, Shelby Co., Mo. 1881 dir.

TOOLE, WILLIAM T.
   (1844 -) MO Arrow Rock, Saline Co., Mo. 1860c. Nephew and apprentice of John Sites Jr.

TRYON, F. J.
   Bolivar, Polk Co. Mo. 1889 dir.-1898/99 dir.

TUCKER, J. W.
   Carthage, Jasper Co., Mo. 1898/99 dir.

TUGHARDT see **JUGHARDT**

TURK, WILLIAM
   (1809-) NC unl. Ohio 1832-1847. Greencastle, In., 1850c.-1855. Columbia, Boone Co., Mo. 1860c., dir.

TURNER, WILLIAM H.
   (1827-) MO Liberty, Clay Co., Mo. 1850c. Missouri City, Clay Co., Mo. 1860c. Liberty, Clay Co., Mo. 1876/77 dir. - 1898/99 dir. Associated with James Keller on 1850c.

Polk's 1883-84 State Directory

U

UNDERWOOD, HENRY
   St. Louis, Mo., 1860 dir.

V

VALENTINE, F.
   (1784-   ) (-1884) ? Alton, Il. 1840-1845. Grafton, Il. 1860c., dir. St. Louis, Mo., 1860 dir.-1864 dir. (Johnson)
VALENTINE, J.
   Franklin Co., Mo., Plains rifles.
VANHORN, JOHN
   (1809-   ) MO? Jackson Co., Mo. 1850c., ic.
      1850 Industrial Census:
         Jackson Co.
Name. John Vanhorn
Name of Business, Manufacture, or Product.
         Gunsmith
Capital invested in Real and Personal Estate in the Business. $ 300
Raw Material used, including Fuel
   Quantities.   Kinds.   Values.
   30   Gun barrels $ 90
   40   Gun stocks $ 10
   50   locks $ 75
Average number of hands employed.
   Male. 2
Wages. Average Monthly cost of male labor.
   $ 90
Annual Product.
   Quantities.   Kinds.   Values.
   48   Guns $ 900

VANCE, W. R.
   Waterville, Ozark Co., Mo. 1883/84 dir.
VERDIER, WASHINGTON
   (1817-   ) VA Mo. 1844. Ralls Co., Mo. 1850c.
VOGELREICH, CONRAD
   Moberly, Randolph Co., Mo. 1891 dir.-1898/99 dir.
VOGELSANG, HENRY
   (1810-   ) GER St. Louis, Mo., 1847 dir.-1850c.-1851 dir. Hermann, Gasconade Co., Mo. 1860c., dir.
VOLKEL, JOHN L.
   Sulphur Springs, Lincoln Co., Mo. Patent # 234,632, Nov. 16, 1860, breechloading firearms. Under lever.
VOLLMER, GUSTAV
   St. Louis, Mo., 1881 dir.-1887 dir.
VON BRECHT, AUGUST see BRECHT
VOLLRATH, ERNST
   (1848-1928) GER St. Louis, Mo. 1870c. with Henry Sonnenschein as Valrat. Son in-law of Henry. Took over shop on Henry's death and operated it under Henry's name until his own death in 1928.

NOTES

W

WACHSHAR?, F.
(1808-   ) GER Canton, Lewis Co., Mo. 1860c.

WACHTER, CASPER
(1834-   ) SWITZ Glasgow, Howard Co., Mo. 1860c. Brother of John.

WACHTER, JOHN
(1833-   ) SWITZ Mo. 1856. Glasgow, Howard Co., Mo. 1860c., dir., 1867/68 dir.-1893/94 dir. As J. Wachter & Bro. 1867/68 dir. & 1870 dir., ic. As Machter on 1860 dir.

1870 Industrial Census
Howard Co.

Name.	Wachter & Bro.
Name of Business, Manufacture or Product.	Gun Shop
Cost of Raw Materials.	$ 70
Number of Employees.	2
Wages	Not Given
Annual Gross Product.	$ 600

WADE, W. F.
Norborne, Carroll Co., Mo. 1898/99 dir.

WAECHLER, LOUIS
St. Louis, Mo., 1847 dir.

WAECHTER, H.
(1808-   ) GER St. Louis, Mo. 1850c. With Geo. Nordheim.

WAECHTER, LOUIS
St. Louis, Mo., 1847 dir.?-1871 dir. Lock and gunsmith. 1866 same address as J. R. Schafer.

Campbell & Richard's 1863 St. Louis Directory

WAGEMAN, THOMAS
(1828-) SWITZ St. Louis, Mo., 1870c., ic.
1870 Industrial Census
St. Louis
Name. Wageman, Thomas
Name of Business, Manufacture or Product.
    Gunsmith (repair)
Cost of Raw Materials.	$ 100
Number of Employees.	1
Wages	Not Given
Annual Gross Product.	$ 800

WAGGONER, ISAAC
Lovejoy, Cape Girardeau Co., Mo. 1891/92 dir.
WAGNER, ALVIN
Jackson, Cape Girardeau Co., Mo. (MB 3-65)
WAIBEL, B.
(1834-) AUS Independence, Jackson Co., Mo. 1860c., dir.
WALKER, H. L.
(1816-) KY Mo. 1848, New Madrid Co., Mo. 1850c. James Howard, residing with him in census.
WALKER, JOHN
(1820-) VA St. Louis, Mo., 1850c. Pistol gallery.
WALLACE, ANDREW JACKSON
(1832-1917) TN unl. Mo. 1854. Armorer Co. I, 11th. Il. Cav. Civil War, residence listed as Tn., Libbey Prison briefly during war. unl. Il. 1871. McNear, Tn. 1873. unl. Ks. 1876. Seneca, Newton Co., Mo. 1879., as J. A. in dir. Mountain Grove, Wright Co., Mo. 1880c. Bismark, Mo. 1883-1892. 1890 Tn. Civil War Vet. Census. 1/2 stock perc. signed "AJW ". (Johnson, Noble)
WALLACE'S PATENT .54 cal. "horse pistol", marked "WALLACE'S PATENT ST. LOUIS ". Maker unknown. Victor M. Wallace, of Vermont, received a patent Aug. 17, 1835 for an in-line hammer pistol.
WALLERICH, MATHIAS
Independence, Jackson Co., Mo. 1870 ic. Perc. 1/2 stock. (Hanson)
1870 Industrial Census
Jackson Co. (Independence)
Name. Wallerich, Mathias
Name of Business, Manufacture or Product.
    Gunsmith
Cost of Raw Materials.	$ 200
Number of Employees.	2
Wages	Not Given
Annual Gross Product.	$ 700

WALSER, EDWARD
St. Louis, Mo., 1893 dir.-1916 dir.
WANDERU?, EMIL
(1831-) GER St. Louis, Mo., 1870c.

WARD, HENRY
(1800-) NY St. Louis, Mo., 1850c.
WARD, JOHN
St. Louis, Mo., 1850c. (MB 11-66)
WARDEN, R. W.
New Haven, Franklin Co., Mo., 1893/94 dir.
WARFIELD, C.
Fruitland, Cape Girardeau Co., Mo. 1889 dir.-1891/92 dir.
WARNER, C. H. JR.
De Soto, Jefferson Co., Mo. 1885/86 dir.
WATT & BENNETT
St. Louis, Mo., 1860-1863? Successors to Wm. S. Hawken by business card at Museum of the Fur Trade, Chadron, Ne. 1860 dir. lists William L. Watt by self. No directory is known for 1861 or 1862. No listing in 1863 dir. Given name unknown for Bennett. This research has turned up a number of Bennetts as gunsmith and the surname has been noted numerous times related to blacksmithing. A Thomas Bennett, grate-maker, is boarding at same address as William L. Watt in the 1860 dir. (Hanson 2)
WATT, WILLIAM L.
(1815-) PA unl. Pa. prior to 1840. Baltimore, Md. 1850c. St. Louis, Mo., 1860c., dir.-1877 dir. 1860 dir. & 1864 dir. shop proprietor at address of Hawken shop. 1865 dir. living at shop but Gemmer listed as proprietor. 1870 dir. listed as still with Gemmer. Business cards state "successor to Wm. S. Hawken". (Hanson 2)
Hartzler notes a William L. Watts in *Arms Makers of Maryland*. The listings given are as follows; 1835-1840 as shotmaker; 1847, 1851 and 1855/56 as gunsmith. It seems probable that these are two men and that the gunsmith listed as Watts is the same as William L. Watt who is listed as a gunsmith in Baltimore on the 1850 census.
WAYMON, COLEMAN H.
Princeton, Mercer Co., Mo. Patent # 631,349, Aug. 22, 1899, ejector. (selective ejectors for double guns)
WEAVER, HUGH
Carthage, Jasper Co., Mo. ?
WEBB, BRISON & CO.
St. Louis, Mo., 1859 dir.
WEBB, CHARLES
St. Louis, Mo., 1855 dir.-1859 dir. As Webb, Brison & Co. 1859. Perc. 1/2 stock. J. McInnes at same address 1859.
WEBER, JACOB
(1844-) SWITZ St. Louis, Mo., 1870c. In city hospital.

WEHRLE, JOHN
St. Louis, Mo., 1857 dir.-1886 dir.

WEILEY, JOHN
St. Louis, Mo., 1885/86 dir. Prob same as abv.

WEINBRECHT, WILHELM
St. Louis, Mo., 1864 dir.-1866 dir. At Arsenal 1865.

WEINER, A. G.
St. Louis, Mo., 1898/99 dir.

WELDAN, BENJAMIN
(1817-) IL unl. Il. 1844-1848. Cass Co., Mo. 1850c. Prob. bro. of Hugh Weldon.

WELDON, HUGH M.
(1825-) TN unl. Il. 1844. Mo. 1846. Cass Co., Mo. 1850c. Prob. brother of abv.

WELLER, GEORGE W.
(1825-) KY Lewis Co., Mo. 1850c. Son of David Weller, noted Kentucky gun maker.

WELLS, G. W.
Oregon, Holt Co., Mo. 1860 dir.

WERKER, EBERT
(1815-) GER St. Louis, Mo., 1850c.

WERNER, DANIEL
St. Louis, Mo. Patent #82,908, Oct. 6, 1868, knife pistol.

WERNER, OTTO F.
Kansas City, Mo. 1889/90 dir.

WERTHON, H.
St. Louis, Mo., 1853. Submitted muskets to Ordnance Dept.

WESSELL, WILLIAM
Concordia, Lafayette Co., Mo. 1883/84 dir. - 1899 dir.

WEST, JOHN W.
(1805-) KY Mo. 1830. Daviess Co., Mo. 1850c.

WEST, ROBERT
(1830-) MO Daviess Co., Mo. 1850c. Son of John W.

WESTERN BICYCLE WORKS
Kansas City, Mo. 1898/99 dir., Stephen Karthago.

WESTON, WALTER
(1829-) ENG Mo. 1863. St. Louis, Mo., 1870c.

WHATT, S. C.
(1815-) NY St. Louis, Mo., 1870c.

WHEELER, CHARLES
Webb City, Jasper Co., Mo. 1893/94 dir.

WHEELER, E. G.
Pleasant Hill, Cass Co., Mo. 1889/90 dir.-1891/92 dir.

WHEELER, J. P.
Kansas City, Mo. 1859 dir.-1860 dir. As J. P. Wheeler & Co. 1860.

WHITESIDES, ALLEN
Hazel Run, St. Francois Co., Mo. 1876/77 dir.

WHITE & JAMES
Sedalia, Pettis Co., Mo. 1889/90 dir.

WHITING, E. D. (Ed)
Winona, Shannon Co., Mo. 1898/99 dir. Sellers reported E. D. on 98 dir., as Ed on 98/99 state dir.

WHITMORE, NOAH, H.
Harpers Ferry, Va., 1822, 1835, St. Louis, Mo. 1848 dir., as armorer.

WICHMANN, JULIUS
Decatur, Il. 1878 dir. Brunswick, Chariton Co., Mo. 1883/84 dir.-1885/86 dir. (Johnson)

WIDEMAN, FRANCIS
(1789-) SC Jefferson Co., Mo. 1850c.

OTTO F. WERNER,
GUNSMITH.
DEALER IN
Guns, Rifles and Pistols.
All kinds of Sporting Materials. Browning Barrel, Chokeboring, Crooking or Straightening Stocks to any desired Drop.
Re-Stocking Fine Guns. Repairing Promptly Done.
536 Delaware Street,
KANSAS CITY, - MISSOURI.

Polk's 1889-90 State Directory

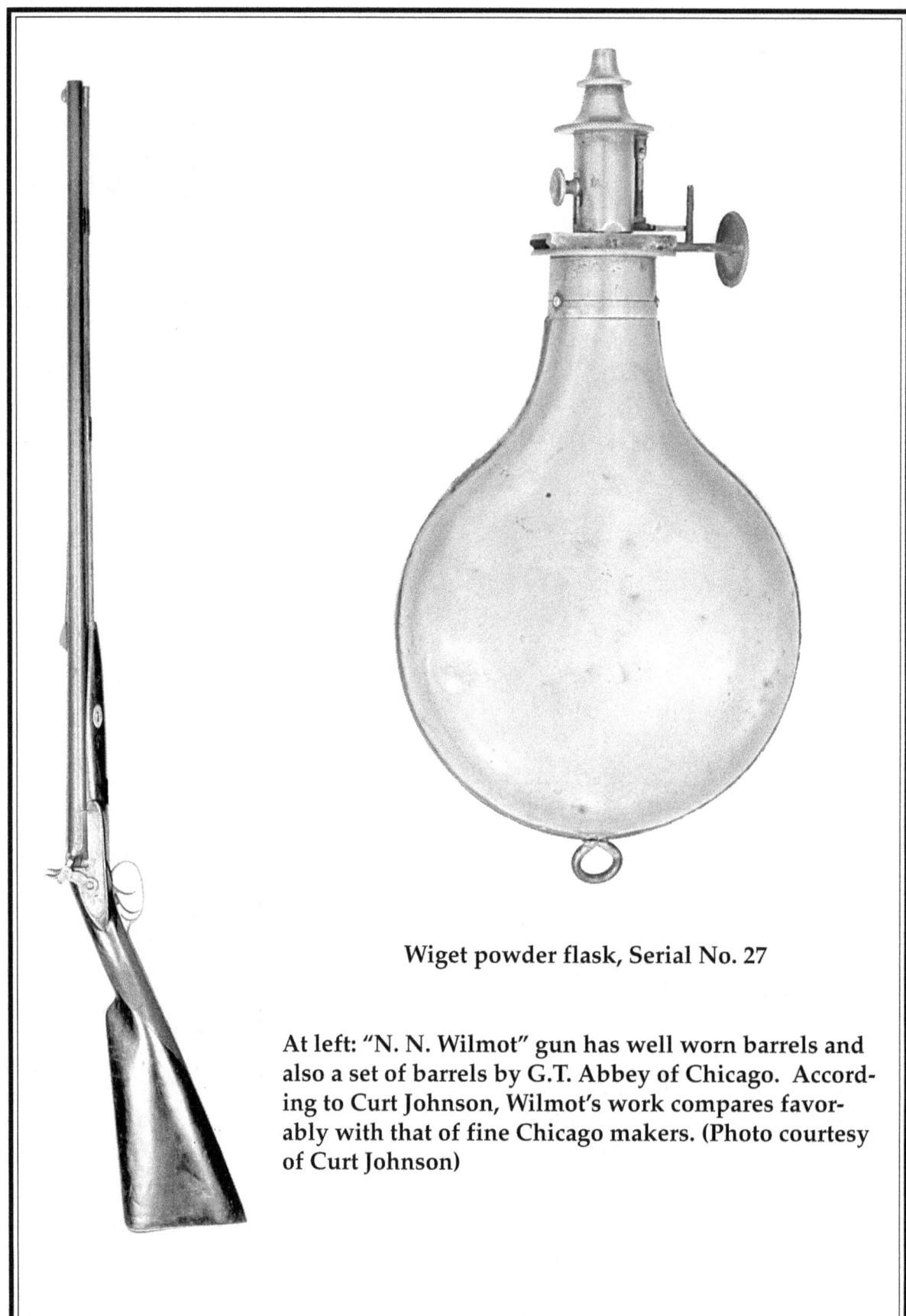

Wiget powder flask, Serial No. 27

At left: "N. N. Wilmot" gun has well worn barrels and also a set of barrels by G.T. Abbey of Chicago. According to Curt Johnson, Wilmot's work compares favorably with that of fine Chicago makers. (Photo courtesy of Curt Johnson)

WIGET, DOMINICK
(1832-1899?) SWITZ? Alton, Il. 1853-1857. Highland, Il. 1857-1885. St. Louis, Mo., 1885 dir.-1899 dir. Patent # 466,209, Dec. 29, 1891, powder flask (measure). Percussion Schuetzen rifles. (Johnson)

WIGET, JOHN L.
(1864-) IL Mendota, Il. 1890 dir.-1898 dir. St. Louis, Mo., reported 1899 dir., first entry found 1906 as hardware, 1908 first found as gunsmith. Son of Dominick. Noted marksman. Also listed as locksmith. (Johnson)

WILCOX, GEORGE C.
Nevada, Vernon Co., Mo. 1891/92 dir. as Wilcox Plumbing.

WILCOX, OLIVER
Stewartsville, DeKalb Co., Mo. 1867/68 dir.

WILKINS, DIDRICK
(1835-) GER Shelbyville, Mo. 1850c., Brother of John. With Frederick Boetcher.

WILKINS, JOHN W.
(1829-) GER Shelbyville, Mo. 1850c. With Frederick Boetcher.

WILKINS, R. D.
(1835-) GER Monroe Co., Mo. 1860c. Same as Didrick above.?

WILL, JULIUS E.
Bethel, Shelby Co., Mo. 1883/84 dir.

WILLARD, ALEXANDER
NH With Lewis & Clark expedition. 1808-1825 Employed by Indian Dept. as blacksmith to Indians in Ia., Il.. & Mo. Mo. 1825.

WILLIAMS, C. & BRO.
Poplar Bluff, Butler Co., Mo. 1898/99 dir.

WILLIAMS, CORDAN
Poplar Bluff, Butler Co., Mo. 1898/99 dir. As C. Williams & Bro.

WILLIAMS, JAMES E.
St. Louis, Mo. 1865 dir.-1869 dir. As master armorer at arsenal.

WILLIAMS, SNOWDEN
(1843-) KY LaFayette Co., Mo. 1860c. As apprentice gunsmith. J. W. Reinhart only gunsmith shown on Co. census.

WILLIAMS, VERNIUS
Poplar Bluff, Butler Co., Mo. 1898/99 dir. As C. Williams and Bro.

WILLIOME, JACOB
St. Louis, Mo., 1877 dir.-1891/92 dir. Jacob prob. given name, Jacques also noted.

WILLIS, JOHN
Wakenda, Carroll Co., Mo. 1883/84 dir.

WILLS, DAVID
Lebanon, LaClede Co., Mo. 1889 dir.-1898/99 dir.

WILMOT, NATHANIEL N.
(1802-) ENG Boston, Ma. 1844-1849. St. Louis, Mo. 1850c., ic., dir.-1860 dir. St. Paul, Mn. 1862-1864. St. Louis, Mo., 1865 dir. Work compares favorably with the fine Chicago, Il. shotgun makers according to Johnson. See ad p. 2 bottom.

1850 industrial census:
St. Louis 3rd. Ward
Name. N. Wilmot
Name of Business, Manufacture, or Product. Gun Maker
Capital invested in Real and Personal Estate in the Business. $ 500
Raw Material used, including Fuel.
Quantities. Kinds. Values.
1000lb. Iron
100lb. Steel   } $ 300
silver, brass
Average number of hands employed. Male. 2
Average Monthly cost of male labor. $80
Annual Product.
Quantities. Kinds. Values.
(not given) Guns, Rifles and Pistols } $ 1,800

WILSON GEORGE W. & CO.
St. Louis, Mo., 1859 dir.

WILSON, E. M.
Savannah, Andrew Co., Mo. 1860 dir.

WILSON, L. F.
Pleasant Hill, Cass Co., Mo. 1879 dir.-1881 dir. Archie, Cass Co., Mo. 1883/84 dir.

WILSON, JAMES
Callaway Co., Mo. 1850c. (MB 11-66)

WILSON, PHILIP
(1824-) KY Andrew Co., Mo. 1850c. Son of Pleasant L.

WILSON, PLEASANT L.
(1795-) SC unl. Ky. 1824-1831. Andrew Co., Mo. 1850c., ic. Pleasant as a given name has been noted with two other Wilsons in Missouri. Relationship, if any, not yet determined.

1850 Industrial Census:
Andrew Co.

Name. "Plasant" Wilson
Name of Business, Manufacture, or Product. Gun Smithing
Capital invested in Real and Personal Estate in the Business. $ 1,000
Raw Material used, including Fuel.
    Quantities.   Kinds.   Values.
    (not given)   Miscellaneous $ 800
Average number of hands employed.
    Male. 4
Average Monthly cost of male labor. $ 60
Annual Product.
    Quantities.   Kinds.   Values.
    (not given)   Guns & Other Articles $ 2,500

WINBRECH, WILLIAM
(1827-) GER Mo. 1859. St. Louis, Mo., 1860c.

WINER, C. H.
Frumet, Jefferson Co., Mo. 1898/99 dir.

WINTER, PETER
New Wells, Cape Girardeau Co., Mo. 1876/7 dir.-1883/84 dir. Schalls, Perry Co., Mo. 1885/86 dir.-1891/92 dir.

WIRSING, CHRISTIAN A.
Cincinnati, Oh. 1855 dir., St. Louis, Mo., 1859 dir.-1864 dir. With Dimick. Ft. Smith, Ar. after. (AR 4-58)

WIRTH, ANTON
St. Louis, Mo., 1879 dir.-1882 dir.

WIRTZ, ABRAHAM
Maryville, Nodaway Co., Mo. 1881 dir-1891/92 dir. Ft. Smith, Ar. 1875-1890. Air guns & perc. rifles. Possibly 2 men. (Hutslar, Elias)

WISEMAN, (OLIVER?) DAVENPORT
Present day Maries Co., Mo. ca. 1830's and 1840's. Nicknamed "Porty".

WISMAN, JOHN
(1813-) GER unl. La. 1844. St. Louis Co., Mo. 1850c.

WOODS, LEE
(1843-) MO Camden Co., Mo. 1870c.

WOODWARD, BENJAMIN F.
(1828-1876) OH Union, Oh. ? Apprenticed to Daniel Sheets? Clarksville, Pike Co., Mo. 1850c. With Sheets family, Daniel had already left for Ca. Napa, Ca. 1866-1876. (Shelton)

WOODWORTH, G.
(1824-) GER St. Louis, Mo., 1850c.

WORKMAN, F.
(1827-) GER St. Louis, Mo., 1850c. Napa, Ca. 1866-1876. (Shelton)

WORSING, CHARLES
(1837-) GER St. Louis, Mo., 1860c. Poss. Wirsing.

WORSING, FREDERICK
(1839-) GER St. Louis, Mo., 1860c. Brother of Charles.

WRIGHT, J. C.
Lincoln, Benton Co., Mo. 1898/99 dir.

WRIGHT, J. M.
St. Joseph, Buchanan Co., Mo. 1889/90 dir. Clinton, Henry Co., Mo. 1893/94 dir. Kirksville, Adair Co., Mo. 1898/99 dir.

WUNDERLICH, CHARLES
Washington, Franklin Co., Mo. 1885/86 dir.-1893/94 dir.

WYANT, ISAAC S.
Lebanon, La Clede Co., Mo. 1881 dir.

Y

YEARWOOD, JOHN
(1824 -) ? Mt. Vernon, Il. 1848-1864. Malden, Dunklin Co., Mo. 1885/86 dir. (Johnson)

YOUNG & BERRY
Liberty, Clay Co., Mo. 1868 dir. (Sellers)

YOUNG, A. J.
Liberty, Clay Co., Mo. 1867-1869 dir. As Young & Berry 1868. (Sellers)

YOUNG, LEWIS V.
St. Louis, Mo. Patent # 104,682, Jun. 21, 1870, breechloading firearm.

YOUNG, WILLIAM
Hannibal, Marion Co., Mo. 1893/94 dir.

Z

ZAMBONI, JOHN
St. Louis, Mo., 1870 dir.

ZEDICK, RODERICK
St. Louis, Mo., 1848 dir., at Arsenal.

ZIEGEL, ANDREW
Hannibal, Marion Co., Mo. 1876/77 dir.

ZIGG, JOSEPH
(1836-) GER St. Louis, Mo., 1850c. Apprenticed to Hoffstether. (Lewis)

ZINGG, JOSEPH
(1820-) SWITZ Mo. 1847. Union, Franklin Co., Mo. 1850c., 1860c., dir. As Zink , Ger. on 50c. Switz. on 60c. Centralia, Marion Co., Il. 1865-1867 prob. same . (Johnson)

ZINK, J.
Panther Valley, Webster Co., Mo. 1881 dir. Prob. John below.

ZINK, JOHN
(1819-) W.VA Marshfield, Webster Co., Mo. 1870c. Webster Co., Mo. 1880c. Associated with Tetyre Couch 1870.

ZINK, JOSEPH see ZINGG

ZINN, H. C.
Leann, Barry Co., Mo. 1898/99 dir.

NOTES

SECTION 2

Section 2 contains additional information about a number of gunsmiths and aspects of the firearms trade. Subjects are covered in section 2 in the following order.

pp. 125-127	St. Louis: Maps
p. 129	Additional information about gunsmiths George Bergner, Joseph Etterle, and John P. Gemmer.
pp. 130-131	Airguns
pp. 133-140	Philip Creamer
pp. 141-144	Hawken: Land purchase, sales and William S. Hawken bankruptcy
pp. 145-148	Industrial Censuses: 1850, 1860, 1870
pp. 149-170	Edward Mead: *Edward Mead's Illustrated Treatise...*
p. 171	H. E. Dimick ad
p. 171	T. J. Albright ad
p. 172	Child & Pratt ad
pp. 173-177	Patents
p. 178	Charles R. Sieber
pp. 179-185	Sites Family
p. 186	Shotguns - House Brands

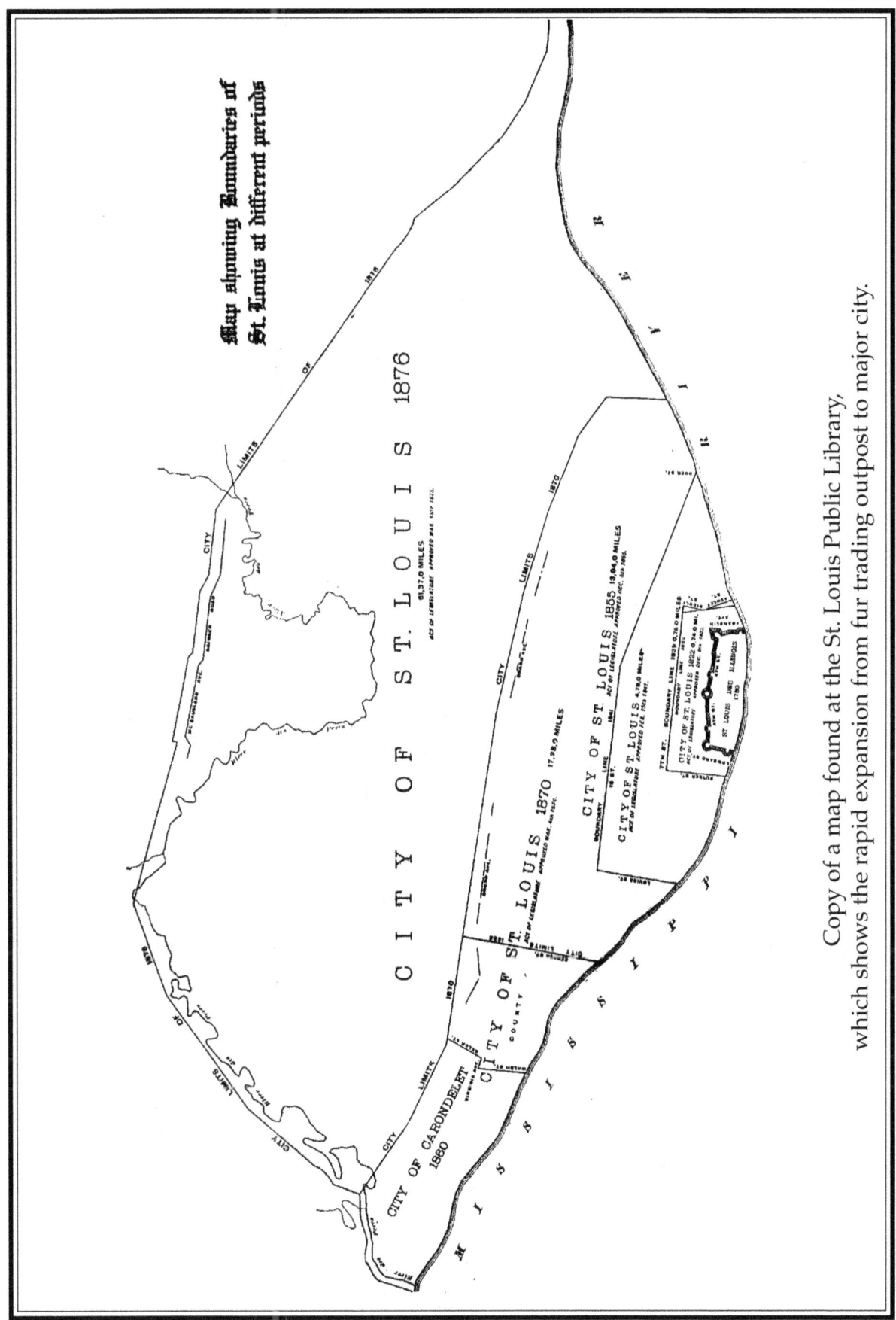

Copy of a map found at the St. Louis Public Library, which shows the rapid expansion from fur trading outpost to major city.

St. Louis

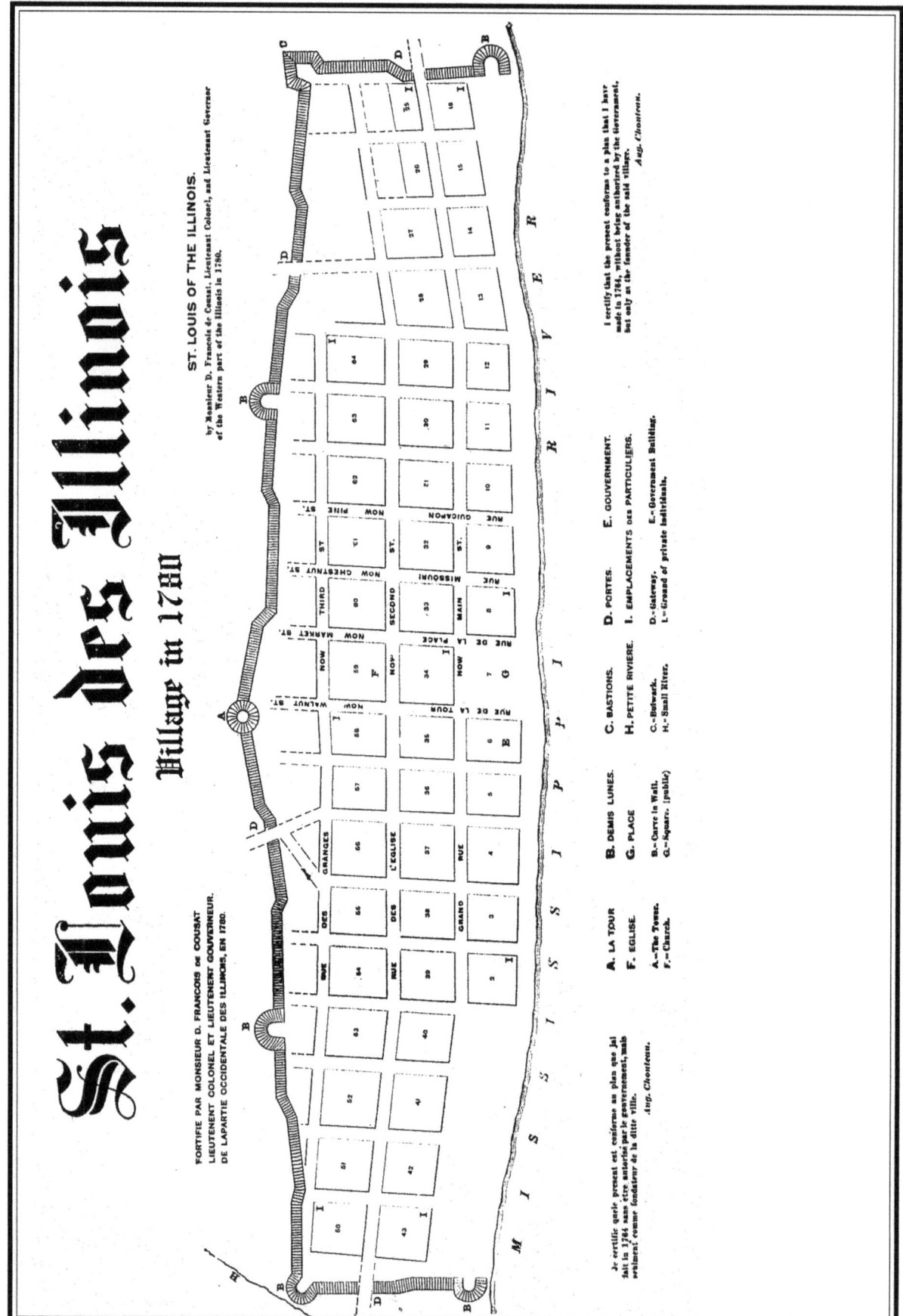

St. Louis

The map opposite is the 1780 plan map for the City of St. Louis and includes the area in which the majority of the gunsmithing and gun dealing took place. Most of this area is now covered by the grounds of the Gateway Arch. The north leg of the Arch is in block 9 and the south leg in block 7.

Of particular interest is block # 12, granted to J. B. Heverieux, a gunsmith from Cahokia, in 1765 by Pierre LaClede the founder of St. Louis. It was still the site of gunsmithing activity sixty years later when Andre Landreville, Louis Soloman Migneron and John Baptiste LeBeau had shops there. Landreville had a store facing Main street and Migneron had a shop next door. Le Beau was behind them "on the levee".

In the early days the block between Main and Front was commonly known as the levee and an ad or statement mentioning "on the levee" could be anywhere on a block not facing Main. Front street was not put through until the latter half of the 1820's, and the cross streets, if they had no other names, were known by letters beginning with A, both north and south of Market street.

When Jacob and Sam Hawken purchased their Laurel street property in 1822 from Thomas H. Benton for $200, no street name was used. The property was facing a cross street north of the square where Mr. Chouteau lived. See p. 141.

A uniform street numbering system was not adopted until after the Civil War, so the exact location of a particular shop cannot always be known from addresses listed in the earlier directories. Odd numbers were usually on the west and even on the east of north-south streets. On east-west streets odd numbers were usually on the north and even on the south. The T. J. Albright ad on page 171 shows one known exception. The ad specifies, "No. 27 Main street, east side."

The cost of land in this area was constantly increasing and the majority of gunsmiths after 1840 appear to have preferred to rent rather than own locations. Shop moves were frequent, see listing below.

Sam Hawken, who sold the property mentioned previously to Robert Campbell in 1853, see p. 141, and Reno Beauvais were among the last to own their own land. A large portion of Beauvais' wealth was based on real estate. The following is a list showing block numbers of gunsmith's and gun dealers in the area shown on the map. Not all locations are listed for each, nor is every dealer or gunsmith listed.

Albright, T. J. 8 (1845) 9 (1849-57) 31 (1860)
Altinger, C. 4 (1851) 33 (1855-60)
Altinger, J. 5
Basler & Denk 56
Beauvais, J. 24 (see p. 142)
Beauvais, R. 12 (1854-66) 29 (1867-72)
Blickensdoerfer, J. 59
Blickensdoerfer & Schilling 34
Bremerman Raschoe & Co. 7
Brown, H. M. 31
Brunner, J. 36
Dimick, H. E. & Co. 31
Dittrich, J. F. 56
Dohrmann, F. 5
Hawken, J & S and successors 27
Hawken J. 24 (1821-see p. 142)
Heverieux, J. B. 12 (1765-75)
Huber & Hoffman 64
Jackson, E. T. 16
Jett, S. C. 31 (1842) 27 (1848-54)
Le Beau, J. B., Sr. 12 (1835+) 39 (1838-45)

Lakenan, J. 24 (see p. 142)
Landreville, A. 12 (1796?-1835?)
Lenzhaner, F. above block 60
Linzel, E. A. 57
Lunsmann, F. 38 (1851) 33 (1852) 37 (1854)
Mead, Edw. & Co. 31
Mcicr, A. & Co. 9 (1838 1854)
Migneron, Louis Solomon 12 (before 1819-1835?)
Nutz, L. N. 60 (1852) 27 (1857)
Pease, J. S. & Co. 33 (1838-42)
Powell, P. & Co. 33 (1838-40)
Roper, J. 36 (1836-38)
St. Louis Indian Affairs gunsmith shop 9
Schaerff Bros. 62 (1851)
Schilling, F. 12 (1852)
Schwarz, F. 27 (1857) 42 (1859-66)
Seiferth, T. F. 57
Shawk, S. North of block 27
Thompson, F. 5
Wilmot, N. N. 32 (1860)

St. Louis

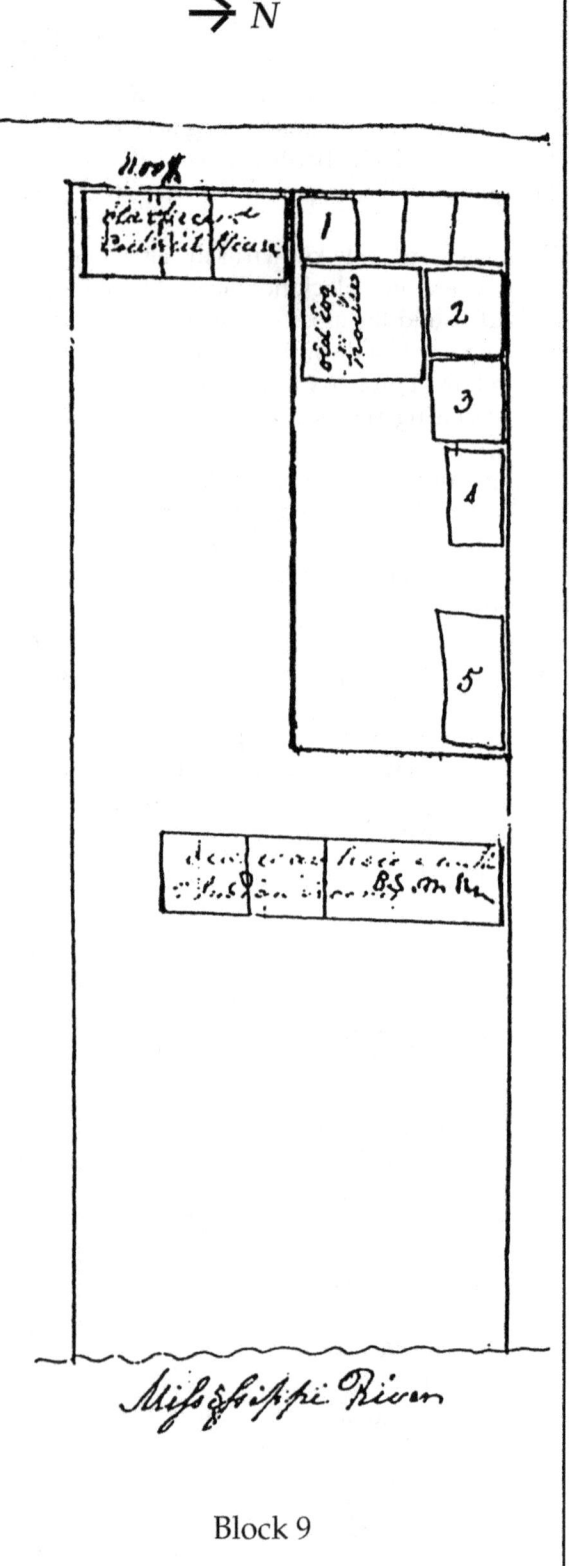

Block 9

It is appropriate that the north leg of the Gateway Arch is located on block 9.

This drawing of block 9 is contained in a letter from William Clark to his superiors in Washington, March 28, 1826.

Among other questions, he asks if the government will pay to repair the buildings recently burned. (Located at S. W. corner of lot, upper left side of map.) He also asks that he be permitted to hire a gunsmith and a blacksmith at St. Louis. (To be housed in the buildings on the lower part of the map.)

On September 1, 1826 Phillip Creamer was hired as gunsmith. Principal duties were to aid those Indians who were being moved West at this time. By 1833 the majority of Indians had been moved and the Superintendency had no further need for a gunsmith shop in St. Louis and it was closed. With the exception of one weeks work in 1827 by John Bte. LeBeau, Phillip Creamer was the only gunsmith found employed for this shop.

In 1826 or 1827 the North part of this block is believed to have been sold.

Among the businesses later found on this block were Adolphus Meier & Co. 1838-1855 and T. J. Albright 1849-1857.

Among the many things we do not know about many of the gunsmiths are their relationships with one another. The rifle at left is marked "S. HAWKEN". Similar rifles marked "J. P. GEMMER" have been noted, though not as fine in fit and finish. It is a light rifle made with a used barrel. It shares some similarities with its better known "big brother', the plains rifle. It was probably made to be a less expensive rifle for the local deer hunters. Although not common, a number of these rifles have been noted in the Midwest. Similar rifles have been noted marked "G. BERGNER".

Although we do not know the exact business relationship between Gemmer and Bergner it is certain that they knew one another. Bergner held a least seven non-firearms patents. One of Bergner's patent applications was witnessed by Gemmer.

While on a visit to the Gemmer gravesite at Bellefontaine Cemetary, St. Louis, Bob Browner, of Missouri, noted the Jos. Etterle gravemarker in Gemmer's family plot. Etterle boarded with Bergner in the 1860 Missouri census, and has been noted in several directories, 1867 to 1871, as a Gemmer employee. It is not known if Gemmer and Etterle were related to one another.

A subject which needs more study is the airgun trade in St. Louis. A style of airgun was dubbed "The St. Louis Type Galley Gun" by Eldon Wolff. The "G. V. Brecht" airgun shown is typical of the type. It was cocked by moving the triggerguard which is actually an underlever which compressed a very strong spring. In 1860 T. Edward Seiferth and in 1865 Frederick E. Seiferth had themselves listed in the St. Louis directory as airgun spring makers.

St. Louis airguns have been noted both unmarked and marked with a number of names. All of those observed have been similar enough to raise the question if they were manufactured in one factory or if they were manufactured by the individuals who marked them. Although some of the embellishments may have been added later, location of both serial numbers and name markings are, in many cases, identical. The engravings shown on a "R. SIEBER & A. HEBERLEIN" and an "A. E. LINZEL" are similar enough to raise the question. In the case of the Linzel, it does not show the degree of skill for which he was noted.

Although there are a number of cases where a gunsmith has changed the spelling of his name over the course of his career it seems unlikely that John Blickensdoerfer would have changed it between airgun number 124 and 125. Number 124 being marked J. BLICKENSDORFER and 125 marked J. BLICKENSDOERFER. Although his name is found with both spellings in print, Blickensdoerfer appears to have been the preferred spelling.

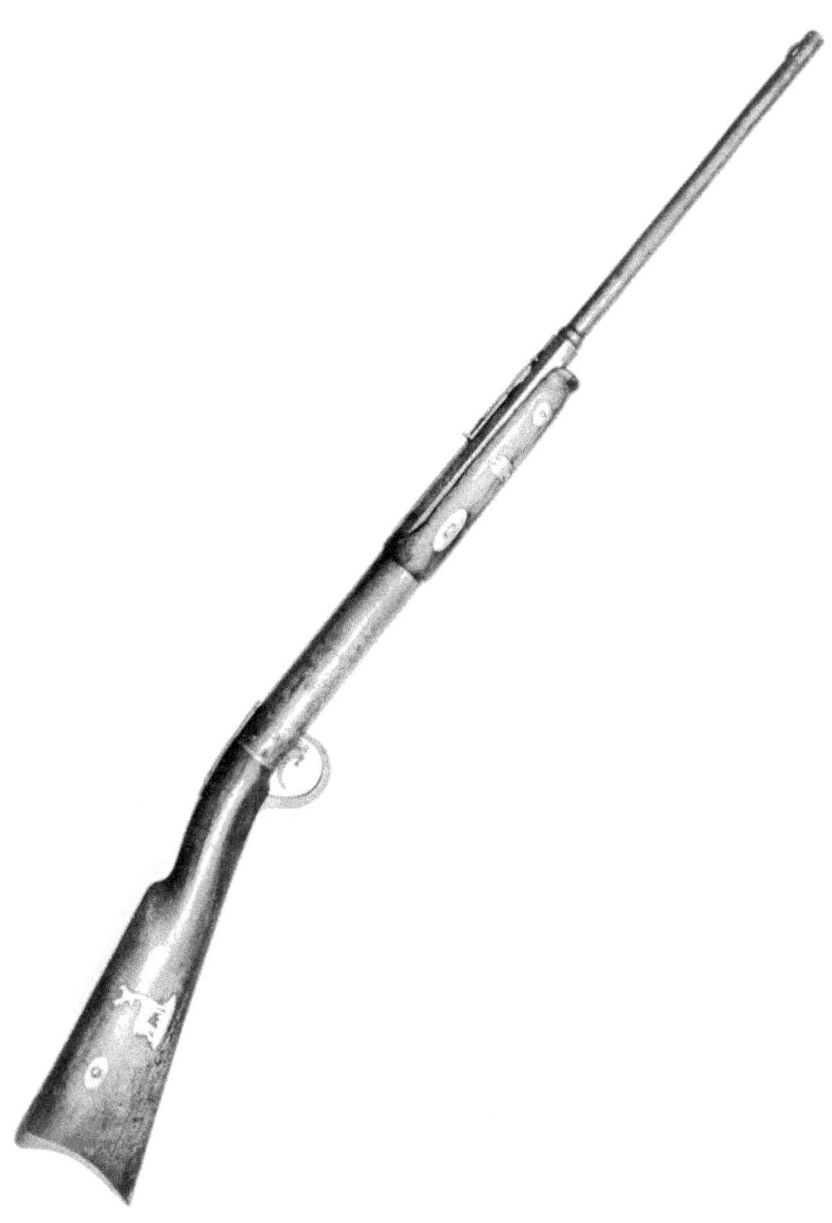

PHILIP CREAMER

The following is the latest version of a compendium which has been placed in numerous research libraries and given to other interested persons. It was not originally intended for publication. However, it is felt that it's inclusion is a valuable addition to this work. Creamer was one of the more important, (but little known) Missouri gunsmiths.

PHILIP CREAMER
pronounced Kramer
(christening name John?)

b. ca. 1775, Frederick Co., Md.
 (possibly Pa. born)
d. ca. 1845, St. Clair Co., Il.
m. Margaret Kane (Cain), b. ca. 1784, d. 1849, of Frederick Co., Md., prior to 1805.
Parents:
 Casper, d. 1802, and Sarah (nee ?, remarried Crouse)
Known Brothers:
 Casper Jr. and Daniel, census indicate a third brother, name unknown, possibly "feeble-minded", about ten years younger than Philip.
Known Adult Children:
 (three infant deaths have been noted in Il.)
Susan Sarah, b. ca. 1804, Md., m. John Anderson 1822 at Kaskaskia, Il. (12 children?)
Joseph N., b. ca. 1810, Il., d. 1856 Il., m. Marie Regi Browner (Brawner) of St. Ferdinand, Mo. (5 children?)
Louis (Lewis), b. ca. 1815, Oh., m. Delilia Clawson, 1839, in St. Clair Co. (she is believed to have died prior to 1850, no known children)
Marie Louise, b. ca. 1816, Il., m. Christian Stimler in St. Clair Co., Il., 1840. (he died prior to 1844)
 m. Daniel C. Deady (Dady) (b. ca. 1812, Md.) 1844 in St. Clair Co., Il. (5 Children?)
 Two other daughters are present on censuses, one in 1800 and one in 1820, names unknown, they are not believed to have lived to adulthood.

Known Locations:
1774, 1778: Casper (father) purchases land in Frederick Co., Md.
1790: Census for Frederick Co., Casper listed.
1792: Frederick Co., Md., a Yeoman/Distiller, Philip Crawmer/Cramer begins having land dealings, he is not believed to be the same. Both Maryland and Pennsylvania had Cramer/Creamers in the gun trade at this time, relationships have not yet been determined.
1799-1805: Active as gunsmith, Taneytown, Md.
 1799: Takes an apprentice.
 1800: Census. Both Philip and Casper listed.
 1801: Purchases lot 17, Taneytown, probable shop location. Purchased improved property.
 1805: Sells out in Md.
1805-1816: St. Clair Co., Il. (Indiana and Illinois Territories) one mile east of the Village of Prairie du Pont in its' Commonfields, (surveys 133-135). It is believed he settled here immediately upon coming west, documented on the land in 1808.
1816: Sells out in St. Clair Co., Il.
1816: Madison Co., Il., presumed, but unknown if he had a shop at this time, sold Dec. 1816.
1817: Creamer begins working for U. S. Indian Agency for Illinois, under agent Richard Graham, employed as a Blacksmith and Gunsmith. The exact location of the shop is unknown. Hired for Peoria he is not believed to have served there. The most likely location is in or near Edwardsville, Il. A second possibility is that it may have been on the Illinois river between its mouth and some distance below Peoria. Least likely is St. Louis. He may have spent some time at Rock Island, Il. and still another possibility is in eastern Madison Co., just west of Highland.
1818-1824: In late 1817 he acquired property in St. Clair Co. (T1N R10W sec. 24). Roughly 2 mi. east of first St. Clair Co. location. He opened a second shop here (late 1818?). He then worked for the Agency part of the year and when the Indians were dispersed, hunting, it is believed he worked his "civilian" shop.
1820: Both population and industrial censuses place him in St. Clair Co., Il.
 Indian Agency receipts show James Bridger (1817) and Samuel B. Lee (1819-1821) as assistants. The 1820 Il. industrial census shows two men employed but does not give names.
1825-1826: The last documentation in the west is April, 1825. He appears on Harper's Ferry, Va. Arsenal records in July, 1825 and March, 1826. Duration of stay in the east as yet unknown. Returned to Il. before Sept. 1, 1826.

Creamer

1826-1835: The next western documentation is Sept. 1, 1826 when he began working as a gunsmith for the Superintendency of Indian Affairs at St. Louis. There 1826-1833. The shop, located on Front just South of Pine, was closed in 1833. Also kept a "civilian shop" at 4th. & Olive, St. Louis. Purchased in 1827, lot 10 on SW corner on intersection.

1835: sells out in St. Louis.

1836-1845: St. Clair Co., Il., same location as second shop (semi-retired?)

1840: Census St. Clair Co., Il. Philip and Joseph listed.

1841: sale of property to son in-law Stimler. (indication of failing health)

1845: approximate death

1846: auction of Stimler Estate (Philip's land) sons Joseph and Louis and son in-law Deady buy.

1847: Margaret releases dowry rights to sons and sons in-law, Anderson included.

1849: Margaret dies.

1850-1860: Various land transactions, all children are on 1850 Il. Census. Joseph N. died 1856, others have not been located on 1860 census for Il.

Creamer was the preferred spelling with Cramer being the most common alternate, only one "K" alternate has been found - others may occur.

Other known alternates are best explained as follows CR (one or more vowels except u) (one or two) M (one or more vowels) R (followed by e if writer was French).

Impression of a Court Seal believed to be one of at least four made by Phillip Creamer. Image size increased for readability.

Courtesy Illionois State Archives

The Creamer House

When Curt Johnson submitted his final draft of his *Gunsmiths of Illinois,* prospects for the Creamer house were looking dim. Various attempts by a number of individuals to acquire and preserve the house, either on location or by moving it, had failed. The roof, damaged by a fire in 1979, had fallen in and it appeared the house was destined to be lost.

A secondary point was the question in the minds of some whether the house had been built by Creamer. Many felt that the house was "Too big to be that early."

Fortunately the house has been acquired by the Historic Daniel Boone Home & Boonesfield Village inc. of Defiance, Mo.

Photos:
> below, as it stood ca. 1983

The house has been dismantled and moved to the Boone location on Highway F, Defiance, Mo. The house probably will not be restored and opened before the year 2000. The Boone House and Village are open for tours between April and November. For further information, their Tour & Event information number is (636) 798-2005.

The Illinois Transportation Archaeological Research Program recently was able to do a survey of the house and nothing in the report by Don Booth, site supervisor, rules out the possibility that Creamer built the house. Having observed five nearly identical houses, in Taneytown, Maryland, within easy walking distance of Creamer's shop location, I never had a doubt. The house received an extensive remodeling about 1850. Originally a two story dogtrot, having an open porch the width of the house in the middle of the ground floor. The openings were filled in at that time of the remodelling

Creamer House

above ca. 1996

almost stripped, 1997

Backside (right side of other photos). A partial lockplate, a broken frizzen spring and a flintlock hammer were found in the floor of this room which was later used as a kitchen.

CREAMER BIBLIOGRAPHY

This abbreviated bibliography is an attempt to list all known sources of information on Creamer

Primary Source:
"Belleville Advocate":
  Notice of Stimler Estate sale (1846).
  Margaret's obituary (1849).
  John Mason Peck article on John Messenger.
Brackenridge, H. M., *Recollections of Persons and Places in the West*, 2nd. ed.
  (many secondary sources use this book as original source).
Bryan and Morrison daybooks and ledgers: "D" ledger and daybooks 6, 7 and 8 of the Cahokia store. "D" ledger original is at the Chicago Historical Society, daybook 6 is property of the Ste. Genevieve Museum, Ste. Genevieve, Mo. and daybooks 7 and 8 are part of the" Pierre Menard Collection" IL. State Historical Library, Springfield, IL.
  The Illinois Historical Survey Library, U. of IL, Champaign, IL has microfilm of all known Bryan and Morrison papers with the exception of daybook 6, which is available on microfilm through the U. of Mo. Western Reserve System #R-176.
Censuses: 1790 & 1800 MD, (1810 & 1818 IL censuses missing or incomplete) 1820 IL, 1830 MO, 1840 & 1850 IL.
Church Records: Holy Family Church, Cahokia, IL (partial search).
  I have not searched St. Louis and was unable to locate appropriate Maryland records.
Court Records: St. Clair Co., IL. (partial search) Madison Co., IL, St. Louis, MO, and Frederick Co., MD.
Illinois Historical Society: Indexed on several lists in society publications Not indexed 1942 article on Col. Stephenson, letter A. C. Dodge to Stephenson (original at Galena Courthouse). "Pierre Menard Coll." daybooks 7 & 8 Bryan & Morrison (Cahokia store) and Christy & Jarrot Flour Mill records.
Kaleb, John & Co., daybook Taneytown, MD.
  (contained in Armsmakers of Maryland).
Land Records: Frederick Co., MD, Madison, Monroe and St. Clair Counties., IL and St. Louis, MO.
"Louisiana Gazette" Supplement, Mar. 28, 1811. Sworn statement by Creamer regarding a dispute between Doctor Reynolds and Doctor Tuttle.
Missouri Historical Society (St. Louis):
  article in "Glimpses",
  "American Fur Co. Ledgers",
  "Richard Graham Papers",
  "Lucas Papers".
"Missouri Republican" letters at Post Office 1827 and delinquent tax list 1827.
Reynolds, John, *Pioneer History of Illinois* , considered inaccurate by historians, was acquainted with Creamer.
St. Louis Business Directory for 1847 (account of the flood of 1844).
U. S. Govt.:Am. State Papers, Indian Affairs, II, p. 366, (this entry questionable).
  "Correspondence of the St. Louis Superintendency for Indian Affairs" M234, rolls 748, 749 & 750, Natl. Archives Microfilm.
Harper's Ferry Arsenal Records.
Public Domain Land Sale Records (at IL State Archives, indexed).

Secondary Source:
   Brink McDonough, *History of St. Clair County Illinois.*
   Garavaglia, L. A. and Worman, C. G., *Firearms of the American West   1803-1865*, U. of New Mexico, (photos).
   Hartzler, Daniel, *Arms Makers of Maryland*, Shumway, article winter 88 Kentucky Rifle Association newsletter and March 89 "Gun Report" (photos).
   Johnson, Bob, indexer, "Court Records of Madison County, Il. 1818-1821".
   Johnson, Curtis, *A Checklist of 18th. & 19th. Century Illinois Gunsmiths*, and *Gunsmiths of Illinois*, both Shumway (photos).
   McDermott, J. Francis, *Old Cahokia*, (records of Nicholas Jarrot Estate sale).
   Paul, Victor A., "Searching for (Young) Old Jim", Museum of the Fur Trade Quarterly, Winter 90. (photos)
   Scharff, J. Thomas, *History of St. Louis City and County.*
   "St. Clair County Genealogical Society Quarterly" (several St. Clair Co. records are indexed as well as Bryan & Morrison "D" ledger and census of 1820).
   Tarbell, Ida, *The Early Life of Abraham Lincoln.*

   Problems:
      Alter, J. Cecil, *Jim Bridger*, U. of Oklahoma.
         Unknown sources for preferred spelling of Creamer and place names not in Dodge (but correct).
      Dodge, Grenville, "Biographical Sketch of James Bridger".
         It is hoped to be generally correct, however many specifics have been proven incorrect or are in question.
      Russell, Carl P., *Firearms Traps and Tools of the Mountain Man*,
         The Am. State Papers entry he mentions is of questionable validity. Believed to be a case of bureaucratic lag, Creamer is thought to have left govt. employ, temporarily, when the Illinois Agency was closed mid-1821. Both of his employees are believed to have left him in 1822.

SPECULATION ON CREAMER

From the three contemporary accounts known, two things may be said about Creamer's personality. He was kind to children and decidedly eccentric. What manner the eccentricities took is unknown. However, they were probably those normally associated with genius. A project which appeals is done with skill and dispatch while no amount of money or time can complete an uninteresting one.

As if having Jim Bridger as an apprentice and being one of the finest gunsmiths of his time were not enough claim to greater notoriety, there have been speculative statements published, which seem to have the intent of making Creamer a "character". Statements suggesting marital problems or infidelities should be treated as extremely speculative. There are more plausible explanations for these speculations. In 1813 an unnamed child, son of Philip, was buried through the Holy Family Church (Roman Catholic) at Cahokia, Illinois. Some speculate that this child was illegitimate. In the days of high infant mortality sickly infants were frequently not named or baptized until it became reasonably certain they would live. This is believed to be the case here. An illegitimate child probably would not have been buried through the church, on "hallowed ground".

The listing for Philip's son, Lewis, on the 1850 Illinois census shows birthplace as Ohio, ca. 1815. This has been taken completely out of historical context and used with the above burial to construe some sort of marital breakup between Philip and his wife Margaret. Presuming the census entry is accurate, there is once again a much more plausible solution to this separation of spouses. Does the War of 1812 ring any bells? Populations dropped all over the frontier as families moved back east to avoid the very real possibility of Indian attack. It would not be at all surprising if Creamer sent his wife and children to a safer location while he remained on the frontier to provide his much needed services to the military and militia units on the frontier. John Reynolds, in his Pioneer History of Illinois, tells us Creamer both manufactured and repaired firearms for the troops during the war. The birth of a daughter, Marie Louise, ca. 1816 suggests this was a "war caused" separation rather than a break up.

The location of Creamer's birth is not known. Brackenridge, in Recollections of Persons and Places in the West (2nd. ed.), says Lancaster, Pennsylvania. One Indian Department document, in 1826, also gives his birthplace as Pennsylvania. John Reynolds, who knew Creamer well, says he was born in Taneytown, Maryland. Casper Creamer, Philip's father, is found buying land in Frederick County, Maryland as early as 1774, roughly the time of Philip's birth. The simplest explanation may be that Casper left his pregnant wife somewhere in Pennsylvania while he prepared suitable housing in Maryland and that Philip was born shortly before the family moved to Maryland.

The location and Master of his apprenticeship is also unknown. Extant "Golden Age" rifles by Creamer show a heavy influence of George Shroyer, who was located in Hanover, Pennsylvania, a short distance from Taneytown. Reynolds tells us Creamer learned gunsmithing at "Harpers Ferry, Maryland" (sic.). Although he has the state wrong for Harpers Ferry he may have provided us with an important clue. Harpers Ferry was founded too late to have been the location of Creamer's apprenticeship. However, it was not the first arsenal in the area. Creamer may have told Reynolds that he had learned the gunsmith trade at the government arsenal in Maryland, and when Reynolds wrote his book he presumed, in 1850, that Creamer meant Harpers Ferry. The first arsenal in the area was operated by Mathias Shroyer at Taneytown, Maryland!

Records are very sparse for this arsenal. However, evidence suggests, arsenals act as magnets to gunsmiths. It would not be any surprise if George Shroyer traveled the 12 or so miles from Hanover to Taneytown, particularily to aid his younger brother Mathias. Although marked Mathias Shroyer guns do not show the degree of skill of his brother, it is believed that either he or one of his employees is the most probable Master. The other possibilities are that Creamer apprenticed at Hanover or with John Armstrong at Emmitsburg, Maryland. The latter is the least probable given that Creamer and Armstrong were nearly the same age. It is more likely they apprenticed side by side than one to the other, Creamer perhaps slightly behind Armstrong.

Hawken Land Records

The following are edited versions of the purchase and sale of the most well known firearms related property in the city of St. Louis.

BOOK L p. 529 St. Louis Land Records

This indenture made at St. Louis on the first day of October, in the year One thousand eight hundred and twenty two between Thomas H. Benton of one part and Jacob and Samuel Hawken of the other part all of the county of St. Louis. Witnesseth: That the said Thomas H. Benton for and in consideration of the sum of two hundred dollars ($200) to him in hand paid by the said party of the second part...doth bargain grant and sell to the said Jacob and Samuel Hawken a certain part of a lot in the town of St. Louis fronting on the cross street on the north side of the square on which Mr. Pierre Chouteau now lives, and which separates it from the said square; bounded on the east by the lot which Mr. Antoine Vincent Bouis purchased at the public sale of Mr. Hyacinth St. Cyr and extending 65 french measure [unreadable] same more or less with said cross street west to the pickets now enclosing the lot about the house of the said Louis Honore' who sold the present bargained premises to Thomas H. Benton on the 8th. day of June 1817 and extending back north fifty five feet, French Measure, to the lot of some person unknown...[part of page bottom missing] ...[530]...
Recorded April 7th., 1824

BOOK T6 p. 73 St. Louis Land Records

This deed made and entered this seventeenth day of September 1853 by and between Samuel Hawken and Martha Hawken his wife parties of the first part and Robert Campbell party of the second part all of the City and County of St. Louis State of Missouri. Witnesseth: that the said parties of the first part for and in consideration of the sum of $ 7300 to them paid by the party of the second part, the receipt of which is acknowledged... a lot of land lying in the City of St. Louis in block # 27 containing a front on Washington Avenue of 35 feet by a depth northwardly of 59 feet 6 inches, bounded south by Washington Avenue, East by an alley running through said block from north to south, North by property now or formerly of Reel and West by property now or formerly of Hawken. The property hereby conveyed having been acquired by said Samuel Hawken of Jacob and Christopher M. Hawken by deed dated 2nd. June 1853...and part of the same lot conveyed to Jacob and Samuel Hawken by Thomas H. Benton by deed dated the first of October 1822...

The land sale followed several transactions between Sam Hawken and Christopher M. Hawken, representing Jacob's heirs, .

Essentially they exchanged five dollars in a legal manner, to straighten out the titles on properties that Sam and Jacob had purchased together. Christopher M. sold a ten foot strip of ground adjoining the property for $2,500, to Robert Campbell. The temporary retirement of Sam Hawken as a gunsmith probably occured quite near the time of this sale. To put the prices in proper perspective, the highest paid gunsmiths working for wages were paid about $ 40 per month in 1850.

It is uncertain when or in what manner the Hawkens built on the above property. There may have been several small buildings on the property, similar to the map on page 68 of Jacob Hawken's property in block 24. The question is raised given the number of times the address of the Hawken shop changed. Addresses 21-37 are believed to have been on the above property. The 1857 directory lists a number of gunsmiths at 31 Washington and they are traditionaly listed as Hawken employees. William S. Hawken's address in that directory is given as 29 Washington. The bankruptcy, in 1857, lists the store at 31 Washington. In the address listing which follows it should be noted that 31 and 37 are often mistaken for each other when written longhand, as the directory agent would have done when taking the listing.

Dir.	Name	Address
1836	S. Hawken	21 Laurel
1838,40	J & S Hawken	31 Laurel
	S. Hawken(res.)	35 Laurel
1842	J & S Hawken	31 Laurel, 35 Laurel
1845-48	J & S Hawken	33 Washington
1845	S. Hawken	37 Washington
1851,52	S. Hawken	37 Washington
1854	Hawken & Campbell	37 Washington
1857	William S. Hawken	29 Washington
1859	William S. Hawken	21 Washington
1860,64	William L. Watt	21 Washington
1865,66	J. P. Gemmer	21 Washington

In 1845 Laurel st. (3 blocks long) was changed to Washington which connected from the West.

#'s 37, 31 and 21 are referred to as the "Old Stand" in newspaper ads in late 1850's.

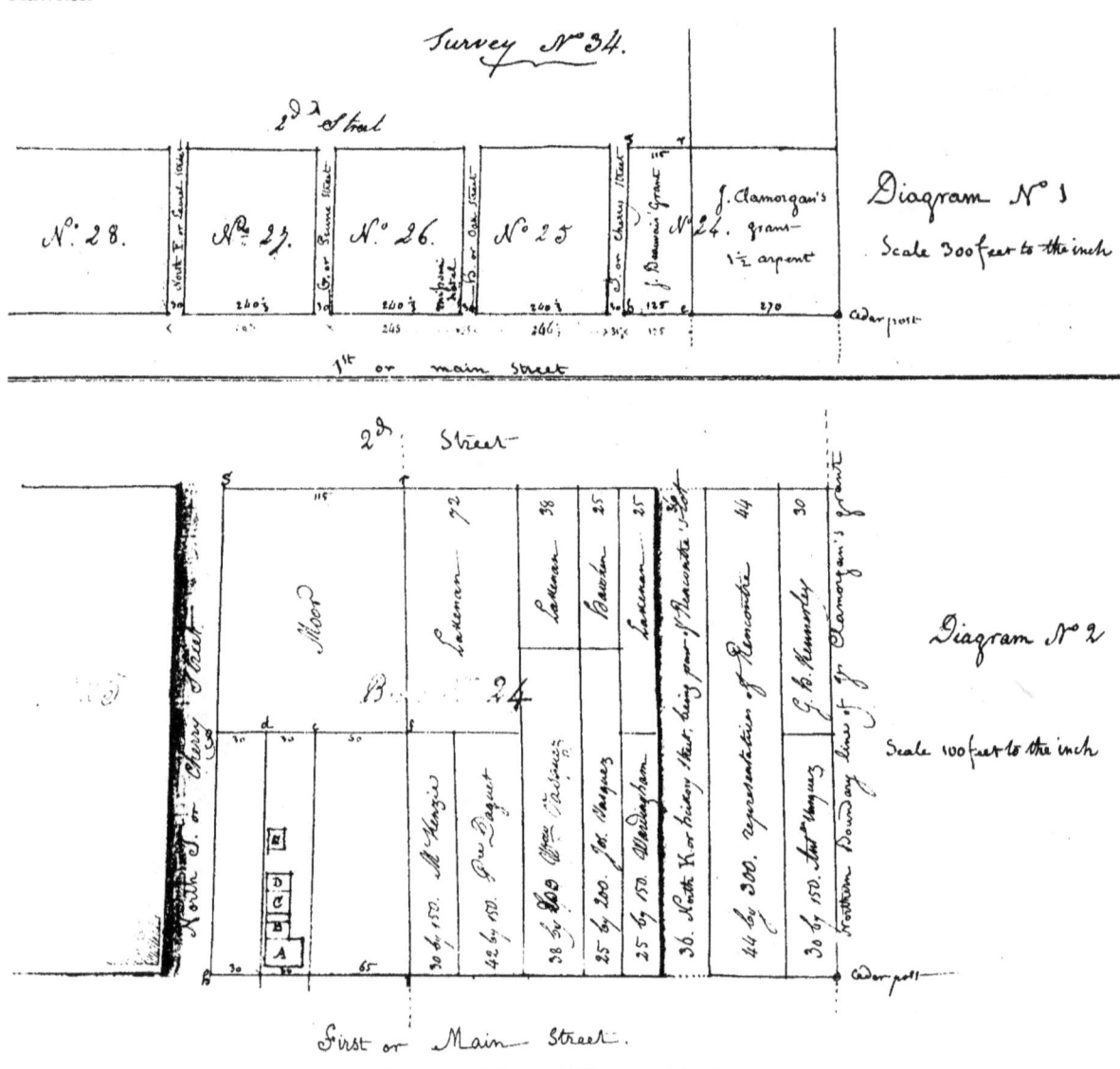

Courtesy Missouri Historical Society

    The above maps were drawn by surveyor Rene Paul, in 1827, to settle a land dispute between Jacob Hawken and Thomas Forsyth. Both claimed the same section of land, part of the original Beauvais grant. (Diagram No. 1) The survey used the N. E. corner of Pierre Chouteau's building, block 28, as the starting point. Jacob won the suit which concerned the section of land which shows buildings "A" thru "E" (Diagram No. 2). The buildings are described as, "A", dwelling house, 25ft. 4in. front by 20ft. 5in. depth. "B" "C" and "D" as back buildings, no dimensions given individually, they extended 39ft. 5in. from the S. E. corner of "A" to the S. W. corner of "D". 15 1/2ft. separated "D" from "E", a smokehouse about 12ft. square.

    Diagram No. 2 also shows the other property of Jacob Hawken and that of the late James Lakenan in block 24.

> Rec'd of Jacob & S Hawken
> Twenty five dollars for the last
> Six months rent
> St Louis July 17, 1827 v v Bouis

> Rec'd of Jacob & S Hawken
> Twenty five dollars in advance

> St Louis July 17th 1832
> Received of J. & S. Hawkins one hundred and
> fifty dollars being for one years rent te-
> rminating the 16 inst. for the tenement he occupies
> belonging to estate of late May T. Biddle
> the lease of which is intended for an[other]
> year to commence this day
> J O'Fallon ag[en]t
> For Mrs Biddle

Courtesy a Missouri Historical Society

The above rent receipts are from the Missouri Historical Society files. The top receipt appears t[o be] for the property of Antoine Vincent Bouis mentioned on page 141 as adjoining the Laurel propert[y on] the east. Quite possibly Jacob and Samuel opened their shop on this property before they built on t[heir] own property.

Thomas Biddle purchased the property at the estate sale of Bouis. The use of the word tenemen[t in] the lower receipt may indicate they resided on this property and worked on their own property, [next] door.

> **'KANSAS'—JUST RECEIVED by** Adams & Co.'s Express, a large and fine assortment of Double and Single SHOT GUNS, which will be sold cheap for cash
>
> We have also on hand an assortment of our own manufacture of RIFLES, so well known for the past thirty years throughout the Western country. Emigrants to Kansas and California should not fail to call at No. 31 Washington avenue, between Main and Second streets, (old stand,) and examine our stock, before purchasing elsewhere.
>
> **WM. S. HAWKEN.**
>
> N. B. Rifles made to order, and repairing done at the shortest notice. mh20

The above ad appeared in the January 10, 1857 issue of the <u>Missouri Republican</u>. It should be noted that the Kansas referred to in the ad included what is now the state of Colorado. He evidently did not sell enough "cheap for cash" as the record of his bankruptcy two months later appears below.

BOOK 185 p. 128 St. Louis Land Records

This deed of assignment made this eleventh day of March in the year eighteen hundred and fifty seven between William S. Hawken of the City of St. Louis, party of the first part, Christopher M. Hawken of the same place, party of the second part and Anna M. Kelly, Mary Egbert, A. W. Spies and Co., Herman Boker and Co., T. H. Bate, Christian Hoffman, The Hazard Powder Co., Laflin N. Smith (sic.), A. C. Williamson and Co., T. S. Reynolds and Co., T. Douglass, W. F. Kelly, Sheldon Hoyt and Co., W. J. Syms and Bros., Morse and Co., Robert Campbell, and certain workmen now in the employ of said William S. Hawken whose names cannot be given, the creditors of the said William S. Hawken, parties of the third part. Witnesseth: That the said party of the first part in consideration of the trust assumed by the party of the second part and in the consideration of the sum of five dollars to him in hand paid by said party of the second part hath bargained sold ...all the real and mixed property to the said William S. Hawken belonging wherever situate or being, including and comprising among other things the following pieces or parcels of land...
Lots 7 & 8 of block 1 of the 2nd. subdivision of the St. Louis City Commons...
Lots 35 & 36 of block 2 of the same
Lots 32 & 37 of block 1 of the 1st. subdivision of the St. Louis City Commons
Frac. section 16 twp. 42 N. of Range 7E described as lot # 6 in block 9 of the subdivision of said section ... Also all debts of said William S. Hawken due and owing whether the same are secured by note or stand on open account. Also all stock in trade of whatever description of the said William S. Hawken, being at the Store number thirty one (31) on Washington Avenue, St. Louis the particulars of which will be ascertained by an inventory thereof according to law...

In Trust however for the following purposes: whereas said William S. Hawken is indebted to the creditors herein before named as parties of the third part in the following sums, Anna M. Kelly $450.00 or thereabout, Mary Egbert $300.00, A. W. Spies and Co. $1981.31, Herman Boker & Co. $279.60, T. H. Bate $294.18, Christian Hoffman $1030.00, Hazard Powder Co. $118.72, Laflin and Smith $84.00, A. C. Williamson and Co. $170.00, H. Boker and Co., in another sum of $279.60, T. S. Reynolds and Co. $139.00, T. Douglass $115.20, W. F. Kelly $234.40, Sheldon Hoyt and Co. $158.75, W. J. Syms and Co. 167.78, Morse and Co. $180.00, Robert Campbell $3334.00 (principal money for which there is a judgement), workmen of said William S. Hawken $180.00 more or less. ... the said party of the second part will, with all convenient speed proceed to collect all debts of the said William S. Hawken owing and to convert into money all the property hereby assigned ...will proceed to pay the same equally and prorata out of the proceeds of this assignment until said claims be paid in full or the said proceeds be exhausted...

Note, among the creditors were two of William S.' sisters; Anna M. Kelly and Mary Egbert as well as W. F. Kelly, his brother in-law. Was Sam one of the workmen "whose names cannot not be given"?

Laflin and Smith was a New York powder dealer, who had an office in St. Louis. A. W. Spies was a New York firearms wholesaler. A. W. Spies also manufactured and wholesaled swords as did H. Boker and Co. With the exception of Robert Campbell and Christian Hoffman, the other names mentioned are presumed to be other wholesalers, though a complete search has not yet been made.

The land mentioned was auctioned on June 30, 1858 and sold for a total of $206.

INDUSTRIAL CENSUSES
1850, 1860, 1870
for Missouri

Industrial Censuses

The map on the previous page shows the distribution of gunsmiths during the period of greatest firearm manufacturing in the state. Population and Industrial censuses of 1850 were used to compile the map, neither census should be considered exact, the number of gunsmiths in the state was probably higher. A number of known gunsmiths were found listed under other occupations such as; farmer, blacksmith, locksmith, etc.

Where a single number is shown the county had gunsmiths only on the population census. The figure for the industrial census is shown following a dash with the first number being that of the population census. Cole county was the site of the state penitentiary and three of the five gunsmiths listed were prisoners.

The following counties had not been organized in 1850 and no population breakdown was possible.

Barton	Christian	Douglas	Iron	Pemiscot	Stone	Worth
Carter	Dent	Howell	Maries	Phelps	Webster	

The industrial census lists those firms or individuals who manufactured goods of any type with value of $500 or more.

Twenty-eight of the firms or individuals listed on the industrial census were involved in firearms production. Approximately ninety-one of the two-hundred gunsmiths found on the population census are indicated as employees. Firearms produced are not shown on every census listing. However, approximately $37,000 in production value is shown. This equates to about 2,500 firearms of all types, nearly half being pistols. Well known names missing from the industrial census include Charles Altinger, Reno Beauvais, H. E. Dimick, Meyer Friede, and John Sites Jr.

Altinger and Sites quite possibly were simply missed by the census takers as, no doubt, were others. There is some question whether Beauvais actually manufactured firearms or purchased them marked with his name, either locally or from the East. Horace Dimick had recently arrived in St. Louis and either had not yet begun manufacture or had not reached full production. The population census lists him as gun store not gun maker. Although Meyer Friede had been in St. Louis he is not believed to have opened his rifle factory until later in the decade. He is the only St. Louis gun manufacturer listed on the 1860 industrial census. The following is a list of gunsmiths based on the 1850 industrial census. Details of their census listing follow their names in the main text.

Andrew
Brown, E. B.
Wilson, Pleasant
Boone
Philips, John G.
Buchanan
Gove, C.
Kemp, A.
Callaway
Gill, Prisley
Clay
Keller, James M.
Cooper
John Sites (Sr.)
Greene
Painter, Jacob*
Howard
Oldham, Gabriel
Jackson
Hockensmith, K. D.
Renick, Abram
Van Horn, John

Lafayette
Palmer, James W.
Stone, Thomas
McDonald
Markham, Carter
Markham, Thomas
Newton
Kendrick, William
Randolph
Riley J.
Ray
Kelsey, John
St. Louis (city)
Albright, T. J.
Brunner, Joseph
Critquelhoef, Wm.
Hawken, Saml.
Lunsmann, Franz
Roper, John
Schaerff, C. & J.
Wilmot, N.

* The only woman thus far found working for wages in the Missouri gun trade is shown on Painter's industrial census listing. Wages shown are $5 per month.

There are other cases where widows took over their husbands businesses and at least one woman, Mrs. A. A. Carlisle, may have managed a business.

The 1860 industrial census is probably less accurate than the 1850 census. A number of the men, listed on the 1850 census, had left the state or retired. Increased pressure of eastern manufacturers certainly affected production as did the "Panic of 1857". However, it does not seem reasonable that the number of firms which produced over $500 fell from twenty-eight to only four.

Prisley Gill, who had moved from Callaway co. to Lincoln co. is the only name found on both industrial censuses. Meyer Friede is the only name found in St. Louis. The other two shown are William Hayes at Warsaw, Benton co. and Joseph Mueller in Gasconade co.

Production figures for the 1860 census are approximately $3,150, less than half of the production figure shown by one manufacturer, T. J. Albright, on the 1850 industrial census.

The material contained in the 1870 Industrial Census for Missouri came as somewhat of a surprise. There appears to have been more manufacturing at that time than has been traditionally thought.

Wilson's History and Directory for Southeast Missouri and Southern Illinois 1875-76 mentions the St. Louis portion of the 1870 Missouri Industrial census. It states that St. Louis had 16 gunsmithing establishments which employed 51 hands, had $35,500 invested, paid wages of $21,874, used $19,435 in materials and produced $80,000 in finished products. In addition there was one factory which employed 14 hands, had $15,000 capital, paid $10,000 in wages, used $23,000 in materials, and had $43,000 in products.

I was able to locate the 16 gunsmithing establishments on the census, which had 2 pages missed when microfilmed and may have other pages missing from the original. I was unable to find the factory listing. Two well known St. Louis names were missing from the census, H. E. Dimick and T. J. Albright & Son. They are both possibilities.

The names were spelled as found on the census. The following is additioal information about the St. Louis names on the list.

Augustus Abe was active in St. Louis 1869 to 1895 by directory listings.

George Duenckel was active 1864 to 1888 by directory listings.

Martin Flesh(Flesch) was active from 1850 to 1870 by population census. No directory listings have been found.

J. P. Gemmer was active in St. Louis 1859 or 1860 through 1915.

Thos. Givens is probably Thomas Gibbons who was listed in various directories 1859 to 1885.

John Hams is probably the same or related to Stephen Hemmes who has various listings in St. Charles, Mo. 1854 thru 1867. No other listing for this or a similar name has been found in St. Louis.

Jno. Harstrotter is probably the same as Frederick Herkstroeter who had listings 1860 to 1874. Listed as Herkstroeter and Stahlberg in the 1870 and 71 directories.

Conrad Homa was listed in an 1867 directory and on the 1870 population census.

John Plickendorf is almost certainly John Blickensdoerfer who was listed 1863 to 1874. Although the firm of Blickensdoerfer and Schilling had been formed in 1869 they apparently maintained two shops for manufacturing and repair. As several distinct types of firearms are found marked "Blickensdoerfer and Schilling" they may have specialized at each shop and shared a common retail store. However, it may be a case of duplicate listings as the only difference in the listings was in the wages paid section.

This was the only listing found for Alois Pohl.

Christian Schann is probably the same as Christian Scham on the 1870 population census, no other listings have been found.

Frederick Schilling is listed 1860 thru 1874, 1869-1874 as Blickensdoerfer and Schilling.

The surname of Henry Sharoz? was difficult to read on the copy I made and I believe him to be the same as Henry Schantz who was found in directories 1857 to 1869.

I have Anton Strecks listed as Strecker on the 1870 population census, no other listings found.

Henry Sonnenschein, listed here as Sunshin, was active in St. Louis 1863 until his death in 1891. His son in-law, Ernest Vollrath, continued to operate the shop under Henry's name until 1928.

Thomas Wageman is also listed on the 1870 population census, no other listings have been found.

Blickensdoerfer and Schilling, Duenckel, and Gemmer are the only names listed in the 1870 Edward's city directory, under the gunsmith heading.

Industrial Censuses

The following is additional information on gunsmiths present on the 1870 industrial census for Missouri. The order is by Counties, with the exception of St. Louis.

This is the only listing in Missouri thus far found for Henry Brundage.

S. L. McKean who was listed in directories 1879 thru 1889, at Mexico, Audrain Co., is probably the same as Samuel McKain listed here.

F. J. Drummond listed here is probably the same or related to N. Siegle Drummond who was listed in directories 1879 thru 1883 at Butler, Bates Co.

Samuel Hays is probably the same or son of William Hays of Warsaw, Benton Co. William Hays is first found on the 1850 population census, listings for him include the 1860 industrial census, population census and directory. There are also directory listings for a William Hays at Warsaw 1883 thru 1893. If these or for the same man he would be age 70 to 80 years old at the time of the listings.

Victor Rudolph is listed at St. Joseph on the 1860 census and has directory listings 1867 thru 1893.

William Dunn arrived in Missouri about 1848, he is listed on the 1860 population census in Callaway Co. His son John H. was apprenticed to him according to the 1860 population census.

James C. Short has directory listings 1870 thru 1876.

Francis X. Roll probably arrived in Missouri ca. 1853, he has been found on the 1860 population census. There are also directory listings 1893 thru 1898.

No other listing has been found for Earnest Schmidt.

William Knaus was active in Otterville 1844 thru 1889. Though primarily a blacksmith, at least one marked pistol is known. Chester P. Sites may be one of the 3 employees listed. Knaus also purchased a number of items at the estate sale of John Sites Sr. at Boonville. see Sites, Section 2.

Flor. Balthaur is almost certainly the same as Floerl Balthasar who was listed at Ste. Genevieve 1879 thru 1891. Preferred spelling of name is not certain, also found as Balthazar and Balthauer.

Joseph Muller/Mueller arrived in Missouri ca. 1846 and has been found on the 1860 population and industrial censuses, also at Hermann.

No other listing for Tal or similar surname has been found in Missouri.

Joseph Batcheller is probably the same as Josiah W. Batcheller Sr. who was listed at Oregon City, Holt Co. on the 1860 population census. He is listed at St. Joseph 1883 thru 1898. Son Josiah Jr. was also a gunsmith.

J. Wachter & Bro. was listed in directories 1867 and 1870 at Glasgow, Howard Co. John and Casper Wachter arrived in Missouri ca. 1856. John was listed on the 1860 population census and has directory listing 1860 thru 1893. The only other listing found for Casper was the 1860 population census.

This is the only listing found for Mathias Wallerich.

Frederick Fredericks was listed in directories 1869 thru 1885.

Charles Miller & Co. was listed 1867 thru 1871 and succeeded by G. C. Miller & Co. thru 1898.

No other listings have been found for Peter Neilson or Nelson & Youngquist though P. W. Nelson listed in an 1871 directory may be the same.

There was a Robert Owsley listed in a 1867 directory at Newark, Knox Co.

No other listing has been found for Burkhard Meyer or for Louis Ganders.

August Anschutz has also been found in directories at Chillicothe, Livingston Co. 1879 and 1881 and at New Frankfort, 1883 and 1885.

Charles O. Miller was found in an 1860 directory and an 1876 directory, both at Hannibal. Several marked guns are known.

No listing has been found for Elijah Brawley. However, Reynolds Co. had a John Brawley on the 1850 population census and I've been unable to document Brawley Bros. at Ellington ca. Civil War.

Fred Butcher is probably the same as Frederick Boettcher, who arrived in Missouri about 1848 and is listed on the 1850 population census and a directory in 1867, both at Shelbyville.

A Frederick Hasenjager was listed in directories at Holstein, Warren Co., 1879 thru 1898.

Joseph Bivens is listed at Woodbury, Warren Co. in an 1860 directory and is also found on the 1870 population census.

*EDWARD MEAD'S ILLUSTRATED TREATISE ON THE RIFLE,
SHOT-GUN AND PISTOL
TOGETHER WITH EDWARD MEAD'S CATALOGUE*

Edward Mead was born in New York ca. 1810. He is first found in business with Edwin Adriance in 1831 in Ithaca, New York as Mead, Adriance and Co. By 1835 they had moved to St. Louis, doing business as Mead & Adriance. In 1840 the frim name was changed and thereafter Mead's business was listed as Edward Mead & Co. Taylor & Crooks *Sketch Book of Saint Louis* (1858) tells us that Mead lost everything in the fire of 1849, when a large part of the commercial district burned. In 1852 he visited Europe to purchase direct rather than using the New York wholesale houses. At that time he had as partners Wm. H. Maurice and Edward H. Mead (his son). The *Sketch Book of St. Louis* fits into the category of a "booster book" so some of the statements cannot be taken at face value. However, it indicates Mead did a thriving business in wholesale firearms. Mead successfully survived the "Panics" of 1837 and 1857 and the 1849 fire. His wife, Phoebe, died sometime between 1860 and 1870, quite possibly in 1861. He sold his house and apparently his business to his son in-law Charles S. Russell ca. 1861, though he continued to work with Russell until 1869. In 1870 Mead and his son Edward H.(1834-) are listed as Edward Mead & Co. 1880 is the last listing found as Edward Mead & Co. No obituary or certain time of death has been found for him. However, he is listed in directories through 1884.

It is not surprising that the maternal grandfather of the famed artist C. M. Russell was somewhat of an artist himself. He was noted for his silver service designs. This pamphlet appears to have been an attempt to gain business from his more affluent and better educated customers. We may forgive him the inability to foresee the development of the cartridge and other firearms advances. Any number of his statements still have as much application today as they had in 1851.

The catalogue portion of the pamphlet shows a stock of goods that was more or less typical of the St. Louis retail/wholesale establishments of the time. Reno Beauvais, Charles Altinger, Stephen C. Jett, T. J. Albright, H. E. Dimick & Co., Adolphus Meier & Co., and Child Pratte & Co., to name a few, all carried a similar stock of goods throughout the 1850's.

Some firms concentrated their efforts heavily in one area, hardware, firearms manufacture, or jewelry and watchmaking. However, the previously named firms and over a dozen additional firms offered similar types of goods from Europe, the East and of local manufacture, catering to local needs, and the wholesale trade throughout the upper Midwest, and at that time the biggest market of all, the Gold Rushes. Page 171 shows newspaper ads of H. E. Dimick and T. J. Albright and page 172 shows a newspaper ad by Child Pratt & Co. for comparison.

EDWARD MEAD'S ILLUSTRATED TREATISE ON THE RIFLE, SHOT-GUN AND PISTOL TOGETHER WITH EDWARD MEAD'S CATALOGUE was self published by Edward Mead in 1851. This reprint of the pamphlet has been made from the only known extant copy. It is uncertain how the original edition was bound, as the only known copy was rebound together with 6 other pamphlets for a private library, marked on the spine "Odds and Ends", which was later donated to the Missouri Historical Society.

Henry W. Williams (1816-1892), a lawyer, reached St. Louis in 1844 and lived there the remainder of his life. His boyhood hobby was collecting books, a hobby he kept his entire life. The unique copy of Mead's Treatise is only one of the extemely rare or unique items contained in his library of about 4500 books, pamphlets, manuscripts and periodicals.

August Gehner (1846-1910), a member of The Missouri Historical Society and local civic leader, acquired Williams' library shortly before Williams' death. Had he not had the foresight to acquire and preserve the library, it probably would have been broken up on Williams' death.

Gehner's daughter, Mrs. Frank Mesker, took the responsibility of the library upon her fathers death. In 1952 the library was donated to the Missouri Historical Society, by Mr. and Mrs. Frank Mesker and their sons Francis A., and John B. G. Mesker, as The Gehner-Mesker Library of Rare Americana.

Mead's Treatise

EDWARD MEAD'S

ILLUSTRATED TREATISE

ON THE

RIFLE, SHOT-GUN AND PISTOL.

ALSO;

THE MATERIALS BEST SUITED FOR THE CONSTRUCTION OF EACH, THE MAKING OF STUB-TWIST, WIRE-TWIST, AND DAMASCUS BARRELS, POWDER, BALLS, &C.

TOGETHER WITH

EDWARD MEAD'S CATALOGUE,

OF

Guns, Watches, Silver-ware, Jewelry, Fancy Goods, &c.

AT

54 MAIN, CORNER PIM-STREET, ST. LOUIS, MO.

PUBLISHED BY
E. MEAD, AT HIS GUN EMPORIUM, ST. LOUIS, MO.

1851.

THE GUN.

THE GUN, considered in all varieties and properties, is among the most remarkable intruments in use. Of the word *GUN* there seems to be no satisfactory etymology. The instrument now called a gun, used for war or sport, has, in the progress of time and the change it has undergone, received various names. We find it called *matchlock, hand-gun, musket, firelock, carabine,* &c. Fire-arms, under one or other of these names, were first introduced in England about the year 1470. In the time of Henry VIII. and his successor Elizabeth, the size and shape of fire-arms were regulated by act of Parliament. Specimens of these guns are now to be seen in the cabinets of the curious, and in the British armories. On a comparison of these ancient arms with those of the present day we are forced to the conclusion that few practical arts have made more rapid advancement than that of gun-making. Competition among gun-makers has been very great, and they have arrived at a degree of perfection which it is almost impossible to surpass.

THE RIFLE.

Of the great variety of small arms in use none, either for accuracy of aim, length of range, or fatal result, can, in any way, compare with the rifle. It may be so perfectly constructed that, with uniformity of temperature, equality in the force of powder, and constancy in the refraction of light, distance on a horizontal plane may be measured by the deflection of the ball with as much accuracy as with a surveyor's chain. The principles on which rifles should be constructed seem to have been well understood by ROBINS, the effect of whose careful experiments, under the liberal patronage of the British government, has been to greatly advance the science of gunnery and projectiles.

The rifle is the most effective of all the small arms used in warfare; its very name is a charm to the soldier who bears it, and terror to the foe—and is destined, judging from its effect on our recent wars, to revolutionize the whole system of warfare.*

---

*At the famous"Battle of Prague," the infantry shared the principal part of the contest. After the battle was over, and the killed and wounded were known, it was ascertained that six millions of musket balls had been fired, and that only *one in six hundred took effect*!! Let this be contrasted with the battle of New Orleans, and that of San Jacinto!.

The great superiority of the rifle over all other fire-arms for most kinds of large game is too well known to require more than a passing notice. Indeed some are so expert with it that for smaller game, such as turkeys, geese, squirrels, and the like, it is used in place of the shot-gun, especially when the shot is a long one. With some the use of the rifle seems a matter of pride, as it evidently requires more skill in a marksman to accomplish the same results with the rifle than with the shot-gun.

With careful training and practice most persons may become skillful marksmen. That no great degree of strength is required is evident from the fact, that we frequently meet with boys from ten to twelve years of age who in this particular may be considered worthy descendents of father BOON.

The principle upon which the rifle is constructed, and in which only it differs from the musket and all smooth-bore fire-arms, is the giving the bullet a rotary or spinning motion round its axis, and keeping that axis, as near as possible coincident with its line of flight or progressive motion, thus enabling the ball to overcome any undue deflection by presenting its irregularities of weight and form, in circular succession, to the friction of the atmosphere during the whole course of its flight.

This is accomplished by cutting grooves or creases in a spiral form along the internal surface of the barrel, through its entire length. The bullet, including the patch used in loading, is somewhat larger than the bore, and fills up the grooves, giving it a rotary motion in its passage through the barrel, the same as the threads on a screw-bolt give a rotary motion to a nut.

A bullet thus projected becomes possessed of two motions—a progressive or forward motion, from the explosion of the powder, and a rotary or spinning motion, caused by the grooves inside the barrel. It is this double motion of the ball which gives the rifle its great superiority over all smooth-bore guns, and but for the effect of gravitation and the atmosphere the track of a ball thus projected would be in a straight line to the mark.

There is a great difference of opinion among those who use, as well as those who make rifles, about the number of rifles necessary for the best instruments. The English and American Rifles also differ materially in their construction; the English being usually made with a large bore, barrels thin and light, unless designed for the American market. Those made in our country are quite the reverse, and this causes, doubtless, the acknowledged superiority of the American Rifle over all others, especially for long shots. Perhaps the great difference in the geographical dimensions of the two countries tended to produce this result, for it would seem hardly possible that the man who had travelled over our widely-extended country and contemplated its magnitude, could measure size and distance by the same guage that he would whose wanderings and views were limited to the British Isle.

In England many of the rifles are made with only two grooves; and in order that the ball should possess the rotary motion it was found necessary to have it cast with projections on the sides, made to fit the grooves; but this plan is not approved of in this country.

From all that we can gather on the subject it is evident that six or seven rifles are the numbers most approved, and that the twist should be one turn in from six to seven feet.

Some years since Edwin Wesson introduced in his improved American Rifle, the increasing or gaining twist, which commences at the breech at about one turn in six feet, and terminates at the muzzle of a 32-inch barrel at the rate of one turn in 3 feet 6 inches. It is obvious that the proper degree of twist is an important point. If too little it will not spin the ball sufficiently quick to make its course certain throughout the entire range; if too much it will increase the friction in the barrel and in the course of its flight, by presenting its surface in too quick succession to the action of the atmosphere. If a ball is started from a state of rest, with a velocity of 4,000 feet per second, its tendency will be to move along the bore in a straight line. If, therefore, the twist at the breech is too quick, it will give to the rifle itself a kind of rotary motion in the direction of the creases, the force of which will depend upon the degree or angle of the twist and the weight of the ball.

Another effect of a too rapid twist at the breech is to cause the ball to break loose altogether from the grooves, the edges of which cut it away to such an extent that it passes over the lands and out at the muzzle the same as it would from a smooth-bore. It was thought that both of these evils would be avoided by the use of the *gaining-twist,* which, while it reduces the angle of the twist at the breech, gives the ball at the time it leaves the muzzle a sufficient rotary motion to insure its steady flight. The gaining-twist is not often found except in fine and costly rifles made for prize and target shooting.

After all, it is still an open question with both rifle-makers and marksmen whether the *gaining-twist* is an improvement on the *regular twist* or not.

MATERIALS FOR THE CONSTRUCTION OF RIFLES.

Of all known metals iron is the most remarkable and useful. Its great strength, malleable and ductile qualities render it invaluable for an endless variety of purposes, not the least of which is its extensive use in the manufacture of guns.

Most rifles are made of wrought iron; but some of the finer and more costly are made of cast-steel, which has some qualities for the purpose superior to iron. It has a finer texture, is more homogeneous throughout, and a rifle made of cast-steel can be used longer than one made of iron, without being re-rifled.

Still, the advantage is small; the quality of the looks, the correct adjustment of the sight, and the general make and finish of the gun is more consequence than that it should be made of cast-steel instead of good wrought iron.

SIGHTS.

It would be useless to notice in detail the different kinds of sights in use, from the fact that almost every one accustomed to the use of the rifle has his own fixed notions on the subject. The kind of sight a man is accustomed to use is doubtless the best for his purpose. Rifles are made with the *telescope, globe, bead, spring* and the plain *crotchet* sight. The latter, for all kinds of game, is most approved, and in common use. The other kinds, all subject to a change of elevation, are used for target and prize shooting, where the range is a long one and the elevation of the sight is adjusted to suit distances, &c. which will be more fully explained in our chapter on "Rifle Practice."

BALLS AND SHOT.

The round ball is the one in more general use; until the last five years no other kind or shape was thought of. Some twelve or fifteen years ago the *zone* or *belted* balls were introduced by Mr. Moore, a rifle-maker of London and are now used in the British service. These no doubt possess some superiority over the round balls.

The invention of the flat-ended picket by Mr. Alvan Clark, of Boston, and designed to be used with his patent loading-muzzle rifle, far exceeds any other kind of ball in use, especially for target-shooting. Mr. Wesson, the celebrated rifle maker, monopolized for some time the right to use Mr. Clark's patent for loading, and they have never been used except on fine and costly rifles.

This ball allows a greater charge of powder, producing a quicker flight, so that with its pointed shape, its increase of weight, and more rapid flight, it is certain to penetrate any substance it may come in contact with much farther than balls of any other shape.

T.O. Leroy & Co's "Compressed Balls and Buckshot," designed as they are for every species of rifle, is a more valuable invention than that of Mr. Clark, which can only be used to advantage with his patent loading-muzzle.

The balls made by Leroy & Co. are not molded, but made from cold lead by machinery, by which they are greatly compressed, made equal in density throughout, and heavier than the molded ones of the same size.

This is an important feature—the specific gravity of the ball having much to do with its force and execution.

THE PATCH AND ITS USE.

This is another distinctive feature in the rifle, and though not used in loading any other kind of gun it is an essential requisite with it. Powder with those who are well acquainted with the rifle would almost as soon be dispensed with as the patch.

The patch in a measure fills up the grooves so that the bullet is not as deeply creased by the lands as it would otherwise be; and yet the rotary motion of the ball is equally certain and its flight more steady than it would be if deeply creased. In loading, the patch carries with it most of the loose grains of powder that adhere to the barrel—especially after it has been used a number of times—thus equalizing the charges by having it all carried down in one body, and placed where it should be, below the ball instead of being scattered, as it would be without the patch, throughout the entire length of the gun. It is also useful in keeping the gun clean, being an excellent wiper in its passage in and out.

RIFLE PRACTICE.

Having briefly noticed the peculiarities of the rifle, we will devote some space to the Rifle-practice, showing its superiority over all other small arms, and illustrating with plates its great capability.

We have examined the experiments of different individuals, and find the result in each case about the same, but prefer that made by Professor Bosworth, which we give somewhat abridged.

RANGE NO.1 FIG 1—SEE PLATE.
[p. 155 here, p. 12 in original]

"The target in this range is distant four hundred yards, and the figure is designed to show the deflection, or fall of the ball, from the line of fire, or first direction.

"In this figure I design the line of sight and the line of fire to be parallel—that is, the sights on the barrel are both to be equidistant from, and parallel to, the bore of the gun. These two lines, on a scale so small as the one represented, run into each other, and consequently they may be considered jointly to form a single line, or the upper line of the figure. The lower line, which is a curved line, exhibits the deflection, or track of the ball in its passage to the target; and the *time* of its passage is here calculated to be one second. Now, as by the law governing falling bodies, a ball from a state of rest will fall sixteen feet in a second of time—if we divide a second into four equal parts, or quarter of seconds, a ball will be found to have fallen through one foot in the first quarter, three feet in the second quarter, five feet in the third, and seven feet in the fourth; making in the four quarters, sixteen feet.

"By inspecting the figure, it will be seen that the range is divided into four equal parts, of one hundred yards each. By following out the lower line, (the track of the ball) it will be found to be distant from the other, at the four divisions, in the proportion of 1, 4,9,16. At the first hundred yards the ball has fallen one foot, at the second hundred yards the ball has fallen three feet more, which added to the previous one makes four. In the next hundred it has fallen five feet, which added to four make nine. In the fourth hundred it has fallen seven feet, added to nine make sixteen.

"Upon all balls projected horizontally terrestrial gravity acts with its full force, the same as when the ball falls from a state of rest; the projectile force having no influence whatever upon it.

"This figure demonstrates the fact that a ball fired in a horizontal direction does not continue in that direction through its course, but begins to fall immediatly as it leaves the gun, by the gravitating influence. There is no part of Rifle-practice that should be more fully impressed on the mind than this. I am aware that those already in the practice may think it unneccessary that I should dwell so particularly upon this; but in so doing I am thinking of the young, the uninitiated in science; and that this is not only a point in his progress essential for him to know at the start, but it leads him to think, and to inquire into the causes that produce effect. He asks, What is gravitation? What is projectile

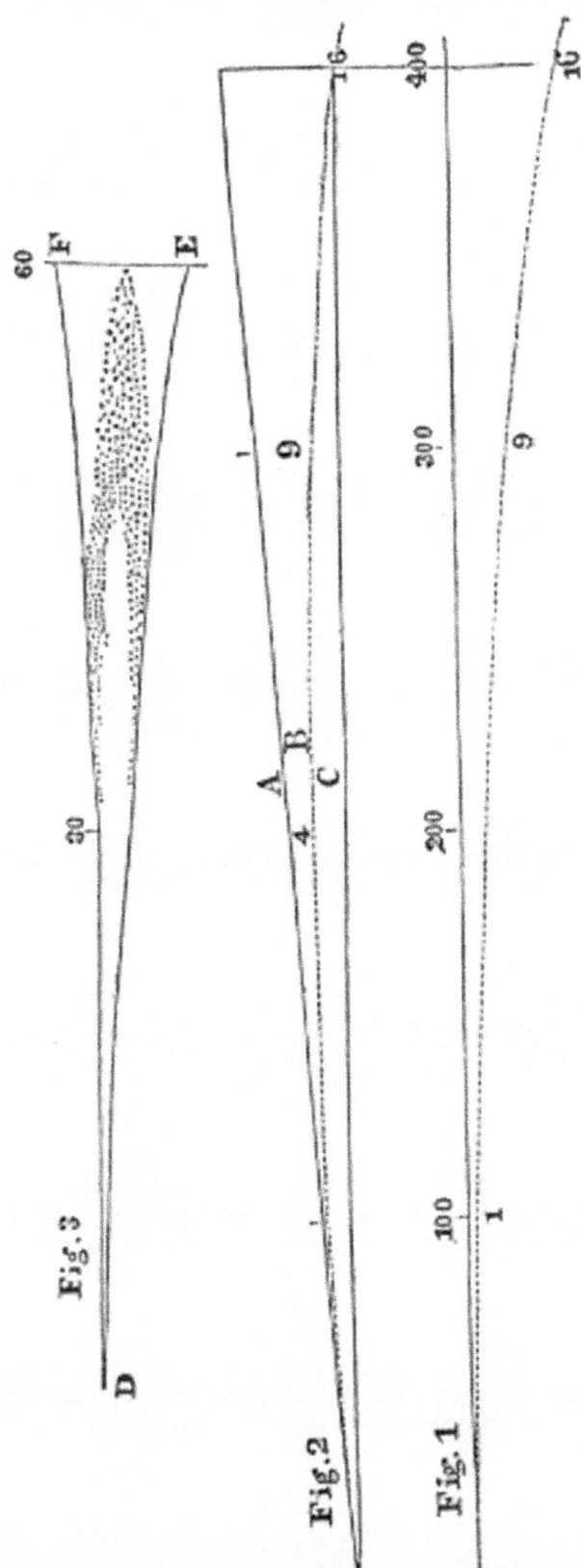

force? and is led on to discover and to learn.

"I have known persons, unacquainted with science, that supposed a ball continued straight onward in the direction of the gun; and some have supposed more than this—even that the ball may rise above its first direction, and overshoot the object aimed at; and they ascribe such an effect to the peculiar 'smartness' or excellence of the gun.

"This is altogether a deception; for if a rifle that 'carries high' be examined, and the top of each sight measured from the center of the bore, the back sight will be found to be considerably the highest, and, as a consquence, the line of fire will be directed above the line of sight. Now, as the line of sight in practice is invariably directed to the object, for all 'point-blank'* distance, long or short, if the line of sight form too great an angle with the line of fire, for any specified distance, the ball must invariably strike above the point aimed at by the line of sight. All other things being right, a gun will carry high or low, within point-blank distance, according as the angle of those lines may be greater or less. To sight a rifle properly, the back sights should be so constructed as to be movable in very small degrees, that an accurate adjustment may be made between the line of sight and the line of fire, so that a point-blank may be formed at any required distance. For this purpose, a spring sight, with a screw to adjust, is considered the best. With such a movable sight. and charger marked in degrees, with powder of uniform strength, a point-blank can be formed at will, at any distance within the range of the piece, which without such means of adjustment would require much time and practice.

"For distances within one hundred yards the line of sight forms but at a very slight angle to the line of fire. Beyond that distance the angle increases in a greater ratio; so that to form a point-blank at four hundred yards the back sight must be raised considerably, that the ball may intersect the line of sight and form a point-blank at that distance. This angle of elevation, in all cases, is subject of calculation, according to the distance between the two sights. To facilitate this, all rifles should have the sights at even number of inches asunder, and not put on carelessly to measure inches and parts, as accident might leave them. Although anything,

---

*Point-Blank (Point-blanc, Fr. from 'white, and point,) means the white spot in the center of a target] In a larger sense, it means the point of intersection of the line of sight with the track of the ball, at the termination of its range. The point-blank, therefore, may be at any distance where such an intersection may take place.

by calculation, may be arrived at, it is far better for all practical purposes to adopt the simple instead of the complex, and whole numbers instead of fractions, whenever the subject will admit of it. The distance, therefore, between the sights, should be in whole numbers of even inches, to facilitate calculation to form the distance of the point-blank.

"I will take occasion here to observe, in regard to the force of the charge and velocity of the ball, that they are points in practice that are not to be carelessly passed over; that although a very small charge may suffice to bring down a squirrel from a tree, yet, when we practice in prize-shooting, where philosophical accuracy is to be attained, even for the shortest distance, the charge must be such that we may *feel* that it has a certain degree of smartness; otherwise a slight difference in the quantity of the charge intended, or a difference in the friction of the patch may disappoint our expectations and disgrace the shot. Hence those in high practice have generally made it a rule, that when they have fixed on the quantity of powder for one hundred yards, they never diminish the charge for any shorter distance, depending entirely upon the adjustment of the sight for any shorter range. They are thus always sure of a quick fire, and, from the simplicity of adjusting from one source instead of two, a high degree of accuracy is attainable.

"Having explained Fig. 1, which is intended to show that a ball projected horizontally can never rise above the line of its first direction, nor keep that direction for a single yard under the influence of gravity, we will next turn to Fig. 2, which exhibits the lines of sight, of fire, and track of the ball, as they exist in perfect practice.

RIFLE PRACTICE CONTINUED—FIG 2.
[p. 155 here, p. 12 in original]

"This figure differs from the first in having a point-blank in the target, which the first had not—that being drawn for the only purpose of showing the fall of the ball from the line of its first direction. The lines of sight and fire were then made parallel to each other, while those same lines in Fig. 2 are drawn at such an angle that the line of sight is made to intersect that track of the ball exactly in the target, and to form a point-blank at the precise extremity of the range.

"In this figure the eye and the target are supposed to be on the same level. The upper line A is the line of fire, or range of the piece. The next line below, the curved dotted line B, is the track of the ball. The third and lowest line G, (C), is the line of sight: this range in point of distance is the same as the first—four hundred yards.

"The velocity of the ball, and its consequent fall, is supposed to be the same. It differs, however, inasmuch as the first diagram was designed to exhibit a theoretical fact in the science—while the latter illustrates the actual practice in the art of target-shooting. In all cases in practice with a gun properly sighted, the line of sight is directed to the object; and when the line of sight to that of fire is adjusted to suit charge and distance, as can be easily done with a spring sight and adjusting the screw, the ball can be made to intersect the line of sight in the target at any reasonable distance within the range of the piece. There is a limit, however, to a point-blank range by the means of the spring sight; for if it be capable of considerable elevation, the adjusting the screw would come in the way of the sight in extreme low angles for short distance. A spring sight, however, may be considered good for a range of four hundred yards.

"For five or six hundred yards, a couple of lifts may be attached to the upper part of the spring, to suit those distances that would be entirely out of the way. These are extreme ranges that seldom occur in practice, but as they are within the effective reach of all good rifles, as has been shown by the best authority, it is proper that the soldier should know, and practice occasionally point-blank shooting to the extent of these ranges.*

"By inspecting these two ranges the track of the ball will be found to be equidistant from the line of fire in both. The upper line in each is the line of fire, and direction of the piece. With a pair of dividers measure the distance of the dotted line, or track of the ball, from the upper line at one, two, three, or four hundred yards, and the distance in each figure will be found to be the same. The only real difference between the two figures being the adjustment of the line of sight to agree with the fall of the ball, so that the point-blank could be formed in the target. To do this, it is evident that the back sight on the rifle must be considerably elevated; that is, the difference of the measure from the top of the two sights to the centre of the bore must be considerable. If we suppose the sights on the gun to be two feet apart— which is rather more than the usual distance—the back sight will require to be *plus* three-tenths of an inch further from the bore than the front sight—very nearly three and a half-tenths of an inch.

---

*When General Gaines was intrenched against the Seminole Indians in Florida, he stated in his report to the War Department that his sentinels on duty were wounded and killed by single shots from the Seminole Rifle at the distance of four and five hundred yards!

"Now take another view of this of this second figure and observe that throughout the range the ball is above the line of sight—it having touched that line only at the start and at the termination of the range. At all intermediate distances the ball being above the line of sight, so that if a gun sighted for this range were to be used at any intermediate distance without changing the sight it must be perfectly plain that the ball would strike above the object aimed at, according to the distance of the target. By inspecting the plate it appears that the greatest elevation of the ball above the line of sight is at the distance of about one hundred and seventy yards; at which place the ball has ranged about four feet above the line, or mark, provided the target had been placed at the distance of one hundred and seventy-five yards.

"This gives a clear illustration of the fact that no single elevation of sight can suit more than one distance for perfect practice; and that, for philosophical accuracy, every rifle should be provided with the means of graduating the sight to the smallest degree. This comes of necessity, on account of the rapid ratio of increase in the fall of heavy bodies, which for equal times is in the ratio of 1, 4, 9, 16, and so on. If the fall of heavy bodies were equal in equal times, then one angle of elevation would suit any distance; but that not being the case, it is easy to discover that the elevation must correspond to the laws of falling bodies; and that to be correct it must follow the same ratio of 1, 4, 9, 16, &c. for all distances within the range of the piece. At any distance there must be some angle between the line of sight and fire; even at the short distance of ten steps some slight elevation must be had, or the ball will fall below the center of aim; though for all distances up to a hundred yards this angle is but small, as the ball falls very little in the first part of its range. All the American Rifles made at our public armories, at least all that I have seen, are made with *fixed* sights, incapable of elevation.

"As I have been particularly careful in the description of the ranges, Figs 1 and 2, they may be considered as containing all the abstract theory for plain rifle-practice, to the extent of the greatest range in the capacity of the gun."

Frequent experiments have been made to test the comparative merits of the rifle and the musket, and the result has usually been that at a distance of one hundred yards the musket was forty to one hundred of the rifle; while at a longer distance the experiment was useless, for beyond that point the shots with the muskets were so uncertain that they might be called random shots; while the rifle, as has been shown by oft-repeated experiments, is certain at a distance of three or four hundred yards. Not that the musket-ball loses all its force at the distance of one hundred yards, but the course of a ball projected from a smooth-bore is, from the nature of the case, uncertain, and not to be depended on, even at that short distance.

Professor Bosworth thus felicitously states an interesting incident in support of his high estimate of his great favorite, the rifle:—

"When a resident of Charleston, having an invitation to visit Pineville, to spend a week at music and the chase, I took with me a rifle of forty to the pound barrel 26 inches long, whole weight of the gun six and a half pounds. Early in the morning, after my arrival, while discoursing upon the beauty of the village, observing several hawks at a distance, in an 'old field,' said I, 'Those are very large hawks, or are they eagles?' 'They are hawks,' replied my friend, 'of the largest species, and we are greatly annoyed by them, as they live on our poultry. They are very sagacious,' he continued; 'they have measured the distance of our rifles, and sit and look at us at the distance you see them, with the most perfect nonchalance.' 'They are not so very far,' said I 'that one nearest, is about three hundred yards.' 'Yes,' said he, 'just about three hundred yards: but that is entirely out of rifle-range.' 'I think I can take that hawk from this piazza,' said I. My friend smiled, doubtingly. I charged and made a point-blank for three hundred yards. The air was clear and calm—the bird fell. 'I am astonished,' said the gentleman; 'it must be an accidental shot—it is entirely out of rifle-distance.' 'It may be accidental,' said I, jocosely, 'but there is another, sitting at the other end of the field, that appears to be a fellow to the one that is down, and distant but a few yards further; perhaps if I take that it might not be esteemed accidental.' 'Certainly not, but there is no rifle in the world which can reach that distance.'

"I charged again, and made a point-blank for three hundred and forty yards. Fortune smiled on the effort, and I took a second bird.

" 'My God!' exclaimed the gentleman, with some degree of ecstacy, 'if you can do so with that little pistol of a gun what ought I be able to do with my splendid rifle?' He then presented one of the highest-finished rifles I ever beheld, of forty inches length. 'You can do,' said I, 'whatever you *will* with that rifle. Much more depends upon *moral decision* than physical force in rifle-shooting.' 'You must show me how,' said he.

"In the course of the day we removed a fixed sight upon the barrel, replacing it with a spring and a screw, by which a point-blank could be formed at all intermediate distances up to four hundred yards. The whole neighborhood become stimulated for rifle-shooting, and before I left I had made many a respectable competitor at the distance of three hundred yards.

"My friend wrote me in Charleston, saying:— The hawks have taken your visit here in high dudgeon, and seldom make their appearance. Indeed, we have so thinned the number that there are few left to annoy us. My country neighbors won't believe anything of such shooting until I show them; and then they appear much astonished.'

"Here was a casualty that twice produced great moral decision, which resulted in the highest success."

THE SHOT-GUN OR FOWLING-PIECE.

The shot-gun presents to us the greatest variety of character—some of which are very mysterious—and experiments without number have been made to ascertain the cause of the great difference in the shooting of guns which, to all appearance, are precisely alike—some shooting strong others weak, with the same charge. Some will throw the shot wide, while others will throw them near; yet even on a close examination they will appear the same *size, weight, finish,* and the quality of the materials used in their construction.

It has often been said by the best gun-makers that "two guns cannot be made, even by the same workman, from the same bar of iron, that shall with *cetainty* possess the same shooting qualities;" and such indeed is an undeniable fact. It is a rare thing that double-barrels, even of high finish, are found to be equal in their shooting properties—sometimes the right and sometimes the left proving to be the better barrel.

This very extraordinary fact pertaining to the construction of shot-guns has become a sort of standing "mystery."

That a good artist can produce two barrels *exactly alike,* so far the workmanship is concerned, no one will deny. We have then but *one thing* left for our investigation, which is, the *substance* of which the barrel is made.

Two barrels made from the same bar of iron are not certain to possess the same shooting qualities, because no bar of wrought-iron has been made entirely homogeneous throughout, and of the same quality in all its parts. Iron was accidently introduced at a very early period, but the ancients possessed but little knowledge of its great usefulness, and it is not until within a few years that it has been well understood. We are much indebted to Germany for chemical information upon this subject; and we feel pleasure in giving a few extracts from the work of Doctor Schafhault, of Munich, who informs us—

First.—"That pure iron cannot be welded—that the welding power of iron depends entirely upon its alloy with the carburet of silicon."

Second.—"It is extremely difficult to produce even a speciman of pure iron unalloyed with foreign substance, and that the purest wrought iron of commerce always contains nearly a half per cent. of carbon."

Third.—He states that "most of the electro-negative metals have an affinity for iron, and enter into its composition, if in contact at the time of its manufacture; that these electro-metals [metaloids, N. B.] are, aluminum, silicon, calcium, potassium, sodium, and some others; that they may exist in the ores, some of them, and others may be added in the form of flux, in the manufacture." To these he mentions other substances, as carbon, azote, and hydrogen.

Fourth.—"That it is extremely difficult to unite silicon alone with iron, without the presence of carbon, aluminum, or other similar bodies."

Fifth.—He ascertained "that carbon, hydrogen and azote, are always present in the remainders of cast-iron; and that azote is a constituent of steel, as also of wrought-iron."

These few extracts from the pen of a scientific writer contain volumes of chemical information, and prove that the iron is use consists of a complicated alloy, which are either mechanically mixed or chemically combined, and the degree of combination being always accidental, has made an almost infinite variety in quality.

Should we wonder, then, that we cannot find two specimens of iron alike, or that the same rod, if of considerable length, should not be alike throughout.

Since these discoveries have been made the gun-makers in England of the higher order have adopted various means to procure iron of greater purity; and for guns of the highest quality it is not unusual for them to work the iron over some fifteen or twenty times, until *ninety per cent of the iron has disappeared,* for the sole purpose of working out the slag and earthly mixtures with which the iron was contaminated in its manufacture.

Within a few years valuable experiments have been made to ascertain the force of the guns made from different qualities or iron. One of the facts arrived at is extremely interesting : it is the discovery that in guns of the same form and workmanship the *difference of force* arises *solely from the mixture of foreign substances in the iron,* and that the different degrees of force are in exact accordance with the mixture.

There seems to be an opinion that the particles or atoms of a gun-barrel are somehow made to vibrate and re-act simultaneously with the charge; that pure metal, without any earthly mixture, constitutes, as it were, a fulcrum of great solidity, which produces this simultaneous vibration that reacts with great effect; that any kind of earthly mixture in the iron would break this continuous solidity, and render the barrel weak in its re-action, by the great number and variety of fulcra which barrel would assume wherever the intervening mixture should break the continuity of the metalic fibers.

This opinion is entertained both in England and in our own country, and seems to be supported by the interesting fact that the force of a gun is as its freedom from earthly mixtures.

This great variation in the quality of iron has clearly caused the long-standing mystery in the unequal shooting of guns, designed by the best makers to be the same. We will now examine more minutely the different kinds of iron used in the making of shot-guns, believing that a description of the process will be both new and interesting to some of our readers.

We have, with much care, gathered it from works published under supervision of some of the best London gun-makers; and will notice, first: *Stub-twist,* of which a much greater quantity is made than of any other kind. We give it in a condensed form, retaining all that is essential to full understanding of the subject.

STUB-TWIST IRON

As we have shown, it has long since been known that the texture of iron was full of veins and fibers, it was, also, discovered that it was much stronger *in the direction of the fibers than across them.* This gave rise in England to the twisting of barrels, so as to make the fibers *encircle the bore,* thereby giving greater *strength to the gun.*

Old horse-nail stubs have, for a great number of years, been considered the best kind of scraps for the purpose of making the best gun-barrels. Numerous attempts have been made to find a composition of scraps to equal it, but as yet without success. When the practice of using old stubs was adopted we have no certain date. From the appearance of the oldest barrels, we should venture to say that it was coeval with their invention.

Before proceeding to manufacture them into iron, women are employed to sort and examine each stub, to see that no malleable cast iron nails, or other impurities, are mixed with them. They are then taken and put into a drum resembling a barrel-churn, through the centre of which passes a shaft that is attatched to the steam-engine which works rolling-mill, bellows, &c. When the machine is set agoing, the stubs are rolled and tumbled over each other to such a degree that the friction completely cleanses them of all rust, and they come forth with the brightness of silver. The steel with which they are mixed (being generally coach-springs) after being separated and softened is clipped into small pieces, corresponding in size to the stubs, by a pair of large shears, worked by steam. These pieces are then, like the stubs, put into the drum, in order to be divested of any rust they may retain, and are subquently weighted out in the proportion of 25 lbs. of stubs to 15 of steel, in quantities of 42 lbs. After being properly mixed together, they are put into an air furnace and heated to a state of fusion, in which state they are stirred up by a bar of the same mixture of iron and steel, until by their adhesion they form a ball of apparently melting metal. During this process the bar has become sufficiently heated to attach itself to the burning mass, technically called a bloom of iron, and by its aid the whole is removed from the furnace to the forge hammer, by which it is reduced down to a bar of iron, now about 40 lbs.— the weight lost being wasted in the process of welding and hammering. From the forge it passes to the rolling-mill, where it is reduced to the size wanted. By this mode of manufacturing the iron and steel are so intimately united and blended that the peculiar properties of each are imparted to every portion of the mass, and the whole receives the degree of hardness and softness required. The process is admirable, and the mixture is calculated to produce a metal the best fitted under the circumstances to answer the purpose of manufacturing gun-barrels of the best description.

The principal superiority of this iron is owing to the steel and iron, when welded into a barrel, being reduced by the action of the hammer and rolling-mill into threads of so minute and fine texture, and so enlongated, that we can compare a bar of this mixture to nothing better than the strands of hemp rope; there being only this difference, the parts of one are separate, those of the other are, as it were, glued into one, though yet a multitude of distinct layers, varying in size, may be observed throughout.

WIRE-TWIST AND DAMASCUS IRON.

Damascus being a variety of mixture, made from the composition named wire-twist iron, we shall describe them both in this chapter. The mode of making the bar of wire-twist is this:—Alternate bars of iron and steel are placed on each other in numbers of six each; they are then forged into one body or bar; after which, if for the making of wire-twist barrels, they are rolled down into rods of 3-8ths of an inch in breadth, and varying in thickness according to the size of the barrel for which they are wanted; if for Damascus, invariably 3-8ths of an inch square. When about twisted into spirals for barrels care must be taken that the edges of the steel and iron shall be outermost, so that when the barrel is finished and browned it shall have the appearance of being welded of pieces the size of wires, the whole length of the barrel.

When about to be converted into Damascus, the rod is heated the whole length, and the two square ends out into heads (one of which is a fixture) of a description of lathe, which is worked by a handle similar to a winch. It is then twisted like a rope or wrung as wet clothes are, until it has from twelve to fourteen complete turns in the inch. By this severe twisting the rod of six feet is shorted to three, doubled in thickness, and made perfectly round. Three of these rods are then placed together, with the inclinations of the twists running in opposite directions. They are then welded into one, and rolled down to a rod eleven-sixteeths of an inch in breadth.

Such, then, is the *modus operandi* of preparing the three kinds of iron most used in the manufacture of guns; and to those not familiar with the working of iron it will seem a complicated and tedious process; some will be inclined to wonder how guns can be sold so cheap when the making of the barrels only is attended with so much trouble; and we must look at the extent of the manufactories, with the aid of machinery, before we can reconcile it with reason; remembering that those engaged in it have been from childhood learning to accomplish the work both well and rapidly, until the great competition in the trade acts as a constant stimulus. Still great care should be used in the selection of a gun, especially of a low price; for the quality of a gun, like all manufactured articles, is in a great measure regulated by its cost; and though it may sometimes happen that a low-priced gun will be found to possess good qualities, and shoot as well as the more costly ones, they are not as *certain* to do this, nor are they usually considered as safe.

The great difference of opinion that exists in the minds of those who have had good opportunities of judging of the relative merits of the three kinds of iron we have described is very natural—because, one man has a very superior and favorite gun of Damascus, another of wire-twist, and a third of stub-twist, and each forms his opinion from the good qualities and peculiarities of his faithful instrument. But we find an equal diversity of opinion among the makers—those who have had every opportunity of seeing the barrels in their different stages, and whose opinions would not be formed on the merits of a single gun, or a number of guns *made from the same kind of iron.* They will point out some fancied superiority of one kind over another, and support their views with arguments. The majority, however, seem to prefer stub-twist, which evidently possesses some qualities superior to the others—one of which is greater strength; while the Damascus it is believed will shoot stronger, and some of these are very beautiful. Being desirous of understanding this subject fully, we have consulted different individuals, and examined the written opinions of many of the best English makers and sportsmen, and the conclusion is irresistible, that the three kinds of iron are equally good, or nearly so, for the purpose—and that the quality of the gun rest solely on the *time, care,* and *skill* employed in making it.

BARREL WELDING

We will briefly notice this stage in the manufacture of guns, which is both interesting and important, and one that requires the utmost skill. The slightest carelessness, even on the part of a skillful welder, would render his work unfit for use. This causes the selling of many barrels as wasters, the iron being full of flaws.

The welding process requires three men: the foreman of the fire, as he is termed—on whose skill all depends—and two subordinates, whose duty it is to blow the bellows, strike, &c.

The quantity of fuel required for welding barrels is very great; the forge of a common smith gives but a faint idea of it. When they have received sufficient orders to employ them the whole day the fire is kindled, and they proceed to weld a dozen or more common guns before the fire and all appliances are in proper condition for welding the finer qualities of barrels, such as the Damascus, wire and stub-twist; all of which are welded in the same manner. These are twisted by the means of two iron bars—one fixed, the other loose. In the latter, there is a notch to receive one end of the rod. When inserted, this rod is turned by a handle; the fixed bar prevents the rod from moving—it is twisted round the other like the wrapping of a whip-handle. The loose bar is then removed, the spiral knocked off and the same process recommenced on another rod. The length of the spirals depend entirely on the breadth of the rod :—for instance, the stub-twist having 16 circles in 6 inches, a rod of 5 feet will only make a spiral of 7 inches long, while iron of an inch in breadth will make a spiral of as many inches long as there are twists. This is the reason that the best barrels have more joints than common ones in the same length.

Having twisted as many as they want, those that are intended for the breech end are heated to a welding heat for about three inches, removed from the fire, and jumped close by striking the end against the anvil. Again they are heated, and again jumped, to insure the perfect welding. They are then beat lightly in a groove, to make them round. The neatest part of the process consists in the joining of the points of the two rods so as to make the barrel appear as if it had been twisted out of one rod. The ends of the two rods are a little detached, brought from the fire, and applied to each other. A gentle tap is then given, and the union is perfect in an instant. The rapid dexterity with which this is accomplished ought to be seen to be duly appreciated. This trouble is only taken with the best barrels.

Having joined the whole of the spiral, three inches are again heated to a welding heat, the mandril is introduced, and the tube hammered in a groove to the size required. This operation is repeated until the whole length is finished. This being done, then follows hammer-hardening; that is, beating the barrel in a groove in the cold state, with light hammers, for the space of half an hour. This is a most important part of the process. It closes the pores, condenses the texture of the metal, compresses a greater substance into the less bounds, increases greatly the strength of the barrel, and renders it more elastic.

The superiority of the genuine Damascus barrels and sword blades can be directly traced to this cause. The effect has been to greatly perplex many who believed the fine quality of the composition to be the secret.

We have been told of the great discoveries they have made of mixtures of platina, and silver, and copper, &c. They have vaunted of their boasted discoveries, and boldly asserted that the excellence of these blades depended on a peculiar mixture in the steel. As if to mock the profundity of their researches, it turns out that this composition consists of nothing more than the mechanical mixture of irons and steels, containing less and more carbon, which men are employed to temper by continually beating for weeks, and in some instances for months together. This long-continued hammering gives a temper which no other means can bestow.

It will be seen that the process of barrel-welding, like that of preparing the iron for the finer qualities of guns, requires both skill and experience, and a careful perusal of this article will convince all that the quality of the gun must depend principally upon the amount of labor bestowed upon it in its different stages.

We have noticed the preparations of iron and the welding of gun-barrels particularly, because the barrel is by far the most important part of the gun, and its quality regulates the finish of every other part. If it did not exceed our intended limits we would describe the manufacture of other parts—such as boring, grinding, and turning barrels, patent breeches, locks, stocking and screwing together, staining of barrels, &c.

THEORY AND PRACTICE OF SHOT-SHOOTING
FIGURE 3.—SEE PLATE
[p. 155 here, p. 12 in original]

The force, direction, and position of a charge of shot in its course to the target will next occupy our attention. As there seems to be no opinion more vague than that which is applied to the length of a gun, we will notice the first. Formerly it was supposed that the longer the gun the farther it would carry; reasoning like children, that "more will produce more," and the longer the gun the greater the effect.

The study of projectiles, which has occupied the attention of philosophers so long, is now so well understood that it may be said that there is a maximum length for every gun, according to the size and *the purpose for which it is intended;* and that if the gun be longer or shorter, the effect would be diminished. There is one important point in respect to this that is little understood—-*that there is no particular length for a gun that will suit all purposes.* Were a gun to be used on all occasions for one exact purpose, one length could be assigned that would suit better than any other. For bird-shooting, at short distances, with a light charge, the barrel should be short, and the powder of a quick-burning property; for a greater distance, and stronger shooting, with the same caliber, the gun must have more length, more charge, and powder of slower burning property. Should the shorter gun be used for a greater distance, and more charge, the force, though increased, would not equal the force of the longer gun, and the shot would not be kept in their former compass, but would cover a much larger space.

For all light shooting, thirty inches has been fixed upon as a very proper length for guns of small caliber; but for strong shooting with the same caliber, the gun should be increased in some cases to nearly four feet, in which case the barrel at the breech should be more strongly fortified, but the thickness from the middle to the muzzle should not be increased, as it is now universally agreed that that half of the barrel should be made as thin as consistent with due strength; it being an established fact that thin barrels, made strong at the barrels, throw shot much stronger and closer than thick barrels.

The operation in the discharge of a gun involves a mechanical principle, which has for its ultimatum pressure and time; hence, in a moderately long gun, the pressure is continued throught greater space, occupying more time; and according to the mode of estimating power, this increase of distance and time, added to an equal pressure, will produce a greater power than in the shorter gun, where the pressure was continued for a less time.

I will now describe a charge of shot in its passage from the gun to the target.

If a charge of shot be fired against a target of soft wood, the shot will be found to have struck the thickest about the centre, becoming more and more dispersed near the outside of the charge. It may also be noticed, that about the centre the shot will have penetrated to more than double the depth of those at the extreme outside.

The force of the shot being proportioned to their velocity, it is evident from the above facts that the shot do not make their exit simultaneously from the gun, but that the central part of the charge is driven onward faster than the rest, and that the collective force of a charge of shot is very unequal in itself.

As the powder and wad are driven through the charge of shot, either before or after their escape from the muzzle, it produces a whirling motion in each single shot, which will be at right angles to their course. The progressive side being next the center of the charge, will have a tendency to cause the shot to be deflected from their true course. FIG. 3, of the diagram, is illustrative of the case. The outer lines of this figure show the extent and breadth of the charge at all points between the gun and the target. The target is distant sixty yards. At half that distance, thirty yards, a screen received the charge in one-fourth of the compass. The hollow cone of the dotted lines in this figure exhibits the charge of shot as it actually exists in its passage—the central part having reached the target, while some of the outside shot have reached but half distance, but which will continue on following out the trumpet-formed track, and ultimately reaching the target.

Many attempts have been made to remedy this irregularity in shot-shooting; the best of which is, perhaps, "Eley's cartridge." This cartridge consists of an open net-work, enclosing the shot, which is made up in separate charges. This is constructed upon philosophical principles, as far as it goes; but we still need something better to insure success.

What we need to perfect the practice of shot-shooting is, first, to be able to cause the shot to make a simultaneous exit from the gun; second, to restrain the charge within proper bounds. This accomplished, there will be but little left undone.

These experiments made with small shot do not apply to buck-shot.

To load correctly with buck-shot they must be "chamber'd;" that is, the size is selected so that three or four (according to taste and circumstances) will exactly fill the caliber; then there is no central part of the charge to be driven faster than the rest. The tendency, however, of buck-shot to scatter is, perhaps, equal to that of the smaller sizes used in bird-shooting. This is caused in a great measure by the friction in their passage through the barrel, which makes them separate as they leave the muzzle, at which point each takes a course for itself, when they move onward as independent of each other as would the same number of balls projected at different times.

THE PISTOL.

The last species of fire-arms we design to notice is the *pistol*, which, though last in order and least in size, is by no means small in importance. The pistol is said to have taken its name from *Pistoia*, a city in Italy, where, as Fauchet tells us, it was first made. The Germans are said to have used them in France before the French, and the horsemen who received them in the time of Henry II. were called *Pistoliers*. The first pistols made and used in England were called *wheel-locks,* from the fact that they were discharged by means of a small steel wheel, in its revolutions, struck a flint and threw the fire into the priming-pan. Contrasting the wheel-lock of the olden time with the percussion, self-cocking, and self-revolving pistol of our day, we are led to conclude that the improvements in this minor branch of fire-arms have been fully equal to these of the gun and rifle. Pistols, as first invented, were, as may be supposed, defective in many particulars. They were clumsy—the barrels large and thin—the bore much too large for the weight of the barrels—the ball so heavy that the recoil was not only disagreeable and dangerous, but the direction of the ball itself very uncertain.

As soon as due attention was given to *proportion*, experience showed that small balls could be expelled with sufficient force to do great execution; they then lessened the size of the caliber, by which means the barrel was made thicker, which increased its steadiness and greatly lessened the recoil. It was a long time, however, before pistols were *rifled*—none believing that so short a barrel could turn the ball upon an axis in the line of fire. This prejudice had to yield; the pistol was rifled, and at once became an instrument of great perfection.

It was found on trial that a well-rifled pistol barrel of not more than four or six inches possessed the qualities peculiar to the rifle. This was highly gratifying to those engaged in its improvement; and were it practicable to obtain a perfect aim with so short an instrument they would be nearly equivalent to, and almost supplant the ordinary rifle. It was by a ten-inch rifled pistol, in the hands of Col. Johnson, that the famous Tecumseh fell. In a public speech delivered at Harrisburg, in 1841, a voice in the crowd was heard to say: "Tell us about the battle of the Thames, and how Tecumseh fell."

The Col. said, as he had been particularly requested he would state in a few words a part of the closing scene of that battle, and the fall of the warrior Tecumseh. "Towards the close of the battle," he said, "we were about to charge upon the enemy, who were not many yards distant. As we advanced." he continued, " I saw a group of some ten or a dozen Indians, as if in council. There was one among them much taller than the rest, who appeared to be a distinguished personage, to whom the others paid deference. From the description I had previously had of Tecumseh, and knowing that he headed his men to battle, and was in the thickest of the fight, I had no doubt but the person I had distinguished was Tecumseh himself. Making my way directly for the group, he leveled his rifle at me and fired. I received the ball in my left hand, which it shattered considerably, but my hand, with the bridle-reins enclosed, became a shield of protection to my body, to which I owe the preservation of my life, as the aim of the ball was central. Keeping my eye upon the same distinguished indivdual I drew a pistol, and with *perfect aim,* fired—and at the same instant saw the warrior fall. Soon after the battle it was rumored that Tecumseh had been killed. I went immediately," he continued, "to view the fallen warrior, and discovered him to be the same distinguished individual with whom I had, not long before, exchanged *effective shots*. My horse," he continued, "the noble animal that had borne me onward thus far, with pride, through the hottest of the fight" (here the colonel made a pause, somewhat affected,) "being perforated with more than twenty balls, survived but a few minutes longer."

No sooner were the merits of the pistol fully understood than they underwent as great and rapid a change in appearance as they had been improved in their shooting qualities. Most of the pistols of the present day are made for self-defence—being generally smaller and more portable than those formerly used—among the most prominent of which are Colt's repeating, Allen's revolving, and the genuine Deringer pistol, the reputation of which is too well established to require more than a passing notice.

GUNPOWDER

Is composed of saltpeter, brimstone and charcoal.

It is important that the ingredients are pure, correctly proportioned, and thoroughly mixed; but this alone will not produce the best article. It must also be well made; the quality depending equally on the time and labor expended in the manufacture as on the quality and correct proportion of the ingredients.

An erroneous opinion is very prevalent that the small grained powder is the best for all purposes; nor is it generally known that gunpowder is made intentionally of different sized grains, degrees of strength and ignition, suited to different puposes.

A grain of powder burns from the surface to the center; the very large grain is comparatively slow in the burning, while the very fine grained is quick—other circumstances being equal. In fact, it burns in point of time in proportion to the size of the grain.

As an ordinary charge will burn nearly in the same time with a single grain, it is evident that the force of a charge of fine grained powder will be more instant and stronger at the start than powder of a coarser grain. The effect of this is to produce an *instant sharp recoil* at the starting of the ball. This is an important consideration, especially with rifle shooting, which should be free from any recoil or jar tending to interfere with the steadiness of the aim. As a general rule in practice, the smaller the ball and the shorter the piece, the finer and quicker may be the powder; and as we increase the size of the ball and length of gun, so must the grain of the powder be enlarged, that it shall occupy time in its combustion to suit the distance allotted to its action.

In using the large-grained powder the force of the charge will remain the same, or perhaps will be rather increased, while the recoil will be diminished. Some have attempted to give one rule for general application in regulating the quantity of powder and proportion of lead to be used in the different kinds of fire-arms, but the almost endless variety of guns now in use precludes the practical application of such a rule, and each individual must fix for himself, by making experiments with his own gun, the size and proportion of the charge best suited to his purpose.

CLEANING, OILING, &c.

We would not presume to give directions for cleaning, oiling, &c. as every one accustomed to the use of gun must have learned this from experience; but as this may fall into the hands of the young and uninitiated we will notice some of the most important things to be observed.

Hot water should be used, making the operation as quick as possible. If the barrel has become *leaded*, and you have not the regular cleaning rod with scraper, scratch-brush, &c. it can be scoured with fine sand, or brick-dust, which should be used with water; this will effectually remove the lead. The effect of hot water is to warm the barrel, which greatly accelerates its being wiped dry, to prevent rust. It should be oiled inside and out after washing; if used soon , the inside oiling may be omitted. The best kind of oil for the purpose is the *pure sperm or bear's oil*. *Sweet oil* should never be used: it contains a vegetable acid that is sure to rust the gun, if allowed to remain for a length of time. When put away, the gun should never stand cocked—which, from its constant strain, tends to weaken the springs. If loaded, the cap should be taken off, and when replaced for use, a few grains of fresh powder should be put in the tube, that the charge may not fail to explode.

CATALOGUE

OF

GUNS, RIFLES, PISTOLS, &c.

Watches, Jewelry, Silver Ware,

CUTLERY, PLATED WARE,

BRITANNIA GOODS,

FANCY GOODS, &c.

FOR SALE BY

EDWARD MEAD,

54 MAIN, CORNER OF PINE, ST. LOUIS, MO.

My Stock is laid in with Cash; and European Goods I import direct; I get my domestic articles direct from the makers, and being satisfied with a small profit offer great inducements to my friends and the public, who are invited to call and examine for themselves.

PUBLISHED BY
E. MEAD, AT HIS GUN EMPORIUM,
ST. LOUIS, MO.

1851.

4*

The above appears as page 41 of the pamphlet. The catalogue portion is on p. 43 to p. 58 (pages 43-46 and p. 58 are reproduced on the following pages, size enlarged for easier reading)

OUR GUN DEPARTMENT.

Under this head we include Shot-Guns, Rifles and Pistols, with all the accompaniments.

We have dealt, to some extent, in Guns for a number of years, and a close attention to this branch of our trade has convinced us that the assortment in our market has never been equal to the demand, and that the *locality* of our city—being in a game country, the inhabitants fond of hunting—with its wide-spread and increasing trade, makes it *the* point for the establishment of a *Gun Emporium on a large scale*, in which will be found guns *suitable for all kinds of game, in every variety of size, style and price.*

Believing that such an assortment, sold at low rates, would command the trade of a large extent of country, we have been eighteen months shaping our plans to that effect, during which time we have made arrangements to obtain Shot-Guns direct from some of the best makers in England, while our American contracts will insure at all times a full assortment of Rifles.

It is impossible to give a list of the *variety* in our stock, while our prices will range for

Double-barrel Shot-Guns, from	$8 00 to $200 00
Single " " "	3 50 " 15 00
Rifles "	8 00 " 75 00
Rifle and Shot-Gun combined, from	20 00 " 60 00

In our assortment will be found the genuine Jo Manton Shot-Guns, and the Wessen Rifle.

Orders from a distance, giving *length*, *size* and *price*, which are uniform, will be promptly filled, subject to a change should the article sent not suit.

All kinds of repairing done in the best manner, including the making of new parts.

PISTOLS.

The genuine Deringer, assorted sizes.
 " English do. do. } and quality.

A great variety of Single-barrel Pistols—some with guards, for the California trade.

Colt's Repeater, assorted sizes.
Wesson's do.   do.   do.
Allen's Revolver, do.   do.
Blunt & Sym's do. do.   do.
Allen's Self-cockers, do. do.
English Stub-twist Revolvers.
   Do.   do.   Double-Barrels.

GUN ACCOMPANIMENTS.

Game-Bags in great variety, from $1 00 to $12 00.
Shot   do.   "   "   "   "   50 to   5 00.
Do.   Pouches, assorted.
Powder-Flasks, from 4 to 16 oz. assorted.
 Do.   do.   for Pistols   "
 Do.   do.   for Rifle and Shot-Gun combined.
Mahogany Gun and Pistol Cases.
Leather   "   "   "
Screw-drivers, assorted.
Tube Wrenches   do.
Extra Tubes   do.
Cleaning Rods   do.
Cap Carriers.
Leather Drinking-cups.
Decoy Ducks.
Powder Magazines, 4 lbs.
Anti-corrosive Oil, prepared expressly for guns.

POWDER.

The Superior American Sporting Powder, manufactured by the Hazard Powder Company.

In Canisters of 1 lb.
" Kegs No. 1 of $6\frac{1}{4}$ lbs.
"   "   " 2 of $6\frac{1}{4}$ lbs.
"   "   " 3 of $6\frac{1}{4}$ lbs.

The number indicates the size of the grain. See article on powder, in the treatise on guns, powder, &c.

BALLS AND SHOT.

T. O. Le Roy & Co's Compressed Balls, assorted, from 17 to 220 per lb. Also, their buck, turkey, and duck shot, with an assortment of drop shot.

WADDING.

Baldwin's Indented Elastic Gun-Wadding.
Ely's   "   "   "   "
Ely's chemically-prepared pink-edged felt Gun-Wadding, (or do. do.)
Ely's chemically-prepared concave felt Gun-Wadding. Six or eight times as many shots can be made with the use of this article without cleaning as with the common paper wad.

PERCUSSION CAPS.

R. Walker's Caps.
Ely's London   do. extra strong.
Westly Richards' Caps, Registered.
Ely's and Walker's do. for Pistols.
G. D.   do. 10th Boxes.

58

TO THE TRADE.

WHOLESALE DEPARTMENT.

WATCHMAKERS and Merchants dealing in my line are respectfully informed that I can supply them with goods on the most reasonable terms. My stock of Tools and Materials is also large and well assorted. I can, therefore, furnish watchmakers with every thing in that line necessary for a successful prosecution of the trade.

MECHANICAL DEPARTMENT.

IN addition to my being a practical Watchmaker, I keep constantly in my employment the best London and Geneva workmen, and can repair or supply new parts to the finest Chronometer, Duplex or Lever Watches, with dispatch. I also employ the best Jewelers and Diamond-Setters, and can execute all orders for new Jewelry in the neatest and most fashionable style.

I have fitted up in my third story a Gun Smith's Shop and Shooting Gallery, and will manufacture new Guns or Rifles to order, or repair Guns or Pistols.

All new Guns will be proved to the satisfaction of the purchaser. And, taking it all in all, I think I have the best arranged Establishment in the Union.

CALL, SEE, AND TRY.

GUNS, RIFLES, PISTOLS, GUN MATERIAL,
SPORTING APPARATUS, FISHING TACKLE, FINE CUTLERY, &c., &c.

DIMICK & CO., 42 NORTH MAIN STREET, ST. LOUIS, invite the attention of Sportsmen, city and country Merchants, and all others, to their large and well selected stock of English and German Guns, single and double.

GUNS, PISTOLS and RIFLES—of all descriptions and qualities, made and imported to order.
PISTOLS—English, German and American, of all kinds.
RIFLES—of various patterns. Cast Steel and best Iron RIFLE BARRELS always on hand.
All the parts used in making Guns, Rifles and Pistols, in the forged, filed and finished state.
Shot Belts, Shot Pouches, Powder Flasks, Powder Horns.
Bowie and Sportsmen's KNIVES, Dram B...les and Game Bags.
Baldwin's improved GUN WADDING; ..ley's GUN WADDING, and Patent Wire Shot CARTRIDGES; Starkey's GUN WADDING.
English and American FLASKS, in great variety.
Cox's, Eley's, G. D., &c., &c., PERCUSSION CAPS.
Every article required for Gunsmiths' and Sportsmen's use always on hand.
A full supply of REVOLVERS and other fire-arms manufactured by Allen & Thurbur constantly on hand.
COLT'S REVOLVERS—of all sizes.

All of the above will be sold at the lowest possible price, and on the most favorable terms.

St. Louis, Mo., Oct. 2

GUNS, RIFLES, PISTOLS, FISHING TACKLE

T. J. ALBRIGHT, Importer and Wholesale Dealer, has now in store and for sale the largest and most complete stock ever before offered suitable for the Western and Southern trade, such as Deer, Ducking, and Bird Guns, Mountain and Target Rifles, U. S. Rifles, Muskets, Sharp's breech loading Rifles, Colt's Pistols, revolving hammer Pistol, Allen's, Deringer's, and other Pistols, Remington Barrels, Locks, Gun material, Screw Plates, Flasks, Pouches, Belts, Percussion Caps, Money Belts, portable Fishing Rods, Reels, silk, grass and other Lines, Artificial Bait, Sook Dologers, gravitation Fish Hooks, &c.

The city and country dealers are invited to examine my stock. My motto shall be quick sales and small profits, at my new store, No. 27 Main street, east side.

☞ Laminated Steel Guns, fine Rifles, &c., made to order by the best of workmen and at fair prices.

m20 6m   T. J. ALBRIGHT.

Missouri Republican 5-11-1854

Child Pratt & Co. Ad

Hardware.

HARDWARE AND CUTLERY.

1854.   SPRING SALES.   1854.

ALONZO CHILD, } E. G. PRATT, } { E. W. FOX,
New York City. } O. W. CHILD, } { S. C. MANSUR.

CHILD, PRATT & CO.,

DIRECT IMPORTERS AND WHOLESALE DEALERS IN

FOREIGN AND DOMESTIC HARDWARE,

CUTLERY, GUNS, RIFLES, &c.,

147 Main street, St. Louis, Mo.,

WILL BE IN RECEIPT, FOR SPRING SALES, OF ONE of the largest stocks and most complete assortment of Goods in our line, ever offered in this market. Importing all our Foreign Goods direct, and purchasing our American Goods from the manufacturers, (at lowest cash prices,) we are enabled to offer Merchants and purchasers, Goods at as LOW PRICES and on as favorable terms as any house East or West. Our stock will embrace a large and very complete assortment.

AGRICULTURAL TOOLS AND IMPLEMENTS,

of the latest and most approved kinds and qualities, of Scythes, Snaths, Forks, Rakes, Handled and Corolina Hoes, Shovels and Spades, Scoops, Hames, Collars, Chains—ox, trace and others, Axes—all makes and kinds, Picks, Mattocks, &c. &c.

HOUSE FURNISHING AND BUILDERS' HARDWARE.

Large and complete assortment of Locks, Latches, Butts, Hinges, Screws, Bolts, Brads, Nails, &c.; Trimmings—great variety.

CARPENTERS' AND BUILDERS' TOOLS.

Planes, Saws, Chisels, Augers, Braces, Bitts, Drawing Knives, Squares, Trowels, Gauges, Bevils, Hatchets, Hammers, Adzes, Board, Burch and Broad-Axes, Gimblets, &c.

BLACKSMITHS' TOOLS, &c.

Bellows, anvils, Vices, Hammers, Screw Plates, Horse Nails, Shoes, Files and Rasps of Butcher's and other makers—all kinds and sizes.

COOPERS' TOOLS.

Large assortment of Knives, Hoops, Planes, &c.

CUTLERY.

A very large stock and assortment of Wostenholmas', Butcher's and others, Table, Pocket, Pen, Butcher and Shoe Knives Razors, Shears, Scissors, Carvers, &c., great variety.

GUNS, RIFLES, GUN TRIMMINGS AND MOUNTINGS.

Single and Double-Barrelled English and German Rifles, Pistols, Mountings and Trimmings—great variety.

Together with a general assortment of other goods usually kept in a Hardware Store. Saws, every variety, Mill, X Cut and Circular, of best quality, furnished at manufacturer's prices. ☞ Orders promptly filled and forwarded.

jan27   CHILD, PRATT & CO.

Missouri Republican 5-20-1854

MISSOURI PATENTS

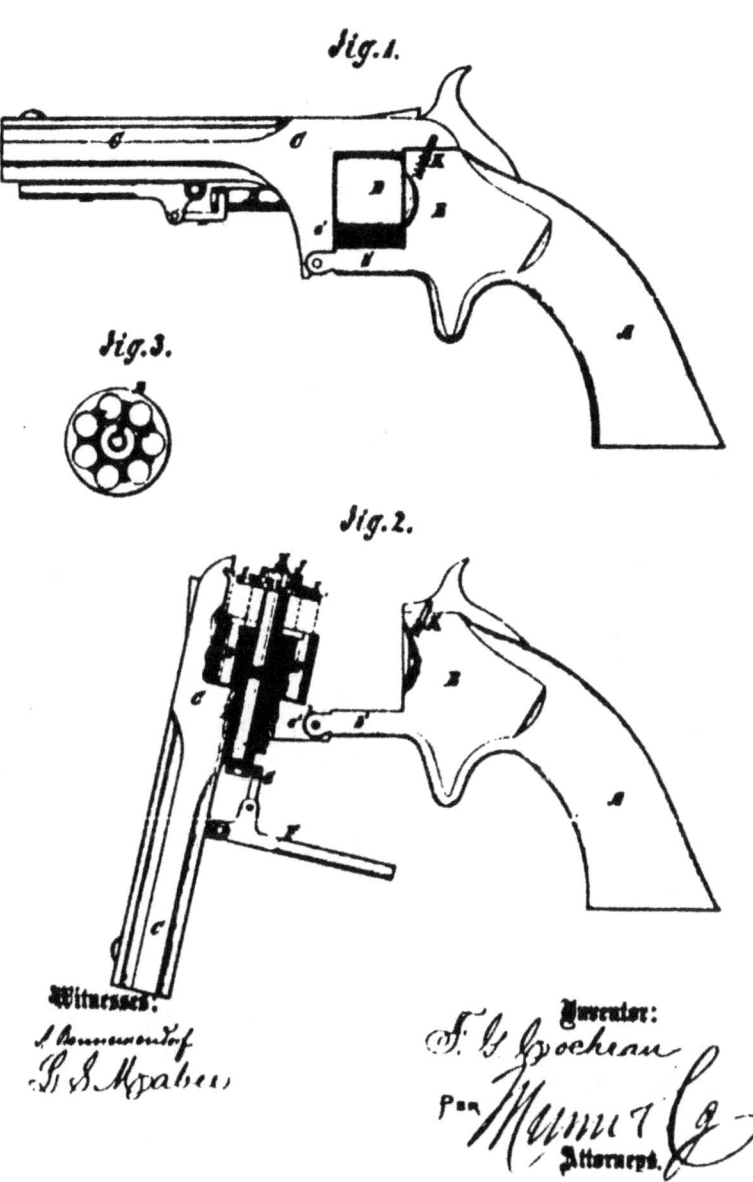

Patents

The following is a list of patents granted to Missouri residents, in alphabetical order.

BLEHA, WILLIAM V.
#633949, Sept. 26, 1899, breechloading firearm. Falling block, open hammer.
#657,052, Aug. 28, 1900, breechloading firearm. Improvement on above patent. Assigned 2/3 to Otto F. Stifel and Gustav Pleus, both of St. Louis.

BRACE, D. R. and CASH, R. W.
#426,916 April 29, 1890, recoil self cocking gun. Hammerless double.

BRUTON, JACKSON W.
#440,538 Nov. 11, 1890, target gun. Not properly a firearms patent. It is for a rubber band gun.

CAMPBELL, TRISTRAM and POORMAN, HENRY B.
#16,327 Jan. 6, 1857, bullet molds. Casting machine. See p. 24.

CASH, ROBERT W. see BRACE.

COCHRAN, FREDERICK G.
#116,559 improvement in revolving firearms. Ejector rod. See p. 173.

COLONEY see McLEAN

CORY, RANDOLPH
#555,432 Feb. 28, 1896, choke attachment for guns. Removable choke attached by means of a lever, for double or single barrel. Assigned 1/3 to Julius Baron, also of St. Louis.
#633,428 Sept.19, 1899, choke-bore attachment for guns. Add-on choke attached by links. Assigned 49/100 to Julius Baron.
#847,911 Mar.19, 1907, choke attachment. Primitive adjustable choke, 2 position, on/off.

DIMICK, HORACE E.
#16,377 Jan. 13, 1857, rifling cannon. See p. 32.
#39,216 July, 14, 1863, cannon projectile. See p. 32.

DIMITT, FRANK
#306,593, Oct. 14, 1884, shotgun. Chambers made from mono-block and threaded for barrels.

ENHOLM, J. H.
#28,977 July 3,1860, alarm gun. Door stop burglar alarm.

EUSTACE, THOMAS F.
#488,627, Dec. 27, 1892, cartridge. "Wad" rings, to hold shot column together.

GERNGROSS, STEPHEN
#110,353 Dec. 10,1870, breech-loading firearm. Needle-fire bolt action. A pistol is at the Smithsonian and is pictured in *FAMOUS GUNS FROM THE SMITHSONIAN COLLECTION*, Hank Wieand Brown, 1966, Fawcett Publications.

GOODMAN, HENRY
#185,912, Jan. 2,1877, Improvement in Breechloading Fire-arms. "Trapdoor", block and hammer have common pin, block rotates up and rearward, cocking hammer and extracting spent shells. Drawing shows double gun. Assigned 1/2 to Lewis Lockwood, also of St. Louis.
#212,459, Feb. 18, 1879, Improvement in Breechloading Fire-arms. Stop lugs for proper alignment on open hammer double. Assigned 1/2 to Daniel P. Kane, also of St. Louis.
#267,876, Nov. 21, 1882, Concealed-hammer Gun. Has essentially all components of modern double-barrel shotgun. Assigned 1/2 to Daniel P. Kane.
#274,093, Mar. 13, 1883, revolver. Swing-out cylinder, ejection by moving cylinder forward. Assigned 1/2 to Daniel P. Kane.
#288,939, Nov. 9, 1883, lock for firearms. Method of depth adjustment for firing pin. Assigned 1/2 to Daniel P. Kane.
#352,185, Nov. 9, 1886, revolver. Mainspring & pawl arrangement. Assigned to Daniel P. Kane.

HASTINGS, GARDNER P.
#576,964, Feb. 9, 1897, magazine firearm. Tube-fed, pump action.

HONEY, JOHN W.
no number assigned, Feb. 10, 1825, shot table.

HOPPENAU, HENRY
#136,998, Mar. 18,1873, Improvement in Breech-Loading Fire-arms. Single shot, slide action.

JANSEN, DIEDERICH W.
#341,751, May 11,1886, breechloading firearm. Similar to Snider action adapted to double gun. See p. 66.

JOHNSTON, COLUMBUS
#32,067, April 16, 1861, shot pouch.
#68512, Sept. 3, 1867, Adjustable shot measure. See p. 68

KACER, MARTIN V. and KRIZ, WILLIAM
#273,288, Mar. 6, 1883, firearm. Side by side shotgun with superposed rifle barrels between, made from a mono-block. Open hammer.
#282,328, July 31, 1883, magazine fire arm. Butt-feed magazine for rifle barrels of above firearm. Trigger guard lever ejection & feed.

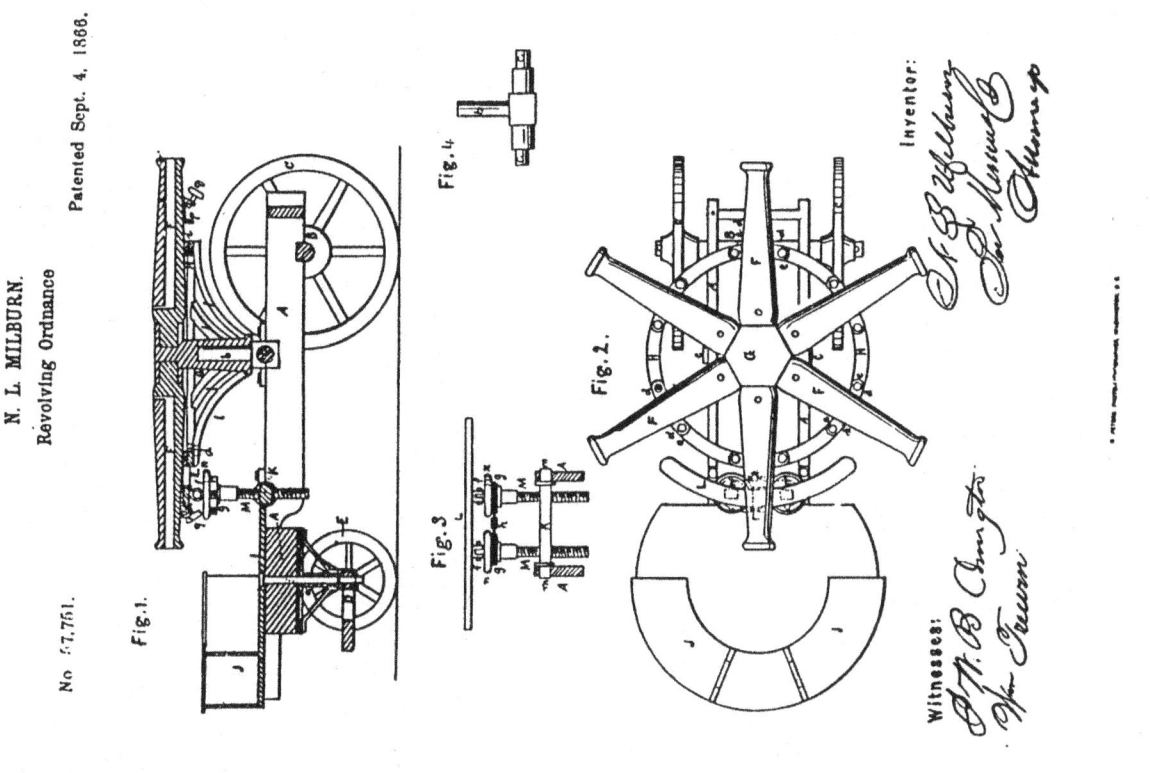
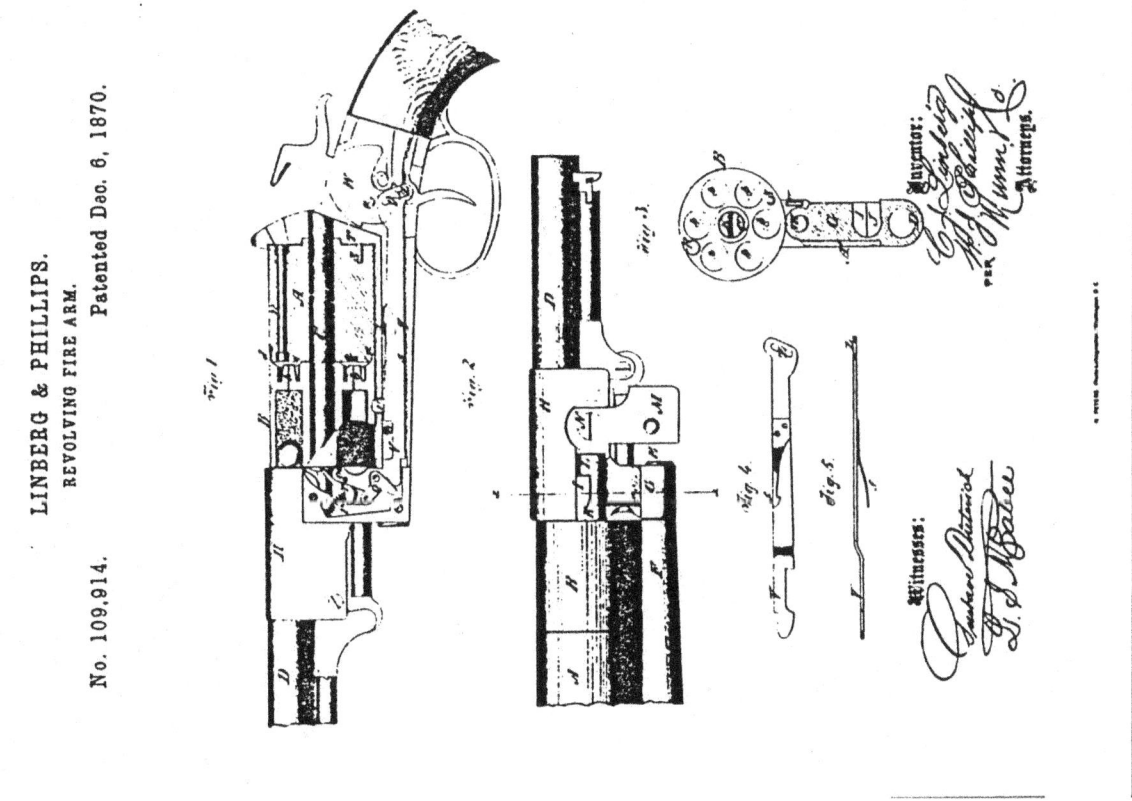

Patents

KLINGLESMITH, JOHN F.
#398,265, Feb. 19, 1889, spring gun. Toy gun.

LARD, ALLEN E.
630,061, Aug. 1, 1899
636,050, Oct. 31, 1899
668,526, Feb.19, 1901
674,508, May 21, 1901
747,191, Dec. 15, 1903
All for single triggers, for double guns.

LEEMAN, JULIUS
295,564, Mar. 25, 1884, magazine firearm. Tube-feed, pump action.

LINBERG, CHARLES J. and PHILIPS, WILLIAM J.
109,914, Dec. 6,1870, revolving fire arm. Percussion double cylinder revolver, cylinders placed inline, each cylinder has a firing pin to be used when in the rear position to fire the forward cylinder. After forward cylinder is emptied the cylinders are switched. See p. 175.

McLEAN, DR. JAMES HENRY and COLONEY, MYRON
282,548, breech loading composite gun. Coastal or Naval gun.
282,549, machine gun. Carriage mount, multi-barrel.

McLEAN, DR. JAMES HENRY
282,550 cartridge. Primer extends, by a tube, to base of bullet or shot capsule, which acts as anvil. Case to be used as head-space guage in conjunction with machine gun patents.
282, 551, machine gun. Multi-barrel with "gumball machine" magazine.
282,552, magazine gun. Gravity magazine-fed revolving rifle.
282,553, machine gun. Multi-barrel multi-magazine.
282,554 magazine gun. Gravity magazine-fed, semi-auto.
all above Aug. 7, 1883
290,905 Dec. 25, 1883, breechloading firearm. Side breech, gravity magazine feed, designed for small arms up to wheel mount cannon.
(All of the above are probably Coloney's inventions.)

MATTHEWS, J. A.
29,437, July 31, 1860, improvement in repeating ordnance. Turret gun with attached rammer. Patent assigned Mathews and S. H. Heraph.

MILBURN, NATHAN
57,751, Sept. 4, 1866, revolving ordnance. Six barrel rotating rail gun. See p. 175.

PHILLIPS, WILLIAM J. see LINDBERG

PRIOR, GEORGE W.
264,899, Sept. 26, 1882, Sight for Firearms. One-piece sight with "sight disks" at each end.

STAUF, C. and STEINBACH, C. J.
34,017, Dec. 24, 1861, improvement in portable battery or platoon guns. See p. 177..

VOLKEL, JOHN L.
234,632, Nov. 16, 1860, Breech Loading Fire Arms. Underlever load and eject. Closed hammer, trigger guard unlatches and rotates forward and down.

WAYMON, COLEMAN H.
631,349, Aug. 22, 1899, cartridge ejector for guns. Selective ejectors for double guns

WERNER, DANIEL
82,908, Oct. 6, 1868, improvement in breech-loading pistols. Folding blade, "pocket knife" pistol.

WIGET, DOMINICK
466,209, Dec. 29, 1891, ammunition charger. Powder flask with adjustable powder measure attached.

YOUNG, LEWIS V.
104,682, Jun.21, 1870, breechloading firearm. Trigger guard lever barrel release, single barrel.

C. STAUF & C. J. STEINBACH.
PORTABLE BATTERY OR PLATOON GUN.

No. 34,017. Patented Dec. 24, 1861.

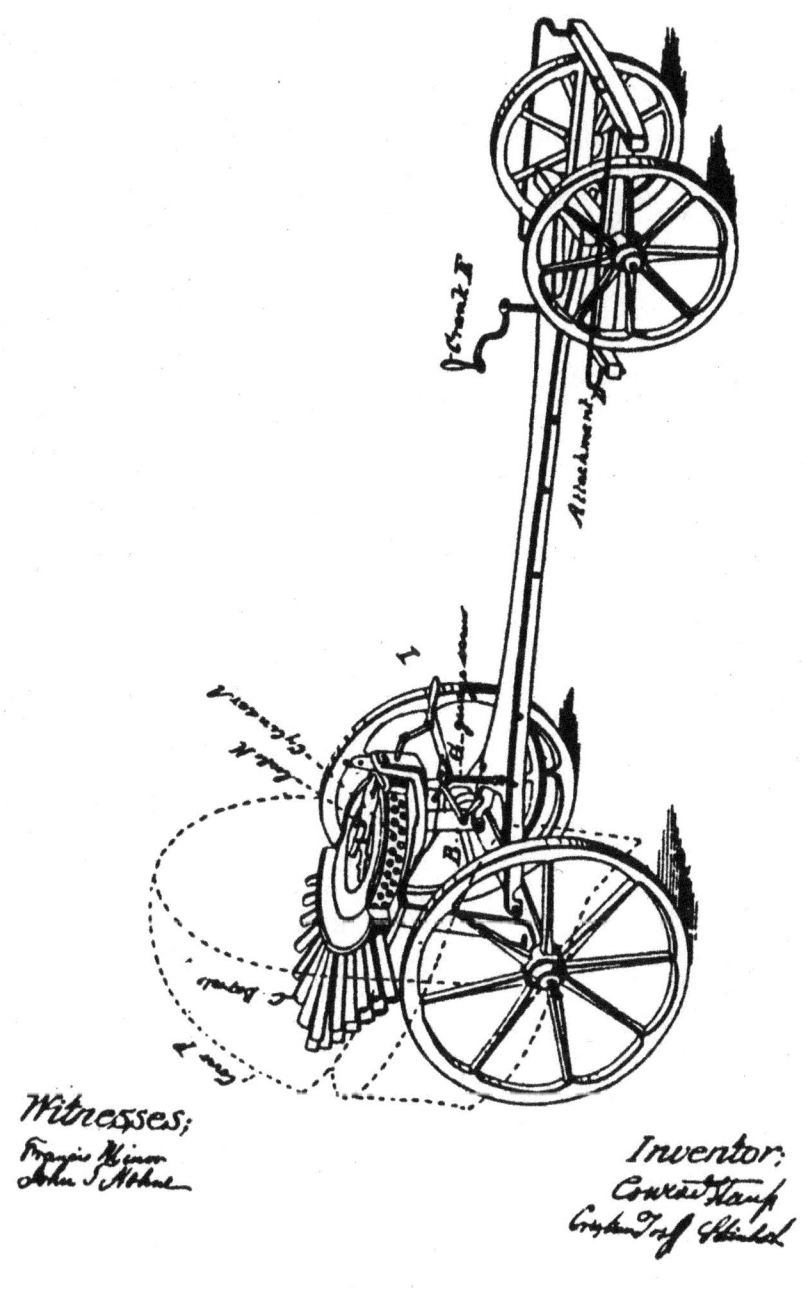

SIEBER

Confusion exists as to which directory listing refers to which Sieber. All listings may refer to one man, Charles R. His full name may have been Charles (Carl) Robert. A common practice among Germans was to drop the first name, the christening name, and use the middle name in everyday life. The various dir. listings may be duplicates. Only a few of the Robert listings show addresses different than those shown for Charles R. and they are in years with no listing for Charles. Some listings may refer to Edward Robert. They may have been brothers and Edward Robert may have lived with Charles R. when in St. Louis. A third possibility is that there was a Robert C., brother to Charles R.

SIEBERS IN ST. LOUIS

Dir.	Name	Address, work or res.
47-55	None	
57	Robert	31 Washington
59-66	None	
67	Charles R.	612 S. 7TH. (res. same)
	Robert	612 S. 7TH. (res.)
68-70	None	
71	Robert (finisher)	620 CERRE (res.)
72	Charles R.	613 CERRE (res.)
73	Charles R. (Albright&Rudolph)	708 S. 7TH. (res.)
74	Robert C. (Albright & Sons)(gunmaker)	708 S. 7TH. (res.)
75	Charles R. (Albright & Sons)	7TH. near Cerre (res.)
	Robert C. (above is near Cerre)	708 S. 7TH. (res.)
76	Carl	506 S. 7TH.
77	Robert	506 S. 7TH.
78	Carl R.	506 S. 7TH.
79	Carl R.	1108 S. 13TH.
	Robert C.	1108 S. 13TH.
80	Carl R.	630 S. 5TH.
81	Carl	620 S. 5TH.
	Robert	630 S. 5TH.
82	Carl R.	630 S. 5TH.
83	Robert	1102 N. 25TH.
84	Charles R.	1506 CLARK AVE.(shop)
85	Charles R.	1506 CLARK AVE.(shop)
	Robert	1506 CLARK AVE.(res.)
86	Charles R.	2021 EUGENIA (res.)
	Robert	2021 EUGENIA (res.)
87	Charles R.	2021 EUGENIA (res.)
88-89	None	
90	Charles R.	19 N. 10TH. (shop) 24 S. 16TH.

Same shop listed as Charles R. or Carl R. through 1906. Residence changes to 226 S. BEAUMONT 91-94, then 4950 MAPLE AVE in 1895. Obituary mentions Maple address.

Name Charles also occurs under various other occcupations. However, they do not appear to be related to the gunsmith.

1886 is the last occurence of the name Robert. Name Robert occurs only as gunsmith or as noted.

SITES FAMILY

January, 1991 letter from Thomas B. Hall III

reprint of July, 1969 article by Thomas B. Hall (II)

additional author's comments

A number of buildings have been restored by the Friends of Arrow Rock Inc. They are open for touring throughout the summer and on weekends spring and fall. They also host various events, including an excellant craft show the second weekend in October. For further information call (660) 837-3231. In addition there is a state historical site open year round.

John P. Sites, Jr. Gunsmith Shop
Arrow Rock, Saline County, Missouri,
1844-1904
Restored and opened to the Public by
THE FRIENDS OF ARROW ROCK, INC.

Thanks largely to the generous assistance of Byron C. Shutz of Kansas City, Missouri, the Friends of Arrow Rock have upgraded and added to the restoration of this historic gunsmith shop since its original restoration by the Friends, 1967-1970. The latest in safety and security protection, temperature and humidity control, and museum displays have been installed. The shop is, as far as we can tell, the only historic working gunsmith shop restoration housed in its original building, in the United States.

In addition to making the improvement of this restoration possible, Byron Shutz has given to the Friends of Arrow Rock an outstanding collection of 19th century Missouri firearms, which the Friends are displaying in memory of Mr. Shutz's grandparents, Max A. Christopher and Sue Hargis Christopher, both of pioneer Missouri families, and the original owners of this collection.

A knowledgeable group of blackpowder shooters, collectors, and gunsmiths has been of great help to me in this second restoration of the Sites gunshop: Herschel Gaddy and Ted Hamilton, both of Saline County, who were on the original committee with my late father, Dr. Thomas B. Hall, Jr., in the first restoration of the shop 1967-1970; John L. Davis, Jr. of Hardeman and St. Louis, Missouri, Jim Duncan of St. Louis, and Lyt Tough of St. Louis and Arrow Rock.

We have learned a good deal more about the Arrow Rock gunsmith, John P. Sites Jr. (1821-1904); he came from at least three generations of Pennsylvania, Maryland, Virginia, and Missouri gunsmiths, including his brother Chester P. Sites (1834 -1899), his father, John P. Sites Sr. (1784 -1853), his grandfather's brother, George Sites (1771-post 1850), and possibly his grandfather, Henry (or Heinrich) Sites (1756-1833), all descended from Johann Peter Seitz, who emigrated from the Palatine region of Germany to Lancaster County, Pennsylvania, in 1727. Sites guns have been located in collections in Pennsylvania, Virginia, Missouri, and every state west of Missouri except Texas.

The Sites gunsmith shop in Arrow Rock will be rededicated at 4:00 PM on Friday, September 27, 1991, during the national meeting of the Santa Fe Trail Association in Arrow Rock; all are invited to attend. For further information about this event, and if any reader knows of the whereabouts of firearms, barrels, locks, or other gun parts marked "SITES", or of Sites or other antique guns or gunsmithing tools you would like to donate to this project, please contact:

        The Friends of Arrow Rock, Inc.
        P. O. Box 124
        Arrow Rock, Missouri 65320
        Telephone: (660) 837-3231

Thomas B. Hall III
January, 1991

TWO MISSOURI GUNSMITHS of the BOONSLICK AREA

JOHN P. SITES SR.
1784 - 1853
JOHN P. SITES JR.
1821 - 1904

by Thos. B. Hall

Reprinted from "Muzzle Blasts", July, 1969, official publication of the National Muzzle Loading Rifle Association, with permission.

Missouri has deservedly been called the Mother of the West. No section of Missouri spearheaded the drive against the last frontier more than the men of the Boonslick region.

Here, as early as 1807 Daniel Boone's sons Nathan and Daniel Morgan Boone made salt extensively at Boon Lick. There is evidence that Daniel spent much time with his sons at this Lick, which they operated for a number of years.

At the forts nearby to Boonslick the "men of Boonslick" held out during the War of 1812, refusing to go to St. Louis, asking only for powder and lead.

Kit Carson, raised in the Boonslick country, crossed the Missouri on the ferry at Arrow Rock in 1826 on his first trip to Santa Fe. Franklin, Missouri was the first place of embarkation for the Santa Fe traders.

The majority of the Boonslick men were second and third generation frontiersmen. Their forebears had pierced the vast and formidable Appalachian range, wrested Tennessee and Kentucky from the Indians, and had started to filter into Missouri before the Louisiana purchase. When the famous physician Daniel Drake stated at Westport in 1844 that "a good rifle was the most indispensable implement for him who embarked on the Western Trail," he was merely repeating a well established opinion. Franklin in its brief existence was the most important town in the Boonslick area. The Franklin Missouri "Intelligencer" in its September 2, 1825 issue describes the Shooting Match as holding first place as a sport. Competition was keen and there is no indication that the plain southern rifles that the contestants had brought from Virginia, Kentucky, and Tennessee were less accurate than the decorated Pennsylvania rifles that occasionally showed up in the community. The rifles of the Boonslick men were often endowed with such names as "Cross Buster", "Hair Splitter", "Panther Cooler", etc.

The famous artist George C. Bingham's picture "Shooting for the Beef" (1850) faithfully depicts this favorite sport.

The man on the frontier wanted his rifle to shoot accurately, to be certain of ignition (the gunsmith who made good and durable springs was sought out), and to have a stock that held together securely the component parts.

Due to encroachment of the Missouri River, Franklin began to decline in the 1820's. Boonville across the river on its high south bank took its place. Here, where the mighty Missouri turns north was the logical place for a town to serve the Western expansion. Soon to develop here was important outfitters and wholesale houses for the Western emigrants. To the south and southwest important freighting roads were established. Over 100 miles away in Springfield, Mo., a street used by these travelers was named Boonville street. This was a logical place for a gunsmith to locate. John P. Sites Sr. (1784-1853) came to Missouri from Virginia in 1834, locating for a short time at Marion in Cole County. He setup his shop in 1835 in Boonville where he remained until his death in 1853.

There is every evidence that J. P. Sites Sr. was an experienced gunsmith when he arrived in Missouri. At that time he was nearly fifty years old. Perhaps some of our readers can enlighten us on John Sites Sr's. career in Virginia. There were at least two John Sites in Rockingham County Virginia, according to Mrs. Dorothy J. Caldwell of the State Historical Society of Missouri. John P. Sites Sr's. wife's name was Martha, according to her death notice in 1847 in Boonville papers.

It has been stated that J. P. Sites Sr. made his own barrels. 1835 seems late for this, but some years prior the Hawkens of St. Louis were making barrels from iron derived from the Massey Iron Works located at Meramec Springs, Mo. Iron from this source is known to have been delivered at Boonville by the steamboats at that time regularly plying the Missouri River. Sites ability to make his rifle "lock stock and barrel" was characteristic of the Virginia mountain gunsmith and is well described in Dillin's book.

In 1837 it is recorded that J. Sites Sr. "fixed"

Senator David Barton's pistols. Barton was Missouri's first Senator and lived in Boonville at the time. Just what "fixing" implies we are not certain, but it is probable that he converted the senator's pistols from flint to percussion.

A group from the east ascending the Missouri River in the early 1830's excited interest among the men along the Missouri River because their guns were percussion.

In 1836 during the so-called Mormon War in Missouri, the Mormons ordered 330 gun flints and a barrel of gunpowder.

Extensive stock of percussion caps were advertised for sale in 1840 in the "Western Emigrant" published in Boonville.

While flintlocks were certainly common in Missouri in the 1830's and 1840's, they could not hold out against a system of ignition that "fired under water."

John Sites Sr. must have worked during the flintlock era while in Virginia, however no flintlock rifles are known to have been made by him, in either Virginia or Missouri. Gluckman and Satterlee list a flintlock rifle by W. Sites. He is thought to be related to the John Sites of Missouri.

J. P. Sites Sr's. shop in Boonville evidently prospered and was in full swing by the time of the roaring forties and early fifties. It is stated that 312 small arms were made in Boonville in one year during these booming times. While there was a gunsmith named Hook in Boonville at this time, the majority of these guns are believed to have been from Sites' shop.

Evidently J. P. Sites Sr. had to have help. Among his helpers was J. P. Sites Jr. (1821-1904) who possibly worked as an apprentice with his father in Virginia and Marion, Missouri before the shop was located in Boonville. The biographer of J. P. Sites Jr. wrote that in 1879 he had, by that time, more than 45 years of gunsmithing experience.

J. P. Sites Jr. was with his father for seven years in Boonville.

Since the father or son apparently never used the name Sites Sr. or Jr. on their guns, there is much uncertainty just who may have made the rifles originating in the Boonville shop.

Sites rifles have turned up in various western states, such as Montana, the mountains of Colorado (barrel only), Oregon, etc. The inventory of John P. Sites Sr's. gunsmithing tools in 1855 is a large one, evidence of a large and busy shop.

At that time it is evident that the making of muzzle loading rifles was a going business. Among those who bought gunsmithing tools of J. P. Sites Sr's. estate is Wm. Knaus of Otterville, Mo. The writer has seen one of the rifles. This was a plain large bore muzzle loading rifle which the Fergusons of Otterville took to Estes Park, Colorado in the 1870's. Ferguson ran a mill on the Lamine river at Otterville and the stone of this wrecked mill was part of the Missouri exhibit at the New Yorks World's Fair in 1939..

For many years this rifle hung over the fireplace of the Brinwood Lodge, Estes Park, operated by Mr. and Mrs. (nee Ferguson) Reid.

The unusual photograph is from a full size 8 1/2 x 6 1/2" tin type. Tin types reversed the image, as did Daguerreotypes. This accounts for the word Democrat being spelled backward. There was a short lived paper in Boonville named the Democrat and the supposition is that Sites had taken over this building for his gunshop. Near the butt plate on the stock of the rifle mounted on the roof is still discernible the name J. P. Sites. Since the tintype was not patented by its inventor H. L. Smith until 1856, it is evident that Sites Sr. (died February 17, 1853) was not living at the time this photograph was taken. (Not pictured here.)

The exact date of this photograph is not known. Obviously it was some time after this process was patented in 1856. We feel that it was probably taken during the period 1856-1859.

The relationship of Sites Sr. to John P. Gemmer (1838-1919), who took over the famous Hawken works in St. Louis in 1862, is an interesting one. John P. Gemmer, according to the biography written by his son). J. P. H. Gemmer in *Arms Collectors of the United States* by Captain Virgil Ney, 1939, arrived with his father William Gemmer from Germany in Boonville in 1855 (two years after the death of J. P. Sites Sr.).

The statement has been frequently made that John P. Gemmer learned the gunsmithing trade in Boonville from J. P. Sites. Even the owners of the Hawken-Gemmer Collection are under this illusion. Gemmer is said to have been in Boonville from 1855-1859, presumably with his father William Gemmer.

Who then are the men in the picture in front of the former J.P. Sites Sr's. gunshop in Boonville?

One at best can only make a partially informed guess. John P. Sites Jr. left Boonville in 1841 and by the time the Gemmers arrived in Boonville in 1855, had a thriving gunsmith's shop in Arrow Rock. John P. Sites Sr's. other son Chester P. Sites (listed as a gunsmith in Boonville, Mo. in the 1850 census, in "Muzzle Blasts," Nov. 1966, "Missouri Gunmakers" by Robert McAfee) could have been trying to carry on his father's well-established gunsmithing business in Boonville. However, at the sale of his father's extensive gunsmithing tools, etc. in 1853, C. P. Sites only bought 2-3 items that could be used in gunsmithing. In contrast, John P. Sites Jr.. at this sale bought many articles, i.e. pistol and rifle barrels, gun mountings, etc.

Chester P. Sites is said by a grandson, Chester B. Collins, to have been at one time a gunsmith at Osceola, Mo. and Otterville, Mo. Over his shop in Otterville his grandson remembers a 15 ft. wooden Kentucky rifle replica closely resembling (possibly the same one) the one shown over the J. P. Sites Sr. shop in Boonville.

The Gemmers, since they do seem to have been connected with the Sites gunshop in some manner, may have tried with C. P. Sites to continue to operate the Sites shop. However, since they left Boonville in 1859, it is apparent that if this was so it was not successful.

We now turn our attention to John P. Sites Jr. John served an apprenticeship of least 7 years with his father. It is probable that he was proficient in all phases of gunsmithing sometime before he left his father's shop in Boonville in 1841.

In 1841 he married Miss Nannie J. Toole, and located in Clifton in Cooper Co., Missouri.

In 1844 he located permanently in Arrow Rock, on the Missouri River in Saline County, Missouri. The move proved a propitious one. This town, established in 1829, by 1844 had developed into a thriving community. The ferry established in 1817 was carrying a steady stream of immigrants. The ferry also gave the relatively numerous inhabitants of Howard County easy access to Arrow Rock. John Stapleton of Howard County, well-known collector of firearms, has handled five Sites rifles. One of these Sites rifles John presented to the Old Arrow Rock Tavern, and it now hangs in the Tavern Museum Room .

In Saline County the rich land had largely been entered and many homesteads established. While the bear and elk (last seen in Saline County in 1836) had been driven out, there were still a great many deer, wild turkeys, a few panthers, and many prairie chicken.

Unbelievable numbers of ducks and geese darkened the skies. John Beauchamp Jones, who established one of the first stores in Arrow Rock, describes well in his book *Wild Western Scenes* the slaughter of ducks and geese who frequented the natural ponds around Arrow Rock.

Three miles almost directly east across the river was Boons Lick, where Daniel Boone formerly frequently stayed with his sons. It is probable that Daniel crossed the river at Arrow Rock to hunt at the numerous salt licks in what was to become Saline County. The 15-20 men working at the Lick making salt for Daniel Morgan Boone and Nathan Boone needed all the game that Daniel's rifle could fetch for them.

While the outfitting post for the Santa Fe and Oregon Trails had been moved to Independence, Mo., this Boonslick area of Missouri was still deeply involved in the Western movement. Phillip Thompson, one of the biggest traders on the Santa Fe Trail, lived at the edge of Arrow Rock. It is said that he came to speak Spanish better than English. Other important Santa Fe traders in the vicinity were the Turleys. Jesse B. Turley was apparently responsible for Kit Carson's autobiography. M. M. Marmaduke was an early trader. There was a Mr. Miller, and others.

John Sites was soon a well established gunsmith, catering to the needs of a wide local area and the wagon trains heading for the west on the Santa Fe Trail. The roaring days of "49" when the white-topped wagons on the nearby Santa Fe Trail were rarely out of sight found him ready for the great amount of work this mass migration brought to him. His reputation was established and any of the western travelers whose guns needed attention were sure to get it from John Sites. An extra main spring for one's rifle lock might prove a good investment on the a decade when the conversion of flintlocks to percussion was in full sway. One of the chief complaints against the flintlocks was the blowing of the priming powder out of the pan by the strong western gales.

John Sites doubtless could harden or reface the frizzen and make any other adjustments necessary for those conservatives who preferred to keep their flintlocks.

Although the western travellers were still in good hickory country (Council Grove was the last place where hickory could be obtained). Sites doubtless had a good supply of hickory rods of various sizes.

John Sites, 40 years old, managed to remain neutral during the dark days of 1861-65.

His brick gunshop (now being restored) and adjoining substantial small brick house have recently been acquired by the "Friends of Arrow Rock" (a non-profit organization.)

Guns of the breech loading type, although well enough known, did not become dominant in this area until after 1890. No doubt tradition and economy were factors here. Missourians were slow to recover after the war and a succession of severe depressions and low agricultural prices made it necessary to economize in every possible way.

There was still considerable work to be done on the old guns. One old timer remembers "Uncle Johnny Sites" recutting a rifle barrel using bits of wheat straw to shim up his saws in recutting the grooves.

Sites was finally forced to sell modern ammunition and guns. It is reported that he acquired a number of cheap 22's which he rented by the day to the "boys." The rifle renters did not clean the barrels properly and they soon became leaded from shooting Lesmoke shells. When Flobert shells were used in these leaded rifles the lead bullet driven with little force often lodged in the barrel, often the careless shooter filling the barrel with lead slugs. For this reason Uncle Johnny strictly forbade the shooting of Floberts. In the 1890's the shooting match was still popular, the muzzle loading rifle being still the favorite weapon. The cross on a blackened board with 1" square white paper as a sighting target was still used. The distance was reduced to 40 yards with rest. At this distance, most of the shots were "in the paper."

Uncle Johnny Sites was a very active man to an advanced age. He is reported to have been able to jump over a rail fence when past 70 years.

Mr. and Mrs. Sites only had one child who died at age 10. Several orphans were a i d e d by them. Uncle Johnny became in his latter years a pillar of the Arrow Rock Christian Church, now restored as the village chapel by the "Friends of Arrow Rock." Besides the present restoration of the Sites property, the "Friends' have restored the Court House, IOOF Hall and printing shop, and the Loom house. The state has restored the Old Tavern, George C. Bingham home, Dr. M. W. Hall home and old jail. All these properties restored by the state are in the Arrow Rock State Park.

During the last period of his life Mr. Sites lived with his nearby nephew, Capt. Tom Sites, who had a steamboat "Nadine" which operated on the Lamine and Missouri Rivers. Uncle Johnny previously had secured walnut planks for stocks from his nephew's farm.

John P. Sites' death occurred in 1904 when he was almost 84 years old. His gunsmithing tools had apparently been disposed of prior to his death. The appraisal of his property at the Saline County Probate Court at Marshall in 1904 shows to what a low state the old time gunsmithing trade had descended. A respected and skillful artisan, his work was no longer appreciated or respected.

Quite a contrast to the probate of his father's gunsmithing tools in Boonville in 1856, when such tools were sought after and brought good prices. In the 1904 probate of the Site property is listed 1 lot of stock blanks 25 cts, 1 bellows, 7 powder flasks $6.00, and here is an eye opener: 22 old guns and rifles, $2.00 for the lot.

One of the old timers here remembers playing with those old guns in a brick shed 9' X 9' which Uncle Johnny had adjoining his gun shop. According to this old timer's description, at least two of these were heavy long barrel flintlock rifles with fancy patch boxes!

With the exception of one rifle, nothing is known of what became of these guns. At the price of less than 10c per gun they were evidently considered practically worthless.

We have been appointed by Mrs. David Eads President of the Friends of Arrow Rock, chairman of a Committee to restore John Sites gunshop in Arrow Rock. My able helpers on this committee are K. Faust (well known for his skillful barrel work on old rifles), Herschel Gaddy (Herschel once won 1st at Friendship in an offhand shoot with a score of 48), Ted Hamilton (he has edited the definitive to date book on gun flints, Missouri Archaeological Society, Columbia, Missouri), Wm. Miller (in charge of construction), and Herb Templeton, the village blacksmith and machinist. Our senior consultant is Victor V. Allen, whose ability to stock and recondition the old rifles and shoot them is well known to many in the Kansas City area.

We hope to make as complete as possible a restoration of Sites' gunshop (circa 1850) as a working gunshop. The shop will be equipped with forge, leather bellows, anvil, vises, all the old time metal and wood working tools, at least two types of rifling rigs, stock blanks, and a display of all the necessary accessories J. Sites sold to the shooter. In short we hope to make this such a complete shop, that Uncle Johnny if he could return would feel able to return to his work as a gunsmith artisan. In 1870 J. P. Sites made an anti-thief gun. This is a formidable looking weapon with a bore of about 12 gauge, a brass breech and mounted in a wooden frame; it has a percussion hammer but no trigger. On the brass breech is stamped J. P. Sites #1. Sites may have patented this anti-thief gun.

We cannot afford and do not intend to have many guns (aside from those made by Sites) in this gunshop restoration.

Wm.. C. Almquist of Montana, well known collector of Western arms, has kindly donated to us a Sites rifle. This rifle is a very interesting piece.

It has been bored and rifled to 48 calibre. According to information obtained by Mr. Almquist it was brought to the gold mine strike in Montana in 1864, by a Mr. Kelly. Considerably battered and altered, what a story it could tell! This rifle is listed in Hanson's The Plains Rifle. Other members of the fraternity and others have made important gifts.

At present we are busy restoring the physical structure of the building. Much brickwork has been required. We hope to have the shop completely enclosed. Kit Carson in his later career is known to have been in Arrow Rock on at least two occasions and in all probability was in this shop. Daniel Boone in his excursion from Boons Lick probably made his rifle crack in earshot of the spot on which the Sites gunshop was to arise in the future. Perhaps on the complete restoration (exterior and interior) of the John Sites gun shop, we can have a Boone-Sites-Carson muzzle loading rifle shooting match in Arrow Rock.

The second restoration of the Sites gunshop at Arrow Rock was completed and the building was rededicated September 27, 1991, complete with a fired salute by members of the restoration committee.

Meanwhile work on this book took more time than anticipated. We were not able to duplicate the photos mentioned in the article in a satisfactory manner. However, additional research has been performed. It was found that John P. Sites Sr. sold his property, in 1846 'with a bed', prior to the death of his wife. This is usually significant of failing health. It is not known how active John Sr. was in his final years. Though not certain it seems possible that Chester P. Sites, age 12 at the time of the sale, had already moved to Otterville and associated with William Knaus, prior to his father's death. It seems probable that the gunsmithing items purchased by William Knaus, primarily a blacksmith, at the auction were for his and Chester P. Sites mutual use.

Some Missouri "House Brands"

The wholesaling of firearms was an integral part of St. Louis business. Henry Von Phul was selling pistols by the case as early as 1810.

The first St. Louis merchant to mark guns made elsewhere, with his name, is not known. However, it was probably done before 1840. By 1850 it was common practice.

As noted, a large number of locks sold with St. Louis marks were manufactured elsewhere. A. Meier & Co., J. S. Pease & Co. and Peter Powell & Co. were among those who followed this practice. Gun manufacturers known to have done so include Dimick and Hawken.

The following list is concerned primarily with shotguns sold after the Civil War. The majority of the list was extracted from Appendix A of *The Golden Age of Shotgunning*, Bob Hinman, Winchester Press, 1971.

As Mr. Hinman notes, H & D Folsom Arms Co. New York, New York was one of the major importers and distributors of "house brand" shotguns. In the 1890's they purchased Crescent Fire Arms Co. of Norwich, Ct.

Henry Folsom kept his St. Louis store until at least 1881 and a number of the names in Hinman's Appendix A were probably sold there. Presumably the Folsoms kept their St. Louis contacts and continued business with them well into the 20th century.

The author received information from Joseph T. Vorisek, publisher of "Shotgun Research Newsletter" P. O. Box 384, Canton, CT. 06019, and it is included here.

Some Missouri "House Brands"

Brand	Source
Berkshire	Shapleigh Hardware (Hinman)
Bridge Gun Works	Shapleigh Hardware, Belgian made (Hinman)
Central Arms Co.	Shapleigh Hardware (Hinman)
Century Arms Co.	Shapleigh Hardware (Sellers)
Diamond Arms Co. of St. Louis	Tobin Arms Co. for Shapleigh Hardware (Vorisek)
Electric City	Wyeth Hardware, St. Joseph (Sellers)
Enders Oak Leaf	Shapleigh Hardware by Crescent (Hinman)
Enders Royal Service	Shapleigh Hardware by Crescent (Hinman)
Expert	Witte Hdw. by Davenport Arms Co. (Sellers)
Hartford Arms Co.	Shapleigh Hardware & Simmons Hardware by Crescent Arms Co. (Hinman)
International	E. C. Meachem (Hinman)
King-Nitro	Shapleigh Hardware (Hinman)
Mississipi Valley Arms Co.	Shapleigh Hardware (Hinman)
MEACHEM, E. C., ARMS CO.	10ga. cart. dbl. by N. R. Davis & Co. for E. C. Meachem, also imported shotguns
NORVELL-SHAPLEIGH	Tobin Arms Co. for Norvell-Shapleigh (Vorisek)
Richards	12ga., Belgian, Lefaucheux Action. From the number seen in the Mississippi valley it seems probable they were sold by Shapleigh or Simmons.
Royal Service	Shapleigh Hardware (Hinman)
St. Louis Arms Co.	Shapleigh Hardware (Hinman)
S. H. Co.	Shapleigh Hardware (Hinman)
Scott's, J. N.	Simmons Hdw. import perc. and cart. dbl., various grades.
Special Service	Shapleigh Hardware (Hinman)
Ten Star	Geller, Ward & Hasner, St. Louis (Hinman)
Ten Star Heavy Duty	Geller, Ward & Hasner, St. Louis (Hinman)
Utica Firearms Co.	Simmons Hardware (Sellers)

APPENDIX I
ORIGINS AND DESTINATIONS
OF MISSOURI GUNSMITHS

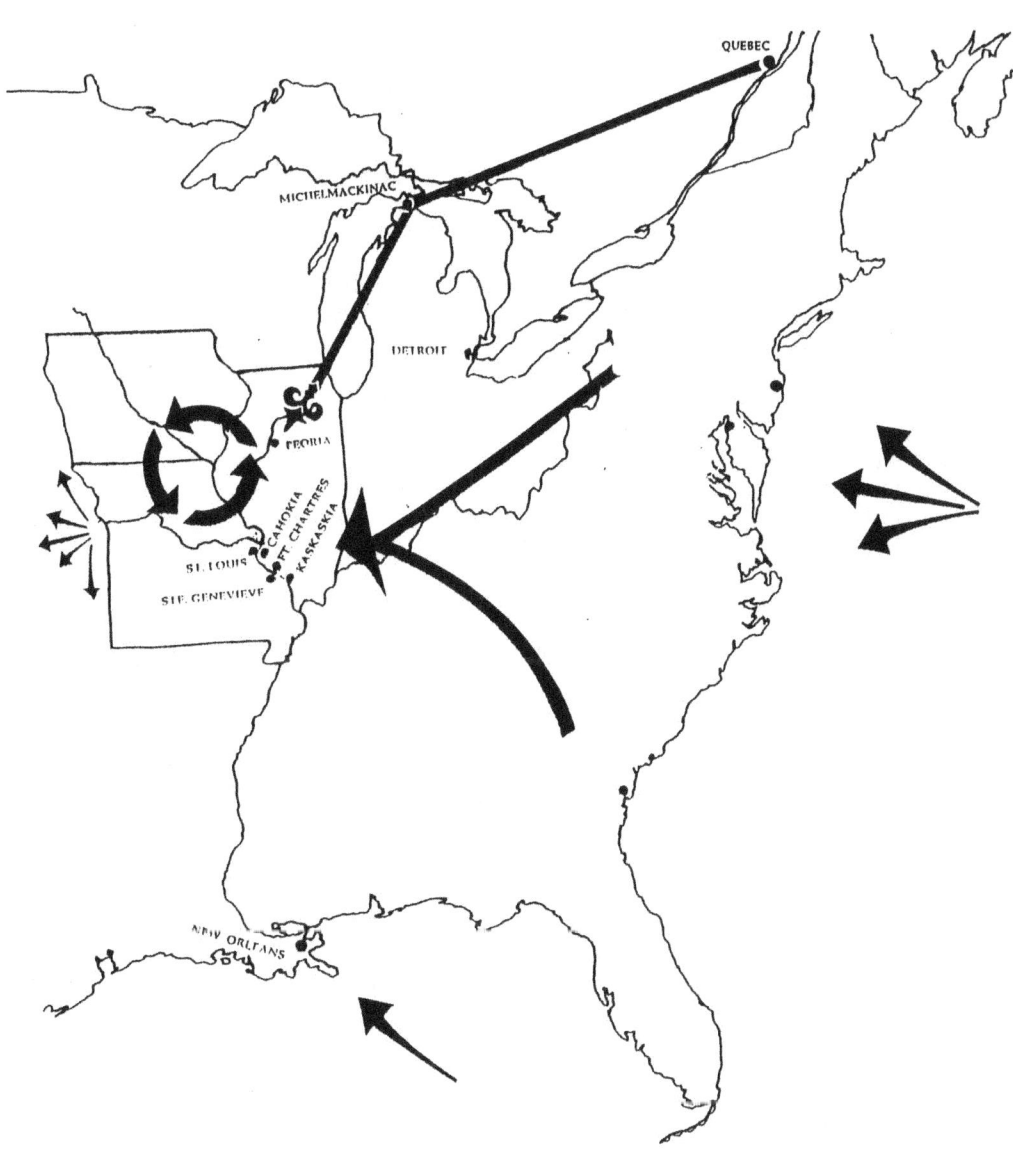

APPENDIX I

The map, previous page, shows the routes used by gunsmiths moving to Missouri.

The early French gunsmiths probably came overland from Canada.

The "American" gunsmiths came from all over the eastern U.S., following the traditional routes of migration, sometimes stopping in Pittsburgh, Cincinatti or Louisville on their way west.

Beginning in the late 1840's a number of immigrant gunsmiths, particularily German, seem to have had St. Louis or Missouri as their destination when they left their homeland as many entered through New Orleans. Numerous German Lutherans entered into Missouri at the "Plymouth Rock" of the Lutheran Church in Wittenberg, Missouri.

The majority of gunsmiths who left Missouri went further west. A number have been found in California, Colorado and other western states. Further research will almost certainly find them spread all along the "Great Trails".

One major exception to the above concerns the states of Iowa and Illinois. The circle of arrows shown at their border with Misssouri indicates a number of gunsmiths who worked in two or all three of these states. A number of these "river jumpers" moved so often it is difficult to pinpoint exactly which state they were in at a particular time.

The following index indicates merely that a gunsmith was in the state listed at some time in his life. Please refer to main listing for dates. This index was compiled from known locations of the gunsmiths and their birth states, as shown on censuses, and the birth states of their children.

Alabama
   Dittrich, John F.
   McKinney, John R.
Arkansas
   Busch, Robert
   Duenckel, Augustus
   Gaylor, Calvin
   Kile?, John
   Linzel, Augustus Edward
   Neal, Alexander
   Wirsing, Christian
   Wirtz, Abraham
California
   Altinger, Charles
   Basler, John
   Breck, William
   Clabrough, John P.
   Eckhardt, Henry
   Flohr, Andrew
   Hellinghaus, Frederick
   Kelsey (Kelsay), John
   Kelsey (Kelsay), Nathaniel
   Kelsey, William
   Kersey, Levi Charles
   McMullen, Thomas S.
   Nordheim, George A.
   Reichling, Frank
   Schade, John
   Sheets, Daniel
   Srefee, Bosemore
   Willard, Alexander
   Woodward, B. F.
   Workman, F.
Colorado
   Campbell, Tristram
   Early, Jacob H.
   Ely, Lewis A.
   Fluhmann, Gottlieb H.
   Gove, Carlos
   Hamilton, John M.
   Hawken, Samuel T.
   Hawken Wm. S.
Connecticutt
   Coloney, Myron
Delaware
   Harris, Robert H.
Georgia
   Bivens, Joseph
   Burns, Joseph S.
   Porter, Alexander A.
   Rigdon, Charles H.

Illinois
   Abbott, Asa McFarland
   Adams, Robert W.
   Altinger, Charles
   Barnett, D.
   Bean, Ahab
   Bean, Joseph R.
   Bishop, Robert
   Black, John
   Bracklow, Theodore
   Brantlinger, D. F.
   Breitenstein, Jacob
   Bridger, James
   Caspari, Frederick
   Chester, M.
   Chismore, H.
   Cook, John W.
   Cox, Jesse R.
   Craig, John W.
   Creamer, Joseph N.
   Creamer, Philip
   Crosier, Jesse L.
   deHodiamont, George
   Drew, Dan
   Duncan, Wilson
   Eaton, Daniel E.
   Hays, Charles
   Head, L. D. (Lorenzo D.?)
   Heverieux, John Baptiste
   Howlett, Robert W.
   Huntington, Chatton Z.
   Hurst, J. Morgan
   Ingalls, Albert P.
   Jackson, John J.
   Kalbitz, Robert
   Kleinhenn, Emanuel
   Knotzel, Anton
   Laird, D. C. (David C.)
   LeBeau, John Baptiste
   Martin, John J.
   Moore, George
   Morgan, Henry
   Musser, Joseph
   Painter, Jacob
   Palmer, Henry C.
   Patterson, John A.
   Pelton, Theodore G.
   Peters, John W.
   Pottorf, George
   Redwine, John F.
   Rinehart, Jessie
   Secor, Oliver P.
   Sieber, Edward Robert
   Staphs?, George E.

   Theide, Fred
   Thompson, Charles I.
   Valentine, F.
   Wallace, Andrew J.
   Weldan, Benjamin
   Weldon, Hugh M.
   Wichmann, Julius
   Wiget, Dominick
   Wiget, John L.
   Willard, Alexander
   Yearwood, John
   Zingg, Joseph
Indiana
   Clawson, George
   Clawson, James
   Cory, Randolph
   Glanz, John
   Heiad, Dan
   Holmes, Samuel C.
   Howard, Lawson H.
   Hurst, J. Morgan
   Jones, Henry
   Jones, Jesse
   Lorenz, Fred
   Lutes, William
   Malkin?, Peter
   Marshof, John G.
   Posegate, Isaac F.
   Reed, Isaac
   Turk, William
Iowa
   Arnold, William
   Breitenstein, Jacob
   Burchet, Theodoric
   Duncan, Wilson
   Gove, Carlos
   Hitton, E. J.
   Klocker, John
   Lafferty, Smith
   Martin, John J.
   Melvin, William T.
   Misner, Benjamin
   Nordheim, George A.
   Parschall, J. T.
   Pelton, Theodore G.
   Southard, A. M.
   Willard, Alexander
Kansas
   Cotton, Wm.
   Early, Jacob H.
   Hoppenau, Henry
   Lash, John
   Pyeatt, James P.
   Redwine, William J.

Kansas (continued)
  Smith, Frank M.
  Sprangle, ?
  Wallace, Andrew J.
Kentucky
  Abbott, Asa McFarland
  Abill, Ross
  Arnold, Thomas
  Beatty, William T.
  Bennett, Joab W.
  Bennett, Thomas
  Betts, Jesse F.p.
  Bishop, Andrew J.
  Botts, William
  Bowling, Justus
  Branham, John
  Brawner, George
  Brown, Evan B.
  Brunty, William
  Carson, Joseph
  Carter, Henry
  Carter, James F.
  Condor, Addison
  Conway, Joseph
  Davenport, James
  Davidson, Alfred
  Dennis, Isaac
  Dennis, William
  Dennison, James
  Dickson, Moses
  Dimick, Horace E.
  Duty, Hiram
  Easter, Allen
  Garrett, Robert A.
  Gibbons, Thomas
  Glore, James R.
  Good, Henry M.
  Good, J. J.
  Hamilton, John
  Harmon, John L.
  Hatfield, R . P.
  Hawkins, William
  Head, L. D. (Lorenzo D.?)
  Herrington, William
  Hockensmith, K. D.
  Hockensmith, William
  Howard, Degratta?
  Howard, James
  Howell, John
  Jett, Stephen C.
  Jolly, William
  Keller, James M.
  Kelsay, John
  Kelsay, Nathaniel
  Kelsey, William
  Kendrick, William
  Kile?, John
  Kinchler, Ezekial
  Lewis, Peter
  Love, Lycian B.
  Lutes, William
  McCallum, David
  McCann, George A.
  McClane, Andrew
  McKinney, John R.
  McMullen, Thomas S.
  Miller, David
  Montgomery, William
  Nowlin, Abram Cephus
  Renick, Abram
  Renick, George
  Richardson, E. G.
  Scaggs, Henry
  Sear?, Zachariah
  Searcy, Bartlett
  Smith, James M.
  Smith, Robert
  Smith, Wiley B.
  Snell, Joseph
  Street, John M.
  Tate, John
  Walker, H. L.
  Weller, George W.
  West, John W.
  Williams, Snowden
  Wilson, Philip
  Wilson, Pleasant L.
Louisiana
  Dittrich, John F.
  Folsom, Henry
  Furlong, Henry
  Jackson, E. T.
  Riley, John F.
  Sonnenschein, Charles
  Sonnenschein, Henry
  Sonnschein, Herman
  Sonnschein, William
  Wisman, John
Maine
  Green. Arthur
  Ingalls, Albert P.
  Jackson, E. T.
  McKinney, John R.
Maryland
  Creamer, Philip
  Drew, Dan
  Earl, Will
  Hawken, Jacob
  Hawken, Samuel T.
  Hellinghaus, Frederick
  Kirlin, Thomas
  Richardson, William
  Watt, William L.
Massachusetts
  Abbott, Asa McFarland
  Buffington, A. R.
  Chamberlin, Howard
  Lewis, Charles L.
  Shaw, Robert
  Talman (Tolman), James
  Wilmot, Nathaniel N.
Michigan
  Dowling, Jesse
  Schammel, John
Minnesota
  Johnson, Gunder
  Schilling, Charles F.
  Wilmot, Nathanial N.
Montana
  Kemp, A. (Alexander?)
  Oldham, Charles
  Oldham, Gabriel H.
Nebraska
  Melvin, William T.
New Hampshire
  Couch, Tetyre
  Eisprich, Charles
  Gove, Carlos
  Willard, Alexander
New Jersey
  Krattli, John
New York
  Basler, John
  Benedict, Albert
  Britton, J.
  Brown, Henry M.
  Brunner, Joseph
  Brunner, Joseph Jr.
  Callender, F. D.
  Chisman, John
  Corey, Chester
  Day, Thomas
  Duffy, Bartholomew
  Duncan, Wilson
  Faxon (Faxton), A. M.
  Holmes, Silvester
  Howe, Oliver R.
  Kersey, Levi Charles
  McFall, James
  Millstead, Alexander I.
  Millstead, Inmet
  Ruggles, James

New York (continued)
   Secor, Oliver P.
   Sharpe, Daniel
   Ward, Henry
   Whatt, S. C
Nevada
   Basler, John
North Carolina
   Abill, Ross
   Albright, Joshua
   Amick, William
   Amrith?, William
   Black, John
   Bradley, Ambrose
   Brawley, John
   Davis, Harman
   Duty, Hiram
   Ellis, William
   Harrison, Marshal
   Harrison, William
   Jett, Stephen C.
   Jones, Henry H.
   Lamb, Joab
   Lutes, William
   McFarland, George W.
   Maples?, William
   Moore, George
   Painter, Jacob
   Palmer, James W.
   Ruhbottom, Ezekial
   Turk, William
Ohio
   Albright Thomas John
   Arn, Edward
   Bargdoll, Joel
   Brantlinger, D. F.
   Coloney, Myron
   Cook, John W.
   Craig, John W.
   Creamer, William
   Eaton, Daniel E.
   Eisprich, Charles
   Ely, Lewis A.
   Farmer, Edwin
   Harrison, William
   Hawken, Samuel T.
   Hayes, William
   Hazlewood, H. B.
   Hitton, E. J.
   Hunt, John
   Hurst, J. Morgan
   Jughardt, Charles
   Kelsey, William
   Kester, John

   Lafferty, Smith
   Lash, John
   Levisy, Simpson
   Lewis, Charles L.
   McCoy, John
   McCoy William
   Newberry, William
   Newcomer, Martin
   Patrick, J. M.
   Peabody, Loren
   Rigdon, Charles H.
   Shaw, James
   Sheets, Daniel
   Turk, William
   Wirsing, Christian A.
   Woodward, Benjamin F.
Oregon
   Hellinghaus, Frederick
   Neal, Alexander
Pennsylvania
   Albright Thomas John
   Albright, William A.
   Appel, Charles
   Campbell, Tristram
   Cohen, John
   Creamer, William
   Gibbons, Thomas
   Hoffman, Christian
   Ingalls, Albert P.
   Kaler, John
   Kemp, A. (Alexander?)
   Lettey, William
   Lindsay, Edward
   McCord, Dorastus
   Miller, Nicholas
   Misner, Benjamin
   Morloch, Jacob
   Musser, Joseph
   Otto, Augustus G.
   Pipes, John
   Pottorf, George
   Reed, Isaac
   Ringe, Frederick
   Secor, Oliver P.
   Smith, Benjamin
   Watt, William L.
South Carolina
   Bradley, Ambrose
   Compton, W. J.?
   Conner, Armstrong
   Holbert, Joshua
   Kendrick, William
   Lewis, Ira
   Porter, Alexander A.

   Wideman, Francis
   Wilson, Pleasant L.
Tennessee
   Baker, Thomas H.
   Bean, Ahab
   Bean, Joseph R.
   Black, John
   Bradley, Ambrose
   Brawley, John
   Compton, W. J.?
   Cox, Jesse R.
   Douglass, Asa B.
   Duty, Hiram
   Early, Jacob H.
   Ellis, William
   Folsom, Henry
   Gaylor Calvin
   Glidewell, William J.
   Gully, John J.
   Harmon, George
   Kelsey, William
   Kennedy, Thomas J.
   Kile?, John
   Lewis, Ira
   Lynch, William
   McKinney, John R.
   Markham, Carter
   Mathews, James
   Mathews, Lemuel C.
   Miller, Noah
   Mills (Wills), George H.
   Neal, Alexander
   Oldham, Charles
   Oldham, Gabriel H.
   Read, O. H. P.
   Rigdon, Charles H.
   Sieber, Edward Robert
   Smith, Wiley B.
   Strahorn, J. K.
   Tilford, Samuel K.
   Wallace, Andrew J.
   Weldon, Hugh M.
Texas
   English, Willy
   Jackson, E. T.
Utah
   Lynch, William
Vermont
   Dimick, Horace E.
Virginia
   Baker, Solomon
   Batcheller, J. W. Sr.
   Blakemore, George
   Bridger, James

Appendix 1: Virginia-German States

Virginia (continued)
  Briscoe, John
  Brown, George
  Brown, John
  Brown. L. J.
  Buffington, A. R.
  Burchet, Theodoric
  Burns, Joseph S.
  Busch, Robert
  Carter, Henry
  Clawson, James
  Cole, William
  Day, James
  Dennison, James
  Drew, Dan
  Dumas, John S.
  Dunn, John H.
  Dunn, William
  Earl, Will
  Engle, E. W.
  Gill, Prisley (Presley)
  Harding, B.
  Hitton, E. J.
  Hook, Elijah
  Hopkins, David
  Howell, William B.
  Jackson, John J.
  Kaler, John
  Lakenan, James
  Lewis, Charles L.
  McCallum, David
  McMillan, Edward
  Markham, Carter
  Markham, Thomas
  Martin, John J.
  Maupin, James
  Maupin, Mosias
  Newcomer, Martin
  Patterson, John
  Penn, Gabriel
  Penn, Samuel
  Phillips, John G.
  Pool, James
  Posegate, Isaac F.
  Priss, Benjamin
  Reinhart, J. W.
  Ridgeway, Zack
  Rinehart, Jessie
  Sheetz, Henry
  Sites, Andrew J.
  Sites, John P.
  Sites, John P. Jr.
  Smith, Robert
  Smith T., John

  Snell, Robert M.
  Sprinkle, George
  Sproulle, R. H.
  Staphs?, George E.
  Stipes, Ezekial H.
  Tanner, William
  Tilford, Samuel K.
  Verdier, Washington
  Walker, John
  Zink, John
Virginia (Harper's Ferry)
  Brison, Benjamin
  Brooks, Joseph
  Burke, William
  Creamer, Philip
  Drew, Daniel
  Hawken, Jacob
  Stedman, Thomas
  Whitmore, Noah
Wisconsin
  Detcheneng, Lawrence
  Phillips, John G.
  Wilcox, Oliver
  Willard Alexander
Austria
  Netser, Frank
  Waibel, B.
Canada
  Beauvais, Gemien
  Migneron, L. S. (Jr.)
Denmark
  Bracklow, Theodore F.
England
  Arnold, William
  Barnett, P.
  Batemann, Thomas
  Bishop, Robert
  Daft, Alexander
  Daft, Robert
  Dimmrick, H. C.
  Dodsworth, Robert
  Gibbons, Thomas
  Green. Arthur
  Hague, James
  Harris, John
  Hawksley, William
  Hazlewood, H. B.
  Howlett, Robert W.
  Millstead, Frederick W.
  Millstead, Inmet
  Morgan, Henry
  Round, George
  Smith, Nathan
  Stone, Thomas

  Weston, Walter
  Wilmot, Nathaniel N.
France
  Gero, Jacob
  Heisel, James
  Lamott, John
  Muller, George F. S.
  Muller, Marcus
  Roll, Francis X.
  Shavierre, Isaac R.
German States
  Adams, Julius
  Altinger, Charles
  Austersnell, Louis
  Barkman, J. C.
  Barth, George F.
  Basler, John
  Bauerichter, Frederick
  Behrle, Joseph
  Bergner, George
  Blickensdoerfer, John
  Boetcher, Frederick
  Brake, William
  Brecht, Gustavus V.
  Brunner, Joseph
  Caspari, Charles
  Caspari, Frederick
  Caspari, William
  Cleff, Henry R.
  Craben, William
  Danne, John F.
  Dietrich, Louis
  Dinkle, Chris
  Dittrich, John F.
  Doell, Gottfried
  Doll, J. A.
  Duenckel, Augustus
  Engels, Nathaniel
  Engles, Dan?
  Etterly, Joseph
  Fisher, Lawrence
  Flesch (Flesh), Martin
  Foggerson, Lloyd?
  Friede, Meyer
  Funk, Folden
  Gemmer, John Philip
  Glanz, John
  Griefelt, Stephen
  Gross, Frederick
  Grueninger?, J.
  Gunteman, Joseph
  Gunteman, William
  Guscoyle, Taylor
  Hauptman, Joseph

Appendix 1: German States-Switzerland

German States (continued)
- Hauptman, Joseph Jr.
- Heeman, Fred
- Hemmes, Stephen
- Hoffstether, F.
- Homa, Conrad
- Huslage, Herman G.
- Huss, John Adam
- Kabler, John G.
- Kalbitz, Justice
- Kalbitz, Robert
- Keehnart, Charles
- Kersteins, Henry
- Kish, Michael
- Kleinhenn, Emanuel
- Knidler?, Julico
- Kohne?, Charles
- Krag, Gustus
- Lange, William
- Lehzahner, Fritz
- Lindsay, Edward
- Linzel, Aug. Edw.
- Long, Robert
- Lorenz, Fred
- Lunsmann, Franz
- Martincaf?, Julius
- Maurer, Bertrand
- Meier, Adolphus
- Mieslang, Joseph
- Misel, George A.
- Morloch, Jacob
- Mueller, Joseph
- Munch, George
- Myer, F. (P.)
- Nathan, Joseph
- Nemoeck, Frank
- Nies, Louis
- Nordheim, George A.
- Otto, Augustus G.
- Peters, John W.
- Petters, John
- Reichard, Edward
- Richart, Edwin
- Ringe, Frederick
- Ringe, Louis
- Roesen, John
- Roesen, William
- Roper, John
- Rudolph, Justus
- Schaerff, Christian
- Schaerff, Christopher
- Schaerff, John
- Scham, Christian
- Schammel, John
- Schilling, Frederick
- Schimpf, John Peter
- Schubert, Martin
- Schwander, Emil
- Schwartz, Frederick F.
- Sieber, Charles R.
- Sonnenschein, Charles
- Sonnenschein, Henry
- Sonnschein, William
- Staph, G.....
- Stardtlep, August
- Stock, Theodore
- Strecker, Anton
- Sunemall, Frank
- Swan?, Frederick
- Thorwald, August
- Valrat?, Edward
- Vogelsang, Henry
- Wachshar?, F.
- Waechter, H.
- Wanderu ?, Emil
- Werker, Ebert
- Wilkins, Didrick
- Wilkins, John W.
- Winbrech, William
- Wisman, John
- Woodworth, G.
- Workman, F.
- Worsing, Charles
- Worsing, Frederick
- Zigg, Joseph

Ireland
- Count, Lawrence H.
- Coyle, James C.
- Duffy, Bartholomew
- Duffy, John
- Greenan, Barney
- Lyon, John
- McPartland, P.
- Morrow, Henry
- Null, Thomas

Scotland
- Fea, Thomas
- McLean, Dr. James Henry

Sweden
- Richner, Frederick

Switzerland
- Ith, Rudolph
- Knotzel, Anton
- Krattli, John
- Masuch, Edward
- Rudolph, Victor
- Wachter, Casper
- Wachter, John
- Wageman?, Thomas
- Weber, Jacob
- Wiget, Dominick
- Zingg, Joseph

APPENDIX II
Chapter XXVIII, *RECOLLECTIONS OF PERSONS AND PLACES IN THE WEST*, 2ND. EDITION
Prefaced and Annotated

RECOLLECTIONS

OF

PERSONS AND PLACES

IN

THE WEST.

BY

H. M. BRACKENRIDGE,

A NATIVE OF THE WEST; TRAVELLER, AUTHOR, JURIST.

SECOND EDITION, ENLARGED.

181165

PHILADELPHIA:
J. B. LIPPINCOTT & CO.
1868.

Appendix II: Brackenridge

Many of the duels fought in the St. Louis area were fought on Bloody Island, an island in the Mississippi river which was not claimed by either Missouri or Illinois. As such it offered the participants immunity from officers of the law, who might wish to interfere with the proceedings.

The main body of this appendix is a reprint of Chapter XXVIII of the enlarged 2nd. edition of *PERSONS AND PLACES IN THE WEST*, H. M. Brackenridge, Philadelphia, 1868. Brackenridge presents a most interesting, contemporary account of the circumstances surrounding the first recorded duel on Bloody Island.

The following list is extracted from a paper entitled "Recorded Duels and Near Duels Occurring in the St. Louis Area" compiled by the late L. G. Osborn, no date.

1. 1750 Two Frenchmen, names unknown, fought over a girl at Ft. Chartres(Il.).

2. 1810 Dr. Bernard G. Farrar and James Graham(the subject of Brackenridge chapter)

3. 1816 Henry S. Geyer and Geo. H. Kennerly, on Bloody Island. Kennerly wounded in knee.

4. 1817 (Aug.) 1st. Benton-Lucas duel, on Bloody Island. Chas. Lucas wounded in neck.

5. 1817 (Sept.) 2nd. Benton-Lucas duel, on Bloody Island, Chas. Lucas killed.

6. 1818 Capt. Ramsay and Capt. Martin of Ft. Bellefontaine, on Bloody Island. Ramsay died of wound.

7. 1819 John Smith T. fought Lionel Browne, a nephew of Aaron Burr, "somewhere near St. Louis". Browne was killed. Smith T. is reputed to have killed numerous men in duels. Three recorded.

8. 1820 Timothy Bennett killed Alphonso Stuart in the "false duel" at Belleville, Il. Bennett was hung, the only case on record of a man hung for killing another man in a duel. The duel was supposed to be an elaborate practical joke. However, Bennett slipped a ball in his rifle after the second handed it to him loaded only with powder. This act of treachery, rather than Stuart's death was the cause for the hanging.

9. 1823 Thomas C. Rector killed Joshua Barton, on Bloody Island.

10. 1831 Major Thomas Biddle and Spencer Pettis, on Bloody Island. As Biddle was nearsighted the duel was fought at five feet! Both participants died. This duel is believed to have given Bloody Island its name.

11. 1842 James Shields challenged Abraham Lincoln, Lincoln's choice of weapons was cavalry sabers at ten feet. Duel was not fought. However, the participants had come as far as Alton, Il., on their way to a meeting place, when they agreed to cancel the duel.

12. 1845 A duel was fought between two gentlemen named Histerhagen and Kabbe. Only details known are that it was fought with swords and neither man was seriously injured.

13. 1855(?) Loring Pickering challenged Frank Blair to a duel over an article published in the Enquirer, no duel was fought.

14. 1857 Thomas C. Reynolds fought B. Gratz Brown near Kimmswick, Mo. Brown was wounded though not seriously.

15. 1860 General D. M. Frost and Edward B. Sayer fought the last recorded duel on Bloody Island. Sayers missed, Frost fired in the air.

CHAPTER XXVIII.

Bad Consequences of Good Society
A Constructive Quarrel and
Fatal Duel between two Friends.

I HAVE said that I took no office, having determined to go farther south before entering in earnest on the labors of my profession; yet some portion of my time was daily passed in the office of my friend Graham, who was well satisfied with his present situation. Having more experience in the law, although some years younger, my assistance was useful to him in preparing his cases and in hunting up applicable authorities. He was peculiarly well adapted to the routine of office business, and would have been successful, although he did not aspire to any high degree of eminence, much less to the palm of eloquence. He inherited from his father, a revolutionary officer, an exalted sense of honor, with not a little of military instinct, which rendered him less averse than I was to duels and personal rencounters. These would have formed no obstacles in his way. His person was fine, and his taste for dress and fashion was great, while he had no relish whatever for mere literary abstractions or enthusiasm, for he actually refused to accompany me to visit the great mound at Cohokia,[1] although I had just before ridden with him to the cantonment of a regiment at Bellefontaine on the Missouri, where there was nothing but the great river itself worth seeing; for the mere parade of a few soldiers, and the music even of a good band, were no objects of curiosity to me. My friend sought that kind of society which I avoided, often passing his evenings with the young officers of the army, and others, who killed time with a social game of cards, - not to the extent of gaming, yet far enough to disqualify a young lawyer for the business of the day by sitting up too late at night, not to speak of the demoralizing tendency. But these were not the worst consequences of such habits, as will appear from the unhappy occurrence I am about to relate. It would have been well for my poor friend if he had had as little relish for good society as I had.

One evening, looking on as an unconcerned spectator while a party was playing a game of cards, Graham saw one of those engaged commit an act deemed highly dishonorable among players, and following only the momentary impulse of correct feeling instead of consulting the prudential advice of La Rochefoucauld, *si j'avais la main pleine de verites, ie m'en garderais bien de l'ouvrir*[2] - which may sometimes render prudence the accomplice of guilt - he at once proclaimed the disgraceful act, regardless of consequences. The party was immediately broken up, and the person thus implicated, who was a lieutenant in the army, a man of honor by profession, gave notice that for this insult he should demand the satisfaction due to him as a gentleman. The officer was of that caste of persons not often nowadays met with in the army, since the military school at West Point has furnished it with young men trained to nobler feelings; at the same time, I do not mean to say that some of our best officers, both of the army and navy, have not been taken at once from among the citizens; I merely make it as a general remark that the character of our officers has been raised by the pains taken with our cadets and midshipmen.

The next morning the challenge came, and it was borne by the individual, a physician,[3] with whom Graham had been more intimate than with any other in the town. This gentleman and the officer had married the daughters of the same person, a respectable citizen of St. Louis; he considered himself thus imperatively called upon to act as the friend of his brother-in-law. The challenge was at once refused, on the ground that the challenged party could not place himself on a footing with one whom he had denounced as a cheat and a swindler. On this, the second declared that the consequence was that he must stand in the place of his friend - that the insult was, by a necessary inference, transferred to him, for if his friend was unworthy the notice of a gentleman, he must be no better for taking up the cause of such a person. Graham assured him that he had every possible respect for him, and disclaimed all intention to call in question his standing as a gentleman. But the other insisted that, according to the laws of honor, and according to correct reasoning, the refusal of the challenge on the ground that the principal was not a gentleman was an insult to the second. The difficulty of the case appeared to both insurmountable, and they separated with mutual expressions of unabated esteem, notwithstanding the unpleas-

---

1 Now Cahokia Mounds World Heritage Site, administered and owned by the State of Illinois. **The museum and the mounds are well worth the visit.**
2 Roughly translated, he who knows the plain/obvious truth should guard his openness.
3 Dr. Benjamin Farrar, Brackenridge, in the style of the times, does not name him

ant position which they were now forced to occupy. This kind of reasoning was not altogether new to me; the duel related in another part of this volume, of which Tarleton Bates was the victim, turned on a similar point of honor.

The colonel of the regiment happening to be in town, was applied to by Graham, and, as a matter of course, the delicate and responsible office was, without hesitation, accepted. The colonel was a man of tried courage, and possessed of the prudence and experience of mature years, qualities deemed very important in a second to a duel. There was no possibility of an accommodation. -Nothing short of an acknowledgment that the officer accused of being a cheat, was a gentleman, could not be received; so this Graham could not give without acknowledging himself a slanderer. The challenger could not yield, because in doing so he would acknowledge himself to be no gentleman, by carrying a challenge for a blackguard. In ordinary cases the principal may, after the first fire, acknowledge himself satisfied for the supposed insult, but in this case nothing short of the surrender of the point in dispute could arrest the progress of the duel; so that it necessarily must be a combat jusqu'a la mort, or until one of the parties be disabled, and even then to be renewed as soon as that party should be able again to take the field.

- All the preliminaries of this deadly duel between two friends, on a constructive insult, under the laws of honor, were now arranged, and the time fixed for the meeting three days ahead. In the mean time, all possible diligence was used by the colonel and his principal in providing the best pistols for the occasion; and, in order to place them in the most perfect condition, they went in search of a celebrated gunsmith,[1] who lived in an obscure place in Illinois; almost in a secluded hermitage, a creature of whim and singularity, of the name of Cramar (sic.), famous for his gunlocks, and originally from Lancaster, Pa. I have known a pair of his pistols, perfectly plain, sell for two hundred dollars, and a rifle for one hundred and fifty, on account of the supposed superiority of his workmanship.[2] Afterward they retired to a ravine to practice; but in none of these excursions did I accompany them. All I can say is that the colonel proclaimed Graham one of the best shots he had ever known, which I did not doubt, for I knew him to be well skilled in the use of almost every kind of weapon; at the same time, I placed more confidence in coolness and firmness of nerve in real danger than the mere correctness of the eye when aiming at a dead mark.

The fatal morning having arrived, the whole party proceeded, after daylight, in the same boat, across the river to Illinois. Excepting a surgeon, no one accompanied them. I was the only person who attended them to the boat, where I shook hands with Graham with all the earnest and anxious feelings which can be better conceived than described. I remained for an hour and a half, waiting the result, and felt that sickness of the heart occasioned by the dread of some deep calamity, rendered more intense by glimpses of hope. I listened in vain to hear the reports of the pistols, the river being too wide for this purpose. At length the boat appeared, and my heart beat audibly as she came near enough to enable me to distinguish persons. I was in a short time enabled to count the whole party, seated on their benches; there might be wounds, but there was no one actually dead. I ran to the boat, and helped my friend Graham out; I saw him pale and bloody, but he set his foot on the ground with a firm step. I soon found, however, that he required the aid of the colonel, as well as mine, to enable him to reach his lodging. He was undressed and placed on his bed, while the surgeon examined his wounds. At the first fire he had received the ball of his antagonist in his side, passing round the back bone, and lodging in the flesh beyond, and when extracted the wound measured nine inches in length. The other party, at the same time, had received a slight flesh wound in the hip; but after this wound, Graham's nervous system must have been so much affected as to prevent him from firing with any certain aim. The next fire the ball passed through the calves of both his legs, and at the third his hand was so severely lacerated that he could no longer hold the pistol. In the mean time, he said nothing of his other wounds, and they were only discovered by the loss of blood, and after he was disabled. The seconds now decided that the

---

1 Creamer's property adjoined Prairie du Pont creek, heavily wooded at that time. It was about one mile east of the Village of Prairie du Pont. One mile southeast of modern day Cahokia, Illinois.

2 Brackenridge accompanied and chronicled Manuel Lisa's 1811 expedition and it is believed these may reflect "Mountain" prices. Extant records indicate Creamer did charge above normal prices for his rifles and pistols.

combat should cease for the present, to be renewed again whenever Graham should be in a condition to do so. After the wounds were dressed, the surgeon directed that he should be left alone, that he might take some repose. The colonel related to me the particulars of the combat, and spoke in raptures of the perfect coolness and firmness of my unfortunate friend.

The next day the other party to the duel called to see the person who had thus suffered by his hand, and offered his services to attend him, which were accepted; and during the whole of his attendance he manifested as much tenderness and solicitude as if he had been a brother. These may be regarded as curious contradictions, but human life is made up of strange compounds of motives and actions. Graham was confined four months to his room. The wound in his back first healed, and then opened afresh, while he gradually sunk, and there is little doubt that the spine was injured. Toward the spring he attempted to return to his native place on horseback, but only succeeded in going one hundred miles, when he was found dead in his bed in the morning. I shall not attempt to moralize on the forgoing; I dislike commonplace, and I should probably not be able to say anything that would not suggest itself to the reflecting mind on reading this unadorned narrative of facts.

I cannot but remark, however, that all this false honor, this barbarous and irrational morality, was in obedience to the public opinion of the place, public opinion possessing little or no influence in assigning to individuals their proper stations in society according to merit or demerit, or frowning down conduct really disreputable and immoral, yet so powerful in what related to the exhibition of mere animal courage. Nothing could more strongly prove the savage state of society. It was exactly that degree of the point of honor which I have witnessed among the Indian tribes, where a warrior will voluntarily travel a thousand miles, at the requisition of his chiefs, to surrender to death, under penalty of being degraded from his station as a brave man; and I have seen the willing victim, while singing his death-song, take his measure in the newly-dug grave, surrounded apparently by his friends, who, after manifesting the greatest regard, for him, have dealt the fatal blow on the spot pointed out by himself. As Mr. Clay justly said, on a late occasion, " It is public opinion which is wrong; it is public opinion which restrains a man, in certain sections of the Union, from resorting to this mode of resenting insults and injuries; and it is the same public opinion which, in other sections of the country, exacts from individuals a resort to this practice, in order to settle their disputes. In these latter sections of the country the only alternative offered to a man who had been injured or insulted is whether he will live in ignominy and disgrace, or expose himself to the loss of life in personal rencounters; and under this alternative there are but too few that feel able to refuse that expense of human life."

There are various accounts of this duel which disagree, slightly, with Brackenridge's version. Some state Farrar was not wounded, and also say Graham died within days of the duel.

The Missouri Historical Society has a letter, in the "William Clark Papers", written by a James Baird to Col. Dunning McNair, dated Jan.13, 1811. At the time of the letter Graham was still alive. According to Baird, Farrar was acting on behalf of a Lt. Campbell. Baird names Col. Bissel as Graham's second and General William Clark as Farrar's second. He states Clark delivered the second challenge the same day Graham refused the first challenge and that the duel took place the following day. He also disagrees with Brackenridge as to the timing of the wound to Farrar, stating that Farrar received it at the second firing. Baird does not state he was an eyewitness. Baird appears to have been a recent arrival to the St. Louis area, from the letter.

APPENDIX III
AN INDEX OF MISSOURI GUNSMITHS BY COUNTIES OF RESIDENCE

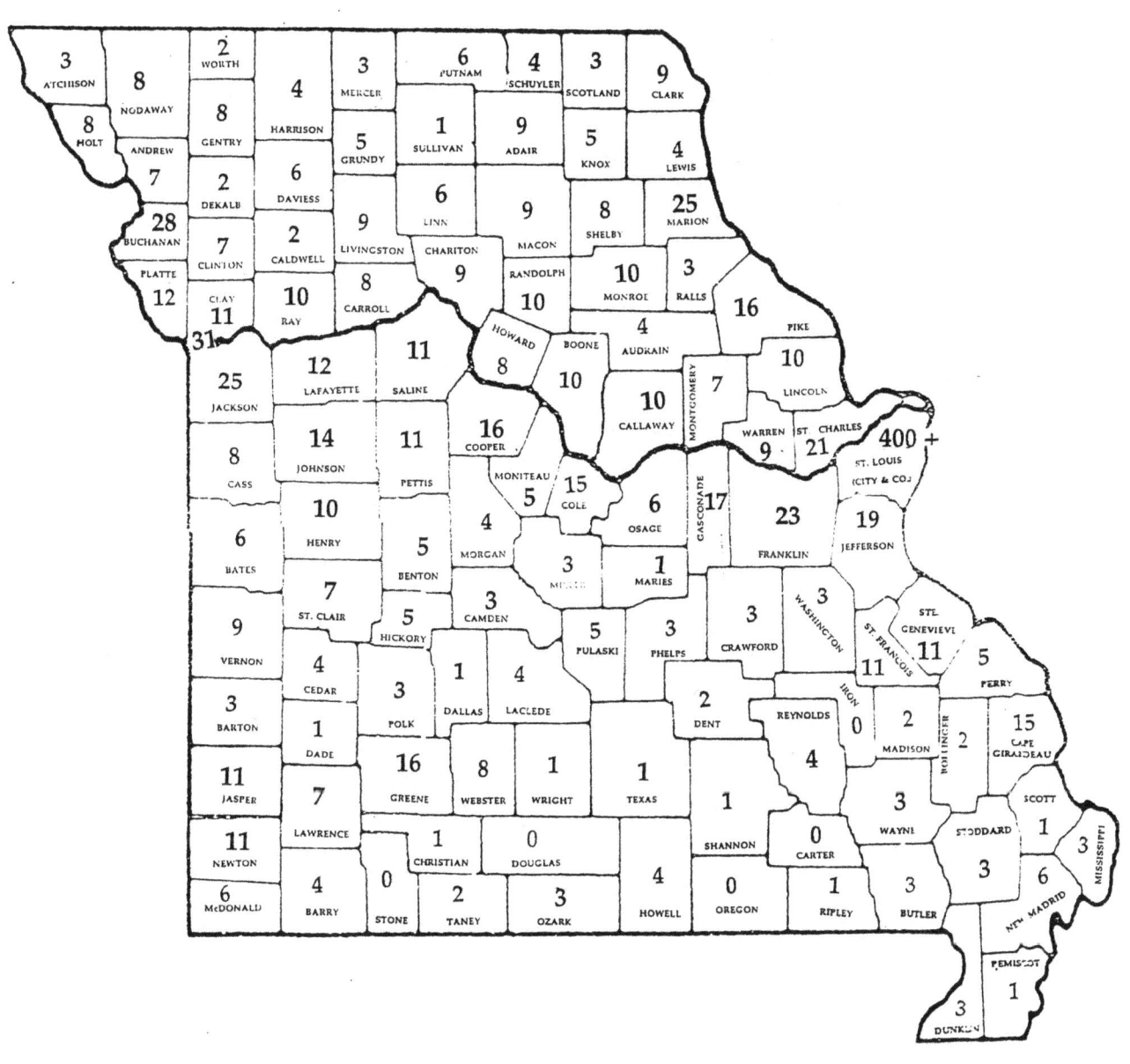

Appendix III

This Index was released in pamphlet form September, 1990 with a yellow cover and again in February, 1991 with a parchment style cover. A revised version of the pamphlet was released, November, 1992, this time with a blue cover. Several errors and number of additions have been found since that release and have been changed in the version which appears here.

On the map, previous page, the number "31" appears at the Clay-Jackson County line. It represents Kansas City which is indexed separately.

Adair
　Beeman, O. H.
　Garrett, Robert A.
　Harris, Robert, H.
　Melvin, William T.
　Notestine, G. W.
　Ruggles, James
　Short, John C.
　Tate, John
　Wright, J. M.
Andrew
　Brown, Evan B.
　Howe, Oliver R.
　Southard, A. M.
　Stiles, John A.
　Wilson, E. M.
　Wilson, Philip
　Wilson, Pleasant L
Atchison
　Blegard, Robert
　Harmon, George
　Kish, Michael
Audrain
　Creasey, Mason
　Greenup. F. M.
　McKean, S. L.
　Wilkins, J. W.
Barry
　Bennett,Richard
　Clifton, William
　Riggins, A. J.
　Zinn, H. C.
Barton
　Hatfield, R .p.
　Markwith, James H
　Parre, J. C.
Bates
　Drummond, N. S.
　Hurst, J. Morgan
　London, Byron
　Marshof, John G.
　Miller, Noah
　Rinehart, Jessie
Benton
　Carter, Henry
　Carter, James F.
　Hayes, William
　Nowlin, Tom
　Wright, J. C.
Bollinger
　Gully, John J.
　James, H.
Boone
　Barton, D. C.
　Brown, John
　Carlisle, A. A. , Mrs
　Carlisle, John W.
　Dimitt, Frank
　Palmer, James W.
　Phillips, John G.
　Phillips, Preston
　Turk, John
　Turk, William
Buchanan
　Ash, S.
　Baldwin, Charles
　Batcheller, J. W. Sr.
　Batcheller, J. W. Jr.
　Beauvais, Francis A.
　Duncan, Wilson
　Eckhardt, Henry
　Eckhardt, William
　Eggelston, C. J.
　Ellinger, Henry
　Ely, Lewis A.
　Goodline, J.
　Gove, Carlos
　Hamilton, John
　Hopkins, Frank G.
　Ireland, J. F.
　Kemp, A.
　Lapthorne, S. J.
　Lard, Allen E.
　Lewis,...
　Moore, George
　Nies, Louis
　Peabody, Loren
　Posegate, Isaac F.
　Posegate, William J.
　Rein,...
　Rudolph, Victor
　Wright, J. M.
Butler
　Lamb, Joab
　Williams, Cordan
　Williams, Vernius
Caldwell
　Everhart, P.
　Mathis, W.
Callaway
　Dunn, John H.
　Dunn, William
　Gill & Blackburn
　Gill, Prisley
　Hawkins, William
　Hays, Charles
　Ith, Rudolph
　Lewis, Charles L.
　Ridgeway, Zack
　Wilson, James
Camden
　Chismore, H.
　Ragg, H.
　Woods, Lee
Cape Girardeau
　Appel, Charles
　Bahn, B. & Bro.
　Buchanan, John
　Bucheit, Joe
　Glidewell, Wm. J.
　Hartung, Gottfried
　Johnson, Gunder
　Lynch, William
　Orrel, John
　Richner, Frederick
　Rickmers, A. F.
　Schaffer, J. C.
　Waggoner, Isaac
　Wagner, Alvin
　Warfield, C.
　Winter, Peter
Carroll
　Brunty, Jesse
Brunty, William
　Montgomery, Wm.
　Ringe,—
　Stemple, Lawrence
　Stemple, Louis
　Wade, W. F.
　Willis, John
Carter
　None
Cass
　Keeney, J. T.
　Mcfarland, George
　Ringe, Fritz
　Short, James C.
　Weldan, Benjamin
　Weldon, Hugh M.
　Wheeler, E. G.
　Wilson, L. F.
Cedar
　Baltzor & Eslinger
　Kaiser, ...
　Misner, Benj.
　Snellings, ...
Chariton
　Barnett, D.
　Brawner, George
　Briscoe, John
　Clever, P. J.
　Malkin?, Peter

Chariton Co. (continued)
   Palmer, A. M.
   Stipes, Ezekial H.
   Theid, Fred
   Wichmann, Julius
Christian
   Corbin, H.
Clark
   Childers, M.
   Clark, Barnes
   Dumas, John S.
   Faxon, A. M.
   Longanecker, H. C.
   Longanecker, J. F.
   Martin, John J.
   Parker, A.
   Texan, A. M.
Clay
   (See Kansas City)
   Carson, Joseph
   Dickson, Moses
   Gero?, Jacob
   Huggins, Calvert
   Keller, James M.
   Kelsay, C. H.
   Laughlin, G. O.
   Roll, Francis X.
   Turner, William H.
   Young & Berry
   Young, A. J.
Clinton
   Crocker, John
   Geesey, J. N.
   Jamison, Allen
   Kelsay, C. H.
   Lamb, Joab
   Lindsay, E. H.
   Parschall, J. T.
Cole
   Beford, Arter
   Chester, M.
   Chisman, John
   Chismore, H.
   Heisel, James L.
   Hirsch, Adam
   Lamott, John
   Mills, George H.
   Misel, George A.
   Pyeatt, James P.
   Redford, Arter
   Roesen, John
   Roesen, William
   Schmidt, William
   Sprinkle, George

Cooper
   Arn, Edward
   Arn, F.e.
   Duenckle, Augustus
   Gemmer, John Philip
   Ginger, George W.
   Hook, Elijah
   Howe, Oliver R.
   Jolly, William
   Kleinhenn, E. ?
   Knaus, William
   Mueller, Fredk,
   Secongost, J. M.
   Sheets, John
   Sites, Chester P.
   Sites, John P. Sr.
   Sites, John P. Jr.
Crawford
   Hardshell, Charles
   Holbert, Joshua
   Souders, Nathan
Dade
   Gibson, L. L.
Dallas
   Lash, John
Daviess
   Reed, Isaac
   Sheets, John
   Sheets, Henry
   Smith, James M.
   West, John W.
   West, Robert
Dekalb
   Palmer, E. B.
   Wilcox, Oliver
Dent
   Dawson, J. G.
   Mcmillian, W. R.
Douglas
   None
Dunklin
   Buchanan, James
   Douglass, Asa B.
   Yearwood, John
Franklin
   Adams, Julius
   Bergner, George
   Busch, Oscar
   Etterly, Joseph
   Funke, Charles
   Hutton, James
   Kasel, G.
   Lewis, J. B.
   McClane, A.

   Maupin, Amos
   Maupin, John
   Maupin, Mosias
   Maupin, William (2)
   Murphy, J. G.
   Poepplemeyer, Wm.
   Reichard, E.
   Tiry, William E.
   Valentine, J.
   Warden, R. W.
   Wunderlich, Chas.
   Zingg, Joseph
Gasconade
   Austersnell, Louis
   Boesch, Jacob
   German, Henry
   Hedrich, C.
   Huxol, Simon
   Kneubuehler, J.
   Krattli, John
   Lohr, Benjamin
   Mcmillan, Edward
   Mcmillian, E.
   Morloch, Jacob
   Mueller, Joseph
   Rudolph, Justus
   Seidner, Philip
   Smith, A.
   Taylor, William
   Thani, Sebastian
   Vogelsang, Henry
Gentry
   Cameron, E. P.
   Dresser, Samuel R.
   Feel, James E.
   Goodspeed, Thomas
   Howell, William B.
   Hunt, John
   Patrick, J. M.
   Riggins, G. W.
Greene
   Altinger, Charles Sr.
   Altinger, Charles Jr.
   Beardon, Elias M.
   Compton, W. J.?
   Hastings, Gardner
   Kile, John
   Magnien, George
   Mason, F. M.
   Painter, Elisha
   Painter, Faelden
   Painter, Jacob
   Painter, John
   Rainey, J. Aug.

Greene Co. (continued)
   Seiler, Charles
   Stanley, C. W.
   Thompson, Chas. E.
Grundy
   Clawson, George
   Clawson, James
   Patterson, John
   Ridgeway, H. C.
   Sprangle,...
Harrison
   Arnold, Thomas
   Burchet, Theodoric
   Hopkins, David
   Lafferty, Smith
Henry
   Adams, Robert W.
   Baker, Solomon
   Beatty, William T.
   Blakemore, George
   Hurst, J. Morgan
   Jackson, George R.
   Krag, Gustus
   Moser, Henry
   Robertson, C. P.
   Wright, J. M.
Hickory
   Black, John
   Bradshaw, Burton
   Calkins, Eli
   Nowlin, Abram C.
   Nowlin, Tom
Holt
   Batcheller, J W. Sr.
   Buckminster, L. W.
   Cotton, Wm.
   De Ford, Isaac
   Harvey, J. M.
   Lowery, M. T.
   Rostock, F. S. Jr.
   Wells, G. W.
Howard
   Amick, William
   Dinkle, Chris
   Knaus, J. H.
   McCann, George A.
   Oldham, Charles
   Oldham, Gabriel H.
   Wachter, Casper
   Wachter, John
Howell
   Cope, James
   Lagrain, William
   Livingston, T. E.
   Rich, A. B.
Iron
   None
Jackson
   (See Kansas City)
   Botts, William
   Conner, Armstrong
   Davenport, James
   Early, Jacob H.
   Fann. J. W.
   Grueninger, J.
   Harmon, David
   Harmon, John L.
   Hockensmith, K. D.
   Hockensmith, Wm C.
   McCoy's & Lee
   McCoy, John
   McCoy, William
   Moore, George
   Renick, Abram
   Renick, George
   Sites, Andrew J.
   Smith, Frank M.
   Sonnenshcein, H.
   Sonnenschein, L.
   Sonnschein, H.
   Sonnschein, Wm.
   Van Horn, John
   Waibel, B.
   Wallerich, M.
Jasper
   Clary, A.
   Farmer, Edwin
   Furlong, Martin
   Jansen, Diederich W
   Karns, H.
   Mckinney, John R.
   Scott, William M.
   Tewksbury, Josiah
   Tucker, J. W.
   Weaver, Hugh
   Wheeler, Charles
Jefferson
   Dohn, N. A.
   Dowling, Jesse
   Dowling, Napolean
   Engle, E. W.
   Harrington, J. C.
   Herrington, John C.
   Herrington, Wm.
   Honey, John W.
   Huber, Felix
   Jones, Henry H.
   Jones, Jesse
   Kalbitz, Justice
   Kalbitz, Robert
   Miller, Nicholas
   Skaggs, J. M.
   Warner, C. H. Jr.
   Wideman, Francis
   Winer, C. H.
Johnson
   Amrith?, William
   Berkly, John R.
   Britton, J.
   Elk, J. F.
   Good, J. J.
   Haas, C.
   Kunkle, J. H.
   Mason, F. M.
   Mathews, James
   Mathews, Lemuel C.
   Porter, A. A.
   Piper, S. P.
   Ratrauff, H G.
   Schnegelscheipen, J. W.
Kansas City
   Allen, Edward
   Berghousen, Chas.
   Billings, F. C.
   Brunn, J. G.
   Buechel, F.w.
   Butcher, F. T.
   Davis, W. P. & Son
   Fredericks, Fredk.
   Hintsche, William
   Hoppenau, Henry
   Johnson, C.
   Karthago, Stephen
   Keissig & Schmidt
   Lockweiler, F. A.
   Long, Robert
   Masuch, Edward
   Menges, E. E.
   Miller, Charles
   Miller, G. C.
   Nelson, F. W.
   Osterman, Charles
   Rickmers, A. F.
   Rolston, James
   Russ, M. B.
   Schaefer, P.
   Schultz, R. A.
   Sieben, Gustav
   Sonnschein, H.
   Stock, Theodore
   Werner, Otto F.
   Wheeler, J. P.

Knox
  Bowen, J. R.
  Cox, Jesse R.
  Owsley, Robert
  Sear?, Zachariah
  Searcy, Bartlett
Laclede
  Atchley, T. V.
  Rogers, George W.
  Wills, David
  Wyant, Isaac
Lafayette
  Bennett, William H.
  Cleff, Henry R.
  Duty, Hiram
  Kinzy, Christian
  Palmer, James W.
  Patterson, H. C.
  Reinhart, J. W.
  Schofield, George L.
  Sheetz, Henry
  Stone, Thomas
  Wessel, William
  Williams, Snowden
Lawrence
  Bennett, Joab W.
  Bennett, R.
  Brown, L. J.
  Lewis, Peter
  Painter, Elisha
  Ryan, Patrick
  Stair, W. H.
Lewis
  Barnes, Erasmus
  Courtney, R. H.?
  Wachshar?, F.
  Weller, George W.
Lincoln
  Baird, James
  Benedict, Albert
  Gill, Prisley
  Glore, James R.
  Goodrich, Asaph
  Head, L. D.
  Heiad, Dan
  Thurstin, A.
  Tilford, Samuel K.
  Volkel, John L.
Linn
  Chapman, W. S.
  Harrison, Marshal
  Harrison, William
  McCallum, David
  Rometsh, ...
  Tanner, August
Livingston
  Anschutz, August
  Bargdoll, Joel
  Bargdoll, Louis
  Brown, George
  Edwin, William J.
  Jackson, George R.
  Redwine, John F.
  Redwine, William J.
  Sanders, Lewis
  Shuler, V.
  Smith, Benjamin
McDonald
  Clark, A. B.
  Cooper, J.
  Hopper, R.
  Lescher, G.
  Markham, Carter
  Markham, Thomas
Macon
  Bruner, J.
  Freeman. J.
  Gibbs, Edwin
  Millstead, Alex.
  Pollard, Phillip
  Powell, C. S.
  Riley, Fielding J.
  Snell, Robert M.
  Thompson, Chas. I.
Madison
  Hartkoff, Daniel
  Stacy, M. H.
Maries
  Wiseman, Davenport
Marion
  Arnold, William
  Brace, D. R.
  Cash, Robert W.
  Condor, Addison
  Conrath, C. H.
  Conway, Joseph
  Dennis, Isaac
  Dennis, William
  Heller, Rudolph
  Heppert, Henry
  Howlett, Robert W.
  Kansteiner, Wm.
  Miller, Charles O.
  Millstead, Alex.
  Millstead, Fredk. W.
  Millstead, Inmet
  Pipino, G. H.
  Powell, R. J.
  Samuels, J. H.
  Schammel, John
  Schwertfeger, C.
  Shadwick, Charles
  Smithers, S. A.
  Young, William
  Ziegel, Andrew
Mercer
  Lutes, William
  Pratt & Sims
  Waymon, Coleman
Miller
  Dresser, Samuel
  Morris, Smith & Bro.
  Reaubert, James
Mississippi
  Howard, Degratta
  Lewis, Ira
  Strahorn, J. K.
Moniteau
  Bolin, William G.
  Husky, D. F.
  Lettey, William
  Nimeck, P. J.
  Palmer, James W.
Monroe
  Branham, John
  Chadwick & Crigler
  Dawson. W. H.
  Holmes, Silvester
  Penn, Gabriel
  Penn, Samuel
  Smith, Robert
  Snell, Joseph
  Wilkins, John W.
  Wilkins, R. D.
Montgomery
  Cardiff?, Dennis
  Davidson, Alfred
  Flood, John
  Laird, D. C.
  Laird, William
  Love, Lycian B.
  Schum, ?
Morgan
  Creamer, William
  Hook, Elijah
  Maples?, William
  Staphs?, George E.
New Madrid
  Blickensdoerfer, J.
  Chedester, Joseph
  Chidester, Martin
  Howard, James

New Madrid Co. (continued)
  Kimball, R. A.
  Walker, H. L.
Newton
  Blackfish, Peter
  Carman, D.
  Coltrin, William H.
  Cornman, David
  Doll, J. A.
  Kendrick, William
  Kennedy, Thomas J.
  McCann, J. E.
  Seagrove, John
  Todd, J. T.
  Wallace, Andrew J.
Nodaway
  Bowling, Justus
  Cook, John W.
  Fletchall, P.
  Levisey, Simpson
  Pipes, John
  Posegate, William J.
  Tanner, William
  Wirtz, Abraham
Oregon
  None
Osage
  Baker, Thomas H.
  Huebler, Reinhart
  Mcfarland, R.
  Nix, Harrison & Co.
  Nix, Thomas
  Prior, George W.
Ozark
  Barnett, P. J.
  Busch, Robert
  Vance, W. R.
Pemiscot
  Schilling, Daniel
Perry
  Behrle, Joseph
  Dietrich, Louis
  Kabler, John G.
  Rhyne, Isaac
  Winter, Peter
Pettis
  Bonker, George
  Dempsey, A. B.
  Easter, Allen
  Gross, A. P. M.
  James. H. A.
  Keating, E. C.
  Kumm, Louis
  Mathews, William
  Porter, A. A.
  Schach, Frank
  White & James
Phelps
  Barnwell, R. M.
  Felton, S.
  Seele, Henry
Pike
  Betts, Jesse F.p.
  Brantlinger, D. F.
  Bruce, Wm.
  Clarke, A. P.
  Douglas, Daniel
  Eldridge, William
  Hitton, E. J.
  Howard, Lawson H.
  Jackson, John J.
  Johnson, James Y.
  Johnston, C.
  Maupin, W. A.
  Newberry, William
  Oyler, Cook
  Sheets, Daniel
  Woodward, B. F.
Platte
  Arnold, Thomas
  Bishop, Andrew J.
  Eberly, J. E.
  Hamilton, John
  Howell, John
  Howell, William B.
  Kessler, John
  Kester, John
  Kohne?, Charles
  Posegate, Isaac F.
  Secor, Oliver P.
  Street, John M.
Polk
  Boutel, S. M.
  Bradley, Ambrose
  Tryon, F. J.
Pulaski
  Bennett, Joab W.
  Bennett, Thomas
  Greenstred, Z.
  Miller, David
  Rest, Freeman
Putnam
  Abill, Ross
  Carns, A.
  Davis, G. W.
  Mannon, R. W.
  Moore, D. A.
  Quigley, E. F.
Ralls
  Hartkoff, Daniel
  Peake, Daniel
  Verdier, Wash.
Randolph
  Ahrens, August
  Bargdoll, Joel
  Craig, John W.
  Grotjan, J. A.
  Kiley, F. J.
  Mayo & Durmial
  Riley, Fielding J.
  Riley, John F.
  Schaefer, Anton
  Shaefer, August
  Vogelsreich, C.
Ray
  Albright, Joshua
  Bartholomew, H. M.
  Danne, John F.
  Hockensmith, Wm.
  Hockensmith, Wm. W.
  Kelsay, John
  Kelsay, Nathaniel
  Kelsey, William
  Smith, Wiley B.
  Thomas, J. E.
Reynolds
  Bramley, E. D.
  Brawley, John
  Corey, Chester
  Scaggs, Henry
Ripley
  Cogshall, Caleb
St. Charles
  Adams , John
  Brecht, Gustavus V.
  Castner, George
  Cherlin, Christ.
  Grisemauer, C.
  Hemmes, Stephen
  Jacoby, Fred
  Mueller, Adam
  Munch, George
  Oberle, ...
  Peers, ...
  Rickmers, Edward H
  Ringe, Frederick
  Ringe, Henry
  Ringe, Louis
  Rubcore, Fred
  Scherlin, Christian
  Schilling, Fredk.
  Schmidt, John

Appendix III: St. Charles Co.- St. Louis City & Co.

St. Charles Co. (continued)
  Thurstin & Jacoby
St. Clair
  Duncan, ,
  Duncan, Wilson
  Gillis, George
  Murphy, J. G.
  Rudolph, J. E.
  Sites, Chester P.
  Sproulle, R. H.
St. Francois
  Day, James
  Dennison, James
  Elvins, Ralph
  Foggerson, Lloyd?
  Gibson, L. L.
  Hamlin, J.
  Kinchler, Ezekial
  McMullen, Thomas S.
  Starkey, C. O.
  Wallace, Andrew J.
  Whitesides, Allen
Ste. Genevieve
  Balthasar, Floerl
  Beauvais, Jemien
  Bean, Ahab
  Bean, Joseph R.
  Bergesoides, R.
  Dave
  Detcheneng?, L.
  Heston, T. J.
  Jicha, Frank
  Jokerst, Emil
  Maurer , Bertrand
St. Louis City & Co.
  Abbott, Asa
  Abe, Augustus
  Albright, Henry T
  Albright Thomas J.
  Albright, Wm. A.
  Aldinger A.
  Alkin, Charles
  Altinger, Adolph
  Altinger, Alex.
  Altinger, Charles
  Altinger, George
  Altinger, Ignatius
  Altinger, Joseph
  Anderson, George
  Anderson, R. S.
  Arnold, Thomas
  Asbeck, Julius
  Baird, James
  Bamberg, Julius

Barber, Ephraim
Barkman, Joel C.
Barth, George F.
Basler, John
Bastmann, Thomas
Bateman, Thomas
Baumannn, Jacob
Baumbach, Henry E.
Beall, Howard C.
Beauvais, Francis A.
Beauvais, Jemien
Beauvais, Jules
Beauvais, Renault
Beckett, William
Behr, Peter N.
Berg, Charles
Bircher, Casper
Bircher, Elizabeth
Bird, Charles
Bischens, Benjamin
Bishop, Robert
Black, Cenas
Black, Henry
Bleha, William V
Blickendoerfer, A.
Blickensdoerfer, J.
Boisaubin, Vincent
Bouis, J. V.
Bracklow, T.
Brake, William
Brecht, Gustav
Breck, William
Breitenbaugh, M.
Breitenstein, Jacob
Brennan, Hugh
Brison, Benjamin
Brison, H. M.
Brooke, Edward
Brooke, John B.
Brooks, Joseph
Brown, Henry M.
Brunner, Joseph
Brunner, Joseph Jr.
Buechel, F. W.
Buffington, H. R., Lt.
Burgan, Emmanuel
Burgess, L.
Burke, William
Burns, William
Callender, F. D.
Campbell, Tristram
Caspari, Charles
Caspari, Frederick
Caspari, William

Chamberlin, H.
Chapin, Charles J.
Child, Alonzo
Clabrough, John P.
Clark, Mathias B.
Clines, John
Cochran, Fredk. G.
Cohen, John
Coloney, Myron
Corbett, Thomas
Corbett, Walter
Cory, Randolph
Cottem, Paul
Count, Lawrence H.
Coyle, James C.
Creamer, Joseph N.
Creamer, Philip
Creissen, Edward
Critquelhoef?, Wm.
Curtain, Joseph
Daft, Alexander
Daft, Robert
Davis, James
Day, Thomas
deHodiamont, G.
Denk, Emmanuel
Dimick, Horace E.
Dimmrick, H. C.
Dittrich, John F.
Dodsworth, Robert
Doell, Gottfried
Dohrmann, Fredk.
Douglas, ...
Drew, Dan
Duchene, John
Duenckel, George F.
Duffy, Barth.
Duffy, John
Duncan, Wilson
Dunseth, A.
Durjk, John
Earl, Will
Eaton, Daniel E.
Eisprich, Charles
Ellinger, Henry
Engels, Nathaniel
Engles, Dan?
English, Willy
Enholm, J. H.
Eterle, Joseph
Eustace, Thomas F.
Evertz, Frederick
Falkenrath, R.
Fea, Thomas

Appendix III: St. Louis City & Co.

St. Louis City & Co. (continued)
Flesch, Martin
Fluhman, G.
Folsom, David
Folsom, Henry
Fopay, Frederick
Fosler, E.
Fricke, Henry
Fricke, Henry (Jr.?)
Fricke, Minna
Friede, Meyer
Froelich, Louis
Funk, Folden
Furlong, Henry
Gemmer, John Philip
Gemmer, Julius
George, J. H.
Gerngross, Stephen
Gertner, Xavier
Gibbons, Thomas
Glanz, John
Gobbels, Mathias
Goeken, Ewald
Goodman, Henry
Green. Arthur
Greenan, Barney
Gridner, Charles
Griefelt, Stephen
Gunteman, Joseph
Gunteman, William
Hague, James
Hamilton, John M.
Harding, B.
Harris, John
Hauptman, Joseph
Hauptman, Joseph Jr.
Hawken, C. M.
Hawken, Jacob
Hawken, James M.
Hawken, Samuel T.
Hawken, William S.
Hawksley, William
Hazlewood, H. B.
Hebb, E. T.
Heberer, Anton
Heberlein, A.
Heeman, Fred
Heiss, Philip
Hellinghaus, Fredk
Henkel, William
Herkstroeter, F.
Herman, John
Heverieux, Jno. Bte.
Hingle, John

Hoffman, C.
Hoffman, J. See
   Hauptman
Hoffstether, F.
Hogan, Joseph
Homa, Conrad
Houdlette, Fredk M.
Huber, Felix
Huber, J.
Huslage, Herman G.
Huss, John Adam
Ingalls, Albert P.
Ingles, David
Jackson, E. T.
Jett, S. C.
Jughardt, Charles
Junker, Edward
Kacer, Martin V.
Kalbitz, Robert
Keehnart, Charles
Kersey, Levi Chas.
Kersteins, Henry
Kirlin, Thomas
Kittredge, Charles
Kleinhenn, E.
Kline, P.
Klinglesmith, John
Klocker, John
Knidler?, Julico?
Knotzel, Anton
Koeppens, Ernst
Kriz, William J.
Kunkle, Mathias
Lakenan, James
Landreville, Andre
Langen, Thomas
LeBeau, John Baptiste
Le Conte
Leeman, Julius
Lehzahnen, Fritz
Leich, George
Lenzhaner, Fredk.
Linberg, Charles J.
Lindsay, Edward
Linzel, Augustus E.
Lorenz, Fred
Lunsmann, Franz
Lutz, D.
Lyon, John
McBlair, W.
McCaughie, Thomas
McClane, Andrew
McCord, Dorastus
McCulloch, James, H.

McDonald, D. W.
McFall, James
McInnes, James
McLanahan, J. K.
McLean, Dr. James H.
McPartland, P
Martincaf, Julius
Matthews, J. A.
Maupin, Mosias
Meachem, E. C.
Mead, Edward
Meier, Adolphus
Merrick, John
Meur, Adam
Meyer, Julius W.
Mieslang, Joseph
Migneron, Francois
Migneron, Louis S.
Migneron, L. S. (Jr.)
Milburn, Nathan
Miller, Charles
Millikin, H. C.
Mitchell, D. D.
Morgan, Henry
Morrow, Henry
Morton, John
Mosch, Herman
Mueller, George F.
Muller, Marcus
Myer, F. (P.)
Nathan, Joseph
Neff, John
Nelzer, F.
Nemoeck, Frank
Netser, Frank
Nordheim, George A
Null, Thomas
Nutz, L. N.
Oppelt, A. E.
Otto, Augustus G.
Overton, Edward
Ovrey, John
Palmer, Henry C.
Pease, J. S. & Co.
Peters, John W.
Petters, John
Phillips, William J.
Poorman, Henry B.
Powell, Peter & Co.
Priss, Benjamin
Pritchard, J. M.
Provost, Peter
Quiney, Frank
Raabe, Julius A.

Appendix III: St. Louis City & Co.- Taney Co.

St. Louis City & Co. (continued)
  Reber, H.
  Reineke, Frederick
  Richardson, Wm.
  Richart, Edwin
  Rigdon, Charles H.
  Riggin, John
  Robinson, John
  Roeber, Henry
  Roper, John
  Round, George
  Round, John
  Rudolph, Thomas W
  Sackwitz, Louis
  Saxton, George S.
  Schade, John
  Schaerff, C.
  Schaerff, John
  Schafer, J. R.
  Schafermeyer, Jos. B
  Scham, Christian
  Schand, Frederick
  Schand, Henry
  Schand, Molty
  Schantz, Henry
  Schertzer, Jules T.
  Schilling, Charles
  Schilling, Fredk.
  Schillinger, Chas.
  Schimpf, John Peter
  Schroeder, Charles
  Schubert, Martin
  Schum, Christian
  Schwander, Emil
  Schwartz, Fredk. F.
  Scott, J. N.
  Seiferth, Fredk. E.
  Seiferth, T. Edw.
  Shamich,   ,
  Sharpe, Daniel
  Shaviere, Isaac R.
  Shaw, James
  Shaw, Robert
  Shaw, Samuel B.
  Shawk, Abel
  Shawk, Samuel
  Shone, George
  Sieber, Charles R.
  Sieber, Robert ?
  Siegmund, Louis
  Smith, T. John
  Smith, Nathan
  Sonnenschein, C.
  Sonnenschein, H.
  Spaedy, Frank
  Speck, Joab
  Stahlberg, William
  Staph, G.
  Stardtlep, August
  Stauf, C.
  Stedman, Thomas
  Stein, Frederick
  Steinbach, C. J.
  Stock, Theodore
  Strecker, Anton
  Sunemall, Frank
  Swan?, Frederick
  Talman, James
  Tegethoff, William
  Thompson, F.
  Thormann, Johann
  Thorwald, August
  Underwood, Henry
  Valentine, F.
  Valrat?, Edward
  Vogelsang, Henry
  Vollmer, Gustav
  Waechler, Louis
  Waechter, H.
  Waechter, Louis
  Wageman?, Thomas
  Walker, John
  Walser, Edward
  Wanderu?, Emil
  Ward, Henry
  Ward, John
  Watt & Bennett
  Watt, William L.
  Webb, Charles
  Weber, Jacob
  Wehrle, John
  Weiley, John
  Weinbrecht, W.
  Weiner, A. G.
  Werker, Ebert
  Werner, Daniel
  Werthon, H.
  Weston, Walter
  Whatt, S. C.
  Whitmore, Noah
  Wiget, Dominick
  Wiget, John L.
  Williams, James E.
  Williome, Jacob
  Wilmot, Nathaniel
  Winberg, John H.
  Winbrech, William
  Wirsing, Christian
  Wirth, Anton
  Wisman, John
  Woodworth, G.
  Workman, F.
  Worsing, Charles
  Worsing, Frederick
  Young, Lewis V.
  Zamboni, John
  Zedick, Roderick
  Zigg, Joseph

Saline
  Chapman, W. S.
  Day, Daniel & Co.
  Dickenson, John
  Holmes, Samuel C.
  McAlister, Albert
  Mitchell, George
  Patterson, H. C.
  Reine, Joseph
  Sites, John P. Jr.
  Stipes, Ezekial H.
  Toole, William T.

Schuyler
  Blurton, John Jr.
  Kaler, John
  Karns, H.
  Lowry, Thomas

Scotland
  Asbill, A.
  Courtney, R. H.?
  Richardson, E. G.

Scott
  Ellis, William

Shannon
  Whiting, E. D. (Ed)

Shelby
  Boetcher, Fredk.
  Butcher, F. T.
  Hodge, G. W.
  Schumate, Kemper
  Tompkins, W.
  Wilkins, Didrick
  Wilkins, John
  Will, Julius E.

Stoddard
  Brentzel, William
  Good, Henry M.
  Newcomer, Martin

Stone
  None

Sullivan
  Creason, Nick B.

Taney
  Gaylor, Calvin

Taney co. (continued)
   Read, O. H. P.
Texas
   Crosier, Jesse C.
Vernon
   Cottet, Eugene
   Ely, Lyman H.
   Hoblit, Lyman
   Hunter, William
   Moss, James
   Oatis, N.
   Pottorf, George
   Robinson, E. A.
   Wilcox, George C.

Warren
   Bauerichter, Wm.
   Craben, William
   Fisher, Lawrence
   Gross, Frederick
   Harrison, William
   Hasenjager, Fredk.
   Lange, William
   Logan, Alexander
   Munch, George
Washington
   Cole, William
   Drew, Andrew
   Fea, Thomas

Wayne
   Green, Alfred
   Huntington, C. Z.
   Ruhbottom, E.
Webster
   Bivens, Joseph
   Bricksey, William
   Burns, Joseph S.Couch, Tetyre
   Doby, Alsey
   Enke, E.
   McMannama,J. B.
   Zink, JohnWorth
   Goodspeed, Thomas
   Hetchall, P.
Wright
   Wallace, Andrew J.

APPENDIX IV

Agreement between Myron Coloney and Dr. James Henry McLean

Filed for record in U. S. Patent Office, Nov. 19th, 1880, Liber C 26, page 27 of transfer of patents.

This memorandum of agreement made and entered into this 15th. day of April A. D. 1878 by and between James H. McLean and Myron Coloney both of the City and County of St. Louis State of Missouri Witnesseth: Whereas by an assignment of ... date herewith the said Coloney has sold and assigned to the said McLean an undivided- seven eights (7/8) of all his right, title and interest in and to certain improvements in
"<u>Time shells</u>" and "Breech-Loading Cannon" and the Letters Patent that may be granted therefore. Now therefore the said Coloney agrees under the direction and subject in all things to the sole direction and control of the said McLean to devote his whole time and attention to the perfecting and bringing into practical operation said inventions and each of them provided said McLean shall furnish the said sums for such expenses, the said Coloney agrees to give his time to said objects as aforesaid, and to be in all things in relation to said matters, subject to the control and direction of said McLean, Should said patents on either of them be obtained said McLean shall have the sole and exclusive right of granting licenses thereunder on selling interests in or the whole of said patents upon such terms as <u>he</u> may deem best, only accounting to me for one eighth (1/8) part of the net proceeds thereof provided he sells the whole of said patents or grants an exclusive interest thereunder and I hereby authorize said McLean to sign my name as my attorney in fact to any such exclusive license or sale of said patents or either of them, hereby notifying any such act or acts of the said McLean in the promises and agreeing that said power hereby granted to sign my name shall be irrevocable for the purposes specifies. Said Coloney further covenants and agrees to keep just and true accounts of all expenditures made by him under this agreement and to make monthly returns thereof to the said McLean during the continuance of this agreement. Said Coloney further agrees that, provided said McLean will furnish the necessary money to procure patents on the said inventions in foreign countries including Canada, England, France, Germany, Austria, Russia, Turkey and any other country where patents are granted he shall have the same interest in such patents and the same right to control the disposal of the same as is provided in relation to the United States patents in this agreement, and the said Coloney will also subject to the conditions aforesaid as to the expenses give to the introduction of such foreign patents such time and attention as the said McLean may direct, it being the intention of this agreement that the said McLean shall furnish all the money necessary for the perfecting and introduction of said improvements - including a reasonable sum for the personal expenses of said Coloney while attending to the same and that the said Coloney so long as said sums of money are furnished by the said McLean shall devote his whole time, attention and energy to the advancement of the said improvements and rendering them a source of profit. The said McLean to be the sole judge of what efforts are necessary and the manner in which the said Coloney best enhance the design of this agreement. It is further understood and agreed that this contract may be annulled at any time by the said McLean. The said McLean further covenants and agrees that during the continuance of this contract, he will pay and allow to the said family of said Coloney, in addition to the personal expenses and other outlays herein before provided for, the sum of seventy five ($75.00) dollars per month payable weekly on the order <u>of said</u> Coloney. This contract it is agreed shall go into effect and the said allowance shall commence on the 22nd. day of April A. D. 1878.

I witness whereof the said parties hereto set their hands the day and year just above written.

Witnesses	(signed)
Saml. S. Boyd	Dr. J. H. McLean
Chas. D. Moody	Myron Coloney

www.ingramcontent.com/pod-product-compliance
Lightning Source LLC
Chambersburg PA
CBHW081222170426
43198CB00017B/2689